Chronicle
of the Year
1988

Chronicle of the Year 1988

Has been conceived and published by Jacques Legrand

Editorial Director: **Clifton Daniel**

Editor in Chief: John W. Kirshon

Correspondents:
Tom Anderson Marjorie Hunter
Benton Boggs Noel Rae
Edward Edelson James Tuite

Staff Writers: Bob Blum, Susan Breen, Kevin Delaney, James Forsht, Philip Farber, John Goolrick, Catherine Hulbert, Marguerite Jones, Nicholas Lee, Jeremy Leggatt, Lilya Lorrin, Erik Migdail, Louis M. Nevin Jr., Tod Olson, Roberta Oster, Karen Rohan, Marianne Ruuth, Julie Siler, Steve Singer, Steven T. Taylor, Pascale Thumerelle, Ken Weinstock

Copy Editor: Ralph Berens

Editorial Research:
Tod Olson *(Editor)*
John Goolrick
Kristie Simco

Photo Research:
Erik Migdail *(Editor)*
Veronique de Saint Andre *(SIPA)*

Production:
Christine Remonté *(Manager)*
Ginny DePaso *(Art)*
Henri Marganne
Rose Ann Caris

System:
Catherine Balouet *(Manager)*
Dominique Klutz *(Software Engineer)*
Darin Hamilton *(DPC)*

ISBN 013 133 737-8
Typesetting: Digital Prepress Center (DPC), Yonkers, N.Y.
Printing & Binding: Connecticut Printers, Bloomfield, Ct.

Distributed in the United States of America by:
Prentice Hall Trade.
A division of Simon & Schuster, Inc.
1 Gulf & Western Plaza
New York, NY 10023

Distributed in Canada by:
Raincoast Books Ltd.
112 East 3rd Avenue
Vancouver
British Columbia V5T 1C8

Chronicle
of the Year
1988

Chronicle

Publications

Mount Kisco, N.Y.

1. Saudi Arabia: As oil revenues continue to decrease, taxes are imposed on foreign businesses and workers.

1. Pasadena: Michigan State over U.S.C. 20-17 in Rose Bowl.

1. San Salvador: United States and human rights advocates condemn blanket amnesty that frees several assassination suspects (→ 3/5).

1. Jerusalem: Israel puts the army on street patrol in Gaza, the West Bank and Jerusalem (→ 9).

1. London: Government discloses Prime Minister Harold Macmillan suppressed account of 1957 nuclear disaster to curb dissent over atomic cooperation with United States.

2. United States: It is reported that, on December 23, 1987, the miltary began secretly testing laser for Strategic Defense Initiative program (→ 16).

2. North America: President Reagan and Canadian Prime Minister Mulroney sign landmark accord to cut trade barriers between United States and Canada.

3. London: On job 3,167 days, Margaret Thatcher passes Herbert Asquith as most durable British premier.

3. Lebanon: Israeli air strike in south kills 21 (→ 4/23).

4. Moscow: Tass reports first major widening of psychiatric patients' rights in 27 years (→ 5).

4. Hemphill, Texas: Three policemen charged with civil rights abuses in beating death of Loyal Garner Jr. during night in jail for drunk driving (→ 2/9).

5. Moscow: Gavril K. Popov, Gorbachev ally, publishes critique of economic reform, calling it "fiction" (→ 15).

6. Washington: Nine, including three ex-Mexican police, charged in 1985 murder of U.S. drug agent (→ 2/13).

DEATH

5. Pete Maravich, leading college basketball scorer, of a heart attack (*6/22/1947).

Israeli army confronts Arab uprising

Stone-wielding Palestinian rebels prepare to confront Israeli troops.

A Palestinian youth is taken into custody by well-armed Israeli soldiers.

Jan 9. Two Gaza Strip skirmishes in the past 48 hours have again pitted stone-throwing Palestinians against a harassed Israeli army, with at least one Arab killed and 12 wounded. The first incident took place the day before the projected start of a United Nations fact-finding tour that grew out of a December 22 resolution. Condemning the Israeli handling of last month's demonstrations, the U.N. said it would explore ways to protect the region's Palestinians. Israel insists, however, that the recent troubles are its own internal business.

At the same time, two West Bank leaders called on Palestinians to begin a civil disobedience movement by boycotting Israeli-made cigarettes. "Gandhi started with salt," one of the leaders said. "We are starting with cigarettes."

The second clash stemmed from a general strike that was called by the Islamic Holy War, a militant group. The group urged Gaza Arabs to stay home "to prove to your sons in prison that you are with them," a reference to the 1,100 Palestinians still jailed because of the December protests, which were also triggered by a general strike. Since December 9, when the new uprisings began, 29 Palestinians have been killed, 200 wounded and many others stunned by rubber bullets. The Israeli army, bridling at its being used as a police force, insists that it fires live ammunition only as a last resort (→ 14).

Soviet restructuring laws go into effect

Jan 1. Are the Soviet Union's days as a workers' paradise ending? That seems to be the case as a new set of laws goes into effect today that will take away much of the economic security Soviet workers have always been assured of, without offering, yet, much in the way of recompense. The new laws transfer a large measure of responsibility from the central government to individual enterprises. A profitable business will be able to give raises to its workers; the unprofitable one will have to consider wage cuts. Since one-quarter of businesses in the Soviet Union operate at a loss or close to a loss, the ramifications could indeed be staggering.

The economic reforms are part of Soviet leader Mikhail S. Gorbachev's policy of "perestroika," or restructuring, which he hopes will energize the sluggish economy. But critics believe the reforms will not succeed until there are goods for Russians to spend money on. A Soviet newspaper reported that one farm worker had increased his earnings to more than 10 times the average wage yet he was not able to buy a better house because they are rationed. The stakes are high: if the economy remains stagnant, the Soviet Union could enter the 21st century as a second-class power (→ 4).

U.S. eating poorly despite food reform

Jan 5. Are you conscious of the cholesterol, fat, salt, sugar, calories, fiber, caffeine and additives in your diet? It seems that food consciousness is on the rise, but according to a nationwide telephone survey by The New York Times, we keep eating junk. The worst sinners when it comes to sugary snacks, soft drinks and french fries are people between the ages of 18 and 29. Overall, women seem more aware of diet and exercise than are men: 46 percent of women said they pay close attention to health needs, but only 31 percent of men said they do.

Computer trading blamed for market crash

Jan 8. A presidential task force blamed two types of computerized trading programs for last October's record-setting 508-point decline in the Dow Jones industrial average.

In a report that was released today, the Presidential Task Force on Market Mechanisms said the computerized trading programs, developed and used by many of the biggest money-management firms in the country for large institutional clients such as pension funds, were a major cause of the collapse of the market last October 19.

The task force reported that two trading strategies which often make use of computers, index arbitrage and portfolio insurance, unleashed huge sell orders on the New York Stock Exchange as well as the Chicago Mercantile Exchange.

"Program trading, on auto-pilot, produced an enormous amount of volume during that time," Nicholas F. Brady, chairman of the task force, said at a press briefing in the White House.

The group's conclusions, which contradict those presented by the Commodity Futures Trading Commission and the Chicago Mercantile Exchange, are expected to prove controversial.

Its major proposal, that a single agency, the Federal Reserve Board, regulate the stock, options and futures markets, drew a cool reception at the White House today, and experts said that it would be bitterly opposed by the Chicago futures industry (→ 2/2).

Pennsylvania oil spill poses major threat

Over a million gallons of diesel fuel have spilled into the Monongahela River as a result of the collapse of a tank which had been storing it.

Jan 6. Water again flows in some of the 13,000 homes in suburban Pittsburgh whose faucets were cut off by one of the worst inland oil spills in American history. The area is returning to normal, but residents along the Ohio River are bracing for a battle. No one yet knows what caused the collapse two days ago of a fuel oil tank at the Ashland Oil Company, 27 miles upstream of Pittsburgh on the Monongahela River. But when the tank buckled, a million gallons of oil were dumped into the waters and began bobbing toward Ohio.

As river boats hurried for home and some hospitals transferred the critically ill, emergency crews put in a round-the-clock containment effort, and intakes in the Ohio River, which the Monongahela flows into, were abruptly shut. Nevertheless, large pockets of oil remain untrapped and these are now near Wheeling, West Virginia, on the Ohio River 100 miles south of the original spill site.

Ohio has declared a state of emergency. Experts expect the spill to leave environmental scars. Fortunately, most birds have gone south for the winter, but fish and water fowl won't be so lucky.

Trevor Howard, who made 70 films, dies

Jan 7. The curtain went down last night for the versatile, powerful actor Trevor Howard, who was 71. He died quietly in his sleep. A man who loved Dixieland jazz and enjoyed life to the fullest, he made some 70 films, including "Brief Encounter," "Ryan's Daughter," "Sons and Lovers," "Gandhi" and "Mutiny on the Bounty." Born in London, he made his debut at the Gate Theatre there in 1934. Playing British officers to perfection, he drew on his own wartime experiences. In World War II, Howard made 22 parachute jumps and was awarded the Military Cross for bravery.

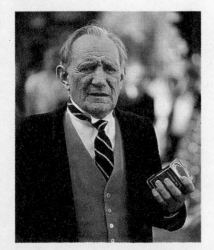

Trevor Howard cut a dashing figure.

Million kids throng Tokyo's Disneyland

Disneyland is fun in any language.

Jan 1. In less than five years Tokyo Disneyland has become Japan's favorite playland, almost a national pilgrimage site. It is reminiscent of the American counterpart with a model of the ideal future family home, a revolving Carousel Theatre, a Cinderella Castle and all. Nevertheless, it has a distinct Japanese flavor. Flawlessly clean and high-tech, this smiling perfection revolves around Mickey-San, that world-famous mouse whose 59th birthday was marked by a 17-day celebration. Japan has again demonstrated a unique ability to take the seeds from other cultures and cultivate them in its own way.

Radon causes death

Jan 5. It may be time to seal up those cracks in the foundation of your house, especially if you are a cigarette smoker. The danger to smokers, and, to a lesser extent, non-smokers, comes from radon gas, a by-product of the natural decay of radium. A new report compiled by the National Academy of Sciences indicates that the odorless gas, which seeps into buildings from underground rocks, is responsible for about 13,000 deaths from lung cancer every year. Cigarette smokers, already at risk of lung cancer, are in the greatest danger from inhaling radon gas. The risk in homes with a radon problem can be reduced by sealing the cracks in the foundation and providing proper ventilation.

Gilbert Stuart's "George Washington" is one of the colonial portraits now at National Gallery.

5

Su	Mo	Tu	We	Th	Fr	Sa
					1	2
3	4	5	6	7	8	9
10	11	12	13	14	15	16
17	18	19	20	21	22	23
24	25	26	27	28	29	30
31						

10. United States: Global demand for U.S. food products at highest level since 1984 (→ 4/27).

11. Chicago: Amoco fined $85.2 million for 1978 oil spill.

11. Washington: Supreme Court bars revival of Hurricane Carter murder case.

11. Bonn: Police announce arrest of Christine G. Endrigkeit, suspect in 1986 Berlin disco bombing; her Palestinian ties cast doubt on U.S. allegations of Libyan connection.

12. New York City: Study shows one in 61 babies here has AIDS antibodies (→ 21).

12. Moscow: United States, Soviets sign scientific cooperation pact, broadest in years (→ 2/12).

13. Washington: Reagan meets with Japanese Prime Minister Noboru Takeshita; they promise to stabilize dollar (→ 2/16).

14. Mideast: P.L.O. vow to recognize Israel if peace talks begin spurned by Israelis (→ 15).

15. Madrid: United States and Spain announce new military pact limiting ties.

15. Moscow: Meeting with Gorbachev, dissident Andrei Sakharov hands him list of prisoners to free (→ 18).

16. San Jose, Costa Rica: Nicaragua agrees to meet directly with contras, asks direct talks with U.S. (→ 21).

16. United States: New seismic data indicates United States held 117 secret nuclear tests in last 25 years (→ 2/8).

16. New York: CBS fires Jimmy "the Greek" Snyder for racist remarks.

DEATHS

11. Isidor Isaac Rabi, Austrian-born, American pioneer in atomic physics (*7/29/1898).

11. Gregory "Pappy" Boyington, head of World War II's Black Sheep Squadron.

13. Chiang Ching-kuo, leader of Taiwan since 1975.

15. Sean MacBride, Irish revolutionary and Nobel Prize winner (*1/26/1904).

Schools given right to censor students

Jan 13. The Supreme Court has ruled that high school administrators have the right to censor student newspapers. Today's ruling, which did not surprise school officials, ends a four-year case in which students at Hazelwood High School in Missouri sued Principal Robert Reynolds for barring articles about divorce and teen-age pregnancy from their paper. Reynolds hopes the court's decision helps other schools gain control of their papers, but many students around the nation are vehement in their disapproval. Gwendolyn Gregory of the National School Board Association says, "Kids don't have the same rights as everyone else. They can't vote. They can't drink. There are all sorts of things they can't do."

"Hitler" painting?

Jan 11. Last week a 9-by-15-inch watercolor of old Vienna that was signed "A. Hitler" was auctioned for $26,000 in Louisville. In 1907 and again in 1908, a young Adolf Hitler applied for admission to the Academy of Fine Arts in Vienna but was rejected. When he became Fuhrer in 1934, he tried to round up his paintings and destroy any forgeries, but hundreds survived. Some Kentuckians voiced their anger over a mass murderer's name making a painting valuable.

Youth is accused of $8 million fraud

Jan 1. David Bloom's savvy got him noticed. The 23-year-old Duke University graduate amassed $5 million in art, $3 million in real estate and he was living opulently just 18 months after earning an art history degree. Today the Securities and Exchange Commission exposed his investment firm as a fraud. Bloom's art buying as well as gifts to Duke were supported by $10 million he collected from 100 investors who believed his bogus statements. In an interview a while back, Bloom said, "First I decide what I want to buy, then I worry about how I'm going to pay for it."

Haitians stage strike on eve of election

Markets are empty because of an opposition call for an election boycott.

Jan 16. A general strike has created an unnatural calm in Haiti's capital of Port-au-Prince as the nation awaits tomorrow's presidential election. Four leading opposition politicians have called on voters to join them in a boycott of the election, charging that the results are certain to be be manipulated by the army. Many of the residents of Port-au-Prince have left the capital in fear of a repeat of last November's violence, when the first Haitian presidential election in 30 years was stopped because gangs and soldiers massacred people who were attempting to vote.

Few Haitians now believe Lieutenant General Henri Namphy is willing to transfer power to a freely elected civilian government. The general has led the provisional government since the ouster of Jean Claude Duvalier's dictatorship almost two years ago. Those opposed to Namphy believe that he wants to make a show of holding democratic elections in order to convince the United States to resume economic and military aid and to give Haitians the impression that the long-promised civilian government is in place, even though he is holding on to the real power (→ 17).

Jan 13. On this date in Washington, D.C., in 1888, 33 prominent men resolved to create an organization to gather and disseminate geographic knowledge, which became the National Geographic Society.

Payton, NFL's leading rusher, ends career

Jan 10. After 13 seasons and 13 miles of yardage, Walter Payton has ended his pro football career. He ended it on a depressing note, though, a yard short of a first down on his final carry and sharing the defeat of his Chicago Bears in the National Football League playoffs.

But his legions of fans will remember the record 17,303 yards that he rushed, the 495 passes he caught and the 4,716 yards they produced. At age 33, Payton was limited to 18 rushes for 85 yards and three pass receptions for 20 yards in his team's 21 to 17 loss to the Washington Redskins.

The best running back in NFL history was emotionally drained as he slumped on the bench at game's end. His teammates rushed by him into the locker room, knowing they had another year to make amends.

Later, Payton removed his uniform, slowly, deliberately. "I'm gonna take my time," he said. "This is the last time I'll take it off." He smiled wistfully as he removed the thigh pads. "Three years in high school, four years college and 13 years here, I've worn the same thigh pads," he said.

In all that time in a grueling sport, Payton has walked away with nothing worse than a scraped elbow. He missed only one game, in his rookie year, 1975. "Overall," he mused, "it's been a lot of fun."

Walter Payton quietly watches the final moments of his career slip by.

Israeli police fight Arabs at Dome of Rock

The Dome of the Rock, revered by Moslems, is the scene of a battle.

Jan 15. An already bleak situation worsened today when stone-throwing Palestinians and Israeli police units clashed at the Dome of the Rock mosque in Arab East Jerusalem. The mosque, one of Islam's holiest places, is on the site where Mohammed is said to have ascended into heaven on a white horse. Some 5,000 Arabs had gathered there on this Moslem Sabbath for special services to mourn protesters killed in the recent uprising, now at 38 following a shooting today in the Gaza Strip.

The scene was tense to begin with as more than 1,000 police, the biggest call-up yet, sealed off the mosque region in anticipation of trouble. The exact cause is unclear, but as the service ended, hundreds of young Palestinians began chanting, "There is no God but Allah!" The police opened fire with tear gas, then began ducking rocks. Several policemen were injured. Doctors at the Arab Mokassed Hospital treated some 70 Arabs, victims of clubbings and tear gas.

Palestinians view the battle as a desecration of a revered site. To Israelis, the violence marks an ominous turn. They had hoped to maintain calm in Jerusalem, their capital, by granting the Arabs wider rights than they would in Gaza or the West Bank. In return, they expect the Jerusalem Arabs to refrain from civil disobedience. Today's police action is regarded by some as a reminder by the Israelis of this tacit agreement (→ 19).

Mexico's capital is called most smog-polluted city in the world

Jan 15. Carlos Fuentes dubbed it Makesicko City in a recent novel and, indeed, Mexico City can make you sick. It has been called the world's most polluted city. Winter mornings are the worst as carbon monoxide, sulfur dioxide, mercury, lead and other foul substances get trapped close to the ground until sunlight warms the atmosphere so they can rise and drift away. Because of this condition, children start school later during the winter months. In 1950, Mexico City had three million residents and 55,000 cars. By 1980, the city's population had grown fivefold, but the number of cars had multiplied by 30, reaching 1.6 million.

Children in Mexico City amuse themselves around a disease-ridden puddle.

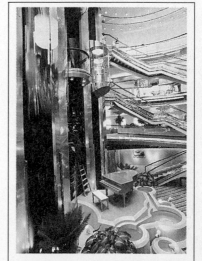

The atrium of the world's largest ocean liner, Sovereign of the Seas. Cruises are thriving again.

Su	Mo	Tu	We	Th	Fr	Sa
					1	2
3	4	5	6	7	8	9
10	11	12	13	14	15	16
17	18	19	20	21	22	23
24	25	26	27	28	29	30
31						

18. Washington: World Bank report says Third World debt hurts living standards (→ 3/5).

18. China: Air crash kills 108.

18. Moscow: Jewish refusnik Josef Begun leaves U.S.S.R. for Israel (→ 21).

18. United States: Daffy Duck back in eight-minute short, "The Duxorcist."

19. Jerusalem: Israel declares emergency powers in East Jerusalem for first time since annexation 20 years ago (→ 2/15).

19. Port Arthur, Texas: On her birth date, Janis Joplin is honored with statue.

20. Washington: United States adds North Korea to list of states sponsoring terrorism, citing role in bombing of South Korean jetliner.

20. New York: The Rev. Al Sharpton accused of being informer in black community.

21. San Jose, Costa Rica: Sandinistas propose international group, with United States, to monitor care of contras who lay down arms (→ 22).

22. Washington: Federal appeals court rules special prosecutor law unconstitutional (→ 6/29).

22. New York: Mistrial declared for jury tampering in Gene Gotti racketeering trial.

22. Managua: Police let protesters break up demonstration demanding amnesty for political prisoners (→ 23).

22. Columbia, Illinois: Sue Zera wins $10 million on lottery ticket she had to buy after pressing wrong button.

23. San Francisco: Arms protester S.B. Willson sued by men driving train that severed his legs.

23. United States: Falling dollar encourages tourism here.

DEATHS

17. Andrija Artukovic, leader of Nazi puppet state of Croatia (*11/29/1899).

18. Bassist Al Hall, first black musician in Broadway theater orchestra (*3/8/1915).

Nicaragua rounds up opposition leaders

After disrupting an opposition rally, a pro-government mob chants slogans.

Jan 23. The Sandinista security police have arrested and temporarily detained several leaders of the opposition. The Nicaraguan government questioned the leaders about a meeting they attended in Guatemala with members of the rebel army, the contras. The action was taken by Interior Minister Tomas Borge without the consent of President Daniel Ortega, who was meeting with regional politicians in Costa Rica. After that summit session, Ortega lifted civil rights restrictions in a conciliatory move, one also aimed at influencing a contra aid bill in the American Congress. Yesterday, violence erupted as Sandinista supporters disrupted an amnesty rally (→ 24).

Million Africans will die of AIDS in decade

Jan 21. The forecast that AIDS will kill one million Africans in the next 10 years has triggered concern over Africa's future. On a continent that sees tens of thousands die each year from curable diseases such as malaria, tuberculosis and sleeping sickness, the rapid spread of AIDS is especially frightening because it is killing many of the young professionals who will be needed if their countries are to develop economically. Because there is no known cure of AIDS and no vaccine to prevent it, African countries have begun public health campaigns in an effort to convince young people to change their life style. In Africa, AIDS is primarily spread through heterosexual intercourse (→ 30).

In African nations, the specter of AIDS haunts women as much as men.

Once-rich Texan loses whole fortune

Jan 22. Rich, powerful and confident, John Connally seemed to epitomize Texas itself. This former secretary of the Navy and former Texas governor, who was wounded by John F. Kennedy's assassin in 1963 and was acquitted on bribery charges while a Treasury secretary, spent $12 million on a run for the 1980 Republican presidential nomination (it netted him one delegate). Now he owes his creditors $49 million, and all he owns — from the gubernatorial chair to the washer and dryer — is being sold at a four-day bankruptcy auction. Silvery head held high, Connally, 70, states that this is neither the demise of the state of Texas nor of John and Nellie Connally. Next he plans to write his autobiography.

Connally and wife: lost the farm.

First tourists come back from Antarctic

Jan 21. Watch out Honolulu, move over Bermuda. The South Pole may be out to take your place as the hot spot for vacationers. Hot spot? Well, maybe not hot, but the Antarctic tundra, where the average summer temperature hovers at 47 degrees below, has received its first tourists. Some 35 travelers paid $35,000 apiece for the round-trip flight and a three-hour tour of the Amundsen-Scott South Pole research facility. Many environmentalists are discouraging the trip to protect the region.

Police surround home of slain polygamist

This Mormon family is awaiting the "resurrection" of John Singer.

Jan 18. Nine years ago today, John Singer, a Marion, Utah, polygamist, was killed by police seeking to arrest him for refusing to send his children to public school. Today, more than 150 armed officers ringed the home of one of Singer's widows, looking for a suspect in a Mormon church bombing. The suspect, Addam Swapp, married to two of Singer's daughters, is one of 14 people, six of them children, who are in the house awaiting the "resurrection" of Singer. The church had excommunicated John Singer for advocating polygamy (banned by the Mormons in 1890). Those inside the compound are armed and have said they will not surrender, whatever the cost (→ 28).

Tyson KO's Larry Holmes in fourth round

Jan 22. Mike Tyson showed no mercy for his grandfatherly opponent, flattening former champion Larry Holmes in the fourth round of a scheduled 12-round bout. Tyson jarred the 38-year-old Holmes with a right to the jaw and floored him for only the fourth time in his 51-fight career. After the first of three knockdowns, Holmes's few punches had no sting as he leaned away from the unbeaten champion.

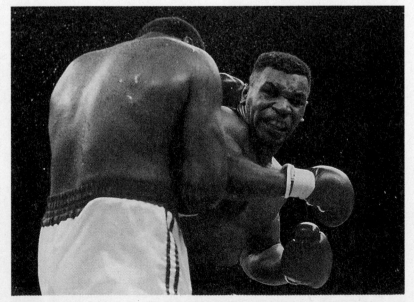

Was it Tyson's look or his fist that delivered Larry Holmes to the mat?

Haitians ballot amid extensive boycott

Jan 17. Today's presidential election in Haiti took place peacefully, unlike the one held seven weeks ago that was halted when rampaging gangs, some made up of soldiers, killed at least 34 people who were trying to vote. A boycott called by opposition leaders appears to have been successful, with one estimate claiming that only about 5 percent of those eligible to vote participated. The opposition had called on Haitians to boycott today's vote to protest the way the government of Lieutenant General Henri Namphy responded to last November's election crisis. The general named new members to an electoral council responsible for the election, replacing the independent civilian body that the constitution called for.

A light voter registration turnout and the failure to set rules governing the operation of polling places created much confusion and led to charges of vote fraud. Many polling places did not require identification of voters, making it easy for people to vote more than once, and for people who were ineligible to vote to take part. And some polling places did not have ballots for each candidate. Many observers believe that Namphy does not want to give up the power that he has held as the leader of the provisional government that came to power after the ouster of dictator Jean Claude Duvalier, and they have accused him of rigging the elections (→ 24).

Optimistic Haitians participating in the democratic process despite boycott.

Homeless, she wins right to roam free

Jan 21. Joyce Brown, New York City's first homeless person forcibly placed in a mental institution by police last October, was freed today. Her story aroused public awareness about Mayor Koch's controversial plan to remove the homeless from the streets, and the New York Civil Liberties Union won her case in court. Miss Brown now lives in a tiny city-run hotel room and says it's "finally good to be treated like a human." The National Coalition for the Homeless reported a 25 percent rise in the homeless count last year, bringing the national total to three million.

Victims of Stalin honored by U.S.S.R.

Jan 21. Nikolai Bukharin was considered the "darling" of the Communist Party in the 1920's. But, his name disappeared from Soviet histories after he was shot in 1939, one of the most prominent of the millions of victims who died during the purges that Soviet leader Joseph Stalin conducted to eliminate "socially alien" elements from society. Today, on the anniversary of Lenin's death, newspapers printed works by Bukharin and other victims of purges as part of Soviet leader Mikhail S. Gorbachev's reexamination of the "painful points" in the nation's history (→ 2/5).

Su	Mo	Tu	We	Th	Fr	Sa
					1	2
3	4	5	6	7	8	9
10	11	12	13	14	15	16
17	18	19	20	21	22	23
24	25	26	27	28	29	30
31						

24. Nicaragua: Plane supplying contras shot down by Sandinista anti-aircraft fire (→ 25).

24. Washington: United States charges Abu Nidal used Warsaw as financial base for terrorist operations.

25. United States: Hertz admits overcharging clients for rental car repairs.

25. Managua: Sandinistas begin formal talks with Meskito Indians (→ 27).

26. New York: "The Phantom of the Opera" opens, with $17 mil. in advance ticket sales.→

27. Washington: Reagan asks for $36 mil. in contra aid (→ 30).

27. Skokie, Illinois: Nutra-Sweet introduces low-calorie, low-cholesterol fat substitute.

27. Moscow: U.S.S.R. reports it scrapped construction of nuclear plant after public opposition from Chernobyl.

28. New Hampshire: Public Service Co., beset by Seabrook nuclear protests, is first public utility to file bankruptcy since Depression (→ 3/20).

28. Washington: Convicted U.S. drug smuggler says he gave Panama's Gen. Noriega millions in bribes (→ 2/5).

28. Washington: Senate passes civil rights bill, reverses Court decision limiting federal anti-discrimination power (→ 2/2).

28. Utah: Polygamist stakeout ends in shootout; one policeman dead (→ 5/9).

29. Chester, Pennsylvania: Amtrak train derails after hitting maintenance equipment on wrong track; 24 hurt; switch operator flees.

30. New York: Cuomo administration agrees to give city addicts free needles to help fight spread of AIDS (→ 3/3).

DEATHS

28. Klaus Fuchs, British physicist and spy, divulged secret of the atomic bomb to the Soviet Union (*12/29/11).

29. James Killian, first presidential assistant for science and technology (*7/24/04).

Museum celebrates 150 years of photos

1839 Paris, through Daguerre's lens.

Jan 31. An exhibit entitled "A Panorama of Photography: 150 Years Since Daguerre" ended today at the Worcester Art Museum in Worcester, Massachusetts. One hundred works from the museum's photography collection were displayed, as well as several early daguerrotypes. Louis Jacques Mande Daguerre of France was one of several men who invented photography in the 1830's. His process, the daguerrotype, which produced a permanent image on a silver-coated copper plate treated with iodine vapor, was greeted with surprise in 1837. Now photography is ubiquitous.

Aspirin is shown to reduce heart attacks

Jan 26. If you are prone to headaches, chances are you won't have a heart attack. A new study by the National Heart, Lung and Blood Institute has demonstrated that regular use of aspirin can reduce the risk of heart attack by as much as 47 percent. This is good news in a country where heart attacks cause 540,000 deaths each year.

The study suggests that, under the supervision of a doctor, many middle-aged men, as well as younger risk-prone men, would be wise to start taking aspirin regularly, as often as every other day. "Thousands of heart attacks will be prevented," says Dr. Lawrence Cohen of the Yale School of Medicine.

A heart attack is often caused when a clot blocks the flow of blood in a coronary artery, depriving the heart muscle of oxygen. The use of aspirin apparently can help keep the blood fluid and thus prevent the formation of clots. According to the new study, aspirin may be good for the heart, but it should be remembered that with some people the use of a mild analgesic can result in a stroke or gastrointestinal trouble.

Jan 31. The final touchdown of the Washington Redskins' 42-10 Super Bowl XXII victory over the Denver Broncos is flown in by Timmy Smith, who set a 204-yard rushing record in a game nicknamed Stupor Bowl.

Reagan opponents targets of spying

Jan 27. The Federal Bureau of Investigation has been spying on people protesting the Reagan administration's policies in Central America. Under the Freedom of Information Act, the Center for Constitutional Rights amassed evidence showing that for more than five years the F.B.I. has been conducting surveillance on groups and individuals at peace rallies. Agents of the bureau photographed protesters and recorded their license numbers. The F.B.I. said it was authorized to conduct investigations into allegations of "criminal activity" (→ 2/2).

Anti-wrinkle drug

Jan 24. Since the report first appeared in The Journal of the American Medical Association, the telephones of dermatologists have been ringing non-stop all across the country. The callers are asking about Retin-A, a vitamin A-based drug that was developed some 17 years ago as a treatment for acne. The new report, it seems, provided proof that Retin-A can actually smooth out wrinkles in the skin and reverse the damage that has been caused by overexposure to the sun. The drug is currently available by prescription only.

Rather versus Bush

Jan 25. Presidential candidate George Bush and CBS News anchor Dan Rather exchanged angry words during a live 10-minute interview on national television last night. When Rather tried to question Bush about his role in the Iran-contra affair, the Vice President said, "I want to talk about why I want to be President." Hostilities intensified when Rather pressed Bush about an apparent policy contradiction — opposing terrorism yet knowing about the arms-for-hostages deal with Iran. Bush then angrily referred to the time last year when Rather walked off a CBS set, leaving the screen dark. The Vice President was offended last night by a taped report concerning his Iran-contra involvement, shown before he was interviewed.

Aborigines protest Australian bicentennial

Aborigines protest the bicentennial. Australia was founded as an alternative penal settlement to the American colonies Britain lost during the Revolution.

Jan 26. More than 20,000 aborigines, the native people of Australia, began a "year of mourning" in a downtown Sydney park. A mile away, some two million of their fellow Australians converged on Sydney Harbor to celebrate the 200th birthday of the penal colony that became Australia.

On January 26, 1788, the first fleet of 11 ships limped in from England with 700 convicts aboard. Brushing aside aboriginal cries of "Warra, warra!" (Go away!), crews, guards and convicts came ashore — and stayed. Now, new immigrants and descendants of those first settlers jostled to see the 11 sailing ships re-enacting that

first arrival — the centerpiece of a parade of tall ships that flocked to Sydney for the festivities. As cannon boomed out a 200-gun salute, the Sydney Sun exulted: "Never has there been a day on which it felt so good to be Australian."

But not everyone cheered. Most aborigines, a tiny 1.4 percent of Australia's 16.5 million population, live in poverty on the fringes of cities, or earn a meager living as stockmen or laborers around rural communities. As the rest of Australia made merry, aborigines went into mourning for what they see as a white invasion of their homeland and the start of two centuries of dispossession.

Sandinista-contra talks end; no gain

Jan 30. Deadlocked. That's the way negotiations between the Nicaraguan government and the contras ended in Costa Rica yesterday. The two sides presented very different proposals to end the six-year war. The Sandinistas detailed a step-by-step plan to disarm the rebels and integrate them into civilian life. However, they refuse to rewrite their constitution or substantially reduce their army as requested in the proposal of the contras. Both delegations realize the talks will influence the upcoming vote of the United States Congress on assistance for the contras. The negotiations are the first direct talks between the opposing sides (→ 2/3).

Tough-guy principal

Jan 31. Principal Joe Clark has stirred a national controversy over the tough law-and-order tactics he has used to get rid of violence and drugs at Eastside High School in Paterson, N.J. The Paterson school board called Clark insubordinate and threatened to fire him for ousting 66 "parasitic" pupils last month without getting board approval. Clark has been praised by President Reagan but criticized by others who say he is dumping unruly students into the streets and a life of despair instead of trying to save them through the school system.

Prosecutor links Meese to pipeline

Jan 30. A special prosecutor, James C. McKay, is investigating purported ties between Attorney General Edwin Meese and an abortive plan to build an oil pipeline from Iraq across Jordan to the Red Sea. The New York Times says the case shows how private commercial interests can "unduly influence decision-making at the highest levels" of the government. In 1985, Meese allegedly arranged for E. Robert Wallach, a friend and a principal in the project, to meet National Security Adviser Robert McFarlane at the White House. Two days later, McFarlane told other officials the plan was important for American security (→ 3/29).

Manigat Haiti victor

Jan 24. A former political science professor, Leslie F. Manigat, has been declared the winner in Haiti's controversial presidential election. The government-appointed electoral council said that 35 percent of eligible voters took part in the election, and Manigat won just over half the votes. The opposition has charged the government with rigging the vote to elect a puppet leader. However, Manigat's choice surprised many because he is viewed as having the best qualifications of any candidate and is known for his independence and ambition (→ 6/20).

Four faces of "The Phantom of the Opera": from left to right, Lon Chaney in the 1925 film classic, Claude Rains in the 1943 movie, Herbert Lom in the 1962 remake and Michael Crawford as the masked menace's latest incarnation — in a Broadway musical that is sold out for a year.

FEBRUARY
Week 5 1988

Su	Mo	Tu	We	Th	Fr	Sa
	1	2	3	4	5	6
7	8	9	10	11	12	13
14	15	16	17	18	19	20
21	22	23	24	25	26	27
28	29					

1. Moscow: Soviets announce death last month of Georgi Malenkov, Stalin's successor, at 86 (*1/8/1902).

2. Washington: Pentagon opens 4,000 jobs to women, demands end to harassment (→ 23).

2. Washington: F.B.I. Director Sessions calls spying on dissenters justified because of their support of "terrorist" groups in El Salvador (→ 3).

2. Montgomery, Alabama: Twelve arrested removing Confederate flag from Capitol (→ 10).

2. Canton, Ohio: Alan Page, Mike Ditka, Fred Biletnikoff, Jack Ham chosen for Football Hall of Fame.

3. Washington: White House says it turned down Soviet proposal to cut aid to Nicaragua if U.S. ends military aid to Central America (→ 3).

3. Washington: Ex-Panamanian official holds that United States asked Panama to set up East bloc arms shipment to El Salvador in attempt to frame Nicaraguan government (→ 8).

3. Trenton, New Jersey: State Supreme Court rules surrogate contracts illegal, but says Baby M can stay with biological dad.

3. Washington: Senate confirms Anthony Kennedy as associate justice of the Supreme Court (→ 18).

3. Washington: House defeats $43 million contra-aid bill (→ 8).

5. Moscow: Special commission decides Nikolai Bukharin, Stalin purge victim, was wrongly convicted and executed (→ 17).

5. San Francisco: Twenty-year-old Robert Wallace Jr. arrested in karate-style killing of businessman in New York.

5. Washington: Patent Office rules firms with patents on new genetically altered animals can charge royalties to farmers for new generations of offspring (→ 4/12).

5. New York: Corporate takeover bids on rise in wake of lower stock prices (→ 3/7).

Noriega indicted by U.S.

Feb 5. The Justice Department has indicted the Panamanian strongman General Manuel Noriega on two charges of drug smuggling in a conspiracy that reportedly dates to at least 1981. Said Leon B. Kellner, U.S. attorney in Miami, "In plain language, he utilized his position to sell Panama to drug traffickers." Among other things, the general is accused of having accepted more than $4.6 million in bribes and kickbacks, and of having assisted a multi-million dollar drug ring in Colombia that is said to account for more than half the cocaine coming into the United States. Because extradition from Panama is restricted, a trial in the United States is not considered likely (→ 27).

Wanted: General Manuel Noriega.

Arizona House votes to impeach Mecham

Enjoying the good will of his constituents is not one of Mecham's pleasures.

Feb 5. Arizona's House of Representatives has voted 46-14 to impeach Republican Governor Evan Mecham. Explaining its decision to bring him to trial, the Republican-dominated House charged that "Mecham has been guilty of high crimes, misdemeanors, and malfeasance in office," adding that the state of Arizona would be improved by his removal.

The 63-year-old Mecham is accused of trying to conceal a $350,000 campaign loan, of borrowing $60,000 of state money to prop up his Pontiac automobile dealership and of attempting to block investigation of a death threat allegedly made by a state official.

Mecham's troubles began soon after he took office in January 1987, antagonizing minorities by canceling the state holiday honoring the Rev. Dr. Martin Luther King Jr. and issuing off-the-cuff ethnic slurs. But throughout his testimony to the select committee considering impeachment, the embattled governor insisted he is innocent of any crime or ethical lapse. He predicted he will be vindicated at his Senate and criminal trials and at the polling booth. "The only way for people to get me out is to strike at my most important asset — my personal integrity," he said (→ 4/4).

Computer trading in stocks is restricted

Feb 2. The directors of the New York Stock Exchange have voted to ban the use of its electronic order system for a form of computerized trading that has been blamed for the market's record-setting 508-point plunge last October.

Under the ban, securities firms that are engaged in a complex trading strategy known as index arbitrage would be prohibited from using the order system whenever the Dow Jones industrial average rises or falls more than 50 points in one day. The Big Board's system, known as the Super Dot, can electronically carry out large blocks of trades almost instantly, making it easier for firms to perform index arbitrage, a strategy that seeks to take advantage of the minor discrepancies in price between stocks and stock index futures.

The chairman of the New York Stock Exchange, John J. Phelan Jr., said in a statement that the ban on the electronic order system was a step toward "limiting potential market volatility caused by program trading and reinforcing investor confidence in the integrity, fairness and efficiency of the exchange marketplace" (→ 5).

What goes 'round comes 'round: The Hula Hoop is once again enjoying a round of popularity; try one for wholesome recreation.

Gunman captured after taking 84 hostages

Harvey said his sympathy for the downtrodden led to his desperate act.

Feb 2. A day without classes sounds like every pupil's dream. But for those attending the West End Christian School in Tuscaloosa, Alabama, the dream became a nightmare when they were held hostage at gunpoint for 12 hours by James Harvey, who has a history of mental illness. After a ruse led to his arrest, he said he had acted to publicize the plight of the hungry and homeless. "This is a political act, not a criminal act," he said. "There are people in the street who don't have a place to sleep or anything to eat." Yesterday, in Lumberton, North Carolina, two Tuscarora Indians also pointed up social inequities by seizing 17 people. They surrendered 10 hours later.

At the Tuscaloosa school, the 80 pupils and four teachers were unharmed, but as one fourth-grader, Mary McCracken, 9, said, "It was sort of scary when we heard him cock his gun." With no lessons to recite, the pupils watched television — and prayed.

Has a picture ever really grabbed you? That's what this new show at New York's New Museum of Contemporary Art by Stephen Taylor Woodrow might do, as real people actually hang on walls and interact with the visitors.

Soviet nationalists get stronger, bolder

Feb 5. With increasingly open demonstrations in the Soviet Baltic, nationalists are pressing Moscow to allow their republics greater autonomy. The demonstrators are turning the language of the Soviet leader, Mikhail S. Gorbachev, against him by asking that he apply the openness and decentralization that he has called for in the economy to their own republics. Anti-Soviet sentiment is particularly strong in this region because the republics of Estonia, Latvia and Lithuania were forcibly annexed by the Soviet Union in 1940. Although the current protests are not very big, the government is reacting quickly to suppress them for fear that they could worsen or lead to more severe demonstrations among the more than 100 other nationalities in the Soviet Union (→ 23).

New Paris fashion star: Christian Lacroix

Classical Paris couture challenged by Christian Lacroix's outrageous designs.

Feb 1. Hail the new prince of couture, Christian Lacroix, who at 37 is witty, frivolous, outrageous, talented, sensuous, wildly creative and fun. He may place a cabbage rose on a woman's derriere or dress a middle-aged lady in a bubble ending at mid-thigh. He mixes vivid colors with swirling prints, enjoying the hard-to-control reds and oranges. A master of excess with an obvious flair for the theatrical, he sees haute couture as a "laboratory of ideas." Next, he is launching a ready-to-wear line and then he plans to expand into men's clothing because he himself "can't find a thing to wear."

In this scene from the Drake Manuscript, exhibited at New York's Morgan Library, the artist depicts himself explaining to his host, an Indian, that faith in Jesus Christ means he need not fear the "evil spirit" who keeps him prisoner in his home at night. Created during one of Sir Francis Drake's trips to the New World, the manuscript has not been shown in 400 years.

Su	Mo	Tu	We	Th	Fr	Sa
	1	2	3	4	5	6
7	8	9	10	11	12	13
14	15	16	17	18	19	20
21	22	23	24	25	26	27
28	29					

7. New York: Rupert Murdoch agrees to sell N.Y. Post to real estate developer Peter S. Kalikow (→ 20).

7. Rio de Janeiro: Floods and mudslides kill 127.

7. Chicago: Michael Jordan scores 40 as East wins NBA All-Star Game 138-133.

8. Miami: Contra leaders open fund in United States to collect private donations, postpone talks with Sandinistas (→ 3/3).

8. Antarctica: Ninety-mile-long glacier heads out to sea at one-tenth of a mile per hour.

8. Cape Canaveral: Unmanned rocket is launched in most elaborate and expensive tests of Strategic Defense Initiative yet (→ 5/4).

8. Vienna: Austrian commission reports that Kurt Waldheim must have known of Nazi atrocities and that he did conceal his past (→ 15).

8. Paoli, Pennsylvania: William Henry Redmond, 66, arrested for 1952 murder of 8-year-old girl.

9. New York: Paintings worth $6 million stolen from Upper East Side gallery, largest New York art theft.

9. Tyler, Texas: Death of black truck driver Loyal Garner Jr. in police beating is ruled a homicide.

10. San Francisco: Appeals court voids Army's ban on gays; first to grant strict constitutional protection to homosexuals (→ 3/14).

10. Washington: Education Department reports that six Southern states have failed to meet desegregation goals (→ 17).

11. Washington: Lyn Nofziger, ex-Reagan aide, convicted on three counts of violating federal ethics law (→ 4/8).

12. Rome: Palestinian gunman Ibrahim Mohammed Khaled convicted of 1985 Rome airport bombing, sentenced to 30 years.

13. Mazatlan, Mexico: President Reagan and President Miguel de la Madrid open summit amid drug-trafficking tensions (→ 19).

Dole, Gephardt win in Iowa; Bush third

Bob doles out Republican wisdom.

Gephardt hammers home his point.

Feb 8. Senator Bob Dole of Kansas won the Iowa Republican caucuses tonight, beating the Rev. Pat Robertson and Vice President Bush. The victor in the Iowa Democratic caucuses was Representative Richard Gephardt of Missouri, trailed by Senator Paul Simon and Governor Michael Dukakis.

While the Dole victory had been expected, based on earlier polls, the relatively strong showing by Robertson, the former television evangelist, was seen by some as a humiliation for Bush, who until now had led the GOP presidential field in nearly all the polls. Dole topped the ticket with 37.4 percent of the vote, followed by Robertson with 24.6 percent and Bush with 18.6 percent. While disappointed by his showing, Bush aides said his strength in the Southern states, most of which vote next month, and his big lead in New Hampshire, which is to vote next week, will win him nomination at the party's national convention this summer.

In the Democratic caucuses, Gephardt won 31.3 percent of the vote to Simon's 26.7 percent, with Dukakis polling 22.2 percent (→ 16).

Small plants lead rust belt revival

Feb 9. Economists have long predicted the eventual demise of small American manufacturers because they lack the economies of scale to compete against low-paying foreign manufacturers. Now, a group of small but successful enterprises in the American rust belt is leading a manufacturing revival. Many companies have thrived without the use of sophisticated technology by producing customized products for highly specialized markets and constantly fine-tuning their production techniques. According to the Small Business Administration, large American manufacturers lost 300,000 jobs between 1976 and 1984, while firms with fewer than 500 workers added about 1.2 million jobs (→ 3/4).

The future is here: Hypermarkets open

Feb 8. Even a Valley Girl could get, like, totally spaced in one of these places. But retail giants like K-Mart and Wal-Mart are betting the hypermarkets, vast "malls without walls" that offer virtually everything and can cover five football fields, are the future of shopping in the suburbs. The new megamalls operate under a simple concept: sell such a huge amount of merchandise that you can discount some items as much as 40 percent below retail. But in reality, the hypermarket experience can prove so complex that one shopper likened it to running a marathon. But progress seems to roll on, with the hypermarkets proliferating from Texas to Montana to Ohio, with many more on the way.

Soviets fix date to leave Afghanistan

Feb 8. The Soviet Union is ready to begin withdrawing its troops from Afghanistan on May 15, Soviet leader Mikhail S. Gorbachev has announced. The pullout would take 10 months and the starting date is contingent on a settlement being reached at the peace talks in Geneva by March 15, he said. The announcement seemed to be aimed at putting pressure on Pakistan and the U.S. to accept the Soviet timetable instead of the eight-month version proposed by Pakistan. Gorbachev said Moscow will not participate in setting up a coalition government. "It is a purely an internal Afghan issue," he said (→ 3/4).

Long-awaited Malle movie in New York

Feb 12. "Au Revoir les Enfants" ("Goodbye, Children") is a cinematic fiction woven out of memory. It recalls life during the German occupation of France, when Louis Malle, the French director-writer, then 12 years old, attended a Jesuit boarding school near Fontainebleau. His best friend and two other Jewish boys were arrested — and disappeared. More than 40 years later, Malle remembers it all on the screen in a moving but never falsely sentimental tale offering performances loaded with naturalness, ease and genuine humor.

Malle with wife, Candice Bergen.

Calgary plays host to the Winter Olympics

Dazzling colors bring up the curtain on the Olympic Games in Calgary.

Feb 12. The longest Winter Olympic Games, with a record number of athletes and countries competing, got under way today after a seventh-grade girl from Calgary stood on her tiptoes and ignited the traditional flame. Robyn Perry, a petite figure skater, was the last of 6,520 Canadians to move the torch on its 88-day journey to the Alberta city. Two billion people watched on television as most of the 1,750 athletes from 57 nations participated in a pageant of pomp and color. Canada's Governor General Jeanne Sauve declared the Games open and the 18-day carnival of sport was on its way (→ 14).

Soviet and U.S. ships in bumping match

Feb 12. Warships in the Black Sea engaged in a high-stakes game of chicken today when a Soviet frigate and destroyer grazed the sides of the American destroyer Caron and the cruiser Yorktown after they strayed within the Soviet 12-mile limit off Sevastopol. Pentagon officials said that the ships were asserting the rights of passage outside the three-mile limit recognized by the United States but conceded that the Caron was carrying advanced intelligence-gathering equipment. Damage to the ships was reported to be slight (→ 3/6).

Although little damage was caused, the bumping of the ships is not what is meant by efforts to bring the United States and Soviet Union closer together.

Nudists versus birds

Feb 8. An unlikely feud has pitted naturist against naturalist in Rhode Island, with the fate of a rare piping plover colony hanging in the balance. Officials last week closed part of Moonstone beach to save four of the birds, whose numbers have dwindled because of the vulnerability of their sandy nests. But since Moonstone is the state's only public beach where one can sun and swim without a bathing suit, angry nudists plan a court fight. Said one: "We're not going to be pushed off beautiful oceanfront property for the sake of four birds."

Farm crisis abating

Feb 13. After six long years of recession, America's farmers appear to be rebounding from their cycle of despair. Though 10 percent of the farmers are still heavily in debt, net cash income for farmers soared to a record $58 billion last year, which is up from $37 billion in 1983, the darkest year of the farm crisis. Overall farm debt has dropped 28 percent since 1983. Some observers, however, fear that too many farmers may be dependent on government subsidies, which the administration is planning to reduce next year (→ 3/1).

Toledo exhibits Picasso linoleum prints

The exhibit is the first comprehensive survey of Picasso's work in linoleum.

The Toledo Museum of Art in Toledo, Ohio, is currently showing the first comprehensive survey of Pablo Picasso's work in the linoleum medium. The exhibition features 71 dazzling color linoleum prints, a form of relief print similar to a woodcut, but usually printed in bright opaque colors.

In 1939, Picasso made his first linoleum cut, but most were done from 1959 to 1963, when the renowned artist was already in his late 70's and early 80's. He made his last linoleum cut print in 1968.

At first, Picasso designed posters in linoleum to publicize the bullfights and ceramic crafts of Vallauris, a village near Cannes on the French Riviera. Soon thereafter, he was developing linoleum still lifes and prints showing musicians and nudes, as well as portraits, many of them of Jacqueline Roque, who in 1961 became his second wife. These include "Woman with a Hat" (a study of Jacqueline Roque), "Lady with a Ruff after El Greco," "Luncheon in the Grass after Edouard Manet" and "Still Life with Watermelon and Cherries."

The Toledo Museum is also currently exhibiting, in an adjacent gallery, its collection of Picasso's illustrated books. From 1910 until shortly before his death, the artist created original print illustrations for 156 publications.

Su	Mo	Tu	We	Th	Fr	Sa
	1	2	3	4	5	6
7	8	9	10	11	12	13
14	15	16	17	18	19	20
21	22	23	24	25	26	27
28	29					

14. Leningrad: Fire ravages library of National Academy of Sciences, damaging some 3,600,000 books.

15. Vienna: Calling criticism "slander," President Waldheim vows he will not resign.

15. Jerusalem: Israel opens inquiry into reports of soldiers burying four Palestinians alive (→ 15).

15. Cyprus: Explosion disables P.L.O. exodus ferry bound for Israel (→ 16).

16. United States: Firestone announces it will sell 75% of tire division to Japanese for $1 billion, largest Japanese investment in United States (→ 3/7).

16. Paris: Arab countries reject negotiations based on Camp David process (→ 24).

17. Moscow: No. 2 party leader charges schools are hindered by central control, poor physical conditions (→ 18).

17. Amherst, Mass.: Black students at Univ. of Massachusetts end five-day occupation of African-American studies building as many racial policy demands are met (→ 3/2).

17. Beirut: Lieutenant Colonel William R. Higgins, U.S. Marine serving with United Nations, is abducted (→ 3/16).

19. Washington: State Department report says national security justifies exempting Mexico and Panama from penalties for lax enforcement of drug laws (→ 3/1).

19. Rome: Pope John Paul II issues encyclical charging ideological rivalry between East and West exploits Third World.

20. New York: Unions agree to $22 million in concessions to save New York Post.

DEATHS

14. Composer Frederick Loewe, wrote "My Fair Lady" music (*6/10/1901).

14. Nora Astorga Gadea, heroine of Sandinistas and delegate to United Nations, dies of cancer at 39.

15. Richard P. Feynan, theoretical physicist, dies at 69 (*5/11/1918).

Bush and Dukakis win New Hampshire

Bush regains ground lost in Iowa.

Feb 16. Bouncing back from his recent crucial defeat in Iowa, Vice President Bush won the Republican presidential primary tonight in New Hampshire, largely by citing his close ties to President Reagan. By defeating Senator Bob Dole, who had topped him in Iowa, the Vice President effectively kept alive his race for the presidency.

Meanwhile, Governor Michael Dukakis won the Democratic contest for his party's nomination, with much of his strength coming from his identification as a regional candidate. The rest of the party's candidates trailed badly.

Conceding defeat just minutes after the polls closed, Dole said that it was but one step along the road and "makes the climb a little steeper," but that he was ready for the next challenge. He criticized Bush for an advertising campaign that suggested Dole would raise taxes.

While the Dukakis victory was a decisive one, it proved little about his ability to win outside his native New England. Representative Rich-

Dukakis, a win on neighboring turf.

ard Gephardt came in second and the Rev. Jesse Jackson did well enough to claim that he has expanded his appeal to white voters (→ 23).

American falls in Olympic speed skating

Feb 14. Dan Jansen, an American speed-skater, fell on the first turn of his 500-meter race at the Calgary Olympics just hours after he learned his sister had died of leukemia. The hearts of millions of Americans watching on television were wrenched when Jansen lost his balance and his bid for a gold medal. They knew that Jane Beres, 27, had died in the family's hometown, West Allis, Wisconsin, and were rooting for one of America's few skating hopefuls. Jansen had offered to be a bone-marrow donor and was ready to leave Calgary if he could help. "Compared to somebody's life," he said, "what is skating a race or running a race or whatever it is you're doing?" (→ 24).

Jansen sees his gold medal hopes dashed as he hits the wall in the 500 meters.

Reagan policy looks contrary to rhetoric

Feb 15. President Reagan gets mixed reviews from conservatives and barbs from liberals over his budget policies of the last seven years. The liberals deplored the rise in arms spending and the braking of domestic programs. Conservatives praised Reagan for ending double-digit inflation, increasing growth, cutting interest rates and moving toward privatization. But they note that the federal civilian work force rose by 150,000 to over three million under Reagan, who swore to cut it, and that federal spending increased by $321 billion to over a trillion dollars under a President who wished to trim spending. They point out that Reagan, a critic of heavy debt, assumed more of it than all previous presidents combined. The debt rose from 26.6 percent of the gross national product in 1981 to 43 percent this year. Most of all, the conservatives lament, Reagan missed a chance to dismantle the welfare state totally; instead, they say, he merely consolidated it, winnowing out minor programs. Liberal economists say the domestic cuts Reagan made hit the poor hard, but spared the middle class.

Kennedy sworn in as new high court judge

Kennedy, after an easy confirmation, is sworn in by Chief Justice Rehnquist.

Feb 18. Judge Anthony M. Kennedy of Sacramento, California, became tho 104th Justice of the United States Supreme Court at swearing-in ceremonies at the court and the White House. He replaces retired Justice Lewis Powell, who frequently cast the swing vote in a court sharply polarized between liberals and conservatives. But Kennedy's views on such issues as abortion, separation of church and state and affirmative action were not immediately known. Kennedy was President Reagan's third choice for the job. His first, Judge Robert Bork, a strong critic of past civil rights decisions, was rejected by the Senate. Reagan's second choice, Judge Douglas Ginsburg, withdrew after it was learned he had smoked marijuana while in law school.

Book warns America of potential decline

Feb 15. The United States may have to learn to accept the status of a second-rate power, warns the Yale professor of history Paul Kennedy in his book "The Rise and Fall of the Great Powers: Economic Change and Military Conflict from 1500 to 2000." In it, Kennedy describes the gloomy prospects for the United States after first examining the patterns of rising and falling powers over the past five centuries. According to the professor, the United States risks "imperial overstretch," and "decision makers in Washington must face the awkward and enduring fact that the sum total of the United States's global interests and obligations is nowadays far larger than the country's power to defend them all simultaneously." In Kennedy's analysis, American dominance is going to fade, not necessarily because the United States is weaker than it was before, but because other powers are becoming relatively stronger.

Western load will ride Soviet rocket

Feb 20. An American firm has contracted with the Soviet Union to allow its clients to conduct pharmaceutical experiments aboard the Soviet space station Mir. This is the first time the Soviet Union will carry an American commercial payload into space. Other American companies are expected to follow suit, which should make the space station a lucrative source of hard currency for the Soviet Union.

With NASA's space shuttle program on hold since the Challenger disaster, the Soviet Union is the only game in town for those companies that need to conduct experiments in space. For that reason, Washington has promoted the construction of a private space station, which should be ready in 1993.

This joint venture did not raise the usual concerns in the United States about technology transfer because the experiments involve protein crystalization, an area in which the Soviet Union is expert ($\rightarrow$ 5/4).

2 guilty of selling fake apple juice

Feb 17. A Beech-Nut chemist called the mixture of sugars and other ingredients a "chemical cocktail," but it was labeled 100 percent apple juice and shipped to 20 states, five countries and the Carribean. Today, two former executives of the Beech-Nut Nutrition Corp., Niels Hoyvald and John Lavery, were found guilty of violating federal laws by buying the concentrate and selling the phony juice to save $750,000. In November, Beech-Nut pleaded guilty and paid a $2 million fine. An assistant U.S. attorney called it "a story of corporate greed and irresponsibility."

Gorbachev revising hallowed Marxism

Feb 18. Marxism must be updated to deal with current domestic and international conditions, Soviet leader Mikhail S. Gorbachev told a meeting of the Central Committee. In a 75-page speech in which Gorbachev sought to provide ideological justification for his economic reforms and better relations with the United States, Gorbachev said key aspects of Communist doctrine had become outdated. Nuclear arms have changed the nature of the threat from capitalism, he said. He also said his land had suffered because of its failure to "unshackle grass-roots initiative" ($\rightarrow$ 3/8).

"Old Pew (Blind Pew)" (1911), by N.C. Wyeth, of the first generation, from Robert Louis Stevenson's novel "Treasure Island."

"Liberty Launch" (1983), by Andrew Wyeth, son of N.C.

Feb 14. "An American Vision: Three Generations of Wyeth Art" leaves Chicago today, bound for Japan. N.C. Wyeth, patriarch of the dynasty, was known as an illustrator. His son Andrew is the best-known of the family. Above is grandson Jamie's "Portrait of Pig" (1970), oil on canvas.

Su	Mo	Tu	We	Th	Fr	Sa
	1	2	3	4	5	6
7	8	9	10	11	12	13
14	15	16	17	18	19	20
21	22	23	24	25	26	27
28	29					

21. Moscow: Soviet President Andrei Gromyko reports in his memoirs that Mao wanted to use Soviet A-bomb on United States soldiers in 1958.

22. Washington: Navy Secretary James H. Webb Jr. resigns over Defense Secretary Frank Carlucci's plan to cut Navy budget.

23. United States: Survey finds women, despite higher percentage in work force, still do almost all grocery shopping and cooking (→ 6/15).

23. Rio de Janeiro: Torrential rainstorms in last week kill 275.

23. Colorado Springs: Five-week-old Rachael Ann White returned to her mother after kidnapping five days ago.

24. Johannesburg: South Africa bans 17 leading anti-apartheid groups, including United Democratic Front (→ 27).

24. Washington: Reagan says there are "intimations" that outsiders are fomenting trouble in West Bank and Gaza (→ 3/1).

24. Calgary: Matti Nykaenen, Finnish ski star, is first to win three gold medals in Olympic ski jumping (→ 27).

26. New York: Rookie police officer guarding drug witness is slain in apparent attempt to intimidate witness.

27. Panama: President Delvalle flees home, goes into hiding as military arrives (→ 29).

27. Pretoria: More than 6,000 rightists rally, urging all-white state (→ 29).

27. Los Angeles: United States indicts four for giving cash and cocaine in radio payola scam.

28. Azerbaijan: Nationalist rioting disturbs major oil and natural gas center (→ 3/2).

29. Cape Town: Archbishop Tutu and two dozen other church leaders arrested in march to protest ban on anti-apartheid groups (→ 3/13).

29. Washington: Environmental Protection Agency reports hazardous conditions in 500,000 buildings due to loose asbestos.

Swaggart quits ministry

Feb 21. "I have sinned against you, and I beg your forgiveness," whispered the television evangelist Jimmy Swaggart in a tearful yet theatrical confession to his hushed congregation in Baton Rouge today. The charismatic preacher, known for stirring his audiences into a devotional frenzy, denounced his rival evangelist Jim Bakker last year as a "cancer on the body of Christ" after a sex scandal rocked Bakker's ministry. But today the 52-year-old Swaggart said that he would relinquish the pulpit because of his own moral failings.

Although the shamed preacher would admit only that his "sin was done in secret," officials at his Assembly of God church were confronted with photographs of Swaggart visiting a prostitute, who has been identified as Debra Murphree.

Swaggart, the undisputed king of hellfire-and-brimstone television, started with a small roadshow and built an empire that reaches 140 nations and earns $140 million per year, enabling the preacher, who has three lavish estates and a personal jet, to live anything but an ascetic life style.

At the end of Swaggart's sermon today, hundreds gathered around the altar in a show of support. But as the decline in donations to other scandal-ridden ministries has shown, many followers may not prove quite so forgiving (→ 3/29).

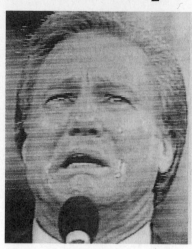

Fallen angel Swaggart, in a familiar outburst of humility, steps down.

Murphree, "the temptress," said Swaggart was "cheap and quick."

David Hockney's "Portrait of an Artist (Pool with Two Figures)" is just one of the works featured in the major retrospective of the artist's career now on tour. Including paintings from all over the world, the show reflects the international reputation this British-born artist has established.

Armenian patriots in major disruption

Feb 23. There has been a severe outbreak of unrest in the southern part of the Soviet Union. Armenian protesters there are urging a redrawing of the country's internal boundaries so that the predominantly Armenian autonomous region of Nagorno-Karabakhs that is now in the Republic of Azerbaijan would instead be attached to the Republic of Armenia. The leadership in Moscow has not been willing to make this kind of change, fearing that one such concession to nationalism might encourage members of the other 100 ethnic groups across the Soviet Union to press their own demands (→ 28).

Cities revive trolley

Feb 28. In 1917, the trolley industry carried 11 billion passengers, used 45,000 miles of track and employed some 300,000 workers. But after World War I, with the advent of autos and buses, the streetcar began to disappear. By the 1960's, trolleys were a rarity. Now cities from Los Angeles to Pittsburgh are resurrecting them to solve a variety of urban transportation problems with an efficient and economical system. The new light rail transit vehicles are sleek, but they still provide service with a style rich in nostalgia.

VCR's replace books

Feb 21. People all over the country are packing up books to make room on their shelves for growing video libraries. They're people like Alan Popper, who keeps his collection of 1,200 titles catalogued on a computer, and Dan Goldberger, who plans to buy a second VCR so he can dub, edit and transform from Beta to VHS. As prices for pre-recorded videos drop, sales are soaring, from $810 million in 1985 to a projected $3.3 billion in 1988. The number of titles has risen 30 percent in a year. Some films have sold more than a million copies — No. 1 is "Top Gun," at three million copies and still climbing. One big seller is children's video, which makes a fine baby sitter.

Dole wins 2 states; Dukakis takes one

Feb 23. Senator Bob Dole scored two victories yesterday, in South Dakota and Minnesota, in his quest for the Republican nomination for President. He easily defeated the Rev. Pat Robertson in the South Dakota primary and topped Robertson and Vice President Bush in the Minnesota caucuses, thus hoping to recoup his loss to Bush last week in New Hampshire. In the Democratic caucuses in Minnesota, Governor Michael Dukakis easily defeated the Rev. Jesse Jackson and others, but in South Dakota he lost by a 12 percent margin to Representative Richard Gephardt (→ 3/5).

Gray power growing

Feb 22. Senior citizens make up 12 percent of the population and as their numbers increase so does their economic and political power. Advertisers seek out their dollars, politicians court their votes and businesses want their expertise. As one older man said, "Aging has become very stylish." But not all the aged are doing well; 55 percent of elderly black women living alone get less than $5,300 a year. Also, as Social Security funds face depletion, there is concern about protecting those who reach 65 in the future.

Rare dinosaur find

Feb 24. Using high-tech X-ray techniques on a 150-million-year-old fossilized egg, scientists have examined what is believed to be the oldest known dinosaur embryo. In a four-inch-long egg, discovered in a Utah quarry in September, it dates to the Jurassic period, which lasted from 210 million to 145 million years ago. With computerized axial tomography, or CAT scanning, researchers from Brigham Young University were able to observe the creature's head, tail and body. The inch-long embryo, in the early stage of development, is believed to be an allosaur, one of the early relatives of the monster-size flesh eater tyrannosaurus rex. If it had lived, it would have grown into a 20-foot-high, three-ton terror of the Jurassic forests.

Winter Olympics end with Russians on top

Feb 27. A Winter Olympics rife with pathos and humor has ended, but with few bright moments for the United States team to remember. The Americans tied for eighth place while the Soviet athletes carried off 29 medals, 11 of them gold. With only six medals, two of them gold, the United States turned in one of its least impressive Olympic performances. Only in 1936 and 1924 did the Americans win fewer medals, four. As a result, the U.S. Olympic Committee named a special overview panel to study the performance and map a new course. George Steinbrenner, the controversial principal owner of the New York Yankees, will head the panel.

600 meters he was skating faster than any of his competitors.

The U.S. suffered another defeat when Debi Thomas was bested by East Germany's Katarina Witt in figure-skating, but an engaging Briton known as Eddie the Eagle captured everyone's imagination.

Michael Edwards, a 24-year-old plasterer whose form and distance as a ski-jumper left something to be desired, finished last and yet made the greatest impression on viewers. His ingenuous replies to questions ("My favorite skier is John Paul II") and modest manner won him television and stage offers. Another conversation piece was the bobsled team from Jamaica, hardly known

Katarina Witt, lithe and sequined, dazzles her audience in Calgary.

The Americans provided their share of drama when Dan Jansen, a speed-skating hopeful, fell in the 500-meter race hours after learning of the death of his sister. Then, with millions of his countrymen rooting him on via television, he fell a second time in the 1,000-meter event, 200 meters short of the finish. At

for its snow depths. The team made up in merchandising what it lacked in bobsledding, offering T-shirts for $15 and sweatshirts for $28. There was even a reggae record for sale. The Canadians were the overall money winners, however, raising a surplus of $20 million to help their sports programs.

Noriega won't quit; picks new President

Feb 29. In the topsy-turvy political scene in Panama, Gen. Manuel Noriega stays firmly entrenched while President Eric Arturo Delvalle is reportedly hiding in or near the capital. Three days ago, when Delvalle dismissed Noriega because of the general's indictment by the United States on drug charges, the opposite promised to be the case. But Delvalle was himself removed by Noriega through the National Assembly and the general chose Education Minister Manuel Palma to be President. The ouster of Delvalle has been condemned by the U.S. and most Latin nations (→ 3/4).

Flynt 1, Falwell 0

Feb 24. Larry Flynt came from behind today to score a victory in his court fight with television evangelist Jerry Falwell. The Supreme Court voted 8 to 0 to overturn a lower-court ruling awarding Falwell $200,000 in damages for "emotional distress" caused by a cartoon in Flynt's Hustler magazine showing a tipsy Falwell boasting of an incestuous relationship with his mother. Chief Justice William Rehnquist said even "outrageous statements of opinion must be protected under the Fifth Amendment."

Exner: Crime link?

Feb 21. Judith Campbell Exner, who made headlines 12 years ago by claiming she had an affair with President Kennedy, now says she served as his link to mobsters in Chicago and Los Angeles. In 1975, she told the Senate Intelligence Committee she had no knowledge of mob activity. But in People magazine this week she reveals she's now dying of cancer and says, "I want to put my life in order so I can die peacefully." Exner says she set up meetings between JFK and the mob chief Sam Giancana that probably led to efforts to fix West Virginia's 1960 Democratic primary. She also says that in 1961 she carried exchanges of messages between JFK, Giancana and mobster Johnny Roselli. Kennedy associates rejected her claims.

MARCH
Week 9 1988

Su	Mo	Tu	We	Th	Fr	Sa
		1	2	3	4	5
6	7	8	9	10	11	12
13	14	15	16	17	18	19
20	21	22	23	24	25	26
27	28	29	30	31		

1. Washington: Farmers Home Administration plans new regulations to relieve 100,000 farmers of $7 billion in debt (→ 6/16).

1. Britain: Post Office, under contract with private evangelist, starts using "Jesus is Alive!" postmark.

1. Brussels: Secretary of State Shultz ends Mideast tour on optimistic note, but little support for peace process (→ 16).

2. Washington: House, 315-98, passes bill overturning Court ruling curbing enforcement of civil rights law (→ 16).

2. Moscow: Soviets report deaths in last Sunday's riots in Azerbaijan; unofficial toll is 17 (→ 5/21).

3. Washington: House, defeating Democratic aid plan 216-208, halts all aid to Nicaraguan contras (→ 19).

3. Massachusetts: A report shows that one in 476 women who give birth in state is infected with AIDS (→ 5).

4. New York: Fourth International Cat Show opens at Madison Square Garden.

4. Washington: United States warns it will not halt arms to Afghan guerrillas until Soviets cut off arms to Afghan government (→ 4/7).

4. Panama: Government orders banks to close until "supply of dollar bills can be regularized (→ 14).

5. San Salvador: Top candidate in ruling Christian Democratic Party accused of misusing $2 million in United States aid.

5. Tibet: Police station hit by protesters in first independence demonstration this year (→ 6).

5. Dhaka: Ruling party wins in Bangladesh after election marred by violence.

5. United States: New Masters and Johnson study causing uproar with judgment that AIDS is "rampant" in heterosexual community (→ 5/26).

5. Chicago: Joe Hertel, collector of Vietnam memorabilia, opens museum to public.

2 U.N. votes heavily favor P.L.O. unit

March 2. The United Nations General Assembly voted almost unanimously against the United States today in response to a move by Congress, over President Reagan's objection, to close the U.N. mission of the Palestine Liberation Organization. In two resolutions, the Assembly held that the American move breached an obligation to the U.N. and said the World Court should decide if the United States must submit to arbitration. Representative Herbert Okun called the U.N. action "premature and inappropriate" because the administration has not yet decided whether to apply the law and shut the mission.

The 1947 Headquarters Agreement says the United States must provide access to the U.N. for those the Assembly invites, such as the Palestinians. A P.L.O. spokesman said that if the court didn't back the Assembly, the U.N. might move, because it could no longer function effectively in New York (→ 4/26).

Latin countries falling deeper into debt

Deeper in debt 1987	Foreign debt (in billions)	Growth per capita	Income	Inflation
Latin America	**$410**	**2.6%**	**0.5%**	**187%**
Brazil	113	3.0	1.0	338
Mexico	108	1.0	−1.2	148
Argentina	54	2.0	0.7	178
Venezuela	32	1.5	−1.1	36
Chile	20	5.5	3.6	23
Colombia	16	5.5	3.1	25
Peru	15	7.0	4.5	105

Source : U.N. Economic Commission for Latin America and the Caribbean.

March 5. With a total foreign debt of $410 billion, inflation at an average 187 percent and the average per capita income 6 percent lower than in 1978, Latin America is now further from paying its debts than it was at the start of the decade. Solutions that seemed possible then, such as debt restructuring and "bridge" loans, have proven illusory, and the debt continues to mount. Nor do these figures tell the whole story. Of the three largest nations, Brazil has an inflation rate of 338 percent, Argentina of 178 and Mexico 148. In Mexico, wages have dropped some 30 percent since 1980. When these nations try to pay off their debt, they face the specter of economic stagnation, even higher inflation and the social unrest that accompanies a rise in already high unemployment. Now, experts are looking for new ideas (→ 6/8).

Rodeos getting richer, but for cowboys it's still "suicide circuit"

Rodeos have traditionally offered their rugged competitors meager pickings. A full-time cowboy enters 50 to 75 rodeos a year and spends up to 45 weeks on the road, taking his horse with him. Unlike most other professional athletes, cowboys pay entry fees to each event and get paid only if they win. But recent increases in corporate sponsorship — from national giants like Coca-Cola and Anheuser-Busch — have driven prize money up. Top stars like saddle bronc rider Louis Feild can earn $160,000 in a year. But bruising competition and thousands of miles of travel take their toll.

Among veterans, professional rodeo is known as the "suicide circuit." Injuries shorten many careers. Every year a few injuries are fatal. Still the cowboys go on. "I've been broke in every state in the country," says one former bareback rider. "If you're not winning, you eat at McDonald's," adds steer wrestler Russell Solberg. "You get a steak occasionally and remember the taste."

Calf-roping, one of the more gentle activities on the "suicide circuit."

The excitement of the stampede.

Radical remedies urged for drug problem

March 1. Reacting to the sharp rise in international drug production in recent years, a report by the State Department has urged extreme measures to stem the tide.

The report painted a dire picture of the vast, expanding global industry in illegal drugs, citing a 10 percent increase in coca production in Bolivia, Colombia and Peru between 1986 and 1987. The world marijuana crop increased by 26 percent and the opium crop rose by 18 percent in the same period, according to the State Department.

The report stressed that the trend should be stopped at its source, by stepping up United States military and economic support to the governments of Latin America in an effort to eradicate crops, destroy processing laboratories and interdict shipments of drugs.

The report also urged increased pressure on governments in places like Switzerland, Hong Kong and Panama, where the drug traffickers launder profits. But the department's description of the rampant corruption in many of the governments suggests that the problems are almost unsolvable (→ 14).

Sphinx showing a new wrinkle

March 1. The fabled 4,600-year-old Sphinx is starting to show its age. Despite restoration begun in 1981, a 700-pound chunk has fallen off, stirring new debate as to how many more years those almond eyes can stare down the elements. Kamal Barakat of Cairo's Egyptian Museum agrees with most experts that the new wrinkle isn't serious but "should be taken as a warning" while more restoration studies are made. Meanwhile, maybe a little tuck here and there?

Jobless rate drops to eight-year low

March 4. The nation's unemployment rate fell to its lowest level in eight and a half years and more than 500,000 new jobs were created last month, the Labor Department reported today. The figures were viewed as a sign that the business expansion, now in its 63rd month, would continue and they allayed fears that the nation would experience a recession. The Labor Department's report was considered good news for presidential aspirant George Bush (→ 4/30).

U2 wins top honors at Grammy Awards

Randy Travis, another winner.

March 2. U2, a rock group that leans more to social conscience than showmanship, topped this year's Grammy Awards ceremony by winning the best album prize for its stirring album "The Joshua Tree," as well as the award for best rock performance by a duo or group. The Irish quartet beat out such contenders as the erstwhile Grammy favorite Michael Jackson, Prince and Whitney Houston. In one highlight of the ceremony, which took place in New York following six straight years in Los Angeles, Aretha Franklin became the all-time female Grammy winner with her two latest awards, one for the album "Aretha," the other for her duet with George Michael.

Magazine must pay $9m for killer's ad

March 3. Soldier of Fortune magazine was ordered to pay $9.4 million in damages to the family of Sandra Black for letting her killer, Wayne Hearn, advertise his services through a classified advertisement. Mrs. Black's husband, Robert, who paid Hearn $10,000, is on death row in Texas and Hearn is serving three life terms in Florida for her death and two other contract killings. Robert Franklin, an attorney for Black's family, said he wants to bankrupt the magazine, which was linked to at least nine more crimes, but he said the suit is no threat to the legitimate press. The magazine plans an appeal.

Bush wins the first Southern primary

March 5. Vice President Bush scored a resounding victory in the South Carolina Republican primary yesterday, defeating Senator Bob Dole and the Rev. Pat Robertson. The Bush showing was viewed by many as a forerunner of a clean sweep of 17 Republican contests to be held next week. Robertson, who has been a television evangelist, had counted on heavy support from fundamental Christians in South Carolina, but he polled less than half as many votes as Bush. An even poorer showing was registered by Representative Jack Kemp, who, according to most strategists, may drop out of the race (→ 8).

Photographer Bruce Davidson's urban realism is now at Washington's National Museum of American Art. This is from his "Subway" series.

These women are "Dressed to Kill": Fashions for terrorists and other criminals, shown in Florida, actually allow concealment of lethal weapons.

Su	Mo	Tu	We	Th	Fr	Sa
		1	2	3	4	5
6	7	8	9	10	11	12
13	14	15	16	17	18	19
20	21	22	23	24	25	26
27	28	29	30	31		

6. Peking: Three reported dead in Saturday's riot in Tibet (→ 4/4.–

6. Antarctica: Rowing expedition reaches Antarctic peninsula after 14-day, 600-mile trip from South America.

7. Washington: Supreme Court expands law requiring companies to disclose merger negotiations to the public (→ 6/27).

7. Washington: Justice Department reports families of Space Shuttle victims received $7.7 million from federal government and Morton Thiokol.

8. Moscow: Gorbachev announces new progressive tax on individuals to curb growing wealth due to private business ventures (→ 4/10).

8. Fort Campbell, Kentucky: Collision of two Army helicoptors kills 17.

9. Fort Lee, Virginia: Rosia Jones and Steven Henderson win United States Army Culinary Competition with dehydrated fish, chef's salad and apple cobbler.

10. United States: Mainstream religious groups announce formation of cable network to advance views but not seek funds.

10. Moscow: Soviets report nine dead in rescue of jet hijacked by family of musicians seeking to go to London.

10. Dedham, Massachusetts: Fifteen-year-old Rod Matthews sentenced to life for killing friend with baseball bat to "see what it felt like to kill."

11. Denver: Gary Hart quits presidential race again (→ 15).

DEATHS

7. Transvestite actor/actress Divine, born Harris Glenn Milstead, at 42.

9. Kurt Georg Kiesinger, ex-prime minister and former Nazi, at 83 (*4/6/04).

10. Glenn Cunningham, leading miler of the 1930's, at 78.

11. Romare Bearden, black-American painter and collagist, at 75 (*9/2/12).

Deaf college students seek deaf president

March 7. At Gallaudet University, the country's only university for the hearing impaired, the students are trying to make themselves heard. But the administration has been turning a deaf ear. The students feel administrators have slighted the community of disabled people by choosing a new president who is not hearing impaired and is only just learning sign language, when two other candidates for the post at the Washington, D.C., school have hearing impairments.

Gary W. Olsen, executive director of the National Association for the Deaf, joined the student protest, and in a sign-language speech said, "The board is further behind on this issue than the population of the country in general. The school educates the deaf to lead, then won't give deaf people a chance to lead. We're tired of oppression and we're going to fight this all the way and make the issue a torch of hope."

The board, headed by Jane Bassett Spilman, chose Dr. Elisabeth Ann Zinser as the new president. Dr. Zinser had been vice president of academic affairs at the University of North Carolina at Greensboro. One focus of a protest that shut the university for a day was a plea to Congress for help, because it funds 75 percent of the school's budget. No response was reported (→ 13).

Making the world listen: Students block the entrance to Gallaudet.

Honda ships autos from U.S. to Japan

March 7. A Honda factory at Marysville, Ohio, built 540 Honda Accord coupes that were subsequently shipped to Japan to be sold there. As a result of the yen making strong gains against the dollar, Japanese products can be produced more cost-efficiently in the United States. This may have spurred Honda's plan to export 4,000 Accords in 1988, equaling the total number of American cars exported to Japan in all of last year. Intent on being the United States's biggest car exporter to Japan, by 1991, Honda will be producing 70,000 Accords per year solely for export (→ 29).

Miniskirts a flop?

March 8. Are knees sexy or not? A year ago they were, as the mini was a must for fashion-conscious women whose knees had not been seen since the 60's. Although short is still chic, the hems are dropping, the mini-mania is ebbing and individual choice is in. The mini was too extreme for American women, designers say. Others say that "women do not obey rules anymore." Or could it be that fashion is a reflection of the national philosophy? Short is flamboyant. But since the mood in the country is uncertain, is the clothing becoming longer and more subdued?

Japanese managers' school, called "hell camp," has U.S. branch

What does it take to be an aggressive manager or sales person? To be able to sing in a public place, imitating a cawing crow? To write speeches and deliver them in stentorian tones? To take a 25-mile hike? Memorize detailed rules of behavior? All of the above and more make up a Japanese training-school curriculum, a veritable "hell camp" for sales people. The Kanrisha Yosei Gakko school was established in 1979 and boasts 100,000 graduates. In its American debut class, eight men and two women in California paid a fee of $2,400 each for 13 intense days, during which they learned methods that were originally designed to break down the traditional Japanese reserve.

Hell camp students study martial arts to train their minds for management.

Soviets shift from offense to defense

March 6. Changes are occurring in Soviet strategic military doctrine that may pave the way for future arms control pacts and a reduction of conventional forces in Europe, according to military experts.

Burdened with a stagnant economy that can barely afford higher expenditures and convinced that neither superpower can win a nuclear war, Soviet leader Mikhail S. Gorbachev has reportedly encouraged a change from the long-standing Soviet offensive military doctrine in favor of one Soviet officials call "a nonoffensive defense."

For example, until now, Moscow has said that if an attack by NATO appeared imminent, Warsaw Pact forces would launch a pre-emptive conventional-force attack against Western Europe. Under the new strategy, the Russians plan to place more emphasis on deterring a war in Europe than in winning it, thus requiring fewer troops (→ 5/31).

Bush sweeps South on Super Tuesday

March 8. Vice President Bush moved closer to the Republican presidential nomination today as he trounced his opponents in primary contests, most of them in the South. After earlier setbacks, in which he and Senator Bob Dole had traded bitter insults, Bush overwhelmed both Dole and the Rev. Pat Robertson, a former television evangelist, by carrying most of the 17 states at stake, including the two largest, Florida and Texas. Only in Missouri and Oklahoma did Dole offer Bush even a close race.

Commenting on the strong Bush showing, Eddie Mahe, a Republican political consultant who supports no candidate, said: "George Bush is the de facto nominee."

The outcome among the Democrats in the so-called Super Tuesday primaries and caucuses was less decisive, with strong showings by Governor Michael Dukakis of Massachusetts, the Rev. Jesse Jackson and Senator Albert Gore.

An elated Bush team celebrates victory from home base in Houston.

Dukakis won in seven states, Texas, Florida, Maryland, Rhode Island, Hawaii, Idaho and his home state of Massachusetts. But he trailed Gore and Jackson in the Deep South. Gore won in his home state of Tennessee as well as in North Carolina and two border states, Kentucky and Oklahoma. Jackson took five states in the Deep South, Alabama, Georgia, Virginia, Mississippi and Louisiana (→ 11).

Andy Gibb, teens' idol, is dead at 30

March 9. Andy Gibb's long downward spiral ended today when the 30-year-old singer died in England of drug-related causes. The one-time teen heartthrob was the younger brother of the Australian group the Bee Gees and starting in 1977 scored big with slick, disco hits like "I Just Want to Be Your Everything." But in the 80's, changing musical tastes left Gibb behind, and he squandered his millions on cocaine.

Gibb, troubled teen heartthrob.

Humans in America for 33,000 years?

March 9. A discovery of charcoal found with 11 ancient stone tools in southern Chile indicates that humans may have inhabited the Americas 33,000 years ago.

If substantiated, the finding could lead to a revision in the accepted story of the first Americans, which says the earliest migrations of people from Asia across the Bering Strait into Alaska occurred 11,500 to 11,000 years ago. This theory is based on early 20th-Century discoveries of stone projectile points near Clovis, New Mexico.

The new discovery, by Tom D. Dillehay of the University of Kentucky, should be taken as a "solid contender" as evidence of an earlier migration, Dillehay says. But one Smithsonian Institution archeologist says, "Everyone is waiting to be convinced of the 33,000 date, and I don't think Tom has done that yet."

Also this week, a stone monument marked with hieroglyphics was found in a river in Veracruz, Mexico, indicating that writing flourished in the New World as early as the second century A.D.

Paris-to-Dakar auto race arouses protest

March 12. The world's longest and toughest motor race, an 8,000-mile grind from Paris to Dakar, Senegal, may have been run for the last time. Opponents of the race, including the Vatican, contend that Africa's proverty-stricken regions are being used as a playground for rich rallyists. The three-week marathon, in January, drew 349 autos, 206 motorcycles and 115 trucks for a total of 2,500 participants. A Paris-based group called Pa'-Dak wants to make the most recent rally the last. The race, which generates $100 million in television, sponsorship and advertising fees, left six dead and 50 hurt. The Ivory Coast and Burkina Faso have barred the event. The Vatican called it "an insult unacceptable to the dignity of man" and a "vulgar display of power and wealth in places where men continue to die from hunger."

From Paris to Dakar over some of the most arid, infertile land on the globe.

Su	Mo	Tu	We	Th	Fr	Sa
		1	2	3	4	5
6	7	8	9	10	11	12
13	14	15	16	17	18	19
20	21	22	23	24	25	26
27	28	29	30	31		

13. Washington: Amid ongoing protest, Gallaudet University chooses I. King Jordan, who is hearing impaired, as new president.

13. Cape Town: Bishop Tutu and the Rev. Allan Boesak call for defiance of hightened repression (→ 21).

13. Miami: One million people in Cuban section form 24-block-long conga line, demonstrating inter-ethnic unity.

14. California: UCLA sanctions Lambda Delta Lambda as nation's first gay sorority (→ 4/1).

14. Panama: Dock workers strike as government withholds pay in cash crisis; teachers tear-gassed while demanding pay (→ 15).

15. United States: Carnegie Foundation report calls urban schools "little more than human storehouses to keep young people off the streets."

15. Atlanta: Eugene Antonio Marino becomes first black Catholic archbishop in U.S.

15. Panama: Police storm hospital as workers protest for pay (→ 16).

16. Belfast: Gunman kills three I.R.A. members in grenade attack at funeral for three I.R.A. guerrillas (→ 19).

16. Washington: Despite override threat in Congress, Reagan vetoes bill reversing 1984 Court decision limiting federal civil rights law (→ 22).

16. Washington: Israeli Prime Minister Yitzhak Shamir ends visit with talks on Mideast peace plan at impasse (→ 20).

16. West Bank and Gaza: Israel severs phone lines to occupied territories in new crackdown on protesters (→ 20).

16. Washington: Friends and relatives mark three years of captivity for hostage Terry Anderson (→ 7/25).

17. Columbia: Plane crashes in mountains with 136 aboard; no sign of survivors.

19. Belfast: Two British soldiers in plainclothes seized driving in crowd at I.R.A. funeral, beaten and killed.

Bush trounces Dole in the Illinois primary

March 15. Vice President Bush defeated Senator Bob Dole today in the Republican primary in Illinois, thus putting himself within reach of the party's nomination for President. At the same time, Senator Paul Simon won the Democratic primary for President in his home state of Illinois, outstripping both the Rev. Jesse Jackson and Governor Michael Dukakis.

A sampling of voters taken by The New York Times/CBS News Poll showed the Vice President ran strongly among those who support President Reagan. Bush also ran well among all groups in his party, outpolling Dole among moderates, conservatives and liberals. Bush, however, did not make a strong showing among women voters and he managed to run only even with Dole among college graduates.

The poor third-place showing by Dukakis was viewed by some observers as a sign that he is less of a front-runner that he seemed in the past. Simon took 43 percent of the vote; Jackson, 31 percent, and Dukakis, just 17 percent (→ 27).

Major cities are battling crack terrorism

![Artist Keith Haring's design, on a playground wall in Harlem, New York.]

Artist Keith Haring's design, on a playground wall in Harlem, New York.

March 14. In the wastelands of America's inner cities, the war on drugs is clearly being lost, as almost an entire generation is swept into a maelstrom of crack addiction and explosive violence.

"We're fighting an impossible fight if our city and other cities continue to be inundated by this drug," said Mayor Coleman Young of Detroit, who in just a few years has seen the ghettos of his city become ravaged as never before by crack and by vicious, heavily armed drug gangs, who roam at will.

Whatever the odds, the fight continues in the country's drug war zones. In Detroit last December and January, police tripled the number of drug arrests compared with the same period a year ago and broke a drug ring reported to have sold $3 million worth of crack per day. In such cities as Miami and Washington, D.C., where violence related to drugs has been responsible for two-thirds of all the homicides this year, federal agents are reinforcing overburdened and outgunned local drug squads.

The rise of organized street gangs in the drug trade, however, has made it ever more difficult for the law to prevail. In Los Angeles, for instance, where brutal "drive by" machine-gun killings are almost commonplace in some areas, last year's 12,000 gang-related arrests barely slowed a gang force totaling more than 70,000 persons.

But the most ominous trend of all may be that those locked in the nightmare world of drugs are extremely young. From machine-gun wielding 16-year-old "enforcers," to 13-year-old dealers, to addicts under 10, the crack underclass is becoming a lost generation (→ 28).

Four are indicted in Iran-contra case

March 16. In a move reminiscent of Watergate days, a federal grand jury in Washington indicted four key figures in the Iran-contra affair on charges of illegally diverting to the Nicaraguan rebels profits from arms sales to Iran. Named were the former National Security Adviser, Rear Admiral John M. Poindexter; Lieutenant Colonel Oliver L. North, former member of the National Security Council; Richard V. Secord, a retired Air Force major general, and Albert Hakim, an Iranian businessman. North protested his innocence (→ 25).

Vast savings rescue

March 17. The Federal Deposit Insurance Corporation will pump $1 billion into First Republicbank Corporation of Dallas to stem a huge outflow of deposits and loss of confidence in Texas's largest bank. In 1987, First Republic lost $656.5 million, mainly from bad real estate loans, and this year has lost nearly $2 billion in deposits. The rate of withdrawals was increasing as reports of the bank's weakened condition spread. F.D.I.C. Chairman L. William Seidman said that First Republicbank's problems stem from the depressed Texas economy, not from mismanagement (→ 6/21).

C.L. Bull's "Nothing is to be heard," at Worcester Museum's American illustration show.

Troops sent to Honduras

82nd Airborne arrives in Honduras.

March 19. For the second time this week, Honduran air force jets struck at Nicaraguan government troops said to have crossed the Honduran border in pursuit of United States-backed Nicaraguan contra rebels. Nicaragua says that the bombs landed on its side of the border. The attack closely follows President Reagan's decision to send 3,000 American troops to Honduras, a move that has stirred angry debate. Claiming the troops would not be near the fighting, Secretary of State George Shultz said they were intended to show the Hondurans that "We are your friend" and that "You can count on the United States." The statement did little to silence critics, and Senate Majority Leader Robert Byrd termed the decision an "overreaction."

American officials said the move is also meant to psychologically intimidate the Sandinistas from further pursuit of the rebels and to persuade Congress to renew aid to the contras. The new troops are actually a reinforcement of the 3,000-man American force already stationed in Honduras (→ 24).

Thousands downcast; Noriega foils coup

March 16. Visions of relief from General Manuel Noriega's cavalier rule were short-lived as a coup led by the police chief, Colonel Leonidas Macias, failed to topple Panama's leader. Shots were heard for more than an hour around Panama City's military headquarters, where Noriega has his office. Colonel Macias and four of his officers were reported "detained'" and Noriega emerged unhurt. Word of the revolt led thousands of Panamanians to stage a mini-coup of their own as they set fire to cars and some buildings and blocked downtown traffic with barricades. The crowd included workers out on strike because the government hasn't paid them. Panama's economy has been cash-starved since March 2, when all banks were closed following United States legal action to freeze $50 million of Panamanian assets (→ 4/1).

Panama strongman Noriega: shaky dictator, ruling by duplicity and drugs.

Man of Steel still young and tough at 50

Superman, at 50, is still fighting for "truth, justice and the American way."

March 14. He is still faster than a speeding bullet, able to leap tall buildings at a single bound, and he doubtless has as little trouble with a bullet train as he did overpowering the more traditional locomotive. In fact, Superman, now 50 years old, is looking better than ever. Despite his advancing years, flying lead still ricochets harmlessly off his chest and the mammoth "S" emblazoned there is stretched more heroically tight than ever.

This month's milestone for one of America's most easily recognizable superheroes will not go unobserved. A party, a retrospective book and an exhibition at the Smithsonian Institution are a tribute to the enduring appeal of the 1938 creation of Jerry Siegel and Joe Shuster. But they are also celebratory rites in honor of an American institution. Years in the public eye, in various comic books, movies, cartoons, radio shows and serials still leave one burning question about Superman: Can the anti-wrinkle cream Retin-A do any good for steel-hard skin?

Darden is executed

March 15. For convicted murderer Willie Darden, 14 years of waiting on death row came to a controversial end today in the electric chair in Starke, Florida. The 54-year-old Darden was convicted of the 1973 murder of a furniture store owner, James Turman, sexually assaulting his wife and shooting a witness in the process. He pleaded his innocence to the end, and he was not alone in his fight. The Rev. Jesse Jackson and Amnesty International were among those who felt that he had an alibi and that the trial was biased in favor of white victims of a black criminal.

The "Icicle Edition," 100 years ago, reported damage wrought by the legendary Blizzard of '88.

MARCH
Week 12 1988

Su	Mo	Tu	We	Th	Fr	Sa
		1	2	3	4	5
6	7	8	9	10	11	12
13	14	15	16	17	18	19
20	21	22	23	24	25	26
27	28	29	30	31		

20. San Salvador: Guerrilla attacks hinder election-day turnout (→ 4/12).

20. Washington: Government officials disclose successful nuclear fusion in secret experiment two years ago.

20. Tokyo: Mike Tyson floors Tony Tubbs in second round; 7th heavyweight title fight leaves record at 34-0.

20. Persian Gulf: Iraqi air attack on Kharg Island oil terminal strikes two supertankers; 54 missing (→ 25).

21. South Africa: More than one million black workers strike to mark 28th anniversary of Sharpeville Massacre (→ 27).

21. New York: Joyce Brown, Mayor Koch's test case for treating homeless as mentally ill, now back on street.

22. Washington: Congress overrides Reagan's veto of bill that restores federal power to enforce civil rights law (→ 4/7).

22. Washington: E.P.A. bars use of data from Nazi experiments in study of effects of phosgene gas.

23. Washington: Court rules strikers can be denied food stamps if they were not poor enough to receive them before work stoppage.

23. New York: Tenth anniversary party for in vitro fertilization draws 168 test-tube babies and their families.

24. Jerusalem: Israeli nuclear technician guilty of treason for revealing that Israel is making atomic bombs.

25. Washington: Reagan declares Iran-contra defendants, who pleaded innocent yesterday, are not guilty (→ 4/7).

DEATHS

20. Gil Evans, jazz composer-arranger second only to Duke Ellington in importance, at 75 (*1912).

21. Dr. Patrick Steptoe, pioneer in test-tube baby technology, at 74 (*6/9/13).

25. Robert Joffrey, founder and artistic director of Joffrey Ballet, at 57 (*12/24/30).

Chambers confesses guilt in girl's death

Chambers exits State Supreme Court after his guilty plea in the Levin case.

March 25. The highly publicized and emotional 13-week murder trial of Robert Chambers ended suddenly today when he pleaded guilty to first-degree manslaughter in the death of Jennifer Levin. Chambers reluctantly stated he intended to injure the 18-year-old Levin seriously. Since her murder 17 months ago, he had claimed that she died accidentally when they were having sex in Central Park. While the jury was still deadlocked after deliberating for nine days, Chambers agreed to a sentence of 5 to 14 years. The case raised issues about racy teen-age life styles as well as victims' and women's rights.

Iraq is accused of gassing Kurdish village

March 25. The scene was reminiscent of World War I. Hundreds, possibly thousands of dead Kurds littered the streets of Halabja, their bodies bloated from the bombs of mustard gas, cyanide and nerve gas dropped by Iraqi warplanes. In the continuing war with Iraq, Iran captured the Iraqi province earlier this month. The gas attack was part of a counterthrust by the Iraqis. The Kurdish people, nominally Iraqi, have been calling for independence, and Iraq apparently decided to deliver a stern object lesson in loyalty. Iraq was condemned by the United Nations in 1986 for chemical warfare against Iran's army (→ 4/26).

A mother and child, both Kurds, are innocent victims of Iraqi poison gas.

Israeli soldier dies, first in uprising

March 20. The Israeli army suffered its first fatality of the current Palestinian uprising when Moishe Katz, 28, was shot dead as he stood guard in Bethlehem in the Israeli-occupied West Bank. Calling the death "murder," the army chief of staff, General Dan Shomron, said, "I don't think from this one incident we can assume we've passed to a new stage of using firearms." Since the demonstrations were renewed on Dec. 9, the Palestinians have chosen to use rocks and occasional gasoline bombs rather than guns, thus gaining sympathy as defenseless protesters rather than armed, active terrorists (→ 4/7).

Largest death grant made in I.B.M. case

March 21. The largest wrongful death award in American history, just under $8 million, was given by a jury to the family of Philip D. Estridge, one of 137 people killed when a Delta Air Lines jet crashed at the Dallas-Fort Worth airport in 1985. In the I.B.M. hierarchy, Estridge was viewed as a rising young star. He oversaw development of the company's personal computer into a billion-dollar operation. The editor of one computer newsletter described Estridge as "a really hot executive, perceived as a real maverick." Estridge was 45 at the time of his death.

Plane hits string of kite, lifting girl

March 20. DeAndra Anrig was flying her glider-type kite in Mountain View, California, today when suddenly the 8-year-old girl went up and away, soaring over her father's head and almost hitting a tree. She was dragged about 100 feet before she let go of the nylon kite line that had been caught by and entangled in one of the propellers of a twin-engine plane approaching the Palo Alto airport. DeAndra is fine, but kite-flying is to be prohibited within five miles of any airport in the state.

Smoking banned on Northwest flights

March 23. Northwest Airlines has banned smoking on almost all its domestic flights. It was the first such move by a major U.S. carrier. "We know we'll lose some passengers, but we believe we'll gain more than we lose," said a spokesman. (Ninety percent of Northwest's passengers already choose nonsmoking seats.) Surgeon General C. Everett Koop was among those lauding the move, but some smokers showed signs of revolt. "It just means I won't be able to fly Northwest," said one smoker at Washington's National Airport. "If I'm going to fly from New York to California I need a cigarette" (→ 4/6).

Du Pont to abandon ozone-harming gas

March 24. A report from NASA scientists demonstrating that the earth's ozone shield has been greatly depleted has prompted the Du Pont Company to announce plans to end production of chlorofluorocarbons (CFC's), the chemical believed to destroy ozone. CFC's are used in refrigerants, cleaning fluids and other products, and Du Pont produces about 25 percent of the world's supply. The company plans to phase out most of the CFC's by the year 2000 (→ 28).

With appetite for food matched only by one for Nielsen ratings, lovable ALF (Alien Life Form) is a big prime-time hit on NBC.

Sandinista-contra cease-fire is reached

March 24. "Is Peace Breaking Out?" asked the headline in the Nicaraguan newspaper Nuevo Diario today. After six years of bloody war, the fighting in this embattled nation will stop. The Sandinistas and the contras have agreed to a cease-fire scheduled to run through May. Whether the cease-fire will endure, only time will tell. But both sides have promised to work diligently for protracted peace.

In an emotional ceremony, President Daniel Ortega and contra leader Adolfo Calero stood side by side. The Sandinista leader said, "We are here together determined to bury the ax of war and raise the olive branch of peace." Calero echoed those words, saying, "Today we have taken a first and firm step to end this fratricidal war."

The terms of the agreement require that the government release 3,300 prisoners, permit the return of deposed National Guard exiles with impunity and guarantee "unrestricted freedom of expression." In return, the contras have promised to recognize the present administration as the legitimate governing body of Nicaragua, to begin to disarm and to refuse to accept military assistance from anyone or humanitarian aid from any partisan groups. If the agreement succeeds, it will bring an end to the attempts by the Reagan administration to overthrow the Sandinista government. The discussions are to continue with more detailed negotiations down the road (→ 27).

Beach losing youths

March 23. Fort Lauderdale, long the "meat market" where college students shop for guys and gals, is nearly bust. After more than 25 years as the No. 1 spring-break hot spot, the Florida resort has fallen behind Daytona Beach. Business owners are suffering. Fort Lauderdale officials expect this season's spending to total less than $50 million, down from $140 million in 1985. Why? "The police were too brutal," says bar owner Joe Dugan. While many believe hostile police treatment drove the crowds away, others say its just a passing shift in preference.

Nicaraguan Defense Minister Humberto Ortega takes copies of the pact from contra chief Alfredo Cesar. Mediator Cardinal Obando y Bravo is at center.

Nancy Spero's "Nicaragua," in a show at New York's Museum of Modern Art. Despite war, Nicaragua is a mecca for many talented graphic artists.

Persian Gulf golfers get first grass course

March 21. Golf has became an expensive reality in the Persian Gulf with the opening of a $10-million grass course, the first of its kind in the region. An engineer for the royal family of Dubai saw one official watching golf on television and asked, "Why not us?" That was in 1985. The course, built on quick-growing grass from Georgia, has artificial lakes and natural sand traps. It was opened by Pakistani President Mohammed Zia ul-Haq. He swatted the first ball with a gold-inlaid club and got to keep not only the club but a solid gold tee as well.

Pakistani President Zia tees off.

Su	Mo	Tu	We	Th	Fr	Sa
		1	2	3	4	5
6	7	8	9	10	11	12
13	14	15	16	17	18	19
20	21	22	23	24	25	26
27	28	29	30	31		

27. Managua: Sandinistas free 100 political prisoners in first step of compliance with truce (→ 30).

27. Mission, South Dakota: Phillip J. Stevens, California businessman who claims to be grandson of Sioux warrior, becomes special chief of Rosebud Sioux, pledging to help them recover land lost after gold was discovered.

27. Washington: Gridiron Club holds annual dinner with string of one-liners and much general hilarity.

28. New York: Brooklyn judge orders convicted heroin dealer to pay $2 million to help drug addicts (→ 31).

28. Washington: Richard Gephardt pulls out of race for Democratic presidential nomination (→ 29).

28. Peking: China announces it will cut bureaucratic staff 20 percent in drive to reduce inefficiency (→ 30).

28. Washington: Scientists say sharper rise in temperature during 1980's confirms greenhouse effect (→ 4/24).

29. Washington: United States firms win right to participate in Japanese public works projects, staving off trade sanctions (→ 4/4).

29. Connecticut: Dukakis scores resounding victory in primary, bouncing back from big loss in Michigan (→ 29).

29. Paris: Dulcie September, spokeswoman for African National Congress, is assassinated (→ 5/11).

30. Washington: House approves $7.9 million in humanitarian aid to Nicaraguan contras (→ 5/6).

30. Peking: Small signs of dissent are seen at the normally unanimous Chinese party congress (→ 4/12).

31. England: Discovery of Lindow man could unlock secrets of Druids.

DEATH

30. Edgar Faure, ex-prime minister of France, at 79 (*8/18/08).

Brawley case still veiled in mystery

March 28. What really happened to Tawana Brawley? The 15-year-old black girl disappeared for four days, then was discovered in a plastic garbage bag, her body smeared with dog feces, the letters "KKK" and the word "nigger" written on her in charcoal. She claimed to have been assaulted by six white men, one of whom showed her a policeman's badge. On the advice of her lawyers, Miss Brawley has been silent about the case, refusing to elaborate in any way on her original, disjointed story. In the meantime, her attorneys, Alton Maddox and Vernon Mason, along with a Pentecostal minister, the Rev. Al Sharpton, have been publicizing the case, turning it into a national civil rights controversy.

Last week, Miss Brawley's lawyers unexpectedly called a news conference where they named a Dutchess County assistant district attorney as one of the girl's attackers. They said they would not provide evidence in support of the assertion until arrests are made. But officials assert they can make no arrests without evidence (→ 5/24).

Six Justice aides resign over Meese

March 29. Attorney General Edwin Meese 3rd was "stunned" and "could barely speak" when he was told of the resignations of Deputy Attorney General Arnold Burns, Assistant Attorney General William Weld and four other top Justice Department aides. The six officials quit amid growing concern over Meese's alleged illegalities. Burns and Weld recently told the White House that department credibility was at risk with the attorney general's continued presence.

The resignations set off speculation that more evidence had been gathered by the special prosecutor investigating the attorney general. Among other matters, prosecutor John McKay is examining Meese's link to an Iraqi oil pipeline proposal and a scandal at the Wedtech Corporation, a military contractor. The President continues to support Meese (→ 4/2).

Jackson outpolls Dukakis 2-1 in Michigan

Jackson cuddles an infant, who perhaps may one day be a future supporter.

March 27. The Rev. Jesse Jackson scored a surprising landslide victory in Democratic caucuses in Michigan, creating further confusion in the party's presidential nomination process. Some top party leaders are now contemplating the possibility that Jackson could wind up with enough votes to earn the nomination, but they voiced doubts that a black candidate could be elected. "I don't know where this leaves us," Robert S. Strauss, the party's former chairman, said.

Of the roughly 200,000 votes that were cast, Jackson won 55 percent, far ahead of Governor Michael Dukakis, who won just 28 percent. Some observers considered the Jackson victory as all the more surprising in that he garnered a substantial vote in white communities. In Michigan, blacks make up just 13 percent of the population (→ 28).

New suburban idea: 19th-century town

Florida resorts are often dominated by row upon row of concrete high-rises. Not Seaside, located in the Panhandle, 100 miles west of Tallahassee. Here, picket fences and front porches are mandatory — in an effort to create a sense of community and sociability. "We're trying to create a sense of neighborliness that doesn't exist in most resort communities," says Robert S. Davis, who developed the town.

Robert Stern, one of the beachfront resort's architects, says of Seaside, "It's a nostalgic evocation of the 19th century translated in the best way for the 1980's. It's not cute in the bad sense. The quality is marvelous. It comes to grips with the car. The car is not allowed to rule the roost. The result is an unusual degree of urbanity."

Bicycles roam freely in Seaside, whose planners favor the human scale.

Toni Morrison gets Pulitzer for novel

March 31. The 17-member Pulitzer board has made its annual selections. The choice in fiction is Toni Morrison's disturbing and passionate novel "Beloved," about a runaway slave who kills her daughter rather than let the child be captured and raised as a slave. Morrison's novel has been a center of controversy since it failed to receive a National Book Award in the fall, prompting 48 black writers to draft an open letter, published in The New York Times Book Review in January. One reviewer said the novel will "reverberate in the readers' minds long after they have finished the book."

More whites resist South Africa draft

March 27. For three years now, the Defense Minister of South Africa has refused to release figures concerning the number of draft evaders. Resisting compulsory conscription has become such a sensitive issue, it is believed, because the number of resisters in the all-white armed forces is increasing dramatically. An organization called the End Conscription Campaign has been formed, in spite of government disapproval, to provide advice for draft evaders (→ 29).

Vanna White will play Venus in NBC's "Goddess of Love."

233 are charged in drug ring inquiry

March 31. American and Italian agents broke the back of a major Sicilian Mafia drug ring today as they disclosed charges against 233 members and arrested 100 suspects in early morning raids in both Italy and the United States. Justice Department officials called the case the largest international drug operation ever for the United States; it was the culmination of two years of undercover work and investigation. The operation epitomized new anti-drug strategies that seek to arrange well-coordinated knockout blows against international drug rings as opposed to the isolated seizure of drug shipments (→ 4/11).

Dole quits, ceding nomination to Bush

March 29. Vice President George Bush virtually clinched the Republican nomination for President today when his chief rival, Senator Bob Dole, dropped out of the race. Dole, speaking in the Senate caucus room, smiled faintly as he told supporters that he was "bloodied but unbowed" as he left the campaign trail. "You come to trust your instincts to tell you when it's over," he said. Despite their angry clashes of the past, the senator said he would work to elect Bush (→ 4/10).

Despite poor results at the polls, Pat Robertson will fight on.

Woman wins third straight dogsled race

March 28. Susan Butcher, 33, braved ice, snow as well as frigid winds to win the grueling Anchorage-to-Nome dogsled race for the third straight time. She survived temperatures as low as 15 below zero in traveling the 1,049-mile course in 11 days and 11 hours. The first prize of $30,000 was presented by the Iditarod Trail Committee, named for an old gold-miners' supply trail. "It didn't seem like I knew what was going on from minute to minute," Miss Butcher said. She credited the courage of the dogs for her victory, especially Granite, the sled leader. There will be lots of extra bones for Granite, as well as for her 150 other dogs.

The dogs get the credit, she says.

And in the lodge, Susan Butcher and friend celebrate the third in a row.

Thinking computers begin to be useful

March 28. The second wave of computer technology has arrived. The hardware and software of the first wave was concerned primarily with data processing; the second wave is concerned with decision-making. This new breed, called knowledge processors or expert systems, is designed to mimic the decision-making processes of human experts, including the ability to deal with ambiguity and less-than-clear-cut judgment. Some 3,000 expert systems are now in daily use, finding applications in a vast array of fields, including government, medicine and finance.

Swaggart is barred from pulpit for year

March 29. When Jimmy Swaggart tearfully confessed last month to "a moral failure" that was said to include paying a prostitute, Debra Murphree, to pose nude, he said he was leaving the pulpit for an "indeterminate time." Today, leaders of his church determined how long. They said that Swaggart would be barred from preaching for a one-year period of rehabilitation. Said one church official: "It is hoped that Jimmy Swaggart will agree to this program of rehabilitation and that such a program will be redemptive and restorative in the life and ministry of our brother" (→ 4/8).

APRIL

Week 14 1988

Su	Mo	Tu	We	Th	Fr	Sa
					1	2
3	4	5	6	7	8	9
10	11	12	13	14	15	16
17	18	19	20	21	22	23
24	25	26	27	28	29	30

1. Washington: United States decides to send 1,300 new troops to Panama (→ 4).

1. Washington: Georgetown University, oldest Catholic college in United States, agrees to fund gay student groups.

4. United States: It is reported that I.B.M. has, for two years, given computer chips to rivals in effort to stay ahead of Japan (→ 10).

4. Peking: China announces Dalai Lama can return to Tibet if he abandons call for independence.

4. Washington: Ex-State Department aide says United States ignored Noriega's drug role in 1986 because of his aid to contras (→ 12).

4. United States: Prudential loses $11 million in loan repayment for typo leaving off three zeros at end of million-dollar figure.

4. United States: It is reported that at least three banks have accepted checks treated with chemicals to make them disintegrate within hours of deposit.

6. Hackensack, N.J.: Mary Beth Whitehead, biological mother of Baby M, wins generous visiting rights.

6. Washington: Reagan denies Japanese request to fish in United States waters on grounds that they violated whaling moratorium.

6. Hanoi: Vietnam asks U.S. for emergency aid to combat growing malnutrition (→ 6/4).

6. New York City: Strict smoking curbs in public places take effect (→ 23).

7. Washington: In testimony to Senate subcommittee, three contra leaders acknowledge that drug dealers supplied them with arms with C.I.A. involvement (→ 6/8).

8. Springfield, Missouri: Assemblies of God defrocks Jimmy Swaggart for rejecting suspension in sex scandal.

9. Bikini Atoll: Elders of Bikini return to island to begin efforts to clean up homeland, rendered uninhabitable by nuclear tests, for eventual return.

Honduras tries to quell anti-U.S. acts

The U.S. Embassy under siege.

April 8. Five Hondurans were killed and at least 10 wounded as anti-American student demonstrators set fire to the United States Embassy in Tegucigalpa, the capital, and burned cars parked outside. The students were protesting the extradition of Juan Ramon Matta Ballesteros, a Honduran accused of drug smuggling and complicity in the death of an American narcotics agent. The Honduran constitution bars such extraditions, and government legislators called the act a "kidnapping." The crowd of about 2,000 also assailed the visit last month of American troops. Honduran guards at the American Embassy put down today's riot with shotguns, tear gas and clubs. The government radio issued appeals to "remain calm" and to "repudiate violence" (→ 7/17).

Seek 10,000 books borrowed by writer

April 4. Gustav Hasford is one writer who loves books, perhaps to the point of hoarding. An Academy Award nominee for the adaptation of his Vietnam War novel, "The Short Timers," into Stanley Kubrick's film "Full Metal Jacket," Hasford may have borrowed but not returned nearly 10,000 books from libraries as far off as Australia. Just last December he checked out 87 volumes and 500 periodicals from California Polytechnic State University. Now its campus police intend to charge the book-loving author with grand theft.

Prosecutor asks no indictment of Meese

April 2. At least for now, Attorney General Edwin Meese 3rd will not be indicted on charges of criminal wrongdoing. According to special prosecutor James McKay, no indictment will be pursued for, among other things, the attorney general's involvement in a $1 billion Iraqi oil pipeline deal or his alleged link to a kickback scandal in the Wedtech Corporation. But McKay did suggest the possibility of internal disciplinary action.

The prosecutor's announcement comes at the end a turbulent week in the department; earlier, six top aides to Meese resigned. Some officials believe that the aides quit in frustration, knowing in advance that McKay would not seek an indictment. While Meese has so far escaped indictment, his legal agenda has been disrupted. The Justice Department had planned to push for a number of conservative programs, including a drive for a federal death penalty, curbs on pornography and Senate confirmation for conservative judicial nominees. But with the investigation draining the time and energy of the department, these goals have been difficult to advance. Although some officials think Meese will resign, most feel he will serve out the rest of President Reagan's term (→ 7/5).

Black who reached North Pole given honors

Henson, with an integrated color guard, gains his proper place next to Peary.

April 6. "We are assembled here today to right a tragic wrong," proclaimed S. Allen Counter, a Harvard professor and student of famous black figures. The professor presided over the re-burial of Matthew Alexander Henson, a co-discoverer of the North Pole. After accompanying Commander Robert Peary on the famous Arctic exploration, Henson lived out his life in obscurity, chiefly because he was a black man in a white society. But today, Henson was given a hero's burial in Arlington National Cemetery. He died in 1955 (→ 10/12).

Arkansas jury acquits 13 white racists

April 7. An all-white jury in Fort Smith, Arkansas, has acquitted 13 white supremacists of plotting to overthrow the federal government and start an all-white nation in the Pacific Northwest, and to kill a judge and a federal agent. Six of the defendants in the seven-week trial were already serving sentences for crimes ranging from racketeering to murder. After the verdict, Ku Klux Klan national chairman Thom Robb said, "The government was going to send the movement a message. The movement sent a message to the government, the same one God told Pharaoh: "Let my people go" (→ 5/10).

Gorbachev agrees to Afghan pullout deal

Mikhail S. Gorbachev conducts talks with Afghan leaders in Tashkent.

April 7. Meeting in the Soviet Central Asian city of Tashkent, the Soviet leader Mikhail S. Gorbachev and the Afghan leader Najibullah announced that the "last obstacles" to concluding the Geneva agreements "have been removed." They have thus implicitly accepted an American compromise solution to the final sticking point of continued Soviet aid to the Afghan government. According to the proposal, as the Russians withdraw, the United States can continue arming the Islamic guerrillas "at an equal and balanced level" with Soviet supplies to the Kabul government. Soviet and American military aid would stop when the Russians begin their troop pullouts on May 15 (→ 5/15).

Women, Third World added to curriculum

April 1. Stanford University now offers its incoming freshmen the course "Cultures, Ideas and Values" as a replacement for the required Western culture course, thereby including the study of non-European cultures and works by women, blacks, Hispanics, Asians and American Indians. The idea is to give students a foundation in global culture. However, it took two years of meetings and discussions for the faculty to reach their non-unanimous decision.

Glasnost has exposed the Soviet public to more than political dissent. Amid new efforts at economic restructuring, Moscow has its first American pizza.

After 60 years, state ousts a governor

After a long campaign to remove him, Mecham was found guilty of two charges.

April 4. The Arizona Senate has removed Republican Governor Evan Mecham from office — the first ouster of a governor in almost 60 years. The Senate found him guilty of two charges of misconduct — attempting to thwart an investigation into a death threat from an aide to a grand jury witness, and channeling state funds into his auto dealership. With the conviction, Arizona Secretary of State Rose Mofford succeeds Mecham. Impeachment prosecutor William French charged that Mecham "has puffed, exaggerated, misremembered, and out and out lied." In 1929, Oklahoma Gov. Henry Johnston was impeached for working with the Ku Klux Klan (→ 6/16).

Israeli girl slain by guard, not Arab stoning

April 7. An Israeli army investigation says that a teen-age Israeli girl was not stoned to death by Arabs as reported yesterday. Instead, the inquiry found, the girl, Tiraz Porat, 15, was accidentally shot by an Israeli guard during a clash between Israelis and stone-throwing Palestinians. A radio version said no weapons were fired by Arabs. Unaware of the new reports, angry Israelis in the West Bank town of El Morah went to her funeral shouting, "Revenge, revenge!" (b4 16).

Former Reagan aide sentenced to prison

April 8. Lyn Nofziger, a former top aide to President Reagan, was sentenced today to 90 days in prison and fined $30,000 for illegal lobbying on behalf of the Wedtech Corporation and other clients after leaving his job at the White House. Federal law bars senior officials from lobbying their former colleagues within a year of leaving government. Nofziger served as White House political director during the first two years of the Reagan administration. Before being sentenced by a federal judge in Washington, Nofziger appeared unrepentant, saying he had done nothing "ethically, morally or legally wrong."

Danny Manning and Kansas are underdog winners of the NCAA title, beating Oklahoma 83-79.

10. Pakistan: Blast at arms depot showers cities of Islamabad and Rawalpindi with rockets and grenades, killing at least 75 and injuring 850.

10. Albany: Governor Mario Cuomo directly asserts for first time he will not accept draft as presidential nominee (→ 5/3).

10. Augusta, Georgia: Sandy Lyle is first British golfer to win Masters.

10. Las Vegas: President Reagan challenges Soviet Union to give access to Western media, lift ban on books (→ 13).

11. Washington: Many experts assert United States attack on drugs is failing because of focus on supply rather than demand (→ 5/13).

11. United States: Committee of United States Roman Catholic bishops issues report calling for expanded role for women in Church (→ 6/27).

11. Bel Air, California: Ronald and Nancy Reagan obtain $2.5 million retirement home through unusual procedure of leasing from group of investors who bought the home for the Reagans.

11. Mesopotamia, Ohio: Fire department bends rules, allowing two Amish volunteers to keep beards.

11. United States: Gun ownership among American women jumped 53 percent from 1983 to 1986, according to Gallup poll.

12. Washington: Robert C. Byrd, 70, announces he will step down as Senate majority leader at end of year.

12. Washington: Pentagon announces United States Marine in Panama was killed by fellow Marine while hunting for intruders at fuel storage base (→ 5/7).

12. El Salvador: Rightist opposition charges fraud in vote tally leaving them one seat short of majority (→ 6/2).

14. Naples: Bomb blast outside U.S.O. club kills five and injures 15, including several United States sailors.

13 Palestinians die in highest one-day toll

Low-tech warfare, reminiscent of the biblical days of David and Goliath.

In Ramallah, Israeli police are kept at bay by a hail of rocks.

April 16. In a day described by a local United Nations spokesman as "total turmoil" and "by far the worst yet," at least 13 rock-throwing Gaza Palestinians were killed by the Israeli army as they angrily protested the assassination of the P.L.O. military commander Khalil Wazir. Commonly known by his code hame, Abu Jihad, he was gunned down early this morning at his home outside Tunis. Today's death toll brings to 141 the Palestinians killed since the uprising surfaced in December. The number wounded today is not yet known, but all 50 of the beds in the local hospital are filled with Palestinian patients who have been shot.

Black banners throughout the Gaza Strip mourned Jihad's passing, and the outlawed Palestinian flag was much in evidence. Jihad was a key guerrilla figure, and his death leaves a major political vacuum in the P.L.O. leadership. Arabs unanimously believe that he was killed by Israelis, most likely by the intelligence service Mossad.

Bassam Shakus, deposed Arab mayor of Nablus, said, "No one else can benefit from his killing, only Israel and the Zionists." In response, Israeli spokesman Avi Pazner said such claims are considered "automatically irrelevant" because "whenever something happens to one of the Fatah people, they always put the blame on Israel." However, rival Palestinian guerrilla factions have buried their differences during the uprising. Their cooperation tends to rule out Arab complicity in Jihad's murder (→ 20).

Harvard gets patent for modified mouse

April 12. The United States Patent and Trademark Office has issued the first patent for a genetically modified higher life form. Patent No. 4,736,866 was awarded to Harvard University for "transgenic non-human mammals," mice developed by Dr. Philip Leder and Dr. Timothy A. Stewart. The new strain, created by injecting genetic material into fertilized mouse eggs, is especially prone to cancer and is intended to help with research on the disease. Some critics denounced the patent as an attempt to set public policy without open debate, but researchers are elated over the development.

Liberace's stuff sold

April 10. A Baldwin Model L grand piano clad in mirrored tiles and with a clear lucite lid brought $42,500, a tiny gold and diamond pin, valued at about $25, went for $900 and so on, all during the first day of the auction of the worldly goods left by Liberace. The flamboyant pianist died of AIDS last year. He was 67. Sequined gowns, furs, goblets, antique bedroom sets, mirrors, dolls, 13 cars, 13 pianos and more glittering and ornate stuff were snapped up so eagerly that the hoped-for $8 million target may be reached. Proceeds of the auction will pay for music scholarships.

Helmsleys indicted

April 14. Real estate tycoons Harry and Leona Helmsley were charged with evading more than $4 million in income taxes by listing vast personal expenditures as business deductions. Purchases included: a $210,000 mahogany card table, a $130,000 stereo system and $500,000 in jade art objects. A total of 235 federal and state indictments were unsealed yesterday and the Helmsleys pleaded not guilty at their arraignment in State Supreme Court in Manhattan. Mrs. Helmsley was also accused of defrauding stockholders by getting $83,333.34 a month in secret consulting fees. The Helmsleys were released without posting bail.

Japan defense spending now third largest

A militaristic revival? Ancient samurai sports increasingly visible in Japan.

April 10. For the first time since World War II, Japan is spending more than 1 percent of its gross national income on defense. This may not seem like much, but it is already more than either France or Britain spend, making Japan the world's third largest military spender after the United States and the Soviet Union.

From Peking, any addition to Japan's military forces looks threatening. Chinese still remember Japanese brutality before and during World War II when hundreds of thousands of Chinese were slaughtered. Japan's new generation does not feel the guilt its

parents felt about those times, say Chinese. There is a rightist, racialist, militaristic tendency among today's Japanese, they say.

Japan's economic dominance is also worrisome to Chinese. China is Japan's Greece and Rome, the source of its language, its art, much of its culture. Now China, awake after years of isolation and a decade of the Cultural Revolution's destructiveness, bitterly envies Japan's towering economic status. Still, to hear the Chinese tell it, the sleeping dragon has awakened, and it is ony a matter of time before China resumes its rightful place at the forefront of Asia (→ 23).

"Last Emperor" wins 9 Academy Awards

April 11. "The Last Emperor," Italian director Bernardo Bertolucci's opulent odyssey of the life of Pu Yi, who, at the age of 3, became the last emperor of China and died a gardener, was crowned with nine Academy Awards tonight. It won in every category for which it had been nominated. Of other films, only the romantic comedy "Moonstruck" won more than one award. In the history of the Academy Awards, only two pictures have won more honors than "Emperor": "Ben Hur" in 1960 with 11 Oscars and "West Side Story" in 1962 with 10. Best-acting honors went to Cher and Michael Douglas, while Olympia Dukakis and Sean Connery were best in the supporting-actor category.

Bertolucci accepts one of nine Oscars.

China names new array of younger leaders

April 12. China's National People's Congress has taken steps to ensure the continuation of the country's economic reforms. The congress approved a new slate of councilors and ministers who were described by the New China News Agency as "a group of technocrats, who are younger in age, pragmatic and enthusiastic in the reform." Li Peng, a 59-year-old engineer who trained in the Soviet Union, was named to be Prime Minister last week. Today's appointments include Qian Qichen as Foreign Minister. Qian is a career diplomat with considerable experience in the Soviet Union and Eastern Europe. His predecessor, Wu Xueqian, will become a Deputy Prime Minister.

In addition, the congress has decided that private enterprise and the sale of land-use rights will be given protection under the constitution. By such a move, the congress seeks to reassure those who do business or are considering doing business in China.

U.S. businessmen meet with Gorbachev

April 13. Soviet leader Mikhail S. Gorbachev held a reception at the Kremlin for some 500 American businessmen in Moscow to attend the 11th annual meeting of the U.S.-U.S.S.R. Trade and Economic Council, a private organization. Gorbachev told the executives that his economic reforms, known as "perestroika," were "an invitation to work out a new system of coordinates in the economic relationship between our socially and ideologically different countries." The invitation was accepted by at least seven of the companies represented, which earlier in the day had established a consortium to encourage joint ventures (→ 21).

Between the different worlds of high art and photojournalism lies a new breed of color photographers, such as Gilles Peress, whose "The eve of the Passion Play" is shown here, from an exhibit at the Toledo Museum of Art.

Speakes loses job over tell-all book

April 15. Larry Speakes resigned from Merrill Lynch & Co. yesterday, less than a week after disclosing that he had fabricated quotations for President Reagan while serving as the White House spokesman. The disclosure came in his new book, "Speaking Out," his memoirs of the Reagan years, and it was promptly criticized by White House officials. Speakes joined the Wall Street investment house as vice president of communications in February of last year after having served in the Reagan administration for more than six years. Previously, he had served as press spokesman for both Presidents Nixon and Ford (→ 5/3).

Su	Mo	Tu	We	Th	Fr	Sa
					1	2
3	4	5	6	7	8	9
10	11	12	13	14	15	16
17	18	19	20	21	22	23
24	25	26	27	28	29	30

17. Washington: Security experts disclose breach in United States military computer security, exploited by a West German for the past two years.

18. Persian Gulf: United States hits two Iranian oil terminals and six navy ships in retaliation for mining of gulf (→ 22).

18. Jerusalem: John Demjanjuk, ex-Nazi extradited from United States, is convicted of war crimes (→ 25).

19. New York: Fourteen postal workers and three others charged with illegally winning $85,000 by pre-dating entries to "Pick the Score" contest.

19. Washington: Supreme Court rules Indian religious practices are not justification for blocking development of land.

20. California: Files on assassination of Robert F. Kennedy are released, revealing that 2,410 photos have been destroyed.

21. New York: "Macbeth" opens on Broadway with Christopher Plummer and Glenda Jackson, after mishaps on the road that seem to confirm tales of curse surrounding the play.

21. Moscow: Politburo demotes Yegor Ligachev in demonstration of support for Gorbachev (→ 24).

21. Washington: University of Chicago, reconsidering a thesis that was ahead of its time, awards Ph.D. to Frank Bourgin, 45 years after he finished his dissertation.

22. Washington: United States to allow Navy in Persian Gulf to protect neutral merchant ships under some circumstances (→ 7/3).

22. Washington: Hoffman-La Roche Inc. charges government report on birth defects caused by acne drug is invalid.

23. Beirut: Car bomb kills 60 at open market (→ 5/8).

23. Tokyo: Farmers burn American car and flag in protest over United States trade demands (→ 5/9).

Dukakis easily wins New York primary

April 19. Governor Michael Dukakis won the Democratic primary in New York state yesterday, outstripping his nearest rival, the Rev. Jesse Jackson, by about 200,000 votes, a 14 percent lead. Senator Albert Gore finished a poor third and is expected to drop out of the race soon. In a campaign that grew bitter because of its emphasis on race and religion, Dukakis did especially well among Catholic and Jewish voters. On the basis of exit polls, it appears that Jackson won about 94 percent of the black vote. Meanwhile, Vice President Bush won the GOP primary easily, having run virtually unopposed (→ 5/3).

Orioles set a record, losing first fourteen

Boddicker watches No. 14 slip away.

April 20. The Baltimore Orioles have carved their place in baseball history, but not in a way the players will want to tell their grandchildren about. The Orioles fell to their 14th straight defeat, a start-of-the-season slump unmatched in big league annals. They dropped nearly 12 games out of first place with 148 games remaining. The record-setting defeat was inflicted by the Brewers on a team that has been one of basebal's most successful. Losing pitcher Mike Boddicker suffered a club-record ninth straight decision without a win (→ 29).

Hijackers get safe passage, free hostages

Hostages debark in Algiers, ending a 15-day ordeal aboard the Kuwaiti jet.

April 20. A 15-day ordeal ended quietly today as 31 hostages were released from a Kuwait Airways jumbo jet in Algeria. Their captors, who hijacked the jet on a flight from Bangkok to Kuwait, evidently were allowed to leave Algeria safely. Algerian officials would not divulge details about the negotiations with the hijackers, but they said that the agreement met with the approval of the Kuwaiti government. The hijackers were demanding the release of 17 Shiite Moslems imprisoned in Kuwait for bombing attacks in 1983. The Kuwaiti policy of refusing to give in to terrorist demands was put to the test with this action: Three members of Kuwait's royal family were among the hostages. The plane first landed in Iran, then flew to Cyprus, where the terrorists threw out the bodies of two Kuwaiti military officers. The hostages believe that the terrorists picked up arms in Iran.

Abu Jihad, P.L.O. hero, buried in Syria

April 20. Chanting "Long live the martyr!" and "We will fight to victory!" a huge, chaotic throng followed the funeral cortege of the slain P.L.O. military commander Abu Jihad through the crowded streets of Damascus. Among other things, Jihad controlled the flow of P.L.O. funds into the Israeli-occupied territories, and his death is a major setback for the Palestinian movement. The Israeli government has not denied reports that Jihad was killed by its commandos. Syrian President Hafez al-Assad's offer to let the funeral take place in Damascus was regarded as a move that might help heal the breach between Assad and P.L.O. chairman Yasir Arafat, who have long been enemies. Arafat has not paid a visit to Syria since the government expelled him in 1983. And when the crowd outside the cemetery heard a rumor that he had arrived, it began chanting his name. But the Palestinian leader stayed away from the funeral, in distant Tripoli, after last-minute efforts to arrange a reconciliation between Syria and the P.L.O. broke down (→ 5/2).

Another life ends in martyrdom.

Air Force shows Stealth bomber pictures

The Stealth seems more like a creation of George Lucas than of the Pentagon.

April 20. For 10 years, the United States Air Force kept information about the Stealth bomber a secret, until today. Pictures of the B-2, its formal name, were released as the Air Force gets ready for the maiden flight of the bomber sometime in the fall. The craft has the capability to fly without being detected on enemy radar.

Senator Sam Nunn of Georgia asserts that the Stealth jet "will render obsolete billions of dollars of Soviet investment in their air defense." While drawings show that the sophisticated bomber looks like a big flying wing with no fuselage, its particulars are still classified, including the maximum payload and the size of the crew. The Air Force has conceded that the cost of producing 132 Stealth bombers will exceed the original estimate of $36.6 billion. The craft marks the return of the flying wing construction to military planes.

Greek pedals ultra-light plane 74 miles

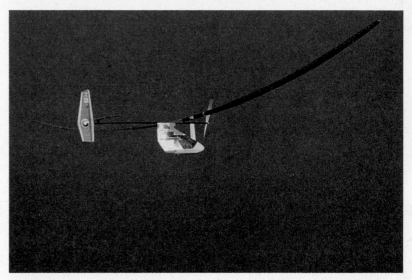

Daedalus flies, bringing the archetypal artificer to life from Greek mythology.

April 23. The strange-looking aircraft collapsed and crashed into the sea, yet its pilot called the flight "a triumph for science, for man and for history." The plane, called Daedalus, was a fragile ultra-light craft that skimmed 74 miles over the choppy Aegean Sea to set three world records for human-powered flight. At its controls was a Greek cycling champion, Kanellos Kanellopoulos, whose churning legs powered the 72-pound airplane between the Greek islands of Crete and Santorini in a little under four hours.

"We have revived the myth," the exuberant pilot said after swimming ashore. He was alluding to the 3,500-year-old Greek myth of Daedalus, who used wings made of wax and feathers to escape from Crete and land safely on the Greek mainland. His son Icarus, according to the myth, fell into the sea after having flown too close to the sun.

Smoking is banned on all short flights

April 23. Smoking was banned today on thousands of domestic airline flights. The new federal regulation outlaws smoking on all flights scheduled to last two hours or less. (Restrictions will remain in effect even if a scheduled flight is delayed and lasts longer than two hours.) The law carries fines of up to $1,000 for smoking and $2,000 for tinkering with lavatory smoke alarms. Cabin crews — what a spokeswoman for Eastern Airlines called the "front-line people" — have been briefed on how to handle recalcitrant smokers. If passengers persist in smoking after being warned they are violating federal law, airlines may arrange for the plane to be met by police at its next stop or even divert the aircraft. But to help passengers conquer the urge to light up, airlines are distributing free candy and gum (→ 5/16).

Louise Nevelson, sculptor, is dead

April 17. Louise Nevelson, 88, has retired into the dark shadows she used structurally and mystifyingly in her huge pieces. Born in Kiev, Russia, she came to the United States as a child, always wanting to sculpt. But she investigated all the arts before returning to her first love. It took three decades of hard work before she was able to make a sale, although her art made a strong impression from the first. With the use of odd pieces of wood, found objects, cast metal and other materials, she constructed huge walls or enclosed box arrangements in complex, rhythmic shapes. She worked almost until the moment of her death, finishing a 35-foot sculpture in black steel. Louise Nevelson has been described as shocking, overwhelming and exhilarating, but never uninteresting, as a person or as an artist.

Anti-acne drug is blamed for defects

April 21. Officials in the Food and Drug Administration are considering taking the anti-acne drug Accutane off the market because it can cause severe birth defects when taken by pregnant women. In a confidential F.D.A. memorandum obtained by The New York Times, it is estimated that from 1982 to 1986 Accutane caused 900 to 1,300 birth defects and 700 to 1,000 spontaneous abortions, while 5,000 to 7,000 women induced abortions "solely because of Accutane exposure and fear of birth defects." Since it was first marketed, in 1982, Accutane has carried a warning to women not to use it if pregnant or if they might become pregnant while using it. Accutane is produced by Roche Laboratories, a division of Hoffman-La Roche. A spokesman says Roche now has better ways to warn the public of Accutane's dangers (→ 22).

After 26 miles and over two hours eight minutes, Kenya's Ibrahim Hussein breaks the tape in the Boston Marathon a mere second ahead of Tanzanian Juma Ikangaa. It was the closest finish in the race's history. Rosa Mota of Portugal took the women's title five minutes ahead of the field. "I like to run by myself," she said.

Su	Mo	Tu	We	Th	Fr	Sa
					1	2
3	4	5	6	7	8	9
10	11	12	13	14	15	16
17	18	19	20	21	22	23
24	25	26	27	28	29	30

24. Washington: Environmental group releases study showing acid rain is bigger threat to Atlantic marine life than previously thought (→ 6/23).

24. New York: Mark Rudd and other ex-radicals gather at Columbia University for 20th reunion of student strike.

24. Washington: C.I.A. report finds Soviet economy stagnating despite Gorbachev reforms (→ 29).

24. Florida: Diesel-powered sub catches fire at sea; 23 crewmen hurt; three missing.

25. United States: Newly published book claims United States plotted to kill Pancho Villa with poisoned coffee.

26. The Hague: World Court rules unanimously that United States should submit to arbitration on closing of New York P.L.O. mission.

26. Saudi Arabia: Saudis break diplomatic ties with Iran over attacks in Persian Gulf and riots in Mecca (→ 7/1).

26. White Plains, New York: Jury rules Mick Jagger did not plagiarize reggae artist Patrick Alley's music in composing "Just Another Night."

26. United States: "America's Most Wanted" series on Fox network has resulted in 11 arrests since February 7 debut.

28. United States: Arena Football League, a risky but promising business venture, plays first regular-season game.

29. Forrest City, Arkansas: First-ever integrated prom result of efforts of four students.

29. Moscow: McDonald's announces deal with Soviets to open 20 restaurants in Moscow to sell the Bolshoi Mak (→ 29).

30. Los Angeles: Judge finds United States guilty of coercing Salvadorans into leaving country in major ruling on immigration rights.

DEATH

26. Frederick Douglass Patterson, founder of United Negro College Fund, at 86 (*10/10/01).

Senate passes trade bill, facing veto threat

April 27. The Senate passed the most comprehensive trade legislation in more than a decade today. But the vote was short of the two-thirds majority that would be required to override a threatened veto by President Reagan. Fifty-two Democrats and 11 Republicans voted in favor of the bill, which bolsters the authority of the President to retaliate against unfair trade practices by foreign companies. The measure contains a wide range of other provisions that were sought by an array of business, labor and farm organizations.

Yet the President has repeatedly threatened a veto because of one provision that would require companies to notify their workers 60 days in advance of plant closings or layoffs. Private industry has fiercely opposed the plant-closing measure as an intrusion by government into its private affairs, while labor groups have lobbied for it. The White House now is expected to push for an agreement that does not include the controversial measure (→ 5/24).

Le Pen alarms France, winning 14% of vote

Le Pen's appeals to racial hatred recall repugnant memories of Vichy France.

April 25. Jean Marie Le Pen's right-wing National Front party grabbed a surprising 14 percent of the vote in French presidential elections yesterday, stirring fears of a wave of extremist politics. The blustering Le Pen (who has dismissed the World War II death camps as a "minor detail" of history) denies he is a racist. But most agree he plays on "immigration, unemployment, crime, and nationalist sentiment." In the traditionally Communist "red belt" around Paris, Le Pen made large inroads by promising to evict Arab and other Third World workers recruited in the 1960's for labor-hungry industry. The boom is over, but the immigrants are still in France (→ 5/8).

"Ivan the Terrible" condemned to death

April 25. "The crimes he committed cannot be forgiven either in the letter of the law or in the hearts of men," said Judge Zvi Tal in Israel as he sentenced John Demjanjuk, the man identified as the Nazi death camp guard called Ivan the Terrible, to death by hanging. Hundreds of spectators, including Holocaust survivors, wept and chanted, "Death! Death!" But Demjanjuk insisted anew that he's the wrong man. A Ukrainian, Demjanjuk, 68, moved to the United States after World War II. Later he lost his citizenship and was extradited to Israel for trial after admitting he'd lied about his wartime activities. He now says he was a war prisoner and not a guard at the Treblinka camp.

Gap grows between U.S. rich and poor

April 30. The rich are getting richer, and the gap between them and the poor is growing, a Census Bureau study shows. A 60,000-home sampling reported an average income of $36,924. Incomes in the top fifth increased from $70,260 to $76,300. But the poorest fell from $8,761 to $8,033. At the same time, there is a new class of employees: temporaries. Instead of traditional job benefits, they may get bonuses or profit-sharing (→ 6/2).

Orioles end streak

April 29. "The public demands certainties," H.L. Mencken once wrote. The sage of Baltimore might have been writing about his hometown folks. For 21 consecutive games, the Orioles seemed certain to lose. Their 21 straight losses set a major league record for start-of-season defeats. The Orioles gave up 129 runs while getting only 44. Baltimore was becoming the butt of even more jokes than Philadelphia. ("Philadelphia is the most Pecksniffian of American cities," Mencken wrote). It all ended last night when the Orioles exploded for a 9-0 victory over the Chicago White Sox. Said Doug Sisk, whose pitching halted the slump, "It's hard to lose that many games in a row."

Lady Bird Johnson says: "With a host of potential calamities hovering over us, how can anybody spend time and resources on flowers? ... how can anyone not?"

Education officer berates U.S. schools

April 24. "Too many students do not graduate from our high schools, and too many of those who do graduate have been poorly educated," said Education Secretary William Bennett in a report issued yesterday called "American Education: Making It Work." Only modest gains have been made despite a five-year drive to improve schools. Bennett said, "Good schools for disadvantaged and minority children are much too rare." He called for "equal intellectual opportunity."

Jet fuselage rips open; one killed

April 28. A heroic pilot safely landed a Boeing 737 at Maui, Hawaii, 15 minutes after an explosion ripped a huge chunk of fuselage off of the forward cabin and swept a flight attendant to her death. The 42-year-old Aloha Airlines pilot, Robert Schornstheimer, landed with one of two engines aflame and 15 to 20 feet of the plane's front cabin exposed. One passenger said she had expected a crash but reported, "It was better than a regular landing." Of the 89 passengers on Flight 243 from Hilo to Honolulu, 60 were reported injured, but most gave credit to the pilot's skill.

Gorbachev promises church more freedom

Marking 1,000 years of Russian Christianity, Gorbachev meets church leaders.

April 29. More than a century ago, Karl Marx condemned religion as the opiate of the masses. But this year is the millennium of the founding of the church in Russia, and out of nationalistic pride and perhaps with an eye on the international propaganda value, the Soviet leader, Mikhail S. Gorbachev, is granting the church new freedoms.

To celebrate the jubilee, which takes place in June, the Kremlin plans to let churches across the land conduct services of thanksgiving. Church buildings and their murals and icons are being restored. Moscow has freed 168 religious prisoners, and it is allotting the Orthodox Church 100,000 new Bibles and is allowing the Baptists to import another 100,000. (This is far short of the demand, however, with the black-market price of a Bible now at $160.)

It is an exhilarating time for the estimated 70 million Christians in the Soviet Union, almost a quarter of the population. Many have long been victims of religious discrimination. Known believers have been barred from party membership, have rarely been admitted to universities and have faced loss of employment and housing.

Christians believe the thaw in relations between church and state is in the party's interest and hope it will continue past the millennium. They hold that persecution of such a large number of citizens saps the country's energy and that an active church could promote better values in a country with high rates of alcoholism, divorce and suicide (→ 5/26).

Sonny Bono wins election as Mayor

Sonny's first lady was Cher.

April 25. Pop culture icon Sonny Bono has found a new world to conquer — politics. Today, he joined the ranks of California's celebrity mayors, which until recently included actor Clint Eastwood of Carmel. Voters in upscale Palm Springs gave Bono the $15,000-a-year post in a landslide victory over his closest rival, an accountant. "I've never been qualified for anything I've done," admitted the singer, songwriter, comedian, restaurateur and recurring guest star on television's "Love Boat." But Bono, who is probably best known as the former husband and partner of Cher, may have been upstaged again. The actress has just won an Academy Award for her performance in "Moonstruck."

John Sloan's "South Beach Bathers" (1908) is one of the artist's works now exhibited at New York's IBM Gallery. Sloan was a leading member of the Ashcan School, which chose as subject matter the drama of everyday life.

Yoichiro Kawaguchi's "Ocean," which is actually only one frame of a film, is an example of how artists are beginning to use modern technology, particularly computers, in the realization of their artistic vision.

Su	Mo	Tu	We	Th	Fr	Sa
1	2	3	4	5	6	7
8	9	10	11	12	13	14
15	16	17	18	19	20	21
22	23	24	25	26	27	28
29	30	31				

1. Poland: May Day protests are smaller but more widely scattered than in recent years (→ 6).

1. Netherlands: Irish Republican Army attack kills three British servicemen (→ 6/14).

1. Chicago: Michael Jordan, with 55, is first to score more than 50 in basketball playoff.

2. Jerusalem: Israel says it sent 2,000 troops into Lebanon to search for P.L.O. infiltrators (→ 4).

2. Sebring, Florida: Largest sinkhole in state opens to 200 feet wide and swallows house.

3. Soweto, South Africa: Forty-member team separates Siamese twins joined at head.

3. Philadelphia: Grand jury acquits everyone involved in 1985 Move bombing.

3. Harrisburg, Pennsylvania: Computer expert and friend charged with printing fake lottery ticket to win $15 million prize.

4. Norway: Officials report 15 tons of "heavy water" that can be used to make nuclear weapons are missing (→ 7/1).

4. Lebanon: Israeli troops destroy village, killing at least 40 Lebanese (→ 6/5).

4. Boston: Mistrial declared in Lyndon LaRouche fraud case after four jurors are excused for hardship.

4. Henderson, Nevada: Over 150 injured in three blasts at space shuttle fuel plant (→ 7/7).

5. United States: Anatomist Randall S. Susman reports that South African fossil hands indicate tool-making not limited to direct human ancestors.

6. Managua: Construction workers call off 10-day hunger strike, saying wage and human rights demands were met by Sandinistas (→ 6/15).

7. Louisville: Winning Colors, with jockey Gary Stevens riding, becomes only third filly to win Kentucky Derby.

DEATH

4. Stanley William Hayter, painter, printmaker, instructor of Miro and Pollock, at 86.

Major strike in Poland

Once again, workers in Poland put down their tools to pick up placards.

May 6. Striking workers at the Nowa Huta steel mill in southern Poland got the government's answer to their demands when riot police swept through the foundry, beating the strikers and arresting key leaders. The raid occurred as mediators appointed by Poland's Roman Catholic bishops met with the strikers following government assurances that no force would be used. The bishops were quick to condemn the hard-line stance.

The current strikes, which began last week, have most prominently hit the Nowa Huta factory and the Lenin shipyard in Gdansk, on the Baltic Sea. They mark the worst labor unrest in Poland since 1982, when the government used similar force to end the strikes and banned the Solidarity trade union.

Most of the demands are for pay increases. Because of a new government program aimed at broad political and economic changes, prices of consumer goods have increased 45 percent, with certain items soaring higher. Even the state-run publications are skeptical about the program. In addition to higher pay, the workers at Gdansk are calling for the reinstatement of Solidarity, the rehiring of workers fired during the earlier unrest and the release of all political prisoners (→ 10).

Jazzfest wakes up sleepy New Orleans

Bop till you drop.

May 1. They call this place "the Big Easy" and this weekend it was easier than ever. The New Orleans Jazz and Heritage Festival, an annual event, is over, but it may be a long time until the hangovers end. For the past 10 days, thousands from across the country were jampacked onto the grounds of the local racetrack to hear an impressive range of music — everything from Dixieland to gospel, with blues, bluegrass, jug bands, rap and rock thrown in. Jazz purists might object to such a melange, but Jazzfest has no object — other than a good time. Buckwheat Zydeco, B.B. King, James Brown, Los Lobos and Little Feat kept everybody's feet moving while crawfish, red beans and rice, gumbo and pralines kept everyone humming.

Dukakis winner in Ohio and Indiana

May 3. Governor Michael Dukakis picked up both Indiana and Ohio today, gaining momentum in his quest for the Democratic nomination for President by garnering a total of 238 delegate votes. However, he was stopped short of a clean sweep in today's primaries when the Rev. Jesse Jackson won the 16 delegate votes in the District of Columbia. At the same time, Vice President George Bush, who already has a majority of the delegates needed to capture the Republican presidential nomination, was the victor in Indiana, Ohio and the District of Columbia today (→ 9).

Pollock work sold for $4.8 million

May 2. Jackson Pollock's work "The Search" has sold at a New York auction for $4.8 million, a record price for contemporary art. Pollock died in a car crash in 1956, giving him a kind of legendary status; but how then to explain why at the same auction "Diver," by the very much alive Jasper Johns, sold for nearly as much, $4.18 million. Christie's is not to question why, just to enjoy the $45.5 million it collected in two days of sales.

Fax changing way business is done

May 5. The advent of low-cost facsimile machines that can send a document across the country in as little as 20 seconds is starting to change the way Americans work, experts say. Fax machines are appearing everywhere, from major corporations to home offices to hotels that offer transmission services to business guests. More than 400,000 fax machines were sold in the United States last year, and sales may reach 700,000 in 1988. Several years ago, a machine that could transmit a document over a telephone line in three minutes cost more than $4,000. Now machines that do a page in 20 seconds are available for as little as $800 in some discount stores.

Bush reportedly heard of Noriega charges

May 7. According to several Reagan administration officials, Vice President Bush knew as far back as 1985 about the drug trafficking activities of General Manuel Noriega of Panama. Although the Vice President, who already has a majority of the delegates needed to win the GOP nomination for President, has repeatedly denied such knowledge, former Ambassador to Panama Edward Everett Briggs said that he had cabled the State Department concerning Noriega's drug trafficking, and had met with Bush in December of 1985.

Bush says that he never saw the cables, and, although he "asked around," could not find anyone who had seen them. Nevertheless, three former administration officials have gone on record as having read the communications. One official told The New York Times, "They were extremely strong. They said ... this was a man who had a history of all these things: drug dealing, gun running, technology transfer, and now he's murdered one of his opponents ..."

It is thought that the Noriega issue could play a part in the upcoming presidential elections, casting doubt on the Vice President's claims to competence in foreign policy, one of his main selling points in his campaign to reach the Oval Office (→ 25).

Paul Gauguin's "When Will You Marry," painted in 1892, is featured in the exhibit "The Art of Paul Gauguin," which opened May 1 at the National Gallery of Art in Washington, D.C. The show, a supreme achievement of curatorial effort, reveals this prolific artist through his work in a variety of media — painting, sculpture, prints, drawings, ceramics — and spans the length of his creative career. Pieces have been obtained from a number of sources, including the Soviet Union, where a great many of Gauguin's later works were bought. The Tahitian spirit abounds at the exhibition.

200 years of American fashion shown

May 3. In a tribute to the city's bicentennial, the Cincinnati Art Museum is presenting women's fashions from the 1770's to the present, in an exhibit called "Simply Stunning: 200 Years of Fashion." Dresses were purchased from Paris and New York and added to the museum's own fine collection; in all, 102 costumes are shown. Highlights include several 19th-century French couturier creations; a French interpretation of an English walking suit from 1886; two pleated Fortuny evening gowns made in Venice before World War II, and contemporary creations by Halston, Bill Blass and Geoffrey Beene. "Trends in fashion ... tell us much about people's desires," explains Otto C. Thieme, curator.

A simply stunning silk dress.

Lost in space: The Reagans and astrology

May 3. In or about 1750 B.C., Hammurabi of Babylonia would summon court astrologers to find out how movements of heavenly bodies influenced his life. In the 1980's, the First Lady of the United States calls her astrologer in San Francisco in order to steer the President's every public move — according to a 376-page account of life in the White House, "For the Record," by former chief of staff Donald T. Regan, who left or was ousted from that position 14 months ago. The President has reacted less than kindly to his former aide's revelation of "the most closely guarded domestic secret of the Reagan White House."

Regan portrays the President as a likable but easy-to-manipulate man, not the least by wife Nancy. Supposedly, she has had a strong interest in astrology for two decades, used to follow the famous seer Jean Dixon but then found Joan Quigley in California in 1981, when the latter showed that the stars had warned of grave danger around the President on March 30, the day John Hinckley Jr. shot and wounded him. The moment of the signing of the intermediate-range nuclear forces treaty on December 8, 1987, at 2 p.m., is said to have been set by Quigley based on her charts of Pisces Gorbachev versus Aquarian Reagan. Regan states that Mrs. Reagan's faith in the astrologer she would refer to as "my friend" wreaked havoc with presidential schedules and sometimes made the world's most powerful man "a virtual prisoner in the White House."

The indication from this account is that the First Lady's concern is with the safety of her husband, almost to the point of obsession.

This rather devastating portrait of a world leader whose moves are dictated by the stars through his wife is chilling to some. Others, however, criticize Regan for a vengeful "kiss and tell" maneuver. The feisty former chief of staff retorts that he has never "been kissed by anybody in the Reagan administration" (→ 23).

Reagan: Lost in the stars.

MAY
Week 19 1988

Su	Mo	Tu	We	Th	Fr	Sa
1	2	3	4	5	6	7
8	9	10	11	12	13	14
15	16	17	18	19	20	21
22	23	24	25	26	27	28
29	30	31				

8. Beirut: Shiite Moslems step up internecine fighting; 125 dead in last three days (→ 27).

9. New York: Office of designer Calvin Klein announces he is undergoing treatment for drug and alcohol abuse.

9. New York: Some 32 Guinness record-holders meet for informal convention; man with most records is follower of Sri Chinmoy who seeks to "go beyond any barriers, mental or physical."

10. Washington: Unreleased study claims oil development in Alaska created widespread environmental damage, threatening administration's plans to open wildlife refuge to oil firms.

10. Washington: Census Bureau reports dropout rate for black high school students fell from 27 to 17 percent from 1975 to 1985 (→ 18).

10. Redwood City, California: Arben Dofti and Reza Eslaminia, members of Billionaire Boys Club, sentenced to life in killing of Eslaminia's father.

11. Washington: Banks raise prime lending rate to 9 percent to stave off inflation.

11. South Africa: Security police arrest four whites said to be A.N.C. guerrillas, seizing largest arms cache ever captured in country (→ 6/5).

11. Washington: Seven in "Communist politico-military organization" indicted in 1983 bombing of Capitol.

11. Pittsburgh: Three-year-old Tabatha Foster, recipient of five-organ transplant, dies.

11. New York: Van Gogh's "Adeline Ravoux" sold at Christies for $13.8 million, six times its price in 1980.

12. Ozark, Arkansas: R. Gene Simmons sentenced to die for two of 16 killings.

13. Washington: Senate votes to expand the military's role in drug enforcement (→ 14).

DEATH

8. Charles Pollock, abstract painter, educator and brother of Jackson, at 86 (*1902).

Mozambique rebels killed 100,000 so far

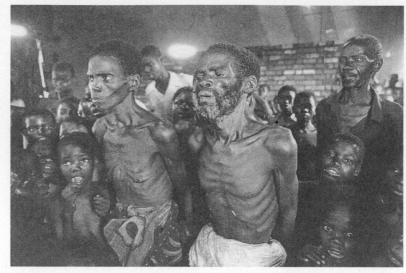

Some of the fortunate survivors of right-wing terror in Mozambique.

May 10. The gentle people of Mozambique have fallen prey to one of the world's fiercest rebel armies — the Mozambique National Resistance, or Renamo. In its campaign to overthrow the nation's Marxist government. Renamo talks of freedom, but its arbitrary and brutal raids have wiped out whole villages and killed at least 100,000 since 1981 and maimed scores of thousands more. The luckier survivors have only their ears cut off.

The raids have led some 900,000 of Mozambique's 14 million people to flee the country and 1.1 million farmers have moved to the safety of the cities. Many health clinics and schools have had to close. With land fallow, some people are starving, and foreign aid has become a vital prop to the lagging economy.

Berlin, who made America sing, is now 100

May 11. Probably the only song sung tonight that he didn't write was "Happy Birthday to You." Irving Berlin, who has composed more than 1,500 tunes, was feted this evening at a 100th birthday bash in Carnegie Hall. Nell Carter sang "Alexander's Ragtime Band," Lena Horne belted out "God Bless America" and Rosemary Clooney crooned "White Christmas." Berlin was grateful, but he wasn't there. He will see the show on television later in the month.

Triad of stars shines for one of the brightest lights in the musical firmament.

Mitterrand elected to his second term

May 8. Francois Mitterrand won a stunning victory in France today, capturing the Presidency for a second seven-year term. It is the first time a President has been re-elected in the 30 years of the current French Republic, and Mitterrand did it in resounding fashion. He captured more than 54 percent of the vote, and that is a landslide by French standards. It was a remarkable comeback for Mitterrand, whose Socialist Party lost control of the National Assembly two years ago. It was also a sharp setback for challenger Jacques Chirac, the rightist challenger. He is expected to step down as Premier.

Stately Socialist Francois Mitterrand is ready to begin his second term as the President of France.

Bush goofs again

May 9. Since their testy season as 1980 Republican primary rivals, President Reagan and Vice President George Bush have smoothed over most of their differences. But the Vice President may have overstated the case somewhat today when he said: "I am proud to be his partner. We have had triumphs, we have made mistakes, we have had sex ..." His remark was met with stunned silence from a crowd in Twin Falls, Idaho, but Bush, who is not without experience in recovering from verbal miscues, was quick to correct himself by saying, "We have had setbacks" (→ 16).

Japan steps up its foreign aid grants

May 9. The Land of the Rising Sun is casting a charitable glow around the world. Japan, formerly considered a miser by the countries of the Third World, will be spending some $10 billion on foreign aid this year, surpassing the United States as the largest philanthropist in the world. The Japanese have used their wealth to fund disparate projects, from helping with farm experiments in Bolivia to providing garbage trucks for Madagascar. While donations by Japan have climbed almost 50 percent against the dollar since 1986, they have grown less than 5 percent in terms of its domestic economy (→ 8/8).

Philby, British spy for Soviets, is dead

May 11. H.A.R. "Kim" Philby, the notorious British double agent who fled to the Soviet Union in 1963, died in Moscow today at the age of 76. As a senior officer for British intelligence during and after World War II, Philby was in a position to channel vast amounts of information to the Soviet government. It was not until 1951 that Philby came under suspicion when a so-called "third man" tipped off two other British spies, Guy Burgess and Donald Maclean, that they were about to be questioned.

Top sci-fi writer, Heinlein, deceased

May 8. Robert A. Heinlein, one of the most successful and revered writers of science fiction, has passed away in his home in Carmel, California. Best known for his sardonic and mystical novel, "A Stranger in a Strange Land," Heinlein still has 64 books in print and has sold over 40 million copies. Born in 1907, Heinlein began writing full time in 1939. His style was always clean and simple; his ideas were always astounding, and often years ahead of his time. Fans will hope that he did not merely die, but has, in the writer's own jargon, "discorporated."

A diamond is not forever same price

May 9. A girl's best friend will cost more next year. De Beers Consolidated, the largest diamond mining company in the world, today announced a 13.5 percent increase in the price of rough-cut gems. This brings to 52 percent the increase in price since 1982 and pushes the cost of a flawless one-carat diamond to $17,000. Among the most eager new customers are the Japanese, who are using their newfound wealth to support a Western custom, the engagement ring. Other new markets for diamonds include the single career woman, who is no longer waiting around for a man to buy her a ring.

Three mayors talk of legalizing drugs

May 14. Dismayed by the continuing futility in the war against drugs, some mayors are considering a once-unthinkable proposal: the legalization of heroin, cocaine and other drugs. Mayors Donald M. Fraser of Minneapolis, Marion S. Barry of Washington and Kurt L. Schmoke of Baltimore said they were talking about the proposal not to sanction drug abuse, but as an admission of the staggering cost in fighting a losing campaign against drug-related crime and to "take the profit out of drug trafficking" (→ 19).

Polygamists lose in bombing trial

May 9. A federal jury found four members of a polygamist clan guilty on 21 counts today as the result of a Mormon-chapel bombing and a 13-day siege at the clan's farm in Marion, Utah. The siege ended in a shootout January 28 that left one policeman dead. Homicide charges are still to be brought against one wheelchair-bound member. Those charged all belong to the family of polygamist John Singer, who was killed in a similar siege at the farm in 1979. Clan members claim that their actions were ordered by God to signify an impending collapse of church, state and nation.

Polish dock strike ends without success

Lech Walesa told workers halt of strike marked a "truce, not a defeat."

May 10. Their efforts checked, grim-faced workers called off their nine-day strike at the Lenin shipyard in Gdansk. The Polish government apparently rejected all their demands, including pay increases and, more significantly, reinstatement of the outlawed Solidarity trade union. Of four other strikes that hit Poland 15 days ago, three ended peacefully. But the fourth, the steel strike at Nowa Huta, was crushed by riot police. Solidarity thus seems to have suffered a major defeat, with its appeal for a national show of support for the Gdansk workers drawing little response. After the shipyard's strike committee voted 13-2 to end the walkout, Solidarity founder Lech Walesa told the workers that the step marked a "truce, not a defeat" (→ 8/31).

Fire ravages site of Louisiana Purchase

May 11. Life in New Orleans's joyous French Quarter was interrupted today by a seven-alarm fire at the historic site of the Louisiana Purchase. The Cabildo, built in 1795, housed both the French and Spanish governments in Louisiana, and in 1803, became the stage for the formal transfer of some 800,000 square miles from France to the United States. Half the city's fire fighting equipment failed to prevent the blaze from ruining valuable antique furniture and paintings.

New Orleans, noted for hot food and hot jazz, goes too far with its museum.

Su	Mo	Tu	We	Th	Fr	Sa
1	2	3	4	5	6	7
8	9	10	11	12	13	14
15	16	17	18	19	20	21
22	23	24	25	26	27	28
29	30	31				

15. Carrollton, Kentucky: Church bus is struck head on by pickup truck, killing 27 in youth group (→ 16).

16. Washington: Supreme Court rules, 6-2, that police can search garbage without warrant if criminal activity is suspected.

16. Washington: Surgeon General warns nicotine as addictive as heroin or cocaine (→ 6/13).

16. Amritsar, India: At least 23 killed in attacks attributed to Sikh militants (→ 18).

16. Carrollton, Kentucky: Pickup truck driver, found to have been intoxicated during bus collision, is charged with 27 counts of murder.

16. Nepal: Mountaineering teams from China, Japan and Nepal leave from opposite sides of Mt. Everest and meet at top in event televised live in Japan.

18. United States: Oakland's Dave Stewart sets major league record with 12th balk of the season.

18. Washington, Missouri: Londell Williams and wife Tammy, members of Nazi terrorist group, are charged with plotting to kill Jesse Jackson (→ 23).

18. United States: In response to the death of a sailor, the Navy Department orders a review of all training procedures involving risk.

19. Jacksonville, Florida: Carlos Lehder Rivas, Colombian drug lord extradited last year, is found guilty of smuggling 3.3 tons of cocaine into United States between 1978 and 1980 (→ 6/10).

19. Riverhead, Long Island: Masked rapist convicted after victims identified his voice from taped "lineup."

21. Baltimore: Risen Star, a son of Secretariat, wins Preakness; Kentucky Derby winner Winning Colors comes in third (→ 6/11).

DEATH

20. Marion G. Romney, head of Mormon Church Council, 90.

Soviets begin leaving Afghanistan

May 15. Soviet soldiers began pulling out of what one called "a beautiful but terrifying place" as a column of 1,200 men rumbled into the Afghan capital of Kabul nine hours after leaving Jalalabad, 100 miles to the east. The men represent the first Soviet withdrawals from Afghanistan called for by the Geneva agreements last month. Some 25,000 to 30,000 men will leave this month and half the total 120,000 will be out by August 15.

Today's pullout comes eight and a half years after a "limited contingent" of Soviet troops arrived to help the Afghan Communist government combat an Islamic guerrilla army. Since then, some 15,000 Soviet have been killed and many more wounded in what has been called the "Russian Vietnam." The war has become increasingly unpopular among Soviet citizens and an unwelcome burden to their already troubled economy. Nor is it likely to evaporate after the Russians pull out. Not only have the mujahedeen rebels not accepted the Geneva accords, but also, on the night before the Soviet convoy withdrew from Jalalabad, they opened a rocket attack on the city as if to emphasize their commitment to the jihad or "holy war."

Experts predict they will intensify their drive on Kabul after the August pullout and they are questioning the government's appetite for a sustained effort. Though the Afghan army has a large stockpile of Soviet arms, its discipline is weak and its desertion rate high. The Moslem rebels — backed by American weapons and $2 billion in covert American aid — have a clear superiority if they can set their own house in order and halt the infighting that plagues their ranks (→ 11/4).

After years of fighting, it is time to bring the boys back home.

Soviet soldiers are leaving what one called "a beautiful but terrifying place."

Pepsi ads in Soviet

May 17. Some 150 million Russians will get a chance to watch Michael Jackson when they catch a five-part television series on America, a prelude to the summit meeting. The show will carry six spots by Pepsi-Cola, the first air time ever sold to an American company on Soviet television. Included will be Jackson flaunting his hit, "Bad.'

Armenian and Azerbaijani chiefs dismissed

May 21. Three months of violent demonstrations and riots in Soviet Armenia and Azerbaijan have led Moscow to dismiss the Communist Party leaders of these southern republics and replace them with men untainted by past problems. The protests began in the Nagorno-Karabakh region of Azerbaijan. The area's Armenians, nearly 80 percent of the population, want it to be annexed by the adjacent Republic of Armenia. Long-standing ethnic tensions between the mainly Christian Armenians and the Moslem Azerbaijanis have led to some bloody exchanges. The worst occurred in Azerbaijan in February when some 30 Armenians were killed in their homes (→ 6/14).

Sitter kills a child at school, then self

May 20. A 31-year-old woman baby sitter walked into an elementary school in Winnetka, Illinois, today, brandishing a .22-caliber pistol, firing at random, killing a boy, 8, and critically wounding five other pupils. The woman, identified as Laurie Wassermann Dann of Chicago, set fire to another elementary school earlier today and to the home where she had worked as baby sitter. After the school shooting, Mrs. Dann fled to a nearby house where she shot and wounded a 20-year-old occupant. After an eight-hour siege, police stormed the house and found Mrs. Dann dead, apparently a suicide.

Cabbage Patch doll maker is in decline

May 16. Out of the seeds of sentimentality the Cabbage Patch doll grew, reaping huge profits in 1985 for its maker, Coleco. But the company, which bought another passing fad in 1986, Trivial Pursuit, is now millions of dollars in debt. Over a third of its managerial staff in West Hartford, Connecticut, and half of its production crew will be laid off.

"Carrie" is $7 million quick theater flop

May 15. All the elements for success were there: The show was a British import like the hits "The Phantom of the Opera" and "Les Miserables"; it was based on a work by the extremely popular master of horror Stephen King, and its singing star was Betty Buckley, whose Streisand-like voice shot her to fame in "Cats." But after an investment of $7 million, dismal reviews and five performances, the musical "Carrie" has failed. Terry Hands, its director and artistic director of the Royal Shakespeare Company, admitted to some inexperience with the Broadway scene. Ironically, someone with no theater experience at all, the pop star Madonna, is doing just fine in David Mamet's play "Speed the Plow."

Sikh militants in Golden Temple surrender

The holy grounds of the Golden Temple are stained with blood.

May 18. The 10-day siege of the Golden Temple of Amritsar ended today with the surrender of 46 militant Sikhs to Indian government security forces. The relatively peaceful end to the crisis is regarded as a major victory for Prime Minister Rajiv Gandhi, whose mother, Indira, was assassinated four years ago following a similar but more violent siege of the Amritsar temple. Damage to the buildings during the present siege was light. But 36 Sikh militants died; at least two of them swallowed poison rather than surrender. Four members of the government security forces were wounded.

Violence in the Punjab has been a long-standing problem for the Indian government, which has refused to yield to Sikh demands for an independent homeland. Government officials now hope that the new head priest of the temple, Jasbir Singh Rode, will be able to moderate the demands of the extremists and negotiate a settlement that does not call for an independent Sikh state. Amritsar itself is still under curfew, but the roads across Punjab are open (→ 6/21).

Poll shows Bush is trailing Dukakis

May 16. A new poll shows Governor Michael Dukakis with a big lead over Vice President Bush in the presidential election to be held in November. The poll of 1,056 registered voters conducted by The New York Times and CBS News found the Massachusetts Governor, the likely Democratic nominee, topping Bush, the expected Republican choice, by 49 to 39 percent. This represented a significant shift from a March poll in which Bush led Dukakis by 46 to 45 percent.

In the latest poll, Dukakis led in all regions, running especially well in the Northeast and Middle West. He held a substantial lead over Bush among blacks, women, union members and Roman Catholics. The poll also found that 28 percent of those who said they voted for President Reagan four years ago now prefer the likely Democratic candidate, while only 9 percent of those who voted in 1984 for the Democrat, Walter Mondale, have switched to Bush.

However, many of the newly polled voters said they were concerned that Dukakis may lack experience, especially in the fields of foreign policy and defense, thus giving the Republicans hope that they will eventually be able to win (→ 6/7).

Garry Winogrand's "The Zoo," a photograph taken in 1962, is part of a retrospective of his work now at New York's Museum of Modern Art. A pioneer in several techniques, including use of the wide-angle lens, Winogrand also created long photo essays; he spent years snapping women on the streets of the city as well as the animals in the Central Park Zoo.

"Syria, Three Soldiers on Camels, 1940," by the famous Life photographer Margaret Bourke-White, part of an exhibit now at the Detroit Institute of Art.

MAY
Week 21 1988

Su	Mo	Tu	We	Th	Fr	Sa
1	2	3	4	5	6	7
8	9	10	11	12	13	14
15	16	17	18	19	20	21
22	23	24	25	26	27	28
29	30	31				

23. Washington: United States official reports Pakistan has tested missile capable of carrying nuclear weapons.

23. Washington: Food and Drug Administration approves cervical cap for birth control.

23. Washington: Commission on Minority Participation in Education and American Life, including Jimmy Carter and Gerald Ford, releases report warning United States commitment to minorities is slipping (→ 7/4).

23. Baltimore: Maryland becomes first state to ban manufacture and sale of cheap handguns often called Saturday Night Specials (→ 8/1).

24. Washington: Pres. Reagan vetoes trade bill; House votes to override (→ 6/30).

24. Poughkeepsie, New York: Tawana Brawley's mother defies grand jury subpoena to testify in daughter's case (→ 6/6).

25. New Jersey: Two Princeton students given jail sentences for serving alcohol to minors after party that put 39 in student infirmary, hospitalized six and put one in coma.

25. Denver: Flight mechanic with no pilot's license steals Lear jet in Virginia, flies to Denver and kills himself.

25. Phoenix, Arizona: Debra Ann Forster, 18, ordered by court to stay on birth control for life for deserting two sons.

25. Los Angeles: Nostradamus's believers breathe easy as date he set for "rumbling of the Earth" in a "new city" passes without earthquake.

26. Washington: Department of Health and Human Services begins mailing "Understanding AIDS" brochure to 107 million households, a $17 million project (→ 6/2).

27. Beirut: Syrian troops move into southern suburbs of Beirut to enforce agreement to end fighting between rival Shiite groups.

27. Hicksville, Long Island: New York State and Long Island Lighting Company reach agreement to close $5.3 billion Shoreham nuclear power plant.

Reagan begins his first visit to Russia

May 31. At the beginning of the Reagan Presidency, few would have predicted the scene today at Moscow State University. President Reagan was surrounded by 600 students and Soviet intellectuals, and he seemed to relish his role. His audience had a good time too.

"Reagan is a simple man, a normal man," one Russian editor told The New York Times when he was asked to explain the warm reaction to the President. "He likes astrology, he was an actor. We want to have a normal man as the leader of our state."

Reagan's visit, the first by an American President to the Soviet Union in 14 years, began very tensely on Sunday. In his first meeting with Soviet leader Mikhail Gorbachev, Reagan was sharply critical of Moscow's record on human rights. White House chief of staff Howard Baker said Reagan and Gorbachev were not great friends to begin with, and sparks flew at their first get-together. A Soviet spokesman was equally blunt. "We don't like it when someone from outside is teaching us how to live and that is only natural," he said.

Reagan continued his human rights campaign yesterday as he met with a group of dissidents at the U.S. ambassador's residence. The President's strident criticisms may quiet right-wing opposition at home to this trip. Conservatives are still wondering what Reagan is doing visiting a country he once condemned as an "evil empire" (→ 6/23).

President Reagan in the heart of what he once called "the evil empire."

Reds rewrite history

May 30. Secondary school students across the Soviet Union are breathing easy because final exams in history have been canceled to allow rewriting of the standard texts. Mikhail S. Gorbachev's candid approach to the Soviet past involves a critical evaluation of Stalin, and the rehabilitation of leaders formerly erased from the books. According to one school director, "We know much more today." Yet some observe the changes with thinly veiled cynicism. "To think," one artist reflected, "after all that nervousness, much of what we studied is turning out not to have been true" (→ 6/3).

Soviet Union to curb Communists' power

May 26. The Communist Party Central Committee admitted quite openly this morning that life is not improving fast enough in the Soviet Union, and it blamed party officials for many of the shortcomings. The committee pledged to clear up the problems by reducing the power of party officials and making their election more democratic.

"Especially intolerable are failures to meet assignments for accelerated growth of consumer goods production," the committee said. "Difficulties remain in food supplies for the population."

The Central Committee would allow the Communist Party to remain the dominant element in Soviet life but would get rid of bureaucrats who have become lazy and entrenched in the system. "Some executives started thinking they had been appointed to their posts for life," the committee said, and "they considered themselves infallible and abused their power."

The committee recommended the term of most party officials be limited to 10 years. The committee's proposals monopolized news coverage in Moscow today. Little was reported about the imminent arrival of President Reagan (→ 30).

Efforts to remove Noriega abandoned

May 25. Secretary of State George P. Shultz has announced that the United States will cease negotiating with Panamanian General Noriega. Last month, a State Department official presented Noriega with an offer to drop federal drug trafficking indictments against the Central American strongman if he would give up his military command and leave Panama. The offer was widely criticized, particularly by members of Congress who opposed a deal that included dropping the indictments. Noriega has refused the offer.

Vice President Bush, who has been accused of delaying action against Noriega since 1985, when Bush was first informed about the general's drug dealing activities, said that he "had some reservations" about the deal but could "certainly understand the Secretary's desire to get the man out of office" (→ 6/17).

Critics find Reagan inattentive, vague

May 23. This has become the era of Reagan bashing, with a number of former top aides, as well as some family members, writing books that describe the President as vague and inattentive to details. In the latest of the spate of books about President Reagan, his former Treasury secretary and one-time top aide at the White House, Donald Regan, has written: "It was a rare meeting in which he made a decision or issued orders ... Nearly everyone was a stranger to this shy President."

Larry Speakes, his former White House spokesman, wrote: "When he does look at a newspaper, the President's habit is to read the comics first." David Stockman, a former budget director, wrote: "Reagan's body of knowledge is primarily impressionistic." And Martin Anderson, another former White House aide, said Reagan resembled a "Turkish pasha, passively letting his subjects serve him."

Armada's 400th raises issues about Drake

The defeat of the Spanish Armada left England as lord of the high seas.

May 23. Tradition has it that Sir Francis Drake was bowling when the Spanish Armada was sighted off the coast of Plymouth 400 years ago this summer. "There is time enough to finish the game and defeat the Spanish, too," Drake was supposed to have said. This account, as well as many others, is being challenged by some British scholars on the anniversary of this greatest of Britain's naval victories. An exhibition presented at the National Maritime Museum would have us believe it wasn't so much a victory by the British as a victory for mother nature. A violent storm in the English Channel apparently caused the Spanish fleet to scatter and prevented any attempt by the Spaniards to put troops ashore.

This debunking has raised the eyebrows and the temperatures of a lot of patriotic Britons. The normally staid Times of London put it this way: "National anniversary festivities should properly be concerned with projecting myths, not recording facts." At Plymouth, where Drake was born, City Councilor Reg Scott was hot under the collar over the treatment of a hero. "It's outrageous of them to play down Drake's role," he said. "I was raised to think of this as a great victory." The British traditionally celebrate the Drake victory with banquets and with bonfires that are lit along the once-threatened coast of Cornwall.

Oilers capture 4th Stanley Cup in five years

May 26. "I think we're one cup away from being recognized as the greatest hockey team of all time," said an exultant Kevin Lowe as the Edmonton Oilers clinched their fourth Stanley Cup in five years. There were few who would argue the point as the Oilers swept the Boston Bruins in four games. This was the first sweep for the Oilers in a final series. Wayne Gretzky played his usual superb game and set a playoff record of 31 assists. He became only the third player ever to win the Conn Smythe Trophy a second time. The Boston coach, Terry O'Reilly, summed it all up by saying his club had "finally come up against a perfect team." The Oilers won the fourth game by 6-3.

Oiler Jari Kurri enjoys a tall, cool one after Edmonton's Stanley Cup victory.

Kadar replaced as leader of Hungary

May 22. Janos Kadar, the 76-year-old General Secretary of the Hungarian Communist Party, has been replaced by Karoly Grosz, who was appointed Prime Minister of the Budapest government last June. Kadar was installed by the Russians in 1956 in the wake of the Hungarian uprising and was widely denounced for his role in the execution of Imre Nagy and others who had been involved in the insurrection. Later, Kadar's policy of allowing increased personal freedom and a higher standard of living made him more popular. Grosz is a 57-year-old party functionary who believes that a revival of the Hungarian economy is more likely through free-market principles than by means of centralized state control.

Myerson is arrested on shoplifting charge

May 27. Bess Myerson, former New York City cultural affairs commissioner and a former Miss America, was arrested for shoplifting today in South Williamsport, Pennsylvania. Two security guards stopped her as she was leaving Hill's Department Store just before 11:30 this morning. Searching her purse and shopping bag, they found several unpaid for items, totaling $44.07. At her arraignment before Justice John M. McDermott, Miss Myerson said, "I was leaving the store to lock my car and come back and pay for the merchandise." The policeman who arrested her said, "She was all upset, she was just sick about it." If found guilty, Miss Myerson would face up to $300 in fines and 90 days in jail (→ 7/15).

Su	Mo	Tu	We	Th	Fr	Sa
			1	2	3	4
5	6	7	8	9	10	11
12	13	14	15	16	17	18
19	20	21	22	23	24	25
26	27	28	29	30		

1. Borken, West Germany: At least 16 people die in a mine explosion which traps 40 others 300 feet underground (→ 2).

2. New York City: Luncheon at Hotel Maxim's de Paris celebrates 60th anniversary of Kraft's Velveeta cheese product.

2. Washington: Rageshree Ramachandran, 13, captures Scripps Howard National Spelling Bee with "elegiacal."

2. Toronto: Mohawk Indians peacefully end two-day blockade of major highway in dispute with government over cigarette trade on reservations.

2. Borken, West Germany: All miners feared dead in explosion.

2. Washington: Salvadoran President Jose Napoleon Duarte is diagnosed as having stomach cancer and related liver problems (→ 9/21).

2. United States: Census Bureau reports that a greater percentage of young people are living with their parents because they cannot afford to move out (→ 10/7).

3. United States: The 100th anniversary of Ernest Lawrence Thayer's "Casey at the Bat" is observed nationwide.

3. Moscow: Andrei Sakharov, in official setting at Foreign Ministry, calls for release of all political prisoners (→ 7).

3. New York: American League baseball umpires, in unprecedented step, vow to take measures to curb N.Y. Yankees manager Billy Martin (→ 23).

4. Cuba: Fidel Castro, in letter to New York Archbishop John Cardinal O"Connor, vows to free all but 44 political prisoners (→ 7/23).

4. Paris: Steffi Graf wins French Open 6-0, 6-0 over Russian Natalya Zvereva, first time since 1911 a Grand Slam finalist has failed to win a game (→ 7/2).

4. Brooklyn, New York: A gunman fires on a crowd at social club, killing two, including a 16-year-old high school student, and wounding five.

Vietnam to pull troops out of Cambodia

June 4. Vietnamese troops, seasoned by almost a decade of jungle fighting, are pulling out of Cambodia, Hanoi announced today. They have fought against an alliance of forces led by the brutal Khmer Rouge, who controlled Cambodia before Vietnam invaded in 1978. Followers of Prince Norodom Sihanouk, who once ruled Cambodia, have also fought against the Vietnamese. In Phnom Penh, supporters of the Communist forces lined the roads as hundreds of officers and men drove to the airport to board Soviet planes headed for Ho Chi Minh City, formerly Saigon. Almost 3,000 of the 50,000 troops scheduled to depart have already left. The war in Cambodia is now officially in the hands of Cambodian leadership, according to government sources in Hanoi. Vietnam has officially conceded, for the first time, that 25,000 soldiers died during the last 10 years. A meeting of Asian leaders in Bangkok, attended by U.S. Secretary of State George Shultz expressed some optimism about the withdrawals.

Vietnamese troops celebrate their going home, sweet home.

America has high rate of abortions

June 1. The United States has a higher rate of abortions than most Western countries, according to a recent survey. The Alan Guttmacher Institute in New York gathered statistics from 20 industrialized nations and reported that although many of them had similar birth rates, the United States had a significantly higher pregnancy rate than most of the countries. It was about 25 percent higher than Canada's, for example. In 1983, the survey found, more than half of the American pregnancies were unplanned, compared to less than a third in Britain. Researchers believe the high rates of unplanned pregnancies and abortion may be the result of a relatively limited choice of contraceptives available on the American market (→ 8/8).

AIDS board breaks with White House

June 2. In a report that clashes with the official White House position, James D. Watkins, chairman of the President's AIDS commission, today suggested strong federal efforts to bar discrimination against infected individuals and AIDS patients. Watkins will ask the 13-member commission to back new federal laws and regulations against AIDS discrimination in its official report, which goes to President Reagan this month.

In his draft report, Watkins said the government's failure to protect AIDS patients against the loss of jobs and other forms of discrimination was "the most significant obstacle to progress in controlling the epidemic." He asked for federal laws protecting AIDS-infected individuals in private life, directives barring discrimination against federal workers and legislation providing confidentiality for people who test positive for the AIDS virus.

The Watkins recommendations agree with those in a report issued yesterday by the National Academy of Sciences. Both criticize the government for failing to provide leadership in fighting the AIDS epidemic and urge major increases in funding of AIDS activities (→ 30).

British still pursue mystery of the Ripper

June 3. Five new books have just been published, a four-hour television miniseries is scheduled for the fall and Ripperology is thriving as the centennial of the sensational murder spree approaches.

It was between August 31 and November 9, 1888, that the unknown psychopath who earned the nickname "Jack the Ripper" killed and mutilated five of the thousand or so prostitutes who walked the slum streets of Whitechapel in London's East End. Scotland Yard investigated, but without result, leading Queen Victoria to comment, "Our detectives must be improved. They are not what they should be."

Evidence amassed by ardent Ripperologists has pointed to a drunken lawyer named Montague Druitt, to Roslyn D'Onston, a dabbler in black magic turned journalist, and to a group of Freemasons under the guidance of the Queen's physician, Sir William Gull. A mad Russian also has his advocates.

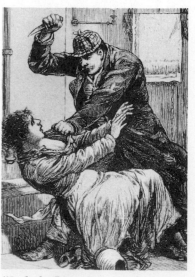

"Jack the Ripper" in action.

Skateboarding has become a U.S. life style

Skateboards may cause some wonderment when future generations dredge them out of time capsules, but there is little doubt about their place in current society. Some 20 million Americans writhe and wriggle their way over sloped swimming pools and anything else that offers a concrete foundation. The sport has its own fashions, its own language and an abundance of tricky moves. It is cool on the West Coast but a pesty annoyance to Chicago police and a bit slow to catch on in New York City. However, an Atlanta entrepreneur insists, "This is no longer a fad. It's gotten to be a life style."

Tony Hawk glides through the air.

Suzuki "jeep" said to roll over easily

June 2. The four-wheel-drive Suzuki Samurai has been declared "not acceptable" and should be recalled from American roads, according to Consumer Reports magazine. The vehicle is prone to roll over if turned quickly, said the magazine as it gave a "not acceptable" rating for the first time in a decade. The publication's testing agency reported that the Samurai will tip over at a speed of less than 40 mph if the vehicle's driver attempts to make a sharp turn in an accident situation.

More wars fought in 1987 than ever

June 2. World Priorities, a research institute based in Washington, says that 1987 was a record year for wars. In a study just released, author Ruth Leger Sivard reports that 25 wars were being fought during the past year. Sivard acknowledged difficulty in accurately estimating the number of casualties, but there were probably about three million killed, she estimated. Four-fifths of them were civilians. Most are "forgotten wars," she explained, because they are not seen on television.

Nostalgic for the 60's? Like, wow, man, psychedelia is back, and you can dig the crazy colors on these cool legs, or pick up some groovy Neo-Max swimwear designed by artist Peter Max to wear at the beach this summer.

Thousand brave rafting thrills and spills

It's like a roller coaster ride on water, and more Americans are doing it every year. From some 25,000 rafting trips a decade ago, the number has now climbed to almost two million a year, despite the inherent dangers to the inexperienced as they paddle over churning rapids. The trips can be as short as a day or as long as a one- or two-week excursion that is combined with fishing and camping, a style most popular in the Far West.

The sport is relatively inexpensive, with the cost ranging up to $100 a day, including meals. "Once you do it, you can't help but feel good about yourself," said Jay Schurman, whose Maine company arranges excursions for more than 10,000 people a year. "It brings strangers together."

Fifteen rafters, a record number, drowned in 1987. But Tom Ellis, a marketing expert, points out that there have been 13 skiing deaths in Colorado alone in the past three or four years, compared with just two deaths on organized rafting trips in the state since 1969. He said that the greatest danger is to people who attempt to raft on their own. Nevertheless, some states are now acting to regulate the sport. They want to require the use of professional guides and a licensing system.

Rafting downriver: Taste the spray, but try not to kiss the rocks.

Polar cap crossed by team of skiers

June 2. A team of Soviet and Canadian skiers has completed a 91-day trip across the polar ice cap, marking the first time anyone has crossed from one country to another via the North Pole. The nine Russians and four Canadians faced icy winds and sub-zero temperatures in a journey from Severnaya Zemlya to Ward Hunt Island, covering 1,100 miles. Air drops of food and equipment assisted the group, which was sponsored by Canadian and Soviet newspapers and had the backing of both governments. The so-called Polar Bridge expedition coincided with the Kremlin's attempts to enlist Canada's support for a nuclear-free Arctic zone.

Music, poetry spur a 1,000-mile runner

June 4. Yiannis Kouros composes music in his head. His mind writes poetry. He plans his life. A lot of people do the same thing, but Kouros does it while running a race 1,000 miles long. What else is there to do in a 1,000-mile race? The 32-year-old Greek immigrant says his role model is the mythological courier Pheidippides, who dropped dead after running 25 miles to Athens with news that the invading Persians had been repulsed at Marathon. Kouros has set records at every distance over 100 miles and last week won a 1,000-mile grind in the borough of Queens in New York. His secret: To keep the mind occupied while running.

JUNE
Week 23 1988

Su	Mo	Tu	We	Th	Fr	Sa
			1	2	3	4
5	6	7	8	9	10	11
12	13	14	15	16	17	18
19	20	21	22	23	24	25
26	27	28	29	30		

5. Jerusalem: Israeli high court upholds expulsion of Palestinian-American Mubarak E. Awad for role in uprising in occupied territories (→ 7).

5. New Haven: Yale alumnus at 30th reunion is arrested for burning wooden shanty erected by students to protest apartheid in South Africa (→ 8).

6. Las Vegas: Iran "Blade" Barkely scores upset knockout over Thomas "Hit Man" Hearns, capturing middleweight title.

6. Poughkeepsie, New York: Glenda Brawley, mother of Tawana, is ordered to spend 30 days in jail for refusing to testify in daughter's case (→ 25).

6. Nepal: Mary Margaret Goodwin is first solo runner to cross Himalayas, a 1,300-mile trek.

6. England: British newscasters go on with broadcast while four women protesting anti-gay laws chain themselves to desk and cameras.

7. Washington: United States officials announce agreement, signed last week in New Zealand, to open Antarctica to international development of oil and mineral resources.

7. El Bireh, West Bank: Mayor Hassan al-Tawil, appointed by Israelis, is stabbed and critically wounded after refusing Arab demands that he resign (→ 7/31).

8. Washington: In blow to prosecution, judge in Iran-contra case rules each defendant must be tried separately (→ 20).

8. Johannesburg: About one million black workers end three-day strike with 10 dead in clashes with police (→ 7/29).

8. Paris: President Mitterrand vows to forgive one-third of African debt, asks other countries to follow (→ 10/17).

10. Washington: Senate passes bill to allow death penalty in drug-related killings; amendment calling for public executions is defeated (→ 12).

11. Belmont Park: Risen Star, son of Secretariat, wins Belmont Stakes in 2:26.4, second only to father's record time.

Throngs battle with police in Seoul

June 10. The worst violence in months reverberated throughout Seoul today. By the time the tear gas cleared, the government was still in control, and South Korean students had been prevented from meeting a North Korean delegation at the border. It took 60,000 police officers to stop the march. Most of them battled with students in the streets. Others fanned out through bus and train stations to prevent students from traveling to the border village of Panmunjom. More than 500 students were arrested. More than 100 people were injured. The worst of the fighting took place at Yonsei University, where students hurled rocks and gas bombs at police. Officers responded with scores of tear-gas canisters. One student was hit in the head and is reported in serious condition.

The tension between the students and the government has been building for several days. The students have rallied at more than 50 universities all over the country to demand the reunification of the two Koreas and the withdrawal of all American forces. "Drive out the Yankees who enforce the partition of the land!" has been the rallying call. The students were planning to press their demands with the symbolic meeting at Panmunjom. They had also planned to organize a sports competition between athletes from the North and South to coincide with the Olympics next month.

The North Korean delegation left

Student demonstrators in Korea let the police know what they think ...

Panmunjom after the students failed to arrive from Seoul. The North Korean press agency blasted the crackdown as "an arbitrary and fascist anti-national criminal act."

Despite the ferocity of the demonstrations, they were less violent than those of last year which forced the government to back down and organize democratic presidential elections. The students also failed to gather the support of key opposition leaders. The latest crackdown came as the government itself was trying to increase contacts with North Korea. Just last week, the government said it would re-open the debate on reunification and resume Cabinet-level talks with officials from the North (→ 7/5).

... and the lawmen reply.

House Speaker hit with ethics charges

June 10. At the urging of Representative Newt Gingrich, Republican of Georgia, the House Ethics Committee has voted unanimously to conduct an inquiry into six allegations against Speaker Jim Wright. In the first investigation of a speaker since the ethics panel was formed in 1967, it will be decided whether Wright committed any violations of House rules. The charges are based on newspaper reports and are not criminal charges, but alleged violations of House rules. Wright denies any wrongdoing.

Electronics change U.S. public libraries

June 6. Videocassettes, computer software and other electronic products are rapidly transforming the American library. Books still are its basic stock in trade, but electronic collections are growing at the fastest rate. An American Library Association study found that 62.5 percent of the nation's 115,000 libraries now lend videocassettes, 49 percent have computers for public use and about 25 percent lend compact disks. The New York Public Library says it now spends 15 percent of its budget on electronic material, including books on tape.

L'Amour, chronicler of the West, is dead

June 10. He once used the name Tex Burns when he thought no one would want to read a western with a French-sounding name on the cover. But Louis L'Amour became synonymous with the genre, and with his passing in Los Angeles, the western itself just might head into the sunset. L'Amour, born March 22, 1908, in Jamestown, North Dakota, was a lumberman, an elephant trainer, a rancher, a sailor who was shipwrecked in the Caribbean and a professional pugilist in the years before he wrote his 86 novels and 14 story collections.

Dukakis clinches presidential nomination

The Massachusetts Governor has Democratic nomination firmly in his grasp.

June 7. Governor Michael Dukakis apparently clinched his bid for the Democratic presidential nomination yesterday, winning the New Jersey and California primaries. He defeated the Rev. Jesse Jackson by a margin of 2 to 1 in New Jersey and 3 to 2 in California. The big victories in these two states, giving him enough delegate votes for nomination at the Democratic National Convention in Atlanta next month, marked the end of a struggle that started four months ago with the first of a long series of primaries and caucuses. However, it also ushered in another struggle over the direction of the Democratic Party and Jackson's possible role in it. In a recent interview, Jackson said he felt Dukakis should offer him the vice-presidential slot on the ticket, even though he might turn it down.

"The constituency I represent has earned its place at the top level of American politics," said Jackson, a civil rights leader who won far more support, particularly in the South, than Democratic leaders had anticipated.

While not ruling out a top spot on the ticket for Jackson, the Massachusetts Governor said he's made no decision on the issue. He said there was plenty of time before the convention to decide (→ 7/12).

Helicopter with speed of jet is unveiled

June 6. The Marine Corps today unveiled its latest flying machine, a helicopter-like craft that can travel as fast as a jet. Called the Osprey, the "tilt-rotor" craft can take off and land vertically by pointing its two 38-foot propellers upward, then speed away by moving them into the forward position.

The Osprey's primary purpose is to carry troops ashore in amphibious assaults. Intended as a replacement for the Marine Corps' aging helicopters, it is designed to carry 24 battle-ready men or five tons of equipment. Marine Corps officials say the Osprey will allow ships to stay further offshore, avoiding enemy fire, and will carry troops deeper into enemy territory. The Navy has overall responsibility for the Osprey program and it will take 350 of the 900 aircraft that are expected to be built, with the rest earmarked for the Marines.

The estimated cost of the program is well over $20 billion, with the first 600 aircraft costing more than $30 million each. That cost has brought criticism. A report by the House Armed Services Committee last year questioned the need for the Osprey, saying, "We may be acquiring the wrong aircraft at the wrong time for the wrong reasons." But a go-ahead for development was given by the Defense Department, with the proviso that the program would be canceled if the costs of the Osprey proved to be too high.

The Marine Corps' new helicopter-like Osprey can fly as fast as a jet.

He flies through the air with the greatest of ease: Sergei Bubka breaks his own pole vault record with a 19-foot, 10.25-inch leap.

June 6. Members of the Kennedy clan pay their respects at the grave of Robert, after a Mass of Remembrance and rededication.

Study of 130 British eccentrics published

June 6. Prince Charles has made an exclusive list from which he may have hoped to be excluded. David Weeks, a clinical psychologist at Royal Edinburgh Hospital, has just released a study of 130 British eccentrics past and present — and Charles qualifies. Reason: The royal heir has been seen chatting with horses, plants and others who do not chat back. Weeks will soon publish the results of profiles on 800 American eccentrics; preliminary findings suggest that they are more gentle-humored than their British counterparts and incline further to the left politically.

Lenin implicated in use of state terror

June 7. Until recently, it was acceptable in the Soviet Union to criticize Stalin and Brezhnev. Lenin, however, was out of bounds. That is beginning to change. A respected Soviet journalist, Vasily Selyunin, writes in a monthly magazine that the creation of labor camps, generally blamed on Stalin, really began under Lenin. Mikhail Gorbachev frequently praises Lenin and even calls his own programs a return to "Leninist principles." Selyunin says that Gorbachev is making economic changes too slowly, and he warns that the country could revert to dictatorship (→ 30).

JUNE
Week 24 1988

Su	Mo	Tu	We	Th	Fr	Sa
			1	2	3	4
5	6	7	8	9	10	11
12	13	14	15	16	17	18
19	20	21	22	23	24	25
26	27	28	29	30		

12. New York City: Police arrest two members of Guardian Angels, now protecting Restaurant Row against drug dealers (→ 16).

13. Luxembourg: European Economic Community agrees on plan to end all curbs on flow of capital between 12 member nations.

13. Nome, Alaska: Alaska Airlines jet, carrying Eskimos, officials and journalists, crosses Bering Strait to Soviet area, reuniting Eskimos (→ 27).

13. Williamsport, Pennsylvania: Dave "Spuds" Bresnahan, fired from AA baseball team for throwing a potato as a wild pitch and tagging baserunner out with ball, gets number retired in belated tribute.

14. Washington: Edwin Meese orders I.R.A. fugitive Joseph Patrick Thomas extradited to face British murder charges (→ 16).

15. Laredo, Texas: Border officials turn away convoy carrying food and medical supplies to Nicaragua (→ 15).

15. Managua: Daniel Ortega lifts Nicaraguan wage and price controls in effort to salvage economy (→ 7/10).

15. Paris: France and Iran announce restoration of diplomatic ties, broken 11 months ago over terrorism.

15. Washington: Census Bureau reports over half of new mothers stay in job market (→ 20).

16. Washington: Senate, 93-3, votes to revise welfare code, requiring jobs for those who are physically able.

16. Tyler, Texas: The Rainbow Family of Living Light, hippie group with thousands of members across country, wins right in court to hold annual meeting in national forest to worship nature.

16. Rutland, Vermont: John A. Zaccaro Jr., son of Geraldine Ferraro, sentenced to four months for selling cocaine (→ 20).

17. Lafayette, Louisiana: U.S. officials indict 170 as members of international drug ring linked to Noriega (→ 7/27).

Use of autos seen as worldwide threat

June 12. Traffic gridlock will become worldwide and health problems from pollution will rise relentlessly unless governments take action to curtail auto use, a study by the Worldwatch Institute predicted today. It urged higher taxes on low-mileage autos and asked governments to encourage use of public transportation instead of autos.

There are now nearly 400 million cars in use and many developing countries are building new factories, according to the institute, which is sponsored by the United Nations. It's absurd, the report said, for poor nations to invest in autos, which benefit only "a small, privileged class with ample purchasing power." It noted that traffic has become so heavy that bicycles move faster than autos in cities such as London and Tokyo, and that research on lowering pollution from cars is not being pursued. The institute acknowleged that some progress has been made. Average mileage for American cars is up to 18 miles per gallon from 13 in 1973, and Japanese and European cars average nearly 30 miles a gallon.

A spokesman for the Motor Vehicles Manufacturers Association in Detroit called the report's conclusions "ludicrous" and said it was not "a serious piece of research."

Soviet republics in territorial deadlock

June 14. Two Soviet republics are struggling for control of a disputed territory, and officials in Moscow have been unable to solve the problem. The dispute centers over an area known as Nagorno-Karabakh. It is controlled by the Republic of Azerbaijan, but almost 80 percent of the residents are Armenians. A two-year campaign by Armenian activists to annex the area has been largely ignored by the central government. Recent riots have left more than 30 people dead in one Azerbaijani city, and the capital of Armenia was paralyzed by a strike. The central government fears it might inflame nationalist sentiment all over the country if it lets Armenia get its way on this issue (→ 7/19).

Worst drought in 50 years means cost rises

Cracked earth, not cracked wheat.

June 16. The drought that struck America's major grain-growing areas this spring will soon cause sharp increases in food prices, Agriculture Department economists say. The drought is the worst to have hit the Midwest, South and Great Plains in 50 years, and its economic effects are worsened because it comes just as U.S. farm policy, aimed at reducing surpluses, has brought grain reserves to the lowest level in years.

More than 78 million acres have been taken out of production since 1985. Wheat stocks have dropped from 52 million metric tons in 1986 to 33.6 million tons this year, with supplies of soybeans and corn at comparably low levels. The price of soybeans has already risen more than 50 percent, to $9 a bushel, while wheat is up from $2.70 to $4 a bushel and corn from $1.85 to $2.50. Meat prices have dropped because ranchers are slaughtering cattle earlier than usual, but they are expected to rise later this year.

Even before the drought began, economists were predicting smaller-than-usual grain crops because of government programs to reduce production. Now the experts say the spring wheat crop will be down by a third from the early predictions. Unless there is rain soon, they say, the fall corn and soybean crops also are in danger.

The drought has revived fears of a world food crisis. In recent years, grain production has been keeping pace with the rise in world population, but a number of nations are reporting decreases. Bad weather has reduced production in India and China, both major grain-growing nations, while the Soviet Union continues to be a major importer, buying 12.8 million metric tons from the United States this year. Washington, which has encouraged grain exports by giving generous subsidies, now is trying to slow the rate of farm export sales (→ 21).

Anselm Kiefer's "Sulamith" (1983) is part of a major show of the German painter's work touring the country. One of the most talented modern artists, he has made a career of exploring the essence of the German psyche.

F.B.I. finds Pentagon aides took bribes

June 15. The Federal Bureau of Investigation has confirmed that six current or former Pentagon officials have been served with search warrants as part of an investigation of alleged bribes accepted by Defense Department procurement officials from military contractors. The searches come as the investigation, which has been proceeding for two years, nears an end, the F.B.I. announced. A senior law-enforcement official claimed there was "direct evidence" that several Pentagon aides had taken bribes, but no names or specific details were released to the public or the press.

For the last few months, it is believed, wiretaps were in place on the telephones of the suspects within the Pentagon. The F.B.I., which is conducting the investigation along with the Justice Department and the Navy's investigative service, provided a list of individuals and companies whose offices were searched, but would not say which of those on the list were suspected of illegal activity.

The list included the McDonnell Douglas Corporation, the nation's largest defense contractor, which said that federal agents had searched its files for information concerning the company's relationship with Melvyn R. Paisley, a former assistant secretary of the Navy for research, engineering and systems. It has not been made clear whether Paisley and the others on the list are suspects in the investigation (→ 7/1).

See it on Walkman

When it comes to turning mobility into marketablity, Sony is still out-running its competitors. In 1979, the Walkman made music portable. In 1982, the Watchman liberated TV from the living room. Last week, Sony announced the Video Walkman, a portable videocassette player. The little traveling tube is no bigger than a book and uses eight-millimeter cassettes (about the size of an audio tape). What will it cost to watch "E.T." on the train? About $1,300.

Worst I.R.A. attack of 80's kills 6 in Ulster

June 16. An Irish Republican Army bomb exploded last night in a British army truck at Lisburn, Northern Ireland, killing six soldiers. It was the worst death toll of the decade from an I.R.A. terrorist strike. Today the group, which is fighting British rule in the strife-ridden country, took responsibility while promising "unceasing war" against British military forces. Because of the severity of the bombing, and because Lisburn, an army garrison town 14 miles southeast of Belfast, had been regarded as safe from attacks by the I.R.A., the British government is beginning a review of its security policy in Northern Ireland (→ 27).

Evan Mecham wins campaign loan case

June 16. After deliberating only six and one-half hours, a Phoenix jury found former Governor Evan Mecham not guilty of six felony counts of perjury, willful concealment and filing false documents. Mecham's brother Willard was also exonerated. The two were accused of hiding a $350,000 campaign loan. If convicted, Mecham and his brother faced 22 years and nine and one-half years respectively. They held that failure to itemize the loan on personal or campaign statements was an innocent error due to Willard's inexperience as an accountant. Mecham was impeached on April 4 by the Arizona House of Representatives.

Civil War buffs seek to preserve Manassas

June 13. The third battle of Manassas is being fought over the same ground that saw two bloody Confederate victories during the Civil War, and this time one of the "generals" is a woman. Annie Snyder of Manassas, Virginia, doesn't believe that a shopping mall should rise where the headquarters of General Robert E. Lee once stood. That is the site proposed by Edward DeBartolo, the country's biggest developer of shopping malls, who wants to build one on 1.2 million square feet of the former battlefield. No way, say such Civil War buffs as Jody Powell and Charlton Heston. Former White House spokesman Powell has nine ancestors who fought at Manassas (or Bull Run). DeBartolo, however, maintains the mall site is "historically insignificant" and is adjacent to the national park where most of the fighting took place. Opponents claim that 155 men died defending the hill that would be bulldozed to make way for a parking lot (→ 11/10).

A center of the Battle at Bull Run: Would asphalt be likely to improve it?

Howard Baker quits as White House aide

Baker will step down.

June 14. In an unexpected announcement, Howard H. Baker Jr., the White House chief of staff, said today that he is resigning as of July 1. Baker had been expected to serve out President Reagan's term. Kenneth M. Duberstein, Baker's deputy, will succeed him. It is known that Baker has not been happy in his job, but he cited "personal circumstances" as the reason for his giving up the post. Apparently, Baker was displeased about Attorney General Edwin Meese having failed to resign. The chief of staff had also been known to oppose military assistance for the Nicaraguan contras. Observers acknowledged, however, that Baker's wife, Joy, is suffering from a long-term illness.

Cigarette company is fined $400,000

June 13. A tobacco company, the Liggett Group, was ordered by a federal jury today to pay $400,000 in damages to Antonio Cipollone, whose wife, a heavy smoker for 40 years, died of lung cancer in 1984. Liggett was found guilty of having failed to warn consumers of the hazards of smoking. Documents discovered by Cipollone's attorneys reveal that tobacco companies were aware of a possible link between smoking and cancer as early as 1946, 20 years before the Labeling and Advertising Act required warnings to be placed on cigarette packs. Despite the award, the jury found Rose Cipollone was largely responsible for her own death (→ 10/18).

JUNE
Week 25 1988

Su	Mo	Tu	We	Th	Fr	Sa
				1	2	3	4
5	6	7	8	9	10	11
12	13	14	15	16	17	18
19	20	21	22	23	24	25
26	27	28	29	30		

20. New York City: Caricaturist Al Hirschfeld is feted by celebrities on night before his 85th birthday.

20. Jay, Maine: International Paper strike, led by Ray Rogers, now a year old.

20. Washington: Supreme Court unanimously upholds New York verdict barring sexual discrimination in large private clubs (→ 26).

20. Washington: Joseph F. Fernandez, ex-C.I.A. chief in Costa Rica, is indicted in criminal charges in Iran-contra affair (→ 23).

20. Brookline, Massachusetts: Curtis Strange wins U.S. Open in playoff against Nick Faldo.

21. Washington: Federal Home Loan Bank Board announces losses of more than $3 billion by savings and loan industry in first quarter 1988 (→ 9/5).

21. Jamestown, North Dakota: Survey shows nearly half of northern Great Plains wheat, barley and oats have been lost to drought (→ 7/19).

21. Punjab, India: Bombs in shopping area kill 22 in latest attack of recent wave of Sikh violence.

23. New York City: Soviet spokesman announces at United Nations that U.S.S.R. is willing to correct imbalance of conventional forces in Europe (→ 7/20).

23. Catak, Turkey: As many as 300 feared dead in landslide.

23. Miami: Federal judge dismisses Christic Institute racketeering suit against 29 government officials and businessmen in relation to 1984 assassination attempt on Eden Pastora of Nicaragua (→ 8/5).

25.: New York: Investigators find tapes alleged to implicate advisers to Tawana Brawley are blank (→ 8/15).

DEATHS

22. Dennis Day, Irish tenor and foil for Jack Benny, at 71 (*5/21/1917).

25. Mildred E. Gillars, nicknamed Axis Sally for her Nazi radio broadcasts, at 87.

General Namphy seizes power in Haiti

Namphy, new dictator in town.

June 20. Flanked by armed guards and brandishing a sub-machine gun, an angry Lieutenant General Henri Namphy appeared on television tonight to announce that he had seized power and declared himself President of a military government. "Everybody is now in the army," he declared, "because it is this army that is going to lead this country as it has to be led." Earlier in the day, General Namphy dissolved the National Assembly and named an 11-member Cabinet of colonels and generals.

The coup led by the 55-year-old general brings to an end the short-lived Presidency of Leslie Manigat, a former political science professor who was put into office in January with the help of the military after elections that had been scheduled for late last year were aborted. Manigat is reported to have fled to safety in the Dominican Republic on the other side of the island.

Although exchanges of gunfire have been heard in Port-au-Prince, the capital, since the coup, there have been no reports of casualties. But any hopes of attaining democracy in this impoverished country seem to have ended for now (→ 9/18).

Economic summit studies anti-drug plan

June 20. Declaring that "the illegal use of drugs and the illicit trafficking in them poses grave risks to the peoples of summit countries as well as the peoples of source and transit countries," the leaders of the seven industrialized democracies have decided to establish a ministerial-level task force to combat the drug trade. The forum for the declaration, which was adopted on the initiative of President Reagan, was the annual economic summit meeting, held in Toronto this year, of the Group of Seven (the United States, Britain, France, Italy, West Germany, Canada and Japan). Although there were no specific measures mentioned by the Western leaders, a campaign to cut down on a multimillion-dollar money-laundering operations of drug kingpins is expected to be among the priorities of the task force (→ 7/20).

Leaders of industrialized democracies looking forward to a drug-free world.

17 Soviet officials barred by Canada

June 20. Eight Soviet officials have been expelled and nine others barred from returning to Canada, in retaliation for an attempt by the Russians to spy on a top-secret military contractor in Montreal. According to a statement issued by Joe Clark, Minister for External Affairs, the activities of the Soviet officials "were a threat to the security of our country." He added that the Canadian Security Intelligence Service in conjunction with the Royal Canadian Mounted Police had forestalled any actual security breach.

Paramax Electronics, the American-owned target of the Russians' attempted espionage effort, is a subsidiary of the Unisys Corporation, a major military contractor with headquarters in Detroit. As part of a substantial expansion of the Canadian navy, Paramax was recently awarded a $1 billion contract for work on six new vessels.

Congress limits use of lie detector tests

June 20. Congress has approved a bill that would drastically limit use of lie detector tests in private industry. The bill essentialy bans routine screening of job applicants or random testing of employees to deter theft. Many business groups and the Reagan administration opposed the measure, but the President is expected to sign it into law.

The administration and many corporations particularly opposed the House version of the bill, which would have put a virtual ban on any business use of polygraphs, or lie detectors. The final bill generally followed the Senate version, which permits lie detector tests after a theft, but only for employees who had access to the scene or were under reasonable suspicion.

Civil liberty groups have been trying to ban polygraph use in the workplace for years. One reason the effort succeeded this year was concern about the growing use of tests and their reliability. Critics said that nearly two million lie detector tests were given in the United States last year and they called them "20th-Century witchcraft."

The greenhouse effect: Has it begun?

Expert studies time wasted for nothing

June 21. A Pittsburgh consulting firm has thrown valuable light on the reason we complain that time goes too fast. According to Priority Management, we waste our lives in the following proportions: five years spent waiting on lines, six years eating, four years doing housework, one year looking for lost possessions, eight months opening junk mail, six months sitting at traffic lights and two years phoning people who are never home, all for a total of 19 years two months frittered away on tasks widely considered tedious. What can we do about it? Eat at Wendy's, found to have faster service than both McDonald's and Burger King.

Lakers beat Pistons to win N.B.A. title

June 20. The Los Angeles Lakers made their coach's prediction come true today, but they did it the hard way. Coach Pat Riley "guaranteed" that his Lakers would win the N.B.A. title for the second time in a row and they did it by surviving a record 24 playoff games. They became the first club in the league's history to win three seven-game series in a year. Their final victims were the Detroit Pistons, who were edged 108-105 in the windup.

Yankees dismiss Martin for fifth time

June 23. In a world of uncertainty, the dismissal of Billy Martin as Yankee manager seems to be as certain as the return of the swallows to Capistrano. It happened for the fifth time today after the Yanks lost their 48-day grasp on first place. Moving into the managerial job was Lou Piniella, who was replaced by Martin last season. Yankee owner George Steinbrenner was said to be unhappy over Martin's role in a fight at a Dallas topless bar and his reported drinking problem. Martin's handling of the pitchers, including the overworking of 45-year-old Tommy John, was also said to have upset the owner.

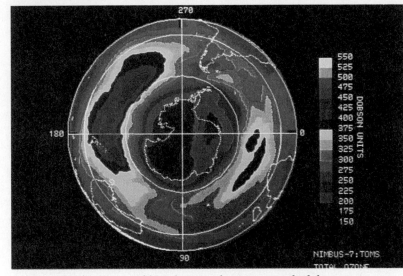

The greenhouse effect could be the most disastrous trend of the century,

Testing climate in a research balloon.

June 23. This year's broiling temperatures across most of the nation are a sign that global warming due to a pollution-caused greenhouse effect has begun, a space agency scientist told a congressional committee today. "It is time to stop waffling so much and say that the evidence is pretty strong that the greenhouse effect is here," James E. Hansen, head of the space agency's Institute for Space Studies, said.

The greenhouse effect results primarily from the release of carbon dioxide in the burning of fossil fuels such as coal and oil. Carbon dioxide traps infrared radiation from the sun, causing the earth's surface to warm. Measuring stations have noted a steady increase in atmospheric carbon dioxide concentrations in recent decades and scientists have predicted an eventual rise in global temperatures.

The four warmest years of the century have been recorded in the 1980's, Hansen said, and so far 1988 is the hottest year ever. The rising temperatures are consistent with those forecast on the basis of the greenhouse effect, he said.

If the buildup of carbon dioxide and other gases in the atmosphere continues at the present rate, world temperatures may rise three to nine degrees Fahrenheit by the middle of the next century. Temperatures are expected to go up the most in the higher latitudes, where the increase would be 20 degrees. Glaciers and polar ice would melt, causing sea levels to rise one to four feet, flooding many coastal areas.

Some of the most damaging effects are predicted for the grain belt of the United States, where higher temperatures will be accompanied by lower rainfall, hurting growing conditions. But Canada and the Soviet Union may benefit as warmer, wetter summers help crop yields. Parts of Africa will suffer as the global temperature rise makes the Sahara expand to the south (→ 7/6).

Civil War raider stirs a new battle

June 24. A Civil War encounter fought 124 years ago is still reverberating in, of all places, the port city of Cherbourg, France. The Alabama, a Confederate privateer that sank 65 Union merchant ships, has been identified off the coast of Normandy, where it was sunk by the Union warship Kearsage. A measure has been introduced in the American Senate declaring that the hulk of the Alabama belongs to the United States. The French claim the ship under international law and plan to transform it into a museum. The Civil War may long be over, but the battle for the Alabama most certainly is not.

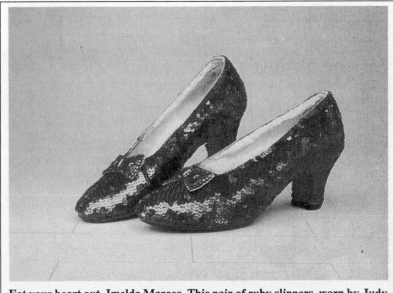

Eat your heart out, Imelda Marcos. This pair of ruby slippers, worn by Judy Garland in "The Wizard of Oz," fetched $165,000 at a Christie's auction.

Su	Mo	Tu	We	Th	Fr	Sa
			1	2	3	4
5	6	7	8	9	10	11
12	13	14	15	16	17	18
19	20	21	22	23	24	25
26	27	28	29	30		

27. Washington: Supreme Court, in 5-4 decision, protects military contractors from suits by injured service personnel if firms followed government specifications and gave warning of danger.

27. New York City: A trader and a Morgan Stanley analyst are charged with insider trading scheme worth more than $19 million (→ 9/7).

27. Collegeville, Minnesota: Nation's Roman Catholic bishops vote to retain controversial statement on AIDS, but acknowledge it needs revision on the condom issue (→ 30).

27. London: Amnesty International releases report charging the British with irresponsibility in using lethal force in Northern Ireland (→ 8/1).

27. Des Moines, Iowa: Some 35,000 people consume 13 tons of pork in The Great Pork BarbeQlossal, opening the first World Pork Expo trade show.

28. Washington: Charging that Teamsters have made a "devil's pact" with organized crime, Justice Department sues to oust union's leadership.

28. Detroit: Motown records sold to MCA for $61 million.

28. Toronto: Canada bans all forms of tobacco advertising.

29. Washington: Supreme Court upholds special prosecutor law in 7-1 decision.

29. New York City: Federal judge rules United States cannot close down P.L.O. mission due to United Nations treaty obligations.

29. West Germany: Three United States F-16 jet fighters crash, killing a pilot and bringing total jet crashes there to five in three months.

30. Chicago: American Medical Association, at annual meeting, urges doctors to breach confidentiality to warn sexual partners of AIDS victims.

30. Fort Erie, Ontario: Remains of 28 American soldiers, killed in War of 1812, are returned to United States amid full military pageantry.

First Soviet Party conference since 1941

Mikhail Gorbachev directs the action at the first televised party conference.

June 30. Political melodramas are nothing new to American audiences, but the publicity around the Communist Party conference is causing a sensation in the Soviet Union. It is the first meeting of its kind in 47 years, and most of it is being broadcast on television. For the first time ever, Soviet citizens are watching snarling bureaucrats call each other names and even accuse each other of taking bribes. It was Soviet leader Gorbachev who called in the TV cameras, and many of the delegates do not like all the exposure. The controversy has eclipsed the debate over Gorbachev's proposal to create a powerful new post of President of the Soviet Union, a job he would presumably keep for himself. Gorbachev also tried to distance himself from recent proposals to dump aging bureaucrats from the party (→ 7/4).

Tyson KO's Spinks, gets $200,000 a second

June 27. Those who showed up late for the bout in Atlantic City missed it. Before latecomers were seated, Mike Tyson had knocked out Michael Spinks a minute and a half into the heavyweight championship fight. A hard right to the head sent Spinks to the floor in one of history's shortest title fights and enabled Tyson to earn $200,000 a second. Said the champ: "No one on earth can come near me."

Mike Tyson, who learned to fight on the streets, is still heavyweight champ.

New Airbus crashes as crowd watches

June 27. Pilot error rather than any technical failure was blamed for the crash last Sunday of an Airbus 320 during an air show in eastern France. According to investigators, the Air France plane was flying at a height of only 30 feet when it brushed some treetops before crashing. Three people were killed and some 50 injured in the accident. The A-320 has a complex computer system that was developed to override many potential pilot errors. However, the investigators believe that the pilot may have turned off these controls before he took off so that he would be free to perform air-show maneuvers.

Death toll in Paris rail crash hits 59

June 28. The death toll from yesterday's Paris train crash rose to 59 today as rescue workers discovered more bodies in the wreckage. The crash occurred when the brakes on a commuter train failed as it arrived at the Gare de Lyons during the evening rush hour and it rammed another crowded train that was about to leave the station. Witnesses said the train was going 50 miles an hour at the time of the collision. Railroad officials said the brakes failed after a passenger pulled the emergency cord as a prank and a backup system failed to work. They promised a full investigation.

U.S. women third in equality in world

June 26. When it comes to equal opportunities with men, American women rank high internationally, according to a report by the Population Crisis Committee, a Washington think tank that studied 99 countries. Women in the United States ranked third, behind Sweden and Finland, by way of superior child care facilities and maternity leave. The survey also found that, unlike men, women all over and in all classes tend to work two shifts: outside the home by day, inside the home with a child by night.

Everybody's making tracks to the train

June 27. If you're worried about air safety or have tired of sitting in traffic, try taking the train next time, but you'd better make your reservations early. Seats on many of Amtrak's Boston, New York and Washington trains and on six other routes across the country are sold out until next fall. Experts say dissatisfaction with air travel and congested roads have caused train travel to jump 8 percent this year. Amtrak trains now serve 30,000 meals a day and 3,000 people bed down in their sleepers every night. Among the famous travelers recently spotted taking to the rails are William F. Buckley and Pearl Bailey.

Eskimos meet again

June 27. Planning a Siberian idyll? Alaskan entrepreneur James Stimpfle has begun regular air contact between Alaska and Soviet Siberia, cut by the 1948 cold war. A "Friendship One" flight inaugurated the operation, shuttling 25 Alaskan Eskimos from Nome to Provideniya and a happy reunion with friends and relatives they had not seen in 40 years. With no hotel and only one restaurant, Provideniya is no rival to the Riviera. But the day-trippers quickly grabbed up the local supply of Revolution T-shirts and Sputnik toothpaste.

Rebel bishop is banned for defying Vatican

Archbishop Marcel Lefebvre at the moment of his fall from grace.

June 30. In the first such schism in the Roman Catholic Church in a century, Archbishop Marcel Lefebvre, the leader of a traditionalist movement based in Switzerland, was excommunicated for consecrating four new bishops in direct defiance of orders from the Pope.

A long-time foe of the reforms introduced by Vatican II, which he has declared to be the work of the devil, Archbishop Lefebvre has vigorously objected to the church's efforts to improve relations with Protestants, Jews, Moslems and other members of what he calls "false" religions. He also opposes celebration of the mass in the vernacular, and collegiality, or a sharing of responsibility for leading the church, between the Pope and bishops. Today's ceremony, which was held at Econe before 7,000 supporters, was conducted in Latin.

Although the excommunication does not invalidate the consecration of the four new bishops, they and the archbishop are expelled from the church and may not receive the sacraments. The archbishop, in a response to the excommunication, said that the Vatican was filled with "anti-Christs" and that the penalties are "null and void."

Vatican officials believe that the Lefebvre movement has 100,000 followers, mostly in France, Switzerland and the United States (→ 7/21).

Foreign holdings in U.S. set a record

June 30. The imbalance between foreign investments in the United States and American investments abroad grew to a new high in 1987, according to figures that have just been released. The purchase by foreigners of American stocks, Treasury bonds, real estate and businesses rose by $195.4 billion, to a record $1.54 trillion. By contrast, investments by American companies abroad totaled $1.17 trillion, resulting in a net investment position of minus $368.2 billion. This is the third year the United States has run such a deficit. It is estimated that foreigners now own 5 percent of the country's assets (→ 9/28).

500,000 Steinways

June 30. In 1853, when Henry Steinway decided to make pianos in New York, he had more than 100 rivals. Today, 135 years and a half million pianos later, only Steinway survives. The company has just put the final, glistening touches on No. 500,000. The preferred choice of some 900 pianists, the Steinway also introduced a unique note to the cultural life of the country. No. 100,000, a 1903 gift to Theodore Roosevelt, now graces the Smithsonian. The one in the White House today, Steinway's 300,000th, has special eagle adornments.

Civil War buffs, 125 years after the event, re-enact the bloody Battle of Gettysburg, the turning point of the war. Real bullets are not used.

Sean Penn and wife, Madonna, at the Tyson-Spinks pre-fight party. Maybe Penn, who is known to throw a mean punch himself, is ready for Tyson.

Su	Mo	Tu	We	Th	Fr	Sa
					1	2
3	4	5	6	7	8	9
10	11	12	13	14	15	16
17	18	19	20	21	22	23
24	25	26	27	28	29	30
31						

1. Washington: Pentagon halts payments to contractors named in bribery scandal (→ 11).

1. Brussels: West German Manfred Worner takes over as secretary general of NATO.

1. Washington: Department of Energy reports cleaning up waste from manufacture of nuclear bombs will cost $40 to $110 billion (→ 9/30).

2. Wimbledon, England: Steffi Graf wins third leg of Grand Slam, 5-7, 6-2, 6-1 over Martina Navratilova (→ 9/10).

4. Washington: Chicago F.B.I. agent admits harassing Don Rochon, a black agent pressing suit against F.B.I. (→ 15).

4. Wimbledon, England: Stefan Edberg defeats Boris Becker 4-6, 7-6, 6-4, 6-2 for Wimbledon crown.

4. Washington: Justice Dept. bars messenger Christopher Stalvey from entering with shirt reading "Experts Agree! Meese is a pig" (→ 5).

5. Houston: J.R. McConnell electrocutes himself in jail while awaiting trial for building real estate empire on fraud.

6. Tokyo: Ex-Prime Minister Yasuhiro Nakasone and other leading Japanese politicians implicated in shady stock deal.

6. Albany: Study finds acid rain has made 25% of lakes in Adirondacks unlivable for fish (→ 8/15).

7. Moscow: Soviets launch Phobos, first spacecraft in 13 years, trying to fly to Mars (→ 9/7).

7. Aberdeen, Scotland: About 165 oil workers dead as oil rig explodes in worst North Sea accident in memory.

7. Moscow: Sotheby's holds first Soviet international art auction, bringing in $3.4 million.

DEATHS

9. Jackie Presser, president of Teamsters, nation's largest union, at 61 (*8/6/1926).

9. Barbara Woodhouse, dog trainer named Britain's TV celebrity of the year in 1980, at 78; she got to know pets by breathing through their nose.

U.S. mistakenly shoots down Iran jet

July 3. An Iran Air passenger jet was shot down by a United States Navy warship in the Persian Gulf today. Iran says 290 people were killed. Admiral William Crowe, chairman of the Joint Chiefs of Staff, says the missile cruiser Vincennes fired on the plane in the mistaken belief that it was a hostile, enemy aircraft. President Reagan, who monitored the crisis from Camp David, said the United States regretted the attack, but he joined Crowe in defending the judgment of the commander of the Vincennes.

Crowe rejected any comparisons between the incident and the shooting down of a Korean passenger plane by a Soviet fighter jet in 1983. Crowe said the KAL jet "was not in a war zone" and "there was no combat in progress." In contrast, Crowe said a helicopter from the Vincennes was fired upon at 10:10 a.m. In response, two Iranian gunboats were sunk at 10:42. The Iran Air jet took off from Bandar Abbas

U.S. cruiser Vincennes.

Iranian depiction of the tragedy.

at 10:47. Officials say it did not follow its flight plan and did not respond to repeated radio warnings. At 10:54, the Vincennes fired two surface-to-air missiles.

Tensions escalated in the Gulf last year after 37 men were killed in the Iraqi attack on the USS Stark. American patrols in the Gulf have also been complicated by Iran's refusal to suspend civilian flights in the area (→ 8).

Iraq admits using chemical weapons

July 1. Iraqi Foreign Minister Tariq Aziz publicly admitted today that Iraqi planes dropped poison-gas bombs during a March attack on the Iraqi town of Halabja in Iranian-held territory. In one of the most horrendous events of the war, some 5,000 Iraqi Kurds were killed by mustard gas and cyanide. The United Nations Security Council condemned the action on May 9 and it urged both Iraq and Iran to refrain from chemical warfare. It alluded to the April finding of the U.N. Secretary General, Javier Perez de Cuellar, that both countries were guilty of such use.

The conflict erupted in 1980 with the Iraqi invasion of Iran. Reiterating Iraqi assertions, Foreign Minister Aziz claimed that the Iranians had been the first to use chemical warfare. "We were victims many times," he asserted, "since the early beginning of the conflict." And in a war-is-hell kind of argument he told Western reporters, "There are different views on this matter from different angles. You are living on a peaceful continent" (→ 20).

Iran disavows revenge against America

July 8. The Speaker of Iran's Parliament announced today that Tehran will not "push for revenge" for the shooting down of Iran Air Flight 655. The comments by Hoja-tolislam Hashemi Rafsanjani contrasted sharply with the remarks yesterday by Iranian President Ali Khamenei. Speaking at funeral services for 72 of the 290 disaster victims, Khamenei said the incident amounted to murder and he called it "one of the biggest crimes of any war." Rafsanjani said today that Iran should wait for action next week by the United Nations Security Council. He is apparently hoping that the council will not only condemn the incident next Tuesday but also apply new pressure on the United States to abandon its patrols in the Persian Gulf (→ 11).

Strong anti-American feelings were evident at funerals for the victims.

Beaches are closed by medical waste

July 6. Sewage and medical debris that washed ashore on beaches in the Northeast have closed them to swimmers in the midst of a searing heat wave. Particularly hard hit are New York's beaches, where swimmers were ordered out of the water along a stretch of more than 15 miles. This area included Jones Beach, which is considered one of the finest in the nation. Syringes, blood vials and other infectious hospital waste washed ashore as concern mounted over the growing problem of ocean dumping.

Beaches in nearby New Jersey, Rhode Island and Massachusetts have also been hard hit by the pollution. Health officials tried to identify the hospital waste on Long Island, where millions use the beaches. A longtime lifeguard at New York's popular Robert Moses State Park said, "It was scary. In the 19 years I have been a lifeguard, I've never seen stuff like this." Beachgoers plucked such "stuff" as surgical sutures from Nassau County beaches, less than 30 miles from New York City. Some of the blood vials tested positive for hepatitis-B virus and AIDS antibodies (→ 8/1).

William Johnson's "Man With a Vest" is part of an exhibit on a nationwide tour, "The Harlem Renaissance, 1919-1929," now at the High Museum of Art in Atlanta. During the 1920's, New York City's Harlem was a mecca for aspiring and talented black painters, poets and other artists.

Communists revise political system

July 4. The most openly contentious meeting in years of the Communist Party has ended in Moscow. While it highlighted major divisions in the bureaucracy, the conference solidified the position of Soviet leader Mikhail S. Gorbachev. He was given almost everything he demanded, including a Presidency with much greater control over foreign and domestic policy. The job will undoubtedly be given to Gorbachev himself.

The conference's resolutions are aimed at decreasing the role of the Communist Party in daily life, transferring some of the party's power to elected legislatures and limiting the office terms of many political leaders to 10 years. Party and government officials who presently hold office, including Gorbachev, would not be affected. Most of the changes were originally proposed by Gorbachev, but he was forced to back down on other proposals aimed at kicking certain aging bureaucrats out of office.

Adoption of the resolutions was seen as a victory for Gorbachev's policies of perestroika, or restructuring, and glasnost, or openness. Gorbachev pointed out, however, that he still has major problems to tackle. He called the shortage of food "the most painful and most acute problem" in the nation.

The new policy of glasnost rubbed off on the style of the delegates. Party members yelled at each other, cheered and shouted questions. They even took off their jackets. The Russians who were watching on television found it all very hard to believe (→ 8/15).

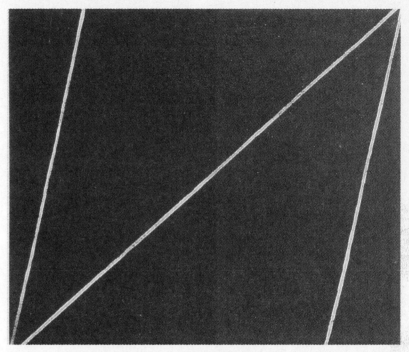

In the current season of reform, artists are finding a kinder climate, too. Rodchenko's "Line" was sold at Moscow's 1st international art auction on the 7th.

Meese quits office, asserting innocence

July 5. Although saying that an independent prosecutor's report on his conduct had "vindicated" him, Attorney General Edwin Meese 3rd has announced his resignation. Citing the allegations against him as "false," Meese said, "I have determined over the past few weeks that it would be advantageous for me to return to private life." Meese acknowledged, however, that he and his lawyers had not yet seen the prosecutor's report which concerned possible unethical conduct by the Attorney General in relation to his dealings with an Army contract for the Wedtech Corporation, and his involvement in a billion dollar scheme to construct a pipeline in Iraq. President Reagan told reporters: "He's a good friend and I'm going to miss him." Meese has not yet disclosed any plans for the future (→ 18).

Seoul planning to quell Olympic violence

July 5. Armed soldiers in full view at the airport. Anti-terrorist squads on the alert. Dogs trained to sniff out explosives. A city under siege? No, just security precautions in Seoul, South Korea, for the 1988 Olympic Games. The Koreans have computerized profiles on 6,000 international terrorists and photographs of some have been distributed to hotel clerks. Recalling the murder of Israeli athletes at the Munich Games in 1972, authorities are taking measures to prevent attacks by North Korean agents of the Japanese Red Army (→ 8/14).

Anti-terrorist forces are training to drop like spiders from level to level.

JULY

Week 28 1988

Su	Mo	Tu	We	Th	Fr	Sa
					1	2
3	4	5	6	7	8	9
10	11	12	13	14	15	16
17	18	19	20	21	22	23
24	25	26	27	28	29	30
31						

10. Nandaime, Nicaragua: Riot police use tear gas, probably for first time under Sandinistas, to break up opposition rally (→ 11).

11. Piraeus, Greece: Nine killed and 53 wounded as gunmen open fire on Greek cruise ship City of Poros, then flee on waiting yacht.

11. Managua: Nicaragua orders United States Ambassador Richard Melton and seven others to leave country for encouraging protests (→ 12).

11. Washington: Pentagon restores payments to all suppliers, citing lack of evidence in bribery cases (→ 8/8).

11. Washington: Two National Security Council clerks have been fired and Secret Service guards suspended for drug use.

12. Washington: United States ousts Nicaraguan Ambassador Carlos Tunnerman and seven others in retaliation (→ 14).

13. New York City: CBS, after worst prime time season, makes two changes in key executives; Howard Stringer becomes broadcast chief and David W. Burke becomes head of news division.

14. San Francisco: Woman arrested after having baby in plane rest room and leaving it there under the sink.

15. Bandar Seri Bagawan, Brunei: Sultan of Brunei, one of the most conspicuously wealthy men in world, celebrates his 42nd birthday with the whole nation.

15. Williamsport, Pennsylvania: Bess Myerson pleads guilty to shoplifting; Justice John M. McDermott fines her $100 plus court fees.

15. Kingston, New York: Police disclose that the letters "KKK" were carved into the body of a 19-year-old black woman who was found murdered (→ 8/5).

DEATH

12. Joshua L. Logan, director of Broadway hits such as "South Pacific" and "Mister Roberts," at 79 (*10/5/1908).

Dukakis picks Bentsen as V.P. candidate

Liberal Dukakis and conservative Bentsen: Odd couple or winning ticket?

July 12. To the surprise of many, Massachusetts Governor Michael Dukakis reached into the party's conservative ranks by choosing Senator Lloyd Bentsen of Texas as his running mate in this fall's presidential election. He thus bypassed the Rev. Jesse Jackson and the others who battled him for the Democratic nomination.

In many ways, Bentsen resembles Vice President Bush, the likely Republican presidential nominee, more than the man who chose him for the Democratic ticket today.

Both Bush and Bentsen have strong Texas ties, both come from wealthy families and earned fortunes of their own in business, and both were decorated heroes in World War II. Also, their political views on such issues as aid to the Nicaraguan contras, tax cuts, abortions, gun control, public school prayer and further production of the MX missile are more closely akin than those of the expected Democratic nominee. But there is one significant difference: Bentsen defeated Bush for a Senate seat in 1970 (→ 18).

Hippies try to keep their life style alive

July 10. The free-spirited 60's were long ago eclipsed by the self-obsessed 70's and the buttoned-down 80's. But for 20,000 dancing, singing, Day-Glo bedazzled visitors to this weekend's 19th annual Country Fair, it might just as well have been the Summer of Love. The event, held each year in the same secluded flood plain 12 miles west of Eugene, Oregon, draws everyone from the novelist and proto-hippie Ken Kesey, still bearing the counterculture torch at 52, to weekday professionals longing to turn on and drop out, if only for a day or two. But among the purple headbands and the painted faces was a serious message: the concerns of the 60's — nonviolence, social consciousness and environmentalism — are still relevant.

Sandinistas seize largest sugar farm

July 14. The largest private business in Nicaragua, the San Antonio sugar plantation, a symbol of capitalism for nearly a hundred years, has been confiscated by the Sandinista regime. Opposition groups believe the move to be part of a political crackdown, but the government describes its reasons as strictly "technical-economic." "If we had not taken this step," said Minister of Agriculture Jaime Wheelock, "the San Antonio complex would deteriorate to the point of disappearance ..." The complex employs 4,500 workers during harvest season. The Nicaraguan regime holds a monopoly on foreign trade, and all sugar is purchased by the government. Some farmers blame insufficient payment from Managua for the farm's demise (→ 17).

Salinas claims win in Mexican voting

July 14. Complete official results of the Mexican presidential election, tainted by allegations of vote fraud, are in and they bring victory to Carlos Salinas de Gortary of the Institutional Revolutionary Party, known as the P.R.I. Salinas received 50.4 percent of the vote. Cuauhtemoc Cardenas of the leftist National Democratic Front came in second with 31.1 percent. Of the more than 38 million Mexicans who registered, only 19.1 million voted. Salinas will be sworn into office on December 1. He will have to overcome the widespread public perception that the election was marred by irregularities.

Salinas (left), victor in Mexico.

U.S. will pay for shooting down jet

July 11. The White House announced today that the United States will compensate the families of the 290 passengers killed when a U.S. warship shot down an Iran Air jet last week. Details of the compensation remain to be worked out, but the White House made it clear that payments will be given to individuals and not to the Iranian government. Administration spokesman Marlin Fitzwater said President Reagan still views the incident as a "justifiable defensive action" but decided upon the payments on humanitarian grounds. The announcement could also defuse the tense diplomatic situation brewing at the United Nations. Iran is seeking condemnation of the United States when Security Council debate begins tomorrow (→ 8/2).

Congress passes 60-day notice of closings

July 13. The House of Representatives approved a mandatory 60-day advance notice to employees for plant closings by a two-thirds majority today. The Senate passed the bill last week and the measure will become law within 10 days unless President Reagan vetoes it.

The President vetoed a trade bill last spring specifically because it included a 60-day notice and said it would impose a "straitjacket of regulations" on the business community. But officials from the Bush campaign are expected to put pressure on Reagan to sign the bill now, to avoid antagonizing labor during the presidential campaign. The bill would require firms with more than 100 employees to notify them of pending layoffs or factory closings.

Lane Kirkland, president of the American Federation of Labor and Congress of Industrial Organizations, said that the measure would give workers the chance "to adequately plan for the future." Many business leaders look upon the bill as an intrusion by government into private affairs and they claim it would give resentful employees the opportunity to sabotage machinery. Senior officials in the administration have been urging the President to veto the bill, but Republican Rep. Marge Roukema of New Jersey has warned that if he goes ahead with the veto, "Vice President Bush will have a problem on his hands in the campaign" (→ 8/2).

Jackie exceeds her own heptathlon mark

July 16. Ignoring the blistering temperatures, Jackie Joyner-Kersee ran and jumped her way to a record score of 7,215 points in the United States Olympic trials for the heptathlon. The thermometer registered just under 100 degrees as the vivacious athlete became the first in history to surpass the 7,200-point mark. She bettered her previous record of 7,158, which was set in 1986, for the seven-event competition. Her closest rival was Cindy Greiner, who piled up 6,226 points. "My motivation was to win, first, and better 7,200 points, so I'm very pleased," said Joyner-Kersee. A foul in the long jump, her specialty, may have prevented her from rolling up an even higher score (→ 17).

One long step for a woman.

United States 01988

July 16. Happy 25th birthday to the ZIP (Zone Improvement Plan) codes! All 43,000 of them! Started in 1963 to allow mail sorting to be done mainly by machines, the ZIP code has become a demographic tool, informing marketing experts where they should open — or close — stores, where folks are likely to buy beer or French wine, a Ford or a Volvo, diapers or laxatives. The ZIP code divides the country into 10 major sections (first digit), sectional hubs (next two digits) and individual post offices or neighborhoods (last two numbers). Combine these with census data and you may be able to classify clusters of individuals and their spending habits.

Chicago and New York: How they grew

The dynamic growth of two great American metropolises, Chicago and New York, is now featured in two architectural exhibitions.

"Chicago Architecture 1872-1922: Birth of a Metropolis," the largest exhibition ever organized by the Art Institute of Chicago's Department of Architecture, surveys the influence of European architects upon the city from the rebuilding after the Great Fire of 1871 to the Chicago Tribune Competition of 1922. French and German influences were important. But the city became known as the capital of American architecture, with the rise of Louis Sullivan's skyscraper and Frank Lloyd Wright's prairie-style single-family house. Representative work by these giants, among others, is on view.

"The Rise and Fall of New York: Building and Unbuilding Manhattan" at the New-York Historical Society includes more than 100 architectural drawings, photographs and prints which focus on the changes in the urban landscape from the mid-19th century to the mid-20th. The techniques of such renowned architects as McKim, Mead and White, and Cass Gilbert are explored. Highlights include such landmarks as Madison Square Garden, Penn Station, St. John the Divine, the Woolworth Building and the Crystal Palace.

Dumping on Africa

July 16. As safety laws in the United States and Europe produce soaring disposal costs, barrels of toxic waste are being dumped on West African countries. For many of these underdeveloped nations, the financial offers, though often 800 percent below dumping fees for American or European sites, can be tempting. However, villagers, one of whom ended up with 10,000 barrels behind his house, are often unaware of the health risks. African newspapers and some leaders are fighting back. In some areas, people caught bringing in waste or aiding disposers, including government officials, face fines or jail. In Nigeria, they can even face a firing squad.

Judge: Excuse me

July 14. In the end, federal Judge Hubert J. Teitelbaum had to apologize to lawyer Barbara Wolvovitz, 36, for having ordered her to use her married name in the Pittsburgh court or face jail. When she, representing two black men in a race-discrimination suit, then asked for a mistrial, the 73-year-old judge said, "What if I call you sweetie?" Ms. Wolvovitz, a practicing lawyer for 10 years and married to Jules Lobel, a law professor, was told, "In this courtroom you will use Mrs. Lobel." When her (male) co-counsel protested, the judge had ruled him in contempt.

The University Club, on Michigan Avenue and Monroe Street in Chicago, as it appeared in 1908.

Only sunlight and a camera shutter break the stillness of Penn Station in New York in this 1911 photograph.

Surrogacy a crime

July 11. While five states have ruled contracts for surrogate parenthood unenforceable, the state of Michigan has gone one step further by deeming it a crime, according to legislation that was signed by Governor James Blanchard last week. Anyone entering into a surrogate contract for pay as well as a spouse condoning such an agreement is liable to a fine of $10,000 and imprisonment for one year. Lawyers and surrogate brokers in Michigan can be branded felons and fined $50,000 and jailed for five years. A surrogate agreement involving no fee is still regarded as legal.

JULY
Week 29 1988

Su	Mo	Tu	We	Th	Fr	Sa
					1	2
3	4	5	6	7	8	9
10	11	12	13	14	15	16
17	18	19	20	21	22	23
24	25	26	27	28	29	30
31						

17. Managua: Sandinistas say recent crackdown was self-protective effort to block U.S. attempt to isolate Nicaragua diplomatically and overthrow regime politically (→ 20).

17. Tegucigalpa, Honduras: Grenade attack kills four American G.I.'s as they leave a disco (→ 29).

18. Washington: Independent prosecutor James McKay releases report charging Meese probably broke tax, conflict-of-interest laws, but says offenses not grave enough to prosecute (→ 8/12).

18. Washington: Workers finish cleaning Constantine Brumidi's 123-year-old painting "Apotheosis of Washington" on ceiling of Capitol.

19. Moscow: Gorbachev, on national television, rejects Armenian demands for territorial changes (→ 8/23).

20. Hollywood: Fundamentalist Christians picket home of Lew Wasserman, owner of MCA studios, which made Martin Scorsese's "The Last Temptation of Christ" (→ 8/12).

20. Washington: United States hails Soviet pledge to tear down Siberian radar station, but denounces requirement that it adhere to strict interpretation of 1972 Anti-Ballistic Missile Treaty (→ 22).

20. Nicaragua: Denouncing shift to right, seven contra commmanders resign over appointment of Colonel Enrique Bermudez to political leadership (→ 8/1).

20. Jacksonville, Florida: Drug smuggler Carlos Lehder Rivas gets life without parole plus 135 years (→ 10/11).

21. Charleston, West Virginia: Barbara Ferraro and Patricia Hussey, Catholic nuns, leave religious order in dispute over advocacy of abortion rights (→ 9/30).

22. Washington: Eight Soviet missile inspectors barred from United States as spies (→ 8/17).

23. Havana: Cubans protesting party thrown by United States diplomats for Cuban dissidents say it was coaching session to prepare for arrival of human rights investigators.

Democrats pick Dukakis and Bentsen

July 21. Promising to lead the nation to "the next American frontier," Governor Michael Dukakis accepted the Democratic nomination for President in Atlanta tonight. By his side, as the cheers rang out through the hall, was his hand-picked running mate, Senator Lloyd Bentsen.

The two are studies in contrast: Dukakis, the coolly cerebral Governor of Massachusetts, the liberal son of Greek immigrants; Bentsen, a wealthy, courtly Texas conservative. As Dukakis put it: "The Republicans are a little confused. They don't know what to make of this ticket."

In his acceptance speech, Dukakis pledged to go beyond what he called the "cramped ideals and limited ambitions" of the Reagan era. He said this election "isn't about ideology; it's about competence. It's not about meaningless labels; it's about American values like accountability and responsibility and respect for the truth."

Bentsen, in accepting the No. 2 spot on the Democratic ticket, also attacked the Reagan administration in which George Bush, the almost certain nominee for President, has served as Vice President. Noting that budget deficits are at an all-time peak, Bentsen said that the administration achieved an illusory prosperity by writing "hot checks" for "$200 billion a year" (→ 8/3).

Hoping to repeat their 1960 victory, Democrats opt for the Boston-Austin axis.

Jesse Jackson seemed to dominate the first two days of the convention.

Native son's success cheered by Greeks

July 21. Dancing, music and plates broken at people's feet were part of the festivities today in Pelopi, Greece. This is the hometown of Governor Michael Dukakis's family, and villagers were celebrating his presidential nomination by the Democratic Party. The Dukakises migrated to the United States from this village on the island of Lesbos during World War I. The villagers are expecting the best because November 8, Election Day, is the feast day of the island's saints and the anniversary of liberation from Turkey. The town plans to pave its dirt road and to open shops and restaurants for American tourists.

Jackson has assumed unprecedented role

July 18. On the surface at least, there appears to be unity within the Democratic Party, as Governor Michael Dukakis and the Rev. Jesse Jackson say they have agreed to cooperate fully in the presidential election battle against the Republicans. And so it was that the two men, Dukakis the winner and Jackson the loser in this year's bid for the nomination, were all smiles as they emerged from negotiations before the Democratic National Convention opened in Atlanta today.

While promising to give Jackson a major public role in the fall campaign and to integrate many Jackson staffers into the Dukakis ranks, the Governor avoided making specific commitments on appointments or on controversial policies. Thus, it is uncertain how closely the two men will work together in the coming months.

Jackson's demand for what he called a "partnership and shared responsibility" was viewed by some as far exceeding what any previous loser in a presidential nomination race had ever sought or been granted. He and his advisers had made it clear just yesterday that he expected to be represented at every level of the Dukakis campaign this fall. Some Jackson supporters had suggested that Dukakis would do well to name him as chief surrogate of the party's campaign or even as cochairman of the Democratic National Committee (→ 21).

Bloody riots drive Ne Win from office

July 23. Burmese leader Ne Win, who served as chairman of the country's only political party for 26 years, resigned today, citing anti-government rioting. In an address to his party's delegates, he said, "Bloodshed in March and June showed the lack of trust and confidence in the government."

Since 1962, when a military coup brought Ne Win to power, his policies of keeping a lid on exports and imports led the country into economic ruin. Burma, which in the past had been one of the leading rice exporters, became one of the 10 poorest countries in the world. Ne Win suppressed all opposition activity and prohibited journalists from entering the country.

The Burmese people, 85 percent of whom are Buddhist, have until recent days kept their frustration mostly silent. But since October student demonstrations have resulted in mass arrests and deaths. The first major protest began after the government took three currency notes out of circulation without warning or compensation, destroying some people's life savings.

Ne Win said a referendum would be held by September to allow the people to chose between single-party and multiparty rule (→ 26).

Farm population is lowest since 1850's

July 19. From 1981 through 1987, our farm population has lost an average of 2.5 percent annually. Last year, 240,000 people left the land, cutting the farm population to its lowest level since before the Civil War. There have been a few surges, such as in 1983, when thousands gave up city living for the country. The farm population is now 97 percent white, 2.5 percent black and the rest other races, while the non-farm ratio is 84.4 percent white, 12.3 percent black and 3.3 percent other races. On farms, there are 109 males per 100 females (93 males per 100 females in the non-farm population). Half the farm people are in the Midwest, 29 percent in the South, 15 percent out West and 6 percent in the Northeast (→ 8/3).

Khomeini accepts ending of Gulf War

Like revolutionaries before him, Khomeini met defeat on the battlefield.

July 20. With the total victory he promised nowhere in sight, Iran's Ayatollah Khomeini has decided to call a halt to his eight-year holy war against Iraq. A statement read over Tehran radio said that he had accepted the United Nations cease-fire plan first proposed a year ago. "Taking this decision was more deadly than taking poison," he was quoted as having said. Acknowledging that he "had promised to fight to the last drop of my blood and to my last breath," he said his decision to end the fighting was "based only on the interest of the Islamic republic" of Iran, which he founded in 1979.

The war, which began in September 1980, has claimed at least a million casualties, laid waste to both nations, impeded navigation through the Persian Gulf and embroiled the United States in several serious international incidents as it tried to protect shipping through the Gulf waters. Gripped by a potentially explosive internal power struggle, Iran is said to stand bankrupt, and its image as the spear-carrier of the Islamic revolution may now be irreparably tarnished.

As for Iraq, it can claim at best only a pyrrhic victory. It has won no new territory and its borders will revert to their previous positions. Blessed with an estimated 100 billion barrels of natural petroleum and an educated citizenry, its impressive pre-war march toward social and economic development has been thwarted, and it finds itself $40 billion in debt. But Khomeini's avowed aim of toppling President Saddam Hussein of Iraq has been foiled, and he has failed to impose on this secular neighbor his brand of Islamic fundamentalism.

According to a Western envoy in Baghdad, the war's achievement is that "both sides look upon things more philosophically. Iran can no longer fight without risking a collapse of its economy and, indeed, its revolution. The war is finished. It is now just a matter of mechanisms, procedures and psychology."

Joyner sets three records for 100 meters

July 17. Florence Griffith Joyner ran faster than anyone expected and set three world records in the United States Olympic trials. Her performance was all the more impressive because it happened in the 100 meters, not her favorite distance. After setting a world record of 10.49 seconds, she followed with a couple of sizzling 100's. She won the semifinal in 10.70 and went on to a 10.61 in the final.

Griffith Joyner (above) and Jackie Joyner-Kersee should win gold in Seoul.

Canadian buys two big American chains

July 17. While many Canadians fret over the prospect of American economic dominance, one entrepreneur is quietly taking over a huge portion of the retail trade below the Great Lakes. Robert Campeau, 64, who bought Allied Stores in 1986 and Federated Department Stores this spring, now owns the largest non-chain group of department stores in the country. Including Abraham & Straus and Bloomingdales, his registers rang up $15 billion in total sales for 1987. Nonetheless, prophecies of doom followed him on a recent tour of his retail empire. A debt of $5.3 billion places him in a precarious position in the retail industry. Some say a small downturn could ruin him. But Campeau is unfazed: "When I built my first 10 houses," he says, "people said I would go broke; and I've built thousands since."

Worst fires of century decimate park

July 27. The first and largest national park in the United States, Yellowstone National Park, its 2.2 million acres crackling dry as the result of the long drought, is experiencing its worst fires in a century. One of the world's largest wildlife sanctuaries, it is home to bears, elk, mountain sheep, bison, moose, a variety of smaller animals and more than 200 species of birds. Now 12 fires have scarred more than 88,000 acres of the evergreen forests that cover 90 percent of the park, and flames are licking at the famed geyser Old Faithful.

"The worst inferno I have seen in 17 years," says one weary firefighter, though spokesmen for the park are quick to point out the positive sides of forest fires. Next summer the tourists — the park attracts 2.5 million each year — will see blackened trees, but the fire will have cleared the forest floor of old needles and dead growth. As the U.S. Park Service's Joe Zarki says, "Life and geysers go on." Pine cones respond to heat by opening and dropping their seeds to begin new tree

Dryness this season kindles flame ...

and thousands of acres are burning.

life. Fire also releases nutrients that have been locked up in old trees, and this natural fertilizer results in luxurious growth.

While smoke billows in seven-mile-high columns, there has not been a mass animal exodus from the fires. Although the area of burning

acreage is vast, there is still plenty of room to roam in the remaining 97 percent of the park.

When is it going to stop? Only sustained rainfall can quell the flames, but it is likely that the fire season is going to continue at least for a few more weeks (→ 9/21).

Last Playboy Club closes in diehard Lansing; Hef to wed Playmate

July 28. The last nine Playboy bunnies will get together for one last party this weekend, and then the Playboy Club of Lansing, Michigan — the last in the country — will close its doors forever.

Life and times and women have changed considerably since 1960,

when the first Playboy Club opened in Chicago. Since that time, there have been 22 Playboy Clubs in America, with some 750,000 members when they were at the height of their popularity. A spokeswoman for Playboy Enterprises said the decision to phase out the clubs was

strictly a business decision. "It was just time for a new thing," she said. "The dance floor was almost empty," added a bunny. "It was sad." Another big change at Playboy is the marriage of founder Hugh Hefner, who has announced he will wed Playmate Kimberley Conrad.

End of the bunny-tail trail.

Hef and Carrie Leigh, his most recent ex, shown here in happier times.

Trump trumps 'em all; his yacht's biggest

July 31. Real estate tycoon Donald Trump calls it "a masterpiece" and "the ultimate toy." Power and Motoryacht magazine describes it as simply the world's "most spectacular yacht." It is the the lavish 282-foot pleasure craft Nabila, recently purchased by billionaire Trump for $29 million.

"I think it's just a hell of a good deal," Trump said. Nearly a third the size of an ocean liner, the Nabila has a discotheque, a hair salon, a cinema with a library of 800 films, a small hospital complete with operating facilities, a helicopter landing pad, 150 phones, a satellite communications system, accommodations for a crew of 52, and enough freezer space to feed 100 people for three months. The original owner, the Saudi arms dealer Adnan Khashoggi, who named the vessel after his only daughter, spent more than $85 million on elaborate construction and garish decor nearly a decade ago. It has been estimated that to build a similar yacht these days a tycoon would have to lay out as much as $200 million.

Trump describes the yacht is "a work of art." Yet his interest in the boat is not purely esthetic. After he spends $8.5 million for renovations, Trump plans to rename his new toy the Trump Princess and to dock her in Atlantic City, where it will be in view of the Trump Castle casino. The yacht is expected to attract not only tourists, but also high rollers to the Atlantic City casinos. "I look for things for the art sake and the beauty sake," Trump said, "and for the deal sake."

Not the sort of boat you can hitch to the back of your Toyota.

Hussein yields Palestine

Jordan's monarch, King Hussein.

July 31. Jordan's King Hussein has dramatically yielded to the Palestine Liberation Organization his country's claim to the West Bank, occupied by Israel ever since its victory in the 1967 war. Describing the P.L.O. as "the sole legitimate representative of the Palestinian people," Hussein said he respected its wish to "secede from us in an independent Palestinian state." To "enhance" the eventual "liberation" of this occupied land, he also announced that Jordan would be severing administrative ties with the West Bank. Stating that Jordan remained committed to its negotiating role in the peace talks, the King said his decision came in response to "the prevailing Arab conviction that such measures would contribute to the struggle of the Palestinian people." While the United States has cast Hussein in the role of principal spokesman for the West Bank Palestinians, the latter have always taken their cue from the P.L.O. chairman, Yasir Arafat. The King's remarks to the contrary, he seems to be disengaging himself from negotiations at a time when the uprising of the Arabs has earned them greater international sympathy and respect. And by his yielding of the West Bank, he has created a vacuum in which Arafat may more validly make his claim to be the true leader of the Palestinian people.

In the past, the relations of the Oxford-educated monarch with the Palestinians have been difficult and his allegiance to their cause often enigmatic. As a child, Hussein saw his grandfather, King Abdullah, killed by Palestinians, and he himself was one of their prime targets during the "Black September" civil war of 1970 (→ 8/4).

Hard-liner takes over stormy Burma

July 26. A retired army general who reportedly commanded troops that repressed student riots has been appointed to succeed Ne Win as the leader of Burma. Sein Lwin, who was selected by the Central Committee of the ruling party, is said to have led soldiers in attacks where more than 100 people were killed, including 40 who suffocated in a police van after being arrested. Though Sein Lwin was a supporter of Ne Win, who retired three days ago after 26 years of rule, the party has suggested rejecting Ne Win's proposal to drop one-party rule. The appointment of Sein Lwin has dashed the hopes of many Burmese people that political reform was at last a possibility (→ 8/12).

Kid with teddy pilots plane across Atlantic

July 24. The smiling pilot turned down the traditional bubbly and opted for a swig of Coke. After all, he was only 11, and had just flown a single-engine plane across the Atlantic, the youngest ever to do so. He hopped off the two pillows that raised him to the level of the plane's window and greeted the crowd at Le Bourget field, just as Charles Lindbergh had done in 1927. Christopher Lee Marshall of Oceano, California, was accompanied by his favorite teddy bear, Charles Lindbeargh. Also aboard was a retired Navy pilot, Duke Cunningham, who served as co-pilot. Marshall has been taking flying lessons since he was 7, while other kids were earthbound on bikes and scooters.

This month's international volcano conference in Kagoshima, Japan, will feature the photographer of this eruption, Tsuyoshi Nishiinoue, who had a premonition one night, and so was able to set up his cameras in time.

Su	Mo	Tu	We	Th	Fr	Sa
	1	2	3	4	5	6
7	8	9	10	11	12	13
14	15	16	17	18	19	20
21	22	23	24	25	26	27
28	29	30	31			

1. Guatemala: Secretary of State George Shultz fails to get Central American nations to concur with denunciation of Nicaragua (→ 17).

1. London: I.R.A. conducts first attack on British mainland in four years, killing one soldier and wounding 10 at army barracks (→ 10/11).

1.: United States: Money magazine rates Danbury, Connecticut, the best place in the country to live.

2. Washington: Defense Department officials disclose that inquiry has found downing of Iranian airbus resulted from error by young crew under battle stress.

2. Washington: President Reagan, bowing to election-year pressure, decides not to veto bill requiring 60 days' notice of plant closings.

2. U.S.S.R.: Defense Secretary Carlucci allowed to inspect state-of-the-art Soviet bomber.

3. Boston: Michael Dukakis reveals medical records to quash rumors that he had sought psychiatric help (→ 18).

3. Moscow: Soviets free Matthias Rust, young German pilot who flew into Red Square unannounced last year.

4. New York City: Ten arrested for "blood-trafficking" scheme, where they paid addicts small sums of money for blood samples, then collected Medicare payments on expensive tests done on blood.

5. Washington: Federal judge puts off Iran-contra trial until after election (→ 9/13).

5. St. Louis: Londell Williams pleads guilty to conspiring to kill Jesse Jackson, saying he was "trying to make a fool out of us white people" by running for president (→ 9/9).

DEATHS

1. John Cardinal Dearden, ex-Archbishop of Detroit and leading liberal voice in Catholic Church, at 80 (*10/15/07).

5. Colin Higgins, screenwriter and director who wrote "Harold and Maude," a victim of AIDS at 47.

Drought cutting grain supplies drastically

Only stunted corn can be squeezed from the painfully parched ground.

Aug 3. America's grain harvest could be below 200 million metric tons for the first time since 1974, down 78 million tons from last year because of the drought, experts say. The outlook for most other grain-producing countries is just as grim because of droughts and other bad weather conditions in China, India as well as the Soviet Union.

World grain production will be down by 76 million metric tons, to 1.521 billion tons, according to Lester Brown, chairman of the World-watch Institute in Washington. The Agriculture Department estimates grain production at 1.672 billion metric tons. The 152-million-ton deficit, the largest ever for a single year, will lower world grain stockpiles to 250 million tons, only a 54-day supply. That is the lowest figure recorded since the early 70's. Prices more than doubled in those years, and comparable increases are likely now, with commodity prices already up by 50 percent this year.

There are a few bright spots, however, with crop increases in Mexico and parts of Africa where rainfall has improved. And speculators at the Chicago Board of Trade, where grain-futures contracts are traded, report an almost unprecedented increase in trading volume caused by the short supplies (→ 11).

Roller coasters designed for more screams

Just don't eat first.

The Arrow Dynamics company of Clearfield, Utah, is busy designing a giant triple clothoid loop. What may sound like an electronic ice cream cone is one of a few designs of roller coasters now being developed through the use of re-applied physics, high-tech computers and new building materials. Designers have the seemingly contradictory goals of making roller coasters safer and more terrifying, replacing the wooden models that hurled riders from side to side with smoother steel constructions that send the riders happily shrieking at 70 mph. The clothoid loop is the main improvement: the tear-shape circle turns roller coaster cars upside down and keeps them safely there by centrifugal force.

Vast Amazon fires poison atmosphere

Aug 6. The Amazon basin is burning. As the annual dry season arrives, over 77,000 square miles of rain forest are set ablaze by farmers seeking new land to cultivate. A possible boon to the farmers, these fires may have serious consequences for the rest of the globe. A new study of satellite data by NASA scientists shows that the fires may account for at least one-tenth of man-made carbon dioxide, a gas believed to be causing a warming of the global climate through the greenhouse effect. The fires may also produce pollutants which diminish the planet's ozone shield.

Air quality drops as result of heat

Aug 3. Levels of ozone, a lung-attacking air pollutant, have soared to record highs this year, according to government monitoring stations. Hot, stagnant air masses are raising pollution levels in many American cities. With present regulations having failed to reduce smog levels, Los Angeles officials are drafting some of the world's toughest pollution rules, including a limit on construction of new plants that could force industries to leave the area.

Hollywood reaches strike settlement

Aug 3. A tentative agreement was reached today between movie and television producers on one side and screenwriters on the other to end the 22-week-old writers' strike. This could mean that the 9,000 striking writers will vote over the weekend and, conceivably, be back at work next week — and the new television season can get rolling. With overseas markets increasing, a key issue to both sides concerns foreign residuals. The writers are said to be asking for 1.2 percent of the gross after a certain amount has been made. This strike, one of the longest in Hollywood's history, nearly split the writers' guild into different camps.

ongressman quits after felony conviction

End of the road for Biaggi.

Aug 5. After 50 years of public service, Democratic Congressman Mario Biaggi of New York City resigned today and announced that he will not seek an 11th term. The announcement came after his second conviction on charges of corruption. Biaggi was found guilty yesterday of extorting $1.8 million in stock from the Wedtech Corporation, a defense contractor, and of turning the company into a racketeering operation to bribe politicians. Many of the congressman's constituents looked upon him as a hero for his personal help and for his ability to pick up the telephone and get things done. Congress was expected to expel Biaggi next month if he did not resign (→ 11/18).

Hussein to stop paying West Bank workers

Aug 4. Jordan has announced that most of its employees in the Israeli-occupied West Bank will be dropped from the government payroll this month. The decision to halt the payment of their salaries followed King Hussein's recent move to abandon Jordan's West Bank claims to the Palestine Liberation Organization, and to sever administrative links with that region. Some 21,000 employees will be officially retired August 16. They include municipal and health workers and teachers.

Israeli officials said their government would "have to decide how to fill the dangerous vacuum which is being created," and they described the matter as "purely a Jordanian affair" in which West Bank residents would suffer. Said one, "It doesn't seem likely that we are going to pay the salaries." Actually, most salary payments are now split between the Israelis and the Jordanians. Jordan spends about $50 million annually to operate its own agencies. Others, such as the school system, are financed by both countries (→ 9/6).

This big cat, whose mother was a tiger and father a lion, celebrates his second birthday this month.

Hertz fined record for consumer fraud

Aug 3. The Hertz Corporation, in a court settlement with the federal government, agreed today to pay a $6.8 million fine for bilking some 110,000 customers and insurance companies by charging fraudulent collision-repair costs. Hertz also will pay $13.7 million in restitution, which may make the figure, $20.8 million in all, the biggest in a criminal fraud case, said Andrew J. Maloney, the U.S. attorney in Brooklyn. Waiving a formal indictment and trial, Hertz pleaded guilty and was sentenced immediately. Frank Olson, its chairman, said the illegal practices were halted in 1986. A spokesman said 20 employees involved in the case had been fired.

Rising pollution threatens world's oceans

Aug 1. Beachgoers around the world are having a bad season, with ocean pollution fouling many of their favorite vacation spots. Beaches on the east coast of the United States have often been closed this summer as medical wastes from unknown sources washed ashore. A study by the European Consumers Union found that such famed beach areas as Deauville in France, Marbella in Spain and Corfu in Greece do not meet standards set by the European Economic Community.

Experts say the problems encountered by vacationers are symptoms of dangerous levels of ocean pollution worldwide. Biologists reported tumors on fish in the North Sea that they link to metals and a variety of pollutants dumped into the Rhine and other rivers flowing into the sea. Some 7,000 seals, half the seal population of the North Sea, have died this year of infections that scientists link to a weakening of immune defenses caused by exposure to pollutants. A fish disaster that occurred in the northern Adriatic last year has also been attributed to industrial pollution.

In 1975, the nations belonging to the European Community promised to clean up their beaches, but little was done. One reason is cost. West Germany estimates that it would cost $12 billion to clean the North Sea, by building better pollution-control equipment and sewage treatment plants.

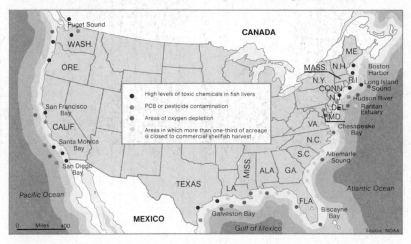

Beside the risks to health caused by the increasing amounts of chemicals and debris, polluted seaports bode ill for a nation that relies on commerce.

Carl Rowan facing illegal gun charge

Aug 1. Carl Rowan, a columnist who has called for "a strict national law to control the availability of handguns," scored a point for the opposite side June 14 when he was arrested for firing at a teen-age trespasser with an unregistered handgun. Charging that he was a hypocrite but that he was also right to take the action he did, pro-gun advocates showed up at his hearing in the District of Columbia Superior Court today. Rowan said that on the night of the incident, he called the police before shooting one of four trespassers in the wrist. Two trespassers were sentenced to 40 hours of community service; Rowan could serve two years (→ 9/29).

Raymond Carver, poet of poor, dies

Aug 2. "I'm a paid-in-full member of the working poor," Raymond Carver once said. Until his death today of lung cancer at age 50, the poet and short-story writer drew on his own experiences, and in a spare writing style created compassionate tales of hard-luck characters, most often set in the Pacific Northwest. During a career wracked by poverty and alcoholism, Carver produced 10 works of fiction and poetry. The most acclaimed, perhaps, was the 1983 story collection "Cathedral." This year, Carver, his body ravaged by cancer, spoke of his hard-won success as a writer: "I feel like the luckiest man around, I really do."

AUGUST

Week 32 1988

Su	Mo	Tu	We	Th	Fr	Sa
	1	2	3	4	5	6
7	8	9	10	11	12	13
14	15	16	17	18	19	20
21	22	23	24	25	26	27
28	29	30	31			

7. Bihar, India: Death toll in ferry crash on Ganges River reaches 400.

8. La Paz, Bolivia: Secretary of State Shultz, on Latin American tour, narrowly escapes assassination attempt as bomb disrupts motorcade.

8. Washington: Pentagon auditors reveal that contractors regularly overcharge for services delivered to Defense Department (→ 9/27).

8. St. Paul, Minnesota: Federal appeals court upholds state law requiring minors to notify parents in order to get abortions (→ 10/27).

8. Pacific Ocean: Scientists doing research 180 miles west of Vancouver find strange, inexplicable glow a mile below surface, suggesting photosynthesis may be possible even at such depths.

8. Baltimore: Astronomers announce discovery of galaxy that is possibly a record 15 billion light years away, at edge of known universe.

9. Washington: Secretary of Education William Bennett resigns; Reagan names Lauro F. Cavazos, president of Texas Tech University, who would be first Hispanic Cabinet member.

9. Tokyo: Japanese announce project to develop commercial jet to travel at five times speed of sound, rival to American project.

12. Washington: Attorney General Meese, on last day in office, signs order requiring that special prosecutors be hired to investigate members of Congress accused of wrongdoing.

13. Fayetteville, North Carolina: Elmo R. Zumwalt 3rd, whose father ordered use of Agent Orange in Vietnam, dies of cancer possibly due to use of the defoliant.

DEATHS

8. Robert Ricci, head of couture house Nina Ricci, at 83.

9. Carl Holman, civil rights leader and president of National Urban Coalition, at 69 (*6/27/1919).

Murdoch purchases TV Guide in big deal

Aug 7. TV Guide and other magazines turned out by Walter Annenberg's Triangle Publications will soon be owned by Rupert Murdoch. The publishing giant has agreed to buy Triangle for $3 billion. The circulation of TV Guide, which has been on newsstands for 35 years, is 17.2 million, surpassing by one million its nearest competitor, The Reader's Digest. Because Murdoch is also owner of the Fox TV network, some critics fear that he will manipulate TV Guide to favor his broadcast investment; but others expect he will do little fine-tuning of the publication.

Beleaguered farms get federal relief

Aug 11. President Reagan signed a $3.9 billion bill to help drought-stricken farmers today, but to qualify the farmers must have lost at least 35 percent of their crops. The ceiling on the federal assistance is $100,000 per farm and it can be used to cover crops, livestock and hired help. The measure is aimed at small- and medium-size farms, and those grossing more than $2 million per year are not eligible. Although the bill will not cover all losses, a spokesman for the American Farm Bureau Federation gave it a B-plus rating and said that it "will provide assistance to people who've been hurt" (→ 9/12).

Crossword's 75th

Aug 9. With fewer than 100 cruciverbalists producing reputable crossword puzzles in the United States, one might expect some unanimity in the pursuit of a common task. But theirs is a two-party system. It pits traditionalists against new-wave constructors who want puzzles renovated to echo modern parlance. Robert Guilbert wants to unite the two camps in an eclectic hall of fame, celebrating 75 years of published crosswords. Now Guilbert has come one step closer to his goal by bringing the two sides together to form a board of directors with equal representation.

Angola cease-fire reached by four nations

Soldiers withdrawing from the battlefield, a promising trend this year.

Aug 8. Four nations have brokered an immediate cease-fire in Angola and nearby Namibia. The United States has been the leader in developing a compromise and timetable for the withdrawal of South African and Cuban troops. Angola joined these three countries in issuing a statement which says that "a de facto cessation of hostilities is now in effect." Some Angolan rebel troops, under the leadership of Jonas Savimbi, insist that they will continue to fight as long as Cuban soldiers remain in Angola. The South African government has further announced that it has suggested a visit by United Nations Secretary General Javier Perez de Cuellar to develop U.N. plans to conduct free elections in Namibia, formerly South-West Africa. The war in Angola has been marked by staggering political complexities.

Disputed "Temptation of Christ" is shown

Aug 12. Martin Scorsese's film interpretation of Nikos Kazantzakis's brilliant novel "The Last Temptation of Christ" opened today despite organized efforts by religious groups to censor it. Scorsese attempts to recreate the introspective Christ who struggles through his self-sacrifice, and even yields to carnal pleasure. The film, as slow moving as it is controversial, is certain to receive a great deal of attention as a direct result of the demonstrations calling for a ban.

To many Christians, "The Last Temptation of Christ" is simple blasphemy.

urma's leader ousted after three weeks

Aug 12. The resignation of Burma's new leader, Sein Lwin, was welcomed with "a huge sense of relief and euphoria," a senior Western diplomat said today. "The mobs, the crowds will have sensed victory." The departure of Sein Lwin comes after violent anti-government protests in all major Burmese cities. There was neither an explanation of why Sein Lwin had stepped down nor word of who his successor might be. The fighting of the last week has declined considerably since the announcement.

At least 95 people were killed in protests this week, according to the government, although diplomats have estimated that the number is in the hundreds. Since the day Sein Lwin, a former army general, was appointed leader of the country, many of the Burmese opposed him for having commanded troops that brutally squelched protests in the past. Students and Buddhist monks have been among those involved in the riots. Last week, the government imposed martial law in the capital city of Rangoon.

The recent demonstrations have been the largest since 1962, when a military coup brought Ne Win to power. Among the reforms that protesters were demanding was a referendum on whether to terminate one-party rule. Ne Win recommended such a reform when he resigned after years of economic decline in Burma (→ 24).

Duchess of York has a royal princess

Aug 8. The British royal family gained yet another member when the 28-year-old Duchess of York, better known to the world as "Fergie," gave birth to a 6-pound, 12-ounce girl in a London hospital. The newcomer, who takes her place behind her uncle, Prince Charles, his two sons, William and Harry, and her own father, Prince Andrew, will be the fifth in line to the throne. A name for the princess has not yet been announced, although Victoria would be a popular choice. Her title will be Princess of York and she is to be formally addressed as "Your Royal Highness" (→ 22).

The law and sports lose a big figure

Aug 13. Edward Bennett Williams, owner of the Baltimore Orioles and one of the best-known lawyers in the country, died of cancer today. Williams soared to fame in the 50's when he defended everyone from Senator Joseph McCarthy to blacklisted film writers. His success was based on his ability to win over a jury. When he defended Jimmy Hoffa in 1957, Williams selected a largely black jury, then arranged for ex-champ Joe Louis to hug Hoffa in the courtroom. Hoffa was acquitted. Williams owned the Washington Redskins before he purchased the Baltimore Orioles.

Nomura richer still

Aug 8. Nomura Securities, which transacts nearly 17 percent of all stock purchases and sales in Japan, is paying $100 million for a 20 percent share of Wasserstein, Perella, a New York investment firm. The move represents a bid by Japan's most profitable firm, with assets of $372 billion, to widen its role in the U.S. Nomura, whose major interest here is in Treasury bonds, is not shy in pursuing foreign business. It was the first Japanese securities firm to return to America after the war, to put a securities unit in China and to get a seat on London's Stock Exchange (→ 9/6).

Queen for a day: Fergie and child.

No joy in Edmonton: Gretzky's leaving

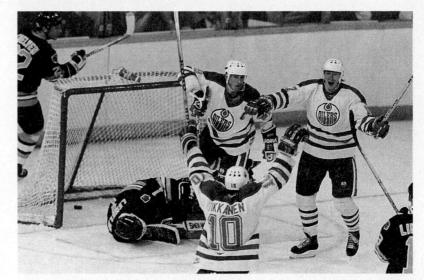
Wayne Gretzky, near cage, in the uniform he won't be wearing next season.

Aug 9. Edmonton's Oilers without the great Wayne Gretzky? That would be like ham without eggs, like Tristan without Isolde — maybe even beluga caviar without champagne. Yet, it has happened. In one of the most shocking trades in the history of sports, Wayne Gretzky has been shipped off to the Los Angeles Kings in exchange for two players, three top draft choices and a mere $10 million.

Oiler fans consider that a small price to pay for their national treasure. In nine seasons with Edmonton, Gretzky was named the National Hockey League's most valuable player eight times. He set 43 league records while leading the Oilers to four Stanley Cup championships. Some experts call him the greatest player ever to don skates.

Why the trade, Oiler fans kept asking. Gretzky explained that he had asked for it so he could be near his actress wife, Janet Jones, in Hollywood. He married Miss Jones on July 16 in a ceremony akin to a royal wedding but said she did not pressure him to change.

Cubs finally play a night game in Chicago

Aug 8. The last bastion against change in baseball has fallen. For the first time in its 73-year history, Wrigley Field was lighted for a night game, 40 years after the previous holdout, the Detroit Tigers, succumbed to modernity. There were 39,012 fans on hand for the Chicago event, but the Cubs' management believes that a million tickets could have been sold. Harry Grossman, who has been attending Cub games since 1906, instructed the crowd to count to three, then say, "Let there be light." And there was light, for the game with the Philadelphia Phillies. "It's emotional that an era is coming to an end," said the Cub first baseman, Mark Grace, "but it's needed."

Wrigley Field under lights: Neither baseball nor Chicago will ever be the same.

AUGUST
Week 33 1988

Su	Mo	Tu	We	Th	Fr	Sa
	1	2	3	4	5	6
7	8	9	10	11	12	13
14	15	16	17	18	19	20
21	22	23	24	25	26	27
28	29	30	31			

14. Seoul: Some 1,500 students arrested trying to march to North Korea to hold talks on reunification (→ 10/18).

14. Delano, California: Cesar Chavez, 61, enters 29th day of his third and longest fast, this one to protest use of pesticides to grow table grapes.

15. New York: Officials say grand jury has rejected advice of State Attorney General Robert Abrams and decided to subpoena Tawana Brawley (→ 9/26).

15. Tallinn, U.S.S.R.: Hitler-Stalin pact of 1938 officially disclosed in Estonia for first time (→ 17).

15. Lubbock, Texas: Some 12,000 gather at St. John Neumann Church for Feast of the Assumption, drawn by reports that parishioners have spoken to Virgin Mary.

15. Washington: In compliance with international ozone treaty, E.P.A. orders limits on certain destructive chemicals.

16. Johannesburg: Lawyer for Nelson Mandela says jailed black leader has tuberculosis, often associated with malnutrition and overcrowding (→ 9/1).

17. Washington: F.D.A. approves Rogaine, first drug cleared in United States for treatment of hair loss.

17. Washington: Administration officials report that White House has ordered government agencies not to cooperate with congressional inquiry into illegal doings of Panama's General Noriega.

17. Moscow: Soviet Culture Ministry denies report libraries have been ordered to purge pre-Gorbachev texts (→ 9/2).

17. Zurich, Switzerland: Butch Reynolds beats world record in 400 meters, with time of 43.29.

17. Managua: Nicaraguan Socialist Party, moving toward social democracy, criticizes Sandinistas as dogmatic and repressive (→ 10/24).

18. West Germany: Three-day bank robbery/hostage drama ends in shootout after bizarre chase in which robbers freely gave interviews and journalists participated in escape.

Republican ticket: Bush and Quayle

Aug 18. Vice President Bush pledged tonight to "keep America moving forward, always forward" as he accepted the Republican nomination for President. But the beginning of his campaign appeared somewhat jeopardized by his choice of Senator J. Danforth Quayle of Indiana as his runnning mate.

Bush's surprise choice of the 41-year-old Quayle, who has little national standing, came yesterday in New Orleans, site of the Republicans' convention. Soon after ter the announcement, word began spreading that Quayle, who comes from a rich and well-connected family, had joined the Indiana National Guard nearly two decades ago in an apparent attempt to avoid being drafted for service at the height of the Vietnam War.

Despite the controversy over the Quayle selection, Bush delivered a rousing acceptance speech tonight, renewing his pledge not to raise taxes, promising to create 30 million

Bush surprised everyone by picking Senator Quayle, 41, as his running mate.

jobs over the next eight years and restating his opposition to abortion and gun control. He depicted Governor Michael Dukakis, his Democratic opponent, as a defeatist who believes in the "long, slow decline"

of the United States. And, seeming to cast himself as something of an underdog in the coming election, Bush promised: "I mean to run hard, to fight hard, to stand on the issues and I mean to win"(→ 18).

Hunts convicted in silver market scam

Aug 20. A commodities company owned by Peru won a legal battle against the Hunt brothers of Dallas today as a federal district court ruled that the tycoons manipulated the silver market in 1979 and 1980. In the civil suit, the jury ordered Lamar, William Herbert and Nelson Bunker Hunt and a Saudi businessman to pay Minpeco, S.A., over $130 million in damages.

With separate agreements by six investment firms to pay Minpeco nearly $65 million in damages, the Peruvian concern made about $40 million more than the $151 million it claimed the market manipulation had originally cost it.

Troubles from class action suits charging similar machinations lie ahead for the Hunts. In addition, they are the target of proceedings started in 1985 by the Commodities Futures Trading Commission.

At the same time, the Hunts have filed a $1.5 billion lending-fraud suit against 22 banks, charging a conspiracy to provide loans that could not be repaid in an effort to buy the brothers' business cheaply.

Quayle's military service becomes an issue

Dan Quayle: saw action in Indiana.

Aug 18. Senator Dan Quayle's use of connections to avoid being drafted during the height of the Vietnam War continues to cause a degree of concern in Vice President Bush's campaign for President. But a top Bush aide insisted that there has been no thought of dropping Quayle from the vice-presidential slot on the Republican ticket.

The latest development in the Quayle matter came today when a retired senior editor of a newspaper owned by the Quayle family said that he had tried to use his influence to help the young man enter the National Guard during the war, a route used by thousands of youths at the time to avoid being drafted and possibly sent to Vietnam. Wendell C. Phillippi, at that time an editor of the Indianapolis News and once a major general in the Indiana National Guard, said he had telephoned a top official of the National Guard on behalf of Quayle. Explaining that he had made such calls for dozens of others, Phillippi said he had long known the Quayle family and viewed Dan Quayle as "a good and qualified man."

The issue has become controversial largely because of Quayle's pro-military positions during his years in the Senate. In a recent interview, the senator said that if his own Guard unit had been called to active duty, "I would have gone and served very proudly in Vietnam." Instead, he spent most of his six-year tour of duty in the Guard turning out press releases (→ 24).

S. and Soviet fire nuclear device

Aug 17. The roomfull of Soviet and American scientists watched intently as a circular patch of ground displayed on a video monitor suddenly lifted about 15 feet. The members of the group smiled quietly at each other, satisfied with the first joint U.S.-Soviet experiment to test nuclear blast verification methods. Then the telephone rang, bringing news from the other group who had been testing the Soviet method of verification from a distance. Finally, the scientists broke into applause.

In 1974 and 1976, American and Soviet officials signed treaties which limited the size of nuclear test blasts, but neither nation ever ratified the treaties because the United States has insisted on on-site verification methods. This experiment will provide data to compare the on- and off-site measurements, which will be analyzed over the next few weeks and carefully compared in Geneva the fall (→ 9/16).

Elvis here, there, or is he anywhere?

Aug 16. In a Michigan laundromat. In a Burger King in Philadelphia. On a carnival parachute ride in Texas. Peering out of a window at Graceland. These are only some of the places that people claim to have spotted Elvis Presley since his death in 1977. As a grieving world sets out on a 12th year without the king of rock and roll, many are beginning to believe that, to paraphrase Mark Twain, the reports of his death were greatly exaggerated.

The current spate of Elvis "sightings" has placed the allegedly dead star in 40 different states, and the intensity with which faith in his continued existence is held by some has reached a near-religious fervor. The believers point to such "evidence" as the factual discrepancies on the death certificate and the disappearance of autopsy documents. Nevertheless, despite the obvious financial incentives for the real Elvis Presley, if alive, to come forward, he has not done so. The king is dead; long live the king.

Pakistan President Zia dies in plane crash

The West loses Pakistan's President Zia, a friend, in a fiery crash.

Aug 17. Only a few minutes after takeoff, the American-made airplane carrying 30 people, including Pakistan's President Mohammad Zia ul-Haq, was engulfed in a ball of fire, somersaulted and tumbled to the ground. The cause of the explosion is unknown, but Gulam Ishaq Khan, the leader of the Senate who assumed power under Pakistani law, said that sabotage could not be ruled out. President Zia, 64, has ruled Pakistan for 11 years, since he took power in a military coup. His government was a leading pro-American force in the area. Arnold L. Raphael, U.S. ambassador to Pakistan, was also killed.

Italian auto magnate Enzo Ferrari is dead

Aug 14. The Italian entrepreneur who made the bright red Ferrari race car a worldwide symbol of elegance and speed is dead at the age of 90. Enzo Ferrari, who was neither a designer nor an automobile engineer, described himself as a "constructor." He oversaw some of the most minute details of design and production until 1977, when he bowed out because of poor health. The early history of the Ferrari race car was marred by the deaths of many drivers as well as of spectators. In later years, Ferrari's cars, handled by some of the world's best drivers, won a reputation for extraordinary performance.

The Ferrari F40, made for the company's 40th year. Wouldn't we all love one!

"Fifth force" could alter Newton's laws

Aug 15. Is Newton's law of gravity subtly wrong? Scientists say an experiment on the Greenland ice sheet indicates there is a fifth force of nature that would alter gravity, one of four known forces (the others are electromagnetism and the strong and weak atomic forces).

The scientists went to Greenland because the ice sheet's even composition allows precise calculation of gravity. Lowering instruments into a mile-deep hole, researchers found their measurements of gravity differed by up to 3.9 percent from what Newton's law predicts. The effect may be explained by a short-range attractive force acting along with Newtonian gravity.

"We appear to have the cleanest evidence to date of something that cannot be explained by Newtonian gravity," said Mark Ander of the Los Alamos National Laboratory. Other physicists say the experiment is so complex and the calculations so difficult that it is too soon to say a fifth force really exists.

U.S. birth rate is highest since 1964

Aug 16. The National Center for Health Statistics reported today that last year the number of births in the United States reached its highest point since 1964. In spite of a recent decline in the marriage rate, an estimated 3,829,000 babies were born in 1987, a figure that surpasses 1986 by nearly 100,000. Experts attribute this rise in fertility to the recent trend among baby boomers to start raising families of their own. The number of women in their childbearing years has been very large lately, and the Census Bureau estimates that births are going to show an annual increase of about 1 percent during the next several years.

The report also states that in 1987 there was a total of 2,127,000 deaths, the highest yearly figure ever recorded. An estimated 12,450 to 13,820 of these deaths were related to AIDS. According to these figures, AIDS would rank as the 15th highest cause of death in the United States.

Su	Mo	Tu	We	Th	Fr	Sa
	1	2	3	4	5	6
7	8	9	10	11	12	13
14	15	16	17	18	19	20
21	22	23	24	25	26	27
28	29	30	31			

21. India and Nepal: Major Himalayan earthquake, 6.5 on Richter scale, kills at least 550.

22. Burundi: Government announces that revival of tribal warfare has claimed at least 5,000 lives in last week.

22. England: The newest member of the royal family is named Her Royal Highness, the Princess Beatrice of York.

23. U.S.S.R.: Demonstrations in three Baltic capitals openly oppose Soviet rule (→ 9/22).

23. San Diego: Officials at San Diego Wild Animal Park say only California condor conceived and hatched in captivity, born April 29, is female.

23. New York City: Heavyweight champ Mike Tyson fractures his hand in late-night street brawl with former ring opponent Mitch Green.

24. New York City: Police Commissioner Benjamin Ward says his department is responsible for August 6 riot in Tompkins Square Park.

24. Washington: Administration officials say that West German and Swedish authorities have detained eight people in connection with a 10-year-old, newly uncovered European spy ring (→ 25).

24. Chicago: Federal grand jury indicts three athletic agents, alleging they used threats and bribes to force college athletes to sign with professional managers.

25. Washington: American Clyde Lee Conrad, former sergeant, is named as key figure in European spy ring.

28. Spa-Francorchamps, Belgium: Belgian Grand Prix is won by Ayrton Senna of Brazil, his fourth Formula One victory in a row.

31. Grapevine, Texas: Ninety-four people emerge alive from the crash of a Delta Airlines Boeing 727 that killed 13.

31. United States: Arbitrator finds major league baseball owners guilty of conspiring against free agents; second violation of collective bargaining agreements in two years.

Day of horror at German air show

Aug 28. Three jets from an Italian air force acrobatic flying team collided today at an air show in West Germany, sending one of the planes careening into a terrified crowd of spectators. At least 46 people were killed while hundreds of others in the audience were injured by flying debris and a fireball of jet fuel.

The shocking event took place at an annual aviation show that attracted about 300,000 people to the American-operated Ramstein Air Base, which is about 60 miles southwest of Frankfurt. Millions more viewed the spectacular collision on West German live television, followed by the scene of devastation and carnage as victims wept in agony amid the rubble and the rapidly spreading flames.

The Italian precision flying team, called the Frece Tricolori, or Tricolor Arrows, followed similar aerial displays by French and Portuguese groups. For their final maneuver, just before 4 p.m., the 10 Italian pilots, in MB-339A fighters that trailed red, white and green smoke to denote the colors of their country's flag, split into two groups of five jets each and swooped toward each other. The planes were at an altitude of only 100 feet when two of them smashed into one of the oncoming planes, sending its exploding mass hurtling toward a field of parked cars and horrified onlookers. West German officials say the death toll will probably rise, because many of the injured suffered severe burns.

Today's tragedy comes at a time of high anxiety in West Germany over plane accidents. Twenty American F-16 fighters have crashed during training flights over the past seven years, and two military craft went down this year near nuclear-power plants. Protests over the air shows have mounted since a Canadian jet crashed in 1983, killing three bystanders, and a U.S. Chinook helicopter fell in 1982, killing 46 people. Today, a statement from the environmentalist Green Party, which had recommended a ban on all low-level training flights and air shows, summed up the catastrophe at Ramstein: "It is terrible when one's fears turn into bitter truth" (→ 9/3).

Their normally flawless flight exhibition gone awry, three Italian air fo[r] jets collide in midair, a moment of frozen horror, with metal flying ...

... and crashing to the ground ... a flaming fuselage bounces ...

... amid horrified spectators, many of whom burn to death instantly.

Long trial of crime figures ends in acquittal

Aug 26. The government suffered a major setback in its fight against organized crime today when 20 reputed members of New Jersey's Lucchese crime family were acquitted at Federal Court in Newark. The trial lasted 21 months, one of the longest in American history.

The defendants were indicted in 1985 after a four-year investigation by the F.B.I., which planted wiretaps at the Hole in the Wall, a Newark luncheonette said to be the headquarters of the Lucchese family crime operations. They were charged with running a vast criminal organization in New Jersey and Florida that was involved in cocaine trafficking, gambling and loan-shark operations. The jurors heard hundreds of hours of wiretap recordings as well as the testimony of government informers, but following 14 hours of deliberations, the foreman read 77 separate not-guilty verdicts as the defendants and their friends and families in the courtroom cheered.

"The jury saw through everything," said Stephen Skoller, the lawyer for reputed Lucchese family boss Anthony "Tumac" Accetturo. Skoller had questioned the credibility of the evidence and the witnesses, while at the same time accusing the government of ethnic bigotry because most of the defendants were of Italian descent.

Samuel A. Alito, the U.S. attorney for New Jersey, seemed unshaken. "This only increases our resolve," he said. "Rest assured, we will continue our offensive against organized crime."

Burma lifts martial law, plans referendum

Aug 24. Burma's government has ended martial law, pulled its troops off the streets and recommended a referendum to end one-party rule. The actions come after weeks of protests against the party that has held power for 26 years.

Maung Maung, the current Burmese leader and one of the few civilians in the Cabinet, was appointed five days ago and said that he would resign if the party rejected his request for a referendum. If the referendum is conducted and the people opt for a multiparty system, elections will take place "as soon as possible," Maung Maung said.

The Burmese people were joyous with the news. "One could say without exaggeration that virtually the whole city of Rangoon was out on the streets today," according to a Western diplomat. "There was a sense that the struggle was nearing a victorious conclusion."

Maung suggested that the troops had been hesitant to oppose fellow citizens. He said soldiers "find it extremely repugnant to confront the people who are their parents." The protesters showed no hostility toward the soldiers, shaking their hands and waving as they withdrew from the capital (→ 9/19).

There is a new sense of freedom in the streets of Rangoon, Burma.

Walesa asks labor peace after official talks

The indomitable Lech Walesa rallies his people with an eye on the future.

Aug 31. After meeting with government officials for the first time since the Solidarity trade union was outlawed in 1981, the union's leader, Lech Walesa, called on Polish workers to end their current strike. Strikes in May led to violent police action and a government rejection of all demands, including the reinstatement of Solidarity. The strikes, renewed August 15, have affected the major ports, coal mines and industries. Walesa said that the round-table talks would continue. He will continue to press for the legalization of Solidarity and direct efforts at achieving a conciliatory accord between government, church and Solidarity aimed at the solution of Poland's many problems (→ 9/3).

Pledge of Allegiance is now campaign issue

Aug 24. Vice President Bush, campaigning in Los Angeles today, stepped up his attacks on Governor Michael Dukakis over the issue of the Pledge of Allegiance to the flag. With President Reagan at his side at a campaign rally, Bush said of his Democratic rival in this fall's presidential election: "What is it about the Pledge of Allegiance that upsets him so much? It is very hard for me to imagine that the Founding Fathers, Samuel Adams and John Hancock and John Adams, would have objected to teachers leading students in the Pledge of Allegiance to the flag of the United States." The crowd roared its agreement.

In his first term as Governor of Massachusetts, Dukakis vetoed legislation that would have imposed fines on teachers for failing to lead their classes in reciting the pledge. In doing so, the Governor cited an advisory opinion rendered by the Massachusetts Supreme Judicial Court which held that the measure would be in violation of the teachers' First Amendment rights to freedom of speech and religion.

Noting that the Massachusetts Legislature had subsequently overridden the Governor's veto, Bush commented today: "I would have signed that bill" (→ 9/9).

A terrible sight, but one that is fraught with hope: The Soviet Union, in compliance with the INF Treaty, destroys an SS-20.

Su	Mo	Tu	We	Th	Fr	Sa
				1	2	3
4	5	6	7	8	9	10
11	12	13	14	15	16	17
18	19	20	21	22	23	24
25	26	27	28	29	30	

1. United States: According to new study, 50% of colon-rectal cancers partly result of genetic predisposition.

2. Belle Glade, Florida: State holds first full-scale alligator hunt in 26 years due to alligator baby boom.

3. Pittsburgh: Robert W. T'Souvas, homeless Vietnam veteran charged in My Lai trial, shot to death in argument over bottle of vodka.

3. Ramstein, West Germany: Two more victims of air show crash die, bringing total to 51; mourners hold memorial.

3. Washington: General Accounting Office report details resurgence of sweatshops in American cities.

4. Moscow: Former Soviet leader Brezhnev's son-in-law goes on trial for corruption.

6. Jerusalem: Israel announces it has arrested dozens of people on charges of bribery to avoid military service (→ 19).

6. Tokyo: All land in Japan calculated at $13.47 trillion, more than all land in U.S.

6. London: Elton John's huge collection of memorabilia goes on sale, 54-inch-tall fiberglass boots from "Tommy" included.

7. Moscow: Soviet astronaut and Afghan companion land spacecraft after being stuck in space for a day with faulty landing equipment (→ 29).

7. Washington: Senator Joseph Biden returns to work after 17-month absence to repair aneurisms on the brain.

7. New York City: Drexel Burnham Lambert accused by S.E.C. of conspiring with Ivan Boesky to defraud clients and trade stocks illegally (→ 10/30).

9. New York City: Iranian sets himself on fire in front of United Nations to protest executions in Iran.

9. Chicago: G.D. Searle told to pay $8.75 million for negligence in distributing intra-uterine device.

DEATH

1. Luis W. Alvarez, scientist, at 77 (*6/13/1911).

Bangladesh flooding is worst in 70 years

International relief from the United States and Japan will help the victims.

Sept 6. At least 400 people have died from drowning, snakebite and building collapses in Bangladesh as a result of the worst flooding in this troubled region in 70 years. The United States is donating some $3.6 million in emergency aid to help the victims of "one of the largest natural disasters of the century," as one official described it. The relief money will purchase high-protein dry foods, water purification pills and medicine to deal with diarrhea and snakebite.

The flooding, caused by heavier-than-usual monsoon rains in June, has left an estimated 28 million people homeless or stranded and has turned the area into "one vast swamp," as a relief worker said. Because of the dire conditions, it will be weeks before the authorities are able to assess casualties and property damage accurately.

Pop stars perform for 72,000 at benefit

Sept 2. "Get up, stand up, stand up for your rights," chanted Senegalese singer Youssou N'Dour today to kick off the Human Rights Now tour before 72,000 fans at Wembley Stadium in London. The six weeks of concerts will be promoting Amnesty International in 13 countries. Today's crowd was roused politically and musically by Bruce Springsteen, Peter Gabriel, Sting and Tracy Chapman.

Beside raising the roof, they're raising consciousness for political prisoners.

Soviet maps false for past 50 years

Sept 2. "Mistrust and spy mania" led the Soviet Union to falsify maps of its country for the past half century, according to the chief Soviet cartographer, Viktor R. Yaschenko. The locations of rivers and towns, and even the streets of Moscow, have been misrepresented on public maps in an effort to confuse bombers and spies. "People did not recognize their motherland on the maps," Yaschenko said. "Tourists tried in vain to orient themselves on the terrain." The Soviet Union now is planning to begin declassification of its accurate maps, which Moscow has regarded as state secrets since the late 1930's (→ 12).

Crippling fines force housing integration

Sept 9. Facing soaring fines of $1 million a day, the city council of Yonkers, New York, has agreed to comply with a federal judge's order to build 800 moderate-income housing units in primarily white neighborhoods. Yonkers' resistance had become a national symbol of efforts to block desegregation. Tonight's vote staves off a "doomsday" austerity plan, scheduled to go into effect tomorrow, that would have laid off 25 percent of the city's work force. Referring to $800,000 in fines already paid, one city councilman called the ordeal "a very expensive civics lesson" (→ 21).

Walesa ends strike of Polish workers

Sept 3. Poland's latest round of labor unrest came to an end today when striking workers reluctantly agreed to Solidarity leader Lech Walesa's request to return to work. The 20-day strike of mine and dock workers was holding up the talks between Solidarity's leadership and the government that Walesa hopes will end the 1982 ban on Solidarity. Mindful that many of the workers felt they were going home empty-handed, Walesa said that he hoped to "push Poland toward reform and agreement" (→ 10/31).

U.S. keeps America's Cup with catamaran

Double-hulled boat used by the U.S. crew to retain the America's Cup.

Sept 9. The America's Cup yacht races were over almost before they started. As the United States sailed to a clear 18-minute victory over New Zealand in the opener, there were hardly any doubts that the Americans would sweep the series off San Diego. Dennis Conner piloted the American catamaran Stars & Stripes to such easy victories that the challenger virtually conceded the best-of-three series. The New Zealanders failed to win a court case in which they contended that the series was a mismatch because it violated the century-old rules that govern America's Cup competition.

Rivals neck and neck as campaign heats up

Sept 9. The race for President has entered a decisive stage with the two candidates locked in a dead heat, according to a new round of surveys of larger states. Vice President Bush has stepped up his attacks on the Democratic nominee, Governor Michael Dukakis, accusing him of a "sorry record" on pollution of Boston Harbor. Meanwhile, Dukakis has tried to energize his campaign by rehiring a key aide, John Sasso, who resigned during the primary race when it became known that he had helped engineer the withdrawal of Senator Joseph R. Biden from the contest for the nomination (→ 25).

Governor Dukakis tries to recapture the flag from Vice President Bush.

Savings-loan rescue is costliest one yet

Sept 5. The nation's groggy savings and loan industry remains on the ropes. In the costliest rescue of a single institution, the Federal Home Loan Bank Board is pledging $2 billion to shore up the American Savings and Loan Association of Stockton, California. The $3 billion bank is the largest insolvent savings and loan operation in the country. The board is selling the bank to a Fort Worth group headed by Robert M. Bass that will pump in $550 million in cash. The most expensive overall rescue effort took place last month, when the board gave $3.5 billion to eight Texas banks that were being combined.

Mandela leaves jail for hospital stay

Sept 1. Nelson Mandela, the imprisoned black nationalist leader in South Africa, was moved last month from Pollsmoor Prison to Tygerburg Hospital to recuperate from tuberculosis. Today, the Pretoria government said that the 70-year-old anti-apartheid leader is to be relocated to a private clinic in Cape Town. The announcement heightened speculation that Mandela may soon be freed, although there has not been any word on this from the government. Mandela has been in prison for 26 years for his role as leader of the outlawed African National Congress (→ 10/19).

U.S. spy satellite fails to gain orbit

Sept 3. A military spy satellite launched yesterday from Cape Canaveral has failed to achieve a successful orbit, informed sources report. The satellite was supposed to be propelled into an orbit 22,300 miles high, which would allow it to hover over the Soviet Union. But the failure of the upper stage of the Titan 34D rocket has rendered the satellite virtually useless. The failure of the mission has left the United States dependent on old, deteriorating satellites to monitor Soviet electronic communications (→ 16).

Steffi Graf wins tennis Grand Slam

Sept 10. For the first time in 18 years, a Grand Slam winner has emerged in women's tennis. Steffi Graf, a 19-year-old West German, added the United States Open to her collection of the Australian and French Opens and Wimbledon to join Maureen Connolly and Margaret Court in the select society of Grand Slam winners. Steffi put away Gabriela Sabatini of Argentina in the U.S. final, 6-3, 3-6, 6-1, and collected $275,000 in prize money as well as a bracelet with four diamonds, one for each Grand Slam event. Graf won more than $1 million in 1988 even before her victory in the U.S. Open.

At 19 years of age, West Germany's Steffi Graf, whose father is her coach, joins the elite of tennis.

Canadian natives get Texas-size area

Sept 5. After a decade of negotiations, Canadian non-whites finally have some land they can call their own. Canada has given the 39,000 Eskimos, Indians and mixed indigenes 260,000 square miles, a plot about the size of Texas and 7 percent of Canada's total area. The agreement, involving the biggest land transfer since the Alaska and Louisiana purchases, also calls for substantial cash settlements. Said an Indian leader: "Once we have our own land, we can make a start on regaining our dignity."

Su	Mo	Tu	We	Th	Fr	Sa
				1	2	3
4	5	6	7	8	9	10
11	12	13	14	15	16	17
18	19	20	21	22	23	24
25	26	27	28	29	30	

11. Flushing Meadows, New York: Mats Wilander defeats Ivan Lendl 6-4, 4-6, 6-3, 5-7, 6-4 to dethrone three-time U.S. Open champ and take top tennis spot in world.

12. Washington: H.R. Haldeman reveals Watergate tapes were made with voice-activated machines only because Nixon was inept with technology; Haldeman was afraid he would forget to turn them on.

12. Washington: Surgeon General's office asks for broad radon testing in homes, calling it major cancer threat.

12. Holland: Dutch virologist Albert Osterhaus finds cause of death of 11,000 seals since April to be same virus that causes distemper in dogs.

12. Washington: Government report says that enrollment in college humanities courses has fallen sharply in the last 20 years due to commercialization of culture.

13. Washington: Congressional report says C.I.A. propaganda campaign on Latin American policy went beyond legal and ethical authority (→ 14).

13. Washington: Reagan, in reversal, says United States will pay some of nearly $600 million owed to United Nations.

14. Washington: F.B.I. disciplines six for unethical surveillance of groups opposing U.S. policy in Central America (→ 20).

15. United States: MasterCard putting out first credit card that features a person, Elvis Presley. A brochure says, "Give your autograph to Elvis. Become part of the legend."

15. Zimbabwe: Hunger Project awards prize to Prime Minister Robert Mugabe for turning Zimbabwe into the "agricultural success story" of Africa.

16. Moscow: Gorbachev offers disputed radar station in Siberia for international use in space exploration (→ 10/5).

DEATH

17. William P. Chrysler, prominent art collector, son of auto tycoon (*5/27/1909).

Gilbert: Fiercest storm of the century

Gilbert is not a welcome tourist in the tropical paradise of Jamaica. The hurricane's destructive power left more than 500,000 persons homeless.

Mexico, which has enough problems, sees the storm destroy everything in sight.

Gilbert's trip across the border to Texas did not go exactly unnoticed.

Sept 17. Hurricane Gilbert seems to be running out of wind in the mountains of northern Mexico after having torn a destructive path through Jamaica and Mexico's Yucatan Peninsula. Packing winds up to 218 miles an hour and churning up 23-foot waves, it is the strongest hurricane to hit the Western Hemisphere in this century. The secret of Gilbert's ferocity lies in its compressed size. The eye of a typical hurricane is 20 to 25 miles in diameter, but this hurricane's eye is only eight miles wide. Its energy is thus highly concentrated, and meteorologists have likened it to a monster tornado. But because it is much bigger than a tornado, its deadly swath is about 50 miles wide, with winds generated some 250 miles from its center.

The hurricane hit Jamaica hard, especially its southern coast, washing away roads and docks, willfully plucking up trees, tearing down power and telephone lines and leaving 80 percent of the homes without roofs. More than 500,000 Jamaicans have been left homeless, with property damage put at over $500 million, and the banana and poultry industries virtually wiped out. Of the 36 people killed in the hurricane thus far, 25 were Jamaicans — most by drowning. International relief agencies have begun flying in food, water and plastic sheets to serve as temporary roofing. Although the physical damage in the Yucatan Peninsula was of a similar nature, Mexican authorities had been forewarned and thus were able to evacuate 100,000 people and prepare plans for the possible transfer of 250,000 more from the northern area in the path of the storm.

As Gilbert headed to its demise in Mexico, southern Texas could breathe a deep sigh of relief. Shops in downtown Brownsville had been boarded up with plywood and tape, and Galveston had approved an emergency measure against scalping after prices for bottled water and plywood shot up 300 percent. The hemisphere's worst storm toll of the century was reported at Galveston in 1900, when 6,000 people were killed. More recently, Hurricane Camille took 256 lives in 1969 when it struck the coasts of Louisiana and Mississippi.

orst of drought ...s passed in U.S.

Sept 12. This summer's drought started to ease, and its effect on ...d prices and farm income will be as bad as feared, the Agricul- e Department said today. But department's experts said crops ...l be down substantially, with ...n 37 percent lower than last ...ar, soybeans down 23 percent and ...eat off 14 percent. Although ... drought is the fourth worst ... record, the department says that ...ge crop yields in other countries, ...cluding France, India and Aus- ...lia, will cushion the effect on the ...ice of food. Farmers who have ...cks of grain will benefit from ...gher prices, the experts say.

ennon biography ttacked, defended

Sept 11. John Lennon, enigmatic ... life, is proving equally elusive ...ght years after his assassination. ... new biography, "The Lives of ...hn Lennon," by Albert Gold- ...an, has been challenged for fac- ...al errors and assailed because of ... lurid depiction of a self-ob- ...essed, violent drug addict. But ...oldman stands by the book, and ... it moves up on the best-seller ...sts fans who revere the ex-Beatle ...r his timeless music are left to sort ...rough a conflicting legacy.

"Apple Pickers" (1937) by Nicolai Cikovsky, from the exhibit "Special Delivery: Murals for the New Deal Era" at Smithsonian's National Museum of American Art.

Seoul Olympics open; spoilers are foiled

Seoul, Korea: Unfortunately, that is not the Olympic torch he's carrying.

Sept 17. Despite threats of terrorist violence, the Olympic Games got off to a peaceful and colorful start in the venerable city of Seoul. With the demilitarized zone just a short drive away and soldiers everywhere, the Olympic spirit of peace prevailed over a schism of hostility that separates South and North Korea. There was an effort by a small group of radical students to block the progress of the Olympic torchbearers through the 600-year-old metropolis, but riot policemen thwarted that threat. One student told of a plan to throw gasoline bombs over the campus wall, but he said police stormed the grounds and forestalled the attack. Some of the riot policemen were said to have suffered burns.

Generally, the students have limited their demonstrations to the campus because they know how eager South Korea is to win the acclaim of the outside world. Demonstrators fear that North and South Korea will be driven further apart because they are not co-hosts of the Games. Meanwhile, Seoul blossomed amid flowers planted along sidewalks and in parks. The Koreans were pleased that the opening ceremonies went off without a hitch, but there was some grumbling over the behavior of American athletes as they took part in the parade into the stadium (→ 24).

Consumers dislike gabby appliances

Sept 17. It is the rare American who hasn't aimed an occasional tongue-lashing at an imperfect car or appliance. But as for machines that talk back, the consumer has spoken again, and the answer is a decided "No!" The loquacious products, from cameras that expound on lighting to washers that proclaim "rinse cycle over" to autos that nag drivers to buckle up, were until recently expected to be the wave of the future. But market researchers have found that though technology may dominate modern life, people have strong reactions against the machines actually telling them what to do.

Gorbachev quizzed by critics in public

Sept 12. The Soviet news program Vremya made news itself by broadcasting an unusually frank encounter between the Soviet leader Mikhail S. Gorbachev and some residents of the Siberian city of Krasnoyarsk. "Go to our stores, Mikhail Sergeyevich, there is nothing there!" one woman shouted. Others complained about housing shortages and high prices. Gorbachev responded calmly to the heckling. "I get your meaning and I know what you're talking about," he said. The broadcast was apparently intended to show Soviet citizens that Gorbachev is aware of their concerns (→ 20).

Mice receive human immune defenses

Sept 14. Separate teams of research scientists at Stanford University and the Medical Biology Institute, an independent research center in La Jolla, California, have succeeded in transplanting the human immune system into living mice. The experiments have been called "remarkable" and "incredible" and, according to leading researchers, will have important applications in the study of AIDS and leukemia, and the testing of vaccines.

Rich tomb of treasures is found in Peru

Sept 13. Archeologists today described the discovery of a pre-Columbian tomb they say contains riches that are comparable to those of King Tutankhamen in Egypt. The 1,500-year-old tomb was excavated 420 miles northwest of Lima by a Peruvian archeological team. It contains the remnants of a warrior-priest of the Moche people, his wives and servants and a dog. The hundreds of objects found in the tomb include a gold face mask, large gold and silver beads in the shape of peanuts and a two-pound gold shield. Said Dr. Christopher B. Donnan of UCLA: "This is the richest tomb ever excavated archeologically in the Western Hemisphere."

Ancient Peruvian statuette.

SEPTEMBER
Week 37 1988

Su	Mo	Tu	We	Th	Fr	Sa
				1	2	3
4	5	6	7	8	9	10
11	12	13	14	15	16	17
18	19	20	21	22	23	24
25	26	27	28	29	30	

18. Baltimore: Federal judge rules in favor of McDonald's, ordering Quality Inns to stop using name "McSleep Inns" for new hotel chain.

19. Jerusalem: Inaugurating space program, Israel launches satellite, raising fears among Arab nations that they will use it for spying (→ 10/5).

20. Moscow: Soviets say new voting rules have created much higher rate of turnover among local officials (→ 30).

20. Fort Worth: In what is believed to be the first conviction of its kind, David Gene Burleson is found guilty of harmful access to computer in which he planted a virus (→ 11/4).

20. Washington: Speaker of House Jim Wright says C.I.A. men have admitted agitating in Nicaragua to provoke government retaliation.

20. New York City: Dante Caputo, Argentine foreign minister, elected President of 43rd U.N. General Assembly.

21. El Salvador: Government troops kill 10 as suspected leftist guerrillas.

21. Yellowstone National Park, Wyoming: Reports indicate park officials kept firefighters from combatting blaze in attempt to protect nature from bulldozers and fire engines (→ 10/21).

21. Shreveport, Louisiana: Hundreds of blacks riot after black bystander is killed by white woman in drug-related argument (→ 10/25).

22. Washington: Environmental Protection Agency issues new guidelines to deal with "staggering" garbage crisis.

23. Washington: Michael Deaver given suspended sentence and fined $100,000 for perjury during ethics trial.

24. Santiago: Hortensia Bussi, Salvador Allende's widow, returns after 15 years in exile (→ 10/6).

DEATH

18. Burton Benjamin, former CBS News producer (*10/9/1917).

Soviet troops subdue ethnic conflict

Armenians raise a nationalist flag.

Heavy armor is rolled out to bring the demonstrators back into line.

Sept 22. Soviet leader Mikhail S. Gorbachev has sent troops to Yerevan, capital of the Soviet Republic of Armenia, in an effort to contain an outbreak of religious and ethnic unrest that is threatening the future of his policy of political openness.

The deployment of troops followed by one day the declaration of a state of emergency in the nearby Nagorno-Karabakh territory and was regarded as an admission by Gorbachev that he had lost control of a spreading nationalist protest that was in large measure inspired by his relaxation of restrictions on political discussions. A new nationalist demonstration took place in the republic of Georgia yesterday, adding to the fears of the Kremlin that the violence in Armenia will ignite other nationalist protests.

At the heart of the dispute is a disagreement about control over the mountainous and remote territory of Nagorno-Karabakh, which is now under the control of the predominantly Moslem republic of Azerbaijan even though its citizens are three-quarters Armenian and for the most part Christian. In February, the territory petitioned the government in Moscow, asking that it be transferred from Azerbaijan and annexed to Armenia. But Moscow refused the request in July.

Two days ago, there was a shootout between the two groups in village near Stepankert, the capit of Nagorno-Karabakh. More tha 50 people were injured and one wa killed, This was the first occasio that either side had resorted t weapons. Widespread protests an rioting followed in Nagorno-Kara bakh, with beatings, looting and ar son. In Armenia, hundreds of thou sands of people walked off thei jobs to take part in the protests. I was at this point that the troop were sent in by Gorbachev (→ 10/9)

Soviet vodka limit is (hic!) raised

Sept 19. Soviet-style prohibition is coming to an end. Three years after having imposed curbs on alcohol consumption in an effort to improve the productivity of workers, Soviet leader Mikhail S. Gorbachev has reversed himself and is allowing an increase in the production of vodka, wine and champagne. Any policy that aims at discouraging the Russians from drinking vodka is bound to prove unpopular. But Gorbachev's policy also had some unintended side effects. For one thing, in 1987 the state lost some 20 billion rubles in income from liquor sales. For another, the rise in moonshine production has resulted in a sugar shortage.

Has the West finally won the Cold War?

Nikita Khrushchev once threatened that communism would bury capitalism. But the new Communist leaders appear more concerned with imitating than destroying their capitalist competitors, leading some observers, including England's Margaret Thatcher, to speculate that the West has won the Cold War. If so, no weapon has proved more deadly in that 40-year competition of ideologies than the sight of the prosperity among capitalist economies compared to the poverty among Marxist ones.

From the Soviet Union to China, with a host of smaller countries in between, socialist leaders are seeking to adapt capitalism to their own societies. Soviet leader Mikhail S. Gorbachev has warned his countrymen that the economy must be reformed if the Soviet Union is to remain a superpower.

Gorbachev's reforms have won the support of many Americans and relations between the superpowers are as good as they have been since World War II. Some 64 percent of Americans surveyed in October 1987 supported a policy of trying harder to reduce tensions with the Russians. But the good feeling could come to an abrupt end. An escalation of ethnic revolts within the Soviet Union or unrest in its Eastern European satellites could force a clampdown. "An empire on the skids can be tempted to take actions out of desperation," warns Richart Burt, U.S. Ambassador to West Germany (→ 10/18).

Johnson, Canadian star, sets dash record

Heavily muscled Ben Johnson, the fastest man in the world.

stitches, scored well on his difficult two final dives.

There was little hope, however, that the Americans would even come close to the Soviet Union in the total medal count at the Games in Korea. Even the United States coach, Mike Jacki, had to acknowledge that the Russians may have fielded "one of the finest sports teams of all time out there, and I'm not talking just about gymnastics." The gymnastic performances by the Russians included seven perfect scores of 10. The American boxing team proved surprisingly strong, collecting eight medals, three of them gold. There had been dire predictions that the squad would prove far inferior to the 1984 team, which won a record nine golds (→ 30).

Sept. 24. Ben Johnson lived up to his reputation as "the fastest man in the world," winning the Olympic 100-meter dash in the record time of 9.79 seconds. The Canadian star outran his arch-rival, Carl Lewis, who set an American record with his time of 9.92 seconds. Johnson had finished third to Lewis in the 1984 Games at Los Angeles.

The defeat of Lewis was another blow to American medal hopes that earlier had been buoyed by the inspiring performance of Greg Louganis in Olympic diving. After a jarring accident in which his head struck the springboard, Louganis came back to capture the three-meter competition. The American diver, his cut closed with temporary

Injured Louganis prepares to dive.

Burmese army in power, quells opposition

With the military in power, it could be a long time before new street demonstrations, like the ones that were broken up, erupt once again in Rangoon.

Sept. 19. The Burmese military has taken over the recently installed civilian government, prohibited all street demonstrations and ordered workers to return to their jobs. All speech-making and the chanting of slogans by more than five people have also been prohibited and a nighttime curfew has been put into effect following six weeks of anti-government demonstrations.

However, thousands of Burmese continue to resist the army's power and have been setting up roadblocks and been protesting in the streets of Rangoon. Today the government reported 23 people dead, but there are some diplomats who estimate that the death toll is probably closer to 100.

The military, which has always

been closely associated with the ruling party, is operating under General Saw Maung, a hard-liner and a close ally of Ne Win, who stepped down as head of the government in July but is believed to continue in control. In radio broadcasts, the military said that it has taken over to restore order and to conduct elections. However, the protesters say they will reject the election proposal unless the present leaders permit the installation of a neutral interim government.

Hundreds of soldiers have defected from the military and have joined in the demonstrations. Students and Buddhist monks are regularly found among the protesters found shot dead. But so are many innocent bystanders.

Los Angeles cops jail 870 in street brawls

Sept. 18. A bloody, real-life version of "West Side Story" has endangered the streets of Los Angeles. But the authorities are fighting back. Police in the metropolitan area swept through many neighborhoods this weekend, arresting 870 people, many of them suspected gang members. The arrests are aimed at bringing a halt to the widespread violence that has overwhelmed city residents. Some 380 police officers combed the city, bringing in droves of suspects on a variety of charges. According to Larry Mazur, a Los Angeles police sergeant, officers issued tickets to hundreds of drivers for traffic in-

fractions and confiscated 66 autos, eight guns, marijuana, cocaine, heroin and other contraband.

Despite the roundup, brutal gang violence has continued. Today, a shotgun blast, delivered from a passing car, killed one man and seriously wounded another in the San Fernando Valley. In another incident, gunfire from a speeding vehicle injured two gang members and an innocent bystander.

In Burbank, a spree of drive-by shootings at a hamburger stand prompted a police stakeout. Police have arrested two reputed gang members in connection with one of the recent attacks there.

Haitian army installs general as President

Sept. 18. Lieutenant General Prosper Avril has been appointed President of Haiti after a coup led by non-commissioned army officers. Lieutenant General Henri Namphy was deposed and headed for the neighboring Dominican Republic, where he has been granted asylum. The leaders of the coup are members of the nation's Presidential Guard, which had helped General Namphy to take power in June from President Leslie F. Manigat, who was the victor in the national election in January. General Avril held important positions during the long years of dictatorship under the Duvalier family.

Lieutenant General Prosper Avril.

Su	Mo	Tu	We	Th	Fr	Sa
				1	2	3
4	5	6	7	8	9	10
11	12	13	14	15	16	17
18	19	20	21	22	23	24
25	26	27	28	29	30	

26. Washington: House-Senate conference agrees on compromise revision of welfare system, first in 53 years.

26. Nashville: The Rev. John David Terry sentenced to death for killing a church handyman, beheading him and setting fire to church.

27. Washington: Lieut. Gen. James A. Abrahamson resigns as head of S.D.I. research to allow fresh approach by new administration (→ 10/6).

27. Niagara Falls, New York: State health commissioner says half of area cleaned up around Love Canal 10 years ago is now safe.

28. Washington: President Reagan vetoes bill limiting textile imports (→ 10/4).

28. Miami: Four convicted on charges of smuggling 243 birds of endangered species into the United States.

29. Seoul: High Olympic official suggests banning weight-lifting after four medal winners are ousted for drug use (→ 30).

29. Washington: Carl T. Rowan, columnist on trial for gun possession, gets mistrial as jury cannot decide.

30. Rome: Pope, in major document on women, defends their right to pursue identity as mothers or virgins, rejects demands for greater church role.

30. Texas: Federal district judge finds F.B.I. guilty of discrimination against Hispanic agents.

30. New York City: Ann Green acquitted of murdering two of her children on grounds she was temporarily insane due to postpartum depression.

DEATHS

25. Billy Carter, 51, brother of ex-President (*3/29/1937).

29. Charles Addams, macabre cartoonist who worked for New Yorker for five decades, at 76 (*1/7/1912).

29. Barney Josephson, owner of Cafe Society jazz club who discovered Billie Holliday (*1902).

American space shuttle flies again

Sept. 29. The space shuttle Discovery was launched successfully from Cape Canaveral today, ending a 32-month shutdown that followed the Challenger disaster of 1986.

Carrying a crew of five, Discovery lifted off at 11:37 a.m., an hour and 38 minutes later than scheduled, watched by an estimated one million spectators on beaches and roads. The delay was caused by unusually light upper-atmosphere winds, which Discovery's computer programs were not designed to handle. The issue was resolved by a quick decision to change the definition of "acceptable" winds.

"I think I had my fingers crossed like everyone else," President Reagan said. Tension in the firing control room reached a peak at the 73-second mark, the moment when Challenger had exploded, then turned into joyous relief as Discovery went into orbit. The solid booster rockets whose malfunction caused the Challenger disaster worked perfectly, and all other major systems were operating well.

Six hours into the flight, the crew successfully released a $100-million communications satellite that was Challenger's main payload. The astronauts, Richard O. Covey, John M. Lounge, Frederick H. Hauck, David C. Hilmers and George D. Nellson, will spend the rest of the three-day flight doing experiments. "This is the first step of a new era," NASA administrator James Fletcher told the astronauts (→ 10/2).

Successful launch of Discovery sends national spirits soaring into space.

The first Americans in space since the Challenger disaster of January 1986.

Pioneer is beatified

Sept. 25. Before a crowd of about 30,000, Pope John Paul II beatified six people, including the Rev. Junipero Serra, an 18th-century missionary and a pioneer of the American West. "His great goal," the Pope said of Serra, "was to bring the Gospel to the native people of America, so that they, too, might be consecrated in the truth." Some people have criticized the beatification, saying that Serra was involved in forcing Native Americans into labor or flogging them if they disputed church dogma. Beatification means that the missionary may now be the object of public prayer and may become a saint.

Grand jury says girl made up rape story

Sept 26. Evidence produced during a seven-month investigation by a New York State grand jury seems to indicate that Tawana Brawley fabricated her story of racism and sexual abuse. Testimony from more than a hundred witnesses, and confidential medical and police reports, have led the grand jury to the conclusion that during her four-day disappearance, Miss Brawley was hiding out in a vacant apartment from which her family had recently been evicted. The investigators say that Miss Brawley, alone or with an accomplice, arranged the shocking condition in which she was found by smearing on dog feces, burning and tearing her clothing, inscribing "KKK" and other racial slurs on her clothing and body and crawling inside a plastic garbage bag. The grand jury also believes that she faked the apparently traumatized behavior that she exhibited during several interviews, refusing to speak or responding to questions monosyllabically.

Tawana Brawley's motives remain unknown to the grand jury since she has, at the advice of her counsel, refused to testify. Her lawyers have charged the state with a cover-up and have accused state officials of crimes, although they have not provided evidence (→ 10/6).

Tested for drugs, Johnson loses gold medal

Sept. 30. Ben Johnson, who was toasted only a few days ago as the fastest human in the world, is on his way back to Canada stripped of his gold medal for having used an anabolic steroid in the Olympics. Johnson's medal was taken away from him and awarded to the second-place finisher, Carl Lewis of the United States. "This is a tragedy, a mistake or a sabotage," said Larry Heidebrecht, Johnson's manager. The Canadian was the seventh and most prominent athlete to fail the Olympic drug test. Lewis, who had earlier suggested Johnson might be on steroids, would not comment except to say that "if there is an incident, I am deeply sorry."

There was no controversy surrounding the magnificent accomplishments of the Joyner family. The 200-meter dash went to Florence Griffith Joyner, who broke the world record twice en route. She won three gold medals and one silver. Her sister-in-law, Jackie Joyner-Kersee, took the grueling heptathlon and went on to win her favorite event, the long jump.

On the negative side for the United States was its crushing defeat in basketball. For only the second time in Olympic history, an American squad failed to win the tournament. The Soviet Union outplayed the United States in every phase and won by 82-76. The biggest individual winner in the Olympics at Seoul was Kristin Otto, the East German swimming star who captured six gold medals (→ 10/2).

Several U.S. nuclear accidents covered up

Sept. 30. Serious accidents at the Savannah River nuclear-reactor facility that produces plutonium for weapons have been covered up for three decades, congressional investigators revealed today. Physicists said the accidents were among the most dangerous ever reported at American nuclear plants.

Memos describing the accidents were released today at a joint hearing of House and Senate committees. One mishap was a fuel-rod meltdown in one of the South Carolina facility's five reactors in December 1970, when operators mistakenly tried to start up the reactor three times after a shutdown because of a cooling-water shortage. Another incident almost led to a runaway chain reaction in January 1960 when operators removed safety units to restart a reactor after it shut down automatically. A similar incident occurred at the Savannah River facility last August.

The Energy Department, which is responsible for Savannah River, denied it was told of the accidents by the plant's operator, E. I. du Pont de Nemours. The department faces the issue of whether to close the plant, now the only source of nuclear weapons material (→ 10/26).

Presidential rivals clash in first debate

Sept. 25. There were taunts and jeers as the two men running for President debated a broad range of social and foreign policy issues in their first face-to-face meeting of the election campaign.

Appearing before a panel of reporters in this first of two debates, held on the Wake Forest University campus in North Carolina, Vice President Bush and his Democratic foe, Governor Michael Dukakis, clashed angrily over who has the experience to run the nation.

Calling Dukakis "the ice man," a reference to the Governor's reputation for being a passionless technocrat, Bush accused him of espousing liberal policies. Dukakis, in turn, called Bush the inheritor of an uncaring administration and a man whose judgment was flawed when it came to such issues as abortion, health care, defense, drug smuggling and how to deal with the Iran-contra affair.

The tensest exchange came when Bush attacked Dukakis as "a card-carrying member" of the American Civil Liberties Union. "I'm not questioning his patriotism," said Bush. "I'm questioning his judgment." An angry Dukakis replied that Bush was indeed questioning his patriotism and said: "I resent it. I love this country" (→ 10/4).

Five Soviet leaders fired

Gorbachev's reforms have now penetrated the highest levels of Soviet society.

Sept. 30. The Soviet Politburo has a new look today following a major shakeup. Gone are four of its oldest members, most of them critics of Soviet leader Mikhail S. Gorbachev's reforms. In their place are three men and one woman whose presence lowers the average age of the Politburo from 71 to 58. With his own people now in dominant positions, Gorbachev's power is considerably strengthened.

The Politburo reshuffling was carried out during an hour-long meeting of the Communist Party's Central Committee. This session was called so urgently that many of its members had to rush back from abroad, giving some Russians the impression that Gorbachev was going to be removed.

In another action, the Central Committee accepted the retirement from the Politburo of Andrei A. Gromyko, the nation's President and a fixture on the Soviet scene for the last half century. In addition, the committee removed the former Soviet envoy to the U.S., Anatoly Dobrynin, from his position as secretary to the Central Committee. And the committee decided to draft plans for a reorganization of the party apparatus (→ 10/1).

U.N. peacekeeping forces win Nobel Prize

Sept. 29. For 40 years, United Nations peacekeeping troops have been dispatched to trouble spots around the world to relieve tensions. Today, their efforts were applauded with the award of the Nobel Peace Prize. The Nobel Committee said the troops "represent the manifest will of the community of nations to achieve peace through negotiations and the forces, by their presence, made a decisive contribution toward the initiation of actual peace negotiations." U.N. troops are now positioned in Lebanon, the Sinai, Cyprus, the Golan Heights and the Iran-Iraq and Afghan-Soviet borders. As the U.N. enters its fifth decade, the award provides a boost to the often-criticized institution (→ 10/13).

With a little help, peace is gaining a toehold in many war-torn regions.

1988 Seoul

Men Athletics

100 M Dash
1. Carl Lewis USA 9.92
2. Linford Christie GBR 9.97
3. Calvin Smith USA 9.99

200 M Dash
1. Joe DeLoach USA 19.75
2. Carl Lewis USA 19.79
3. Robson Da Silva BRA 20.04

400 M Dash
1. Steven Lewis USA 43.87
2. Butch Reynol USA 43.93
3. Danny Everett USA 44.09

800 M Run
1. Paul Ereng KEN 1:43.45
2. Joaquim Cruz BRA 1:43.90
3. Said Aouita MOR 1:44.06

1,500 M Run
1. Peter Rono KEN 3:35.96
2. Peter Elliott GBR 3:36.15
3. Jens-Peter Herold GDR 3:36.21

5,000 M Run
1. John Ngugi KEN 13:11.70
2. Dieter Baumann FRG 13:15.52
3. Hans Joerg Kunze GDR 13:15.73

10,000 M Run
1. M. Brahim Boutaieb MOR 27:21.46
2. Salvatore Antibo ITA 27:23.55
3. Kipkemboi Kimeli KEN 27:25.16

3,000 M Steeplechase
1. Julius Kariuki KEN 8:05.51
2. Peter Koech KEN 8:06.79
3. Mark Rowland GBR 8:07.96

110 M Hurdles
1. Roger Kingdom USA 12.99
2. Colin Jackson GBR 13.28
3. Tony Campbell USA 13.38

400 M Hurdles
1. Andre Phillips USA 47.19
2. El Hadj Dia Ba SEN 47.23
3. Edwin Moses USA 47.56

High Jump
1. Guennadi Adveienko URS 2.38 M
2. Hollis Conway USA 2.36 M
3. Rudolf Povarnitsine URS 2.36 M
Patrick Sjoeberg SWE 2.36 M

Long Jump
1. Carl Lewis USA 8.72 M
2. Mike Powell USA 8.49 M
3. Larry Myricks USA 8.27 M

Pole Vault
1. Serguei Bubka URS 5.90 M
2. Rodion Gatauline URS 5.85 M
3. Grigori Yevgorov URS 5.80 M

Triple Jump
1. Christo Markov BUL 17.61 M
2. Igor Lapchine URS 17.52 M
3. Alexandre Kovalenko URS 17.42 M

Shotput
1. Ulf Timmermann GDR 22.47 M
2. Randy Barnes USA 22.39 M
3. Werner Gunthoer SUI 21.99 M

Discus Throw
1. Jurgen Schult GDR 68.82 M
2. Romas Ubartas URS 67.48 M
3. Rolf Danneberg FRG 67.38 M

Hammer Throw
1. Serguei Litvinov URS 84.80 M
2. Youri Sedykh URS 83.76 M
3. Youri Tamn URS 81.16 M

Javelin
1. Tapio Korjus FIN 84.28 M
2. Jan Zelezny TCH 84.12 M
3. Seppo Raty FIN 83.26 M

Marathon
1. Gelindo Bordin ITA 2:10:32
2. Douglas Wakihuru KEN 2:10:47
3. Ahmed Salah DJI 2:10:59

Decathlon
1. Christian Schenk GDR 8,488 pts
2. Torsten Voss GDR 8,399 pts
3. Dave Steen CAN 8,328 pts

400 M Relay
1. URS 38.19 (Bryzguin, Krylov, Mouraziev, Savin)
2. GBR 38.28 (Bunney, Regis, McFarlane, Christie)
3. FRA 38.40 (Marie-Rose, Sangouma, Quenerhve, Moniniere)

1,600 M Relay
1. USA 2:58.16 (Everett, S. Lewis, Robinzine, Reynolds)
2. JAM 3:00.30 (Davis, Morris, Graham, Cameron)
3. FRG 3:00.56 (Dobeleit, Itt, Vaihinger, Luebke)

20 km walk
1. Jozef Pribilinec TCH 1:19:57
2. Ronald Weigel GDR 1:20:00
3. Maurizio Damilano ITA 1:20:14

50 km walk
1. Vlasheslav Ivanenko URS 3:38:29
2. Ronald Weigel GDR 3:38:56
3. Hartwig Gauder GDR 3:39:45

Women Athletics

100 M Dash
1. Florence Griffith Joyner USA 10.54
2. Evelyne Ashford USA 10.83
3. Heike Drechsler GDR 10.85

200 M Dash
1. Florence Griffith Joyner USA 21.34 (world rec.; prev. rec. 21.71 by Koch and by Drechsler)
2. Grace Jackson JAM 21.72
3. Heike Drechsler GDR 21.95

400 M Run
1. Olga Brysguina URS 48.65
2. Petra Mueller GDR 49.45
3. Olga Nazarova URS 49.90

800 M Run
1. Sigrun Wodars GDR 1:56.10
2. Christine Wachtel GDR 1:56.64
3. Kim Gallagher USA 1:56.91

1,500 M Run
1. Paula Ivan ROM 3:53.96
2. Lailoute Baikauskaite URS 4:00.20
3. Tatiana Samoilenko URS 4:00.24

3,000 M Run
1. Tatiana Samoilenko URS 8:26.53
2. Paula Ivan ROM 8:27.15
3. Yvonne Murray GBR 8:29.02

10,000 M Run
1. Olga Bondarenko URS 31:05.21
2. Elizabeth McColgan GBR 31:08.34
3. Helena Joupieva URS 31:19.82

100 M Hurdles
1. Jordanka Donkova BUL 12.38
2. Gloria Siebert GDR 12.61
3. Claudia Zaskiewicz FRG 12.75

400 M Hurdles
1. Debbie Flintoff-King AUS 53.17
2. Tatiana Ledovskaia URS 53.18
3. Helen Fiedler GDR 53.84

High Jump
1. Louise Ritter USA 2.03 M
2. Stefka Kostadinova BUL 2.01 M
3. Tamara Bykova URS 1.99 M

The Olympic flame.

Long Jump
1. Jackie Joyner-Kersee USA 7.40 M
2. Heike Drechsler GDR 7.22 M
3. Galina Tchistyakova URS 7.11 M

Shotput
1. Natalia Lissovskaia URS 22.24 M
2. Kathrin Neimke GDR 21.07 M
3. Meisu-li CHN 21.06 M

Discus Throw
1. Martina Hellman GDR 72.30 M
2. Diana Gansky GDR 71.88 M
3. Tzvetanka Hristova BUL 69.74 M

Javelin
1. Petra Felke GDR 74.68 M
2. Fatima Whitbread GBR 70.32 M
3. Beate Koch GDR 67.30 M

400 M Relay
1. USA 41.98 (Brown, Echols, Griffith Joyner, Ashford)
2. GDR 42.09 (Moller, Behrendt, Lange, Gohr)
3. URS 42.75 (Kondratieva, Maltschugina, Jirova, Pomochtchnikova)

1,600 M Relay
1. URS 3:15.18 World rec.; prev. rec. 3:15.92 (Ledovskaia, Nazarov, Piniguina, Bryzguina)
2. USA 3:15.51 (Howard, Dixon, Brisco, Griffith Joyner)
3. GDR 3:18.29 (Neubauer, Emmelmann, Busch, Muller)

Heptathlon
1. Jackie Joyner-Kersee USA 7,291 pts (World rec.; own prev. rec. 7,215 pts)
2. Sabine John GDR 6,897 pts
3. Anke Behmer GDR 6,858 pts

Marathon
1. Rosa Mota POR 2:25:40
2. Lisa Martin NZL 2:25:53
3. Kathrin Doerre GDR 2:26:21

Men Rowing

Single Scull
1. Thomas Lange GDR 6:49.86
2. Peter-Michael Kolbe FRG 6:54.77
3. Eric Verdonck NZL 6:58.66

Pair Oars with Coxswain
1. G. Abbagnale, C. Abbagnale ITA 6:58.79
2. M. Streit, D. Kirch GDR 7:00.63
3. S. Redgrave, A. Holme GBR 7:01.95

Double scull
1. R. Florijn, N. Rienks HOL 6:21.13
2. B. Schwerzmann, U. Bodenmann GDR 6:22.59
3. A. Martchenko, V. Iakoucha URS 6:22.87

Pair Oars without Coxswain
1. A. Holmes, S. Redgrave GBR 6:36.94
2. D. Neagu, D. Dobre ROM 6:38.06
3. B. Presern, S. Mujkic YUG 6:41.01

Four Oars with Coxswain
1. GDR 6:10.74 (K. Schmeling, B. Niezecke, B. Eichwurzel, F. Flawonn)
2. ROM 6:13.58 (V. Tomoiaga, V. Robu, I. Snep, D. Popescu)
3. NZL 6:15.78 (I. Whight, G. Johnston, C. White, G. Keys)

Quadruple Sculls with Coxswain
1. ITA 5:53.37 (A. Abbagnale, D. Tizzano, G. Farina, P. Poli)
2. NOR 5:55.08 (A. Hansen, R. Rhorsen, V. Vinjer, L. Bjonness)
3. GDR 5:56.13 (J. Koeppen, H. Habermann, S. Zuehlke, S. Bogs)

Quadruple Sculls without Coxswain
1. GDR 6:03.11 (O. Foerster, R. Brudel, T. Greiner, R. Schroeder)
2. USA 6:05.53 (R. Kennelly, D. Krmpotich, T. Bohrer, R. Rodriguez)
3. FRG 6:06.22 (V. Grabow, J. Puttlitz, G. Grabow, N. Kesslau)

Eight Oars
1. GDR 5:46.05 (T. Moellenkamp, M. Mellinghaus, E. Schultz, A. Wessling, A. Eichholz, T. Domian, W. Maennig, B. Rabe)
2. URS 5:48.01 (V. Bout, N. Komarov, V. Tikhanov, A. Doumtchev, P. Gourkovski, V. Didouk, V. Omelianovitch, A. Vassiliev)
3. USA 5:48.26 (M. Teti, J. Smith, T. Patton, J. Rusher, P. Nordell, J. McLaughlin, D. Burden, J. Pescatore)

Women Rowing

Single Scull
1. Jutta Behrendt GDR 7:47.19
2. Anne Marden USA 7:50.28
3. Magdalena Gueorguieva BUL 7:53.65

Pair Oars without Coxswain
1. O. Homeghi, R. Arba ROM 7:28.13
2. L. Berberova, R. Stoyanova BUL 7:31.95
3. L. Hannen, N. Payne NZL 7:35.68

Double scull
1. M. Schroeter, B. Peter GDR 7:00.48
2. V. Coeanu, E. Lipa ROM 7:04.36
3. S. Madina, V. Ninova BUL 7:06.03

Four Oars with Coxswain
1. GDR 6:56.00 (M. Walther, G. Doberschuetz, C. Hornig, B. Siech)
2. CHN 6:58.78 (S. Zhou, X. Yang, Y. Hu, X. Zhang)
3. ROM 7:01.13 (D.L. Balan, H. Anitas, V. Necula, M. Trasca)

Quadruple Sculls without Coxswain
1. GDR 6:21.06 (J. Sorgers, B. Schramm, K. Mundt, K. Foerster)
2. URS 6:23.47 (A. Doumtcheva, I. Frolova, S. Mazyi, I. Kalimbet)
3. ROM 6:23.81 (E. Lipa, V. Cogeanu, A. Minea, A. Balan)

Eight Oars
1. GDR 6:15.17 (A. Strauch, J. Zeidler, K. Haacker, U. Wild, A. Kluge, B. Schroer, R. Balthasar, U. Stange)
2. ROM 6:17.44 (D.L. Balan, M. Trasca, V. Necula, H. Anitas, A. Bazon, M. Armasescu, R. Arba, O. Homeghi)
3. CHN 6:21.83 (X. Zhou, Y. Zhang, Y. He, Y. Han, X. Zhang, S. Zhou, X. Yang)

Basketball

Men	Women
1. Soviet Union	1. United States
2. Yugoslavia	2. Yugoslavia
3. United States	3. Soviet Union

Boxing

48 kg
1. Ivailo Hristov BUL
2. Michael Carbajal USA
3. Robert Isaszegi HON
Leopoldo Serantes PHI

51 kg
1. Kwang-Sun Kim KOR
2. Andreas Tews GDR
3. Timofei Skriabin URS
Mario Gonzalez MEX

54 kg
1. Kennedy McKinney USA
2. Alexandar Hristov BUL
3. Phajol Moolsan THA
Jorge Julio Rocha COL

57 kg
1. Giovanni Parisi ITA
2. Daniel Dumitrescu ROM
3. Abdelhack Achik MOR
Lee Jae-huyk KOR

60 kg
1. Andreas Zuelow GDR
2. George Cramne SWE
3. Nerguy Enkhbat MGL
Romallis Ellis USA

63.5 kg
1. Viatcheslav Janovski URS
2. Graham Cheney AUS
3. Lars Myrberg SWE
Reiner Gies FRG

67 kg
1. Robert Wangila KEN
2. Laurent Boudouani FRA
3. Jan Dydak POL
Kenneth Gould USA

71 kg
1. Park Si-Hun KOR
2. Roy Jones USA
3. Raymond Downey CAN
Richard Woodhall GBR

75 kg
1. Henry Maske GDR
2. Egerton Marcus CAN
3. Chris Sande KEN
Hussain Shad Syed PAK

81 kg
1. Andrew Maynard USA
2. Nourmagomed Chanavazov URS
3. Henryk Petrich POL
Damir Skaro YUG

91 kg
1. Ray Mercer USA
2. Baik Hyun-Man KOR
3. Arnold Vanderlijde HOL
Andrzej Golota POL

Over 95 kg
1. Lennox Lewis CAN
2. Riddick Bowe USA
3. Janusz Zarenkiewicz POL
Alexandre Mirochnitchenko URS

Men Canoeing

Canadian-1 (500 M)
1. Olaf Heukrodt GDR 1:56.42
2. Mikhail Slivinskii URS 1:57.26
3. Martin Marinov BUL 1:57.27

Canadian-2 (500 M)
1. V. Reineski, N. Jouravski URS 1:41.77
2. M. Dopierala, M. Lbik POL 1:43.61
3. P. Renaud, J. Bettin FRA 1:43.81

Canadian-1 (1,000 M)
1. Ivan Klementiev URS 4:12.78
2. Joerg Schmidt GDR 4:15.83
3. Nikolai Boohlov BUL 4:18.94

Canadian-2 (1,000 M)
1. V. Reineski, N. Jouravski URS 3:48.36
2. O. Heukrodt, I. Spelly GDR 3:51.44
3. M. Dopierala, M. Lbik POL 3:54.33

Kayak-1 (500 M)
1. Zsolt Gyulay HUN 1:44.82
2. Andreas Staehle GDR 1:46.38
3. Paul McDonald NZL 1:46.46

Kayak-2 (500 M)
1. I. Ferguson, P. McDonald NZL 1:33.98
2. I. Nagaev, V. Denissov URS 1:34.15
3. A. Abraham, F. Csipes HUN 1:34.32

Kayak-1 (1,000 M)
1. Greg Barton USA 3:55.27
2. Grant Davies AUS 3:55.28
3. André Wohllebe GDR 3:55.55

Kayak-2 (1,000 M)
1. G. Barton, N. Bellingham USA 3:32.42
2. I. Ferguson, P. McDonald NZL 3:32.71
3. P. Foster, K. Graham AUS 3:33.76

Kayak-4 (1,000 M)
1. HUN 3:00.20 (Z. Gyulay, F. Csipes, S. Hodosi, A. Abraham)
2. URS 3:01.40 (A. Motouzenko, S. Kirsanov, I. Nagaev, V. Denissov)
3. GDR 3:02.37 (K. Bluhm, A. Wohllebe, A. Staehle, H.-J. Bliesener)

Women Canoeing

Kayak-1 (500 M)
1. Vania Guecheva BUL 1:55.19
2. Birgit Schmidt GDR 1:55.31
3. Izabella Dylewska POL 1:57.38

Kayak-2 (500 M)
1. B. Schmidt, A. Nothnagel GDR 1:43.46
2. V. Guecheva, D. Paliiska BUL 1:44.06
3. A. Derckx, A. Cox HOL 1:46.00

Kayak-4 (500 M)
1. GDR 1:40.78 (B. Schmidt, A. Nothnagel, R. Portwitch, H. Singer)
2. HUN 1:41.88 (E. Geczi, E. Meszaros, E. Rakusz, R. Koban)
3. BUL 1:42.63 (V. Guecheva, D. Paliiska, O. Petkova, B. Ivanova)

Men Cycling

100 km Team Time Trial
1. GDR 1:57:47 (U. Ampler, M. Kummer, M. Landsmann, J. Schur)
2. POL 1:57:54 (J. Halupczok, Z. Jaskula, M. Lesniewski, A. Sypytkovski)
3. SWE 1:59:47 (B. Johansson, J. Karlsson, M. Lafis, A. Jarl)

Team Pursuit
1. URS 4:13.31 (V. Ekimov, A. Kaspoutis, D. Melubine, G. Umaras)
2. GDR 4:14.09 (S. Blochwitz, R. Hennig, D. Meier, C. Wolf)
3. AUS 4:16.02 (B. Dutton, S. McGlede, W. McCarney, D. Woods)

Sprint
1. Lutz Hesslich GDR
2. Nikolai Kovch URS
3. Gary Neiwand AUS

1,000 M
1. Alexandre Kiritchenko GDR 1:04.499
2. Martin Vinnicombe AUS 1:04.784
3. Robert Lechner FRG 1:05.114

Individual Pursuit
1. Giantauras Umaras URS
2. Dean Woods AUS
3. Bernd Dittert GDR

30 km Points Race
1. Dean Frost DEN
2. Leo Peelen HOL
3. Marat Ganeev URS

Individual Road Race
1. Olaf Ludwig GDR 4:32:22
2. Bernd Groene FRG 4:32:25
3. Christian Henn FRG 4:32:46

Women Cycling

Sprint
1. Erika Salumiae URS
2. Christa Rothenburger-Luding GDR
3. Connie Paraskevin-Young USA

Individual Road Race
1. Monique Knol HOL 2:52:00
2. Jutta Niehaus FRG
3. Laina Zilporitie URS

Equestrian Sports

Grand Prix Jumping Individual
1. Pierre Durand/"Jappeloup" FRA 1.25 pts
2. Greg Best/"Gem Twist" USA 4 pts
3. Karsten Huck/"Neponuk" FRG 4 pts

Grand Prix Jumping Team
1. FRG 17.25 pts (Beerbaum, Brinkmann, Hafemeister, Sloothaak)
2. USA 20.50 pts (Best, Jacquin, Kursinski, Fargis)
3. FRA 27.50 pts (Bourdy, Cottier, Robert, Durand)

Individual Dressage
1. Nicole Uphoff/"Rembrandt" FRG 1,521 pts
2. Margitt Otto-Crépin/"Corlandus" FRA 1,462 pts
3. Christine Stueckelberger/"Gauguin de Lulle" SUI 1,417 pts

Team Dressage
1. FRG 4,302 pts (Klimke, Linsenhoff, Theodorescu, Uphoff)
2. SUI 4,164 pts (Hofer, Stueckelberger Ramseier, Schatzmann)
3. CAN 3,969 pts (Ishoy, Pracht, Smith, Nicoll)

All-Around Individual Competition
1. Mark Todd/"Charisma" NZL 42.60 pts
2. Ian Stark/"Sir Wattie" GBR 52.80 pts
3. Virginia Leng/"Master Craftsman" GBR 62.00 pts

All-Around Team Competition
1. FRG 225.95 pts (Erhorn, Baumann, Kasparéit, Ehrenbrink)
2. GBR 256.80 pts (Phillips, Straker, Leng, Stark)
3. NZL 271.20 pts (Todd, Knighton, Bennie, Pottinger)

Men Fencing

Foil Individual
1. Stefano Cerioni ITA
2. Udo Wagner GDR
3. Alexandre Romankov URS

Sabre Individual
1. Jean-François Lamour FRA
2. Janusz Olech POL
3. Giovanni Scalzo ITA

Epée Individual
1. Arnd Schmitt FRG
2. Philippe Riboud FRA
3. Andrei Chouvalov URS

Foil Team
1. URS (Romankov, Mamedov, Aptsiaouri, Ibraguimov, Koretskil)
2. FRG (Gey, Weidner, Behr, Schreck, Endres)
3. HUN (Ersek, Szekeres, Szelei, Gatai, Busa)

Sabre Team
1. HUN (Nebald, Szabo, Consgradi, Bujdoso, Gedeovari)
2. URS (Mindirgassov, Bourtsev, Pogossov, Alchan, Koriakine)
3. ITA (Cavaliere, Scalzo, Marin, Dallabarba, Meglio)

Epée Team
1. FRA (Lenglet, Srecki, Riboud, Henry, Delpha)
2. FRG (Borrmann, Fischer, Gerull, Pusch, Schmitt)
3. URS (Chouvalov, Tichko, Kolobkov, Reznitchenko, Tikhomirov)

Women Fencing

Foil Individual
1. Anja Fichtel FRG
2. Sabine Bau FRG
3. Zita Funkenhauser FRG

Foil Team
1. FRG (Fichtel, Funkenhauser, Bau, Weber, Klug)
2. ITA (Vaccaroni, Zalaffi, Traversa, Gandolfi, Bortolozzi)
3. HUN (Janosi, Stefanek, Szocs, Kovacs, Tuschak)

Soccer

1. Soviet Union
2. Brazil
3. Federal Republic of Germany

Men Gymnastics

All-Around Individual Competition
1. Vladimir Artemov URS 119.125 pts
2. Valeri Lioukine URS 119.025 pts
3. Dimitri Bilozertchev URS 118.975 pts

All-Around Team Competition
1. URS 593.35 pts (Nouvikov, Gogoladze, Bilozertchev, Lioukine, Artemov, Charkov)
2. GDR 588.45 pts (Kroll, Tippelt, Buchner, Behrendt, Hoffmann, Wecker)
3. JPN 585.60 pts (Yukio, Mizushima, Sato, Konishi, Yamada)

Horizontal Bar
1. Valeri Lioukine URS 19.900 pts
Vladimir Artemov URS 19.900 pts
3. Holger Behrendt GDR 19.800 pts
Marius Gherman ROM 19.800 pts

Sidehorse
1. Dimitri Bilozertchev URS 19.950 pts
Zsolt Borkai BUL 19.950 pts
Lubomir Gueraskov URS 19.950 pts

Flying Rings
1. Dimitri Bilozertchev URS 19.925 pts
Holger Behrendt GDR 19.925 pts
3. Sven Tippelt GDR 19.875 pts

Horse Vault
1. Lou Yun CHN 19.875 pts
2. Sylvio Kroll GDR 19.862 pts
3. Park Jong-Hoon KOR 19.775 pts

Parallel Bars
1. Vladimir Artemov URS 19.925 pts
2. Valeri Lioukine URS 19.900 pts
3. Sven Tippelt GDR 19.750 pts

Floor Excercise
1. Sergei Kharkov URS 19.925 pts
2. Vladimir Artemov URS 19.900 pts
3. Lou Yun CHN 19.850 pts
Yukio Iketani JPN 19.850 pts

Women Gymnastics

All-Around Individual Competition
1. Elena Chouchounova URS 79.662 pts
2. Daniela Silivas ROM 79.637 pts
3. Svetlana Boginskaia URS 79.400 pts

All-Around Team Competition
1. URS 395.475 pts (Baitova, Chevtchenko, Straieva, Lachtchenova)
2. ROM 394.125 pts (Voinea, Golea, Popa, Potorac, Dobre)
3. GDR 390.875 pts (Jentsch, Schieferdecker, Fahnrich, Klotz, Kersten, Thummler)

Horse Vault
1. Elena Boguinskaia URS 19.905 pts
2. Gabriela Potorac ROM 19.830 pts
3. Daniela Silivas ROM 19.818 pts

Floor Exercise
1. Daniela Silivas ROM 19.937 pts
2. Svetlana Boguinskaia URS 19.887 pts
3. Diana Doudeva BUL 19.850 pts

Beam
1. Daniela Silivas ROM 19.924 pts
2. Elena Chouchounova URS 19.875 pts
3. Phoele Mills USA 19.837 pts
Gabriela Potorac ROM 19.837 pts

Uneven Bars
1. Daniela Silivas ROM 20.000 pts
2. Dagmar Kersten FRG 19.987 pts
3. Elena Chouchounova URS 19.962 pts

Apparatus
1. Lobatch URS 60.000 pts
2. Dounavska BUL 59.950 pts
3. Timoshenko URS 59.875 pts

Rhythmic Competition
1. Lobatch URS 60.000 pts
2. Dounavska BUL 59.950 pts
3. Timoshenko URS 59.875 pts

Weightlifting

52 kg
1. Sevdalin Marinov BUL 270.0 kg
2. Chun Byung-Kwan KOR 260.0 kg
3. He Zhuoqiang CHN 257.5 kg

56 kg
1. Oksen Mirzoian URS 292.5 kg
2. He Yinqiang CHN 287.5 kg
3. Liu Shoubin CHN 267.5 kg

1988 Seoul

60 kg
Naim Suleymanoglou TUR 342.5 kg
Stefan Topourov BUL 312.5 kg
Ye Huanming CHN 287.5 kg

67.5 kg
Joachim Kunz GDR 340.0 kg
Israel Militosian URS 337.5 kg
Li Jinhe CHN 325.0 kg

75 kg
Borislav Guidikov BUL 375.0 kg
Ingo Steinhoefel GDR 360.0 kg
Alexander Varbanov BUL 357.5 kg

82.5 kg
Israil Arsamakov URS 377.5 kg
Istvan Messzi HUN 370.0 kg
Lee Hyung-Kun KOR 367.5 kg

90 kg
Anatoli Khrapatyi URS 412.5 kg
Nail Moukhamediarov URS 400.0 kg
Slawomir Zawada POL 400.0 kg

100 kg
Pavel Kouznetsov URS 425.0 kg
Nicu Vlad ROM 402.5 kg
Peter Immesberger FRG 395.0 kg

110 kg
Youri Zakharevitch URS 455.0 kg
Jozsef Jacso HUN 427.5 kg
Ronny Weller GDR 425.0 kg

Over 110 kg
Alexandre Kourlovitch URS 462.5 kg
Manfred Nerlinger FRG 430.0 kg
Martin Zawieja FRG 415.0 kg

Handball

Men	Women
1. Soviet Union	1. South Korea
2. South Korea	2. Norway
3. Yugoslavia	3. Soviet Union

Field Hockey

Men	Women
1. Great Britain	1. Australia
2. Federal Republic of Germany	2. South Korea
3. Netherlands	3. Netherlands

Judo

60 kg
1. Kim Jae-Yup KOR
2. Kevin Asano USA
3. Shinji Hosokawa JPN
Amiran Totikachvili URS

65 kg
1. Lee Kyung-Keun KOR
2. Janusz Pawlowski POL
3. Bruno Carabetta FRA
Yosuke Yamamoto JPN

71 kg
1. Marc Alexandre FRA
2. Sven Loll GDR
3. Gueorgui Tenadze URS
Michael Swain USA

78 kg
1. Waldemar Legien POL
2. Frank Wieneke FRG
3. Torsten Brechot GDR
Bachir Varaev URS

Kristin Otto of East Germany won 6 gold medals.

86 kg
1. Peter Seisenbacher AUT
2. Vladimir Chestakov URS
3. Akinobu Osako JPN
Ben Spijkers HOL

95 kg
1. Aurelio Miguel BRA
2. Marc Meiling FRG
3. Robert Van de Walle BEL
Dennis Stewart GBR

Over 95 kg
1. Hitoshi Saito JPN
2. Henry Stoehr GDR
3. Cho Yong-Chul KOR
Grigori Veritchev URS

Graeco-Roman Wrestling

48 kg
1. Vincenzo Maenza ITA
2. Andrzej Glab POL
3. Bratan Tzenov BUL

52 kg
1. Jon Ronningen NOR
2. Atsuji Miyahara JPN
3. Lee Jae-sute KOR

57 kg
1. Andras Sike HUN
2. Stoyan Balov BUL
3. Charalambos Holidis GRE

62 kg
1. Kamandar Madjidov URS
2. Jivko Vanguelov BUL
3. An Dae-hyun KOR

68 kg
1. Levon Djoufalakian URS
2. Kim Sung-moon KOR
3. Tapio Sipilae FIN

74 kg
1. Kim Young-nam KOR
2. Daoulet Tourlykhanov URS
3. Jozef Tracz POL

82 kg
1. Mikhail Mamiachvili URS
2. Tibor Komaromi HUN
3. Kim Sang-kyu KOR

90 kg
1. Atanas Komchev BUL
2. Harri Kosteka FIN
3. Vladimir Popov URS

100 kg
1. Andrezj Wronski POL
2. Gerhard Himmel FRG
3. Dennis Koslowski USA

130 kg
1. Alexandre Kareline URS
2. Ranguel Guerovski BUL
3. Tomas Johansson SWE

All-In Wrestling

48 kg
1. Takashi Kobayashi JPN
2. Ivan Tzonov BUL
3. Serguei Karamchatzov URS

52 kg
1. Mitsuru Sato JPN
2. Saban Trstena YUG
3. Vladimir Togouzov URS

57 kg
1. Sergei Beloglazov URS
2. Mohammadian IRN
3. Noh Kyung-sun KOR

62 kg
1. John Smith USA
2. Stephan Sarkissian URS
3. Simeon Chterev BUL

68 kg
1. Arsen Fadzaev URS
2. Park Jang-soon KOR
3. Nate Carr USA

74 kg
1. Kenneth Monday USA
2. Adlan Varaev URS
3. Rakhmad Sofiadi BUL

82 kg
1. Han Myung-woo KOR
2. Nemci Gencalp TUR
3. Joseph Lohyna TCH

90 kg
1. Makharbek Khardartsev URS
2. Akira Ota JPN
3. Kim Tae-woo KOR

100 kg
1. Vasile Puscasu ROM
2. Leri Khabelov URS
3. Bill Scherr USA

130 kg
1. David Gobedjichvili URS
2. Bruce Baumgartner USA
3. Andreas Schroeder GDR

Men Swimming

50 M - Freestyle
1. Matt Biondi USA 22.14 (world rec.; prev. rec. 22.23 by Jager)
2. Tom Jager USA 22.33
3. Guennadi Prigoda URS 22.71

100 M - Freestyle
1. Matt Biondi USA 48.63
2. Christopher Jacobs USA 49.08
3. Stephan Caron FRA 49.62

200 M - Freestyle
1. Duncan Armstrong AUS 1:47.25 (world rec., prev. rec. 1:47.44 by Gross)
2. Anders Holmertz SWE 1:47.89
3. Matt Biondi USA 1:47.99

400 M - Freestyle
1. Uwe Dassler GDR 3:46.95 (world rec.; prev. rec. 3:47.38 by Wojdat)
2. Duncan Armstrong AUS 3:47.15
3. Artur Wojdat POL 3:47.34

1,500 M - Freestyle
1. Vladimir Salnikov URS 15:00.40
2. Stephan Pfeiffer GDR 15:02.69
3. Uwe Dassler GDR 15:06.15

100 M - Backstroke
1. Daichi Suzuki JPN 55.05
2. David Berkoff USA 55.18
3. Igor Polianski URS 55.20

200 M - Backstroke
1. Igor Polianski URS 1:59.37
2. Frank Baltrusch GDR 1:59.60
3. Paul Kingsman NZL 2:00.48

100 M - Butterfly stroke
1. Anthony Nesty SUR 53.00
2. Matt Biondi USA 53.01
3. Andy Jameson GBR 53.30

200 M - Butterfly stroke
1. Michael Gross FRG 1:56.94
2. Benny Nielsen DEN 1:58.24
3. Anthony Mosse NZL 1:58.28

100 M - Breaststroke
1. Adrian Moorhouse GBR 1:02.04
2. Karoly Guttler HUN 1:02.05
3. Dmitri Volkov URS 1:02.20

200 M - Breaststroke
1. Josef Szabo HUN 2:13.52
2. Nick Gillingham GBR 2:14.12
3. Sergio Lopez ESP 2:15.21

200 M - Medley
1. Tamas Darnyi HUN 2:00.17 (world rec.; own prev. rec. 2:00.56)
2. Patrick Kuehl GDR 2:01.61
3. Vadim Tarotchouk URS 2:02.40

400 M - Medley
1. Tamas Darnyi HUN 4:14.75 (world rec.; own prev. rec. 4:15.42)
2. David Wharton USA 4:17.36
3. Stefano Battistelli ITA 4:18.01

400 M Medley Relay
1. USA 3:16.53 (Jacobs, Dalbey, Jager Biondi, world rec.; prev. rec. 3:17.08)
2. URS 3:18.33 (Prigoda, Bachkatov, Evteev, Tkachenko)
3. GDR 3:19.82 (Richter, Fleming, Minneburg, Zesner)

800 M Medley Relay
1. USA 7:12.51 (Dalbey, Cetlinski, Gertsen, Biondi, world rec.; prev. rec. 7:13.10)
2. GDR 7:13.68 (Dassier, Lodziewski, Fleming, Zesner)
3. FRG 7:14.35 (Hochstein, Fahrner, Hentzel, Gross)

400 M Medley
1. USA 3:36.93 (Berkoff, Schroeder, Biondi, Jacobs)
2. CAN 3:39.28 (Tawesbury, David, Ponting, Goss)
3. URS 3:39.96 (Polianski, Volkov, Yarocht-chouk, Prigoda)

Water-Polo
1. Yugoslavia
2. United States
3. Soviet Union

Women Swimming

50 M - Freestyle
1. Kristin Otto GDR 25.49
2. Yang Wenyi CHN 25.64
3. Katrin Meissner GDR 25.71
Jill Sterkel USA 25.71

100 M - Freestyle
1. Kristin Otto GDR 54.93
2. Zhuang Yong CHN 55.47
3. Catherine Plewinski FRA 55.49 (France rec.; own prev. rec. 55.53)

200 M - Freestyle
1. Heike Friedrich GDR 1:57.65
2. Sylvia Poll CRC 1:58.67
3. Manuela Stellmach GDR 1:59.01

400 M - Freestyle
1. Janet Evans USA 4:03.85
2. Heike Friedrich GDR 4:05.94
3. Anke Moehring GDR 4:06.62

800 M - Freestyle
1. Janet Evans USA 8:20.20
2. Astrid Strauss GDR 8:22.09
3. Julie MacDonald AUS 8:22.93

100 M - Backstroke
1. Kristin Otto GDR 1:00.89
2. Krisztina Egerszegi HUN 1:01.56
3. Cornelia Sirch GDR 1:01.57

200 M - Backstroke
1. Krisztina Egerszegi HUN 2:09.29
2. Kathrin Zimmermann GDR 2:10.61
3. Cornelia Sirch GDR 2:11.45

100 M - Butterfly stroke
1. Kristina Otto GDR 59.00
2. Birte Weigang GDR 59.34
3. Qiuan Hong CHN 59.45

200 M - Butterfly stroke
1. Katleen Nord GDR 2:09.29
2. Birte Weigang GDR 2:09.91
3. Mary T. Meagher USA 2:10.80

100 M - Breaststroke
1. Tania Dangalakova BUL 1:07.95
2. Antoaneta Frankeva BUL 1:08.74
3. Silke Hoerner GDR 1:08.83

200 M - Breaststroke
1. Silke Hoerner GDR 2:26.71
2. Huang Xiaomin CHN 2:27.49
3. Antoaneta Frankeva BUL 2:28.34

200 M - Medley
1. Daniela Hunger GDR 2:12.59
2. Helena Dendeberova URS 2:13.31
3. Noemi Lung ROM 2:14.85

400 M - Medley
1. Janet Evans USA 4:37.76
2. Noemi Lung ROM 4:39.46
3. Daniela Hunger GDR 4:39.76

400 M Medley Relay
1. GDR 3:40.53 (Otto, Meissner, Hunger, Stellmach)
2. HOL 3:43.39 (Ma. Muis, Mi. Muis, Van Bentum, Brienesse)
3. USA 3:44.25 (Wayte, Kremer, Walker, Torres)

400 M Medley
1. GDR 4:03.73 (Otto, Hoerner, Weigang, Meissner)
2. USA 4:07.90 (Barr, McFarlane, Jorgensen, Wayte)
3. CAN 4:10.49 (Melien, Higson, Kerr, Nugent)

Synchronized Swimming Individual
1. Carolyn Waldo CAN 200.150 pts
2. Tracie Conforto Ruiz USA 197.633 pts
3. Mikako Kotani JPN 191.850 pts

Synchronized Swimming Duet
1. Canada 197.717 pts
2. United States 197.284 pts
3. Japan 190.159 pts

Men Diving

Springboard Diving
1. Greg Louganis USA 730.80 pts
2. Tan Liangde CHN 704.88 pts
3. Li De Liang CHI 665.28 pts

High Diving
1. Greg Louganis USA 638.61 pts
2. Xiong Ni CHN 637.47 pts
3. Jesus Mena MEX 594.39 pts

Women Diving

Springboard Diving
1. Gao Min CHN 580.23 pts
2. Li Qing CHN 534.33 pts
3. Kelly McCormick USA 533.19 pts

High Diving
1. Xu Yannei CHN 445.20 pts
2. Michele Mitchell USA 436.95 pts
3. Wendy Williams USA 400.44 pts

Modern Pentathlon

Individual
1. Janos Martinek HUN 5 404 pts
2. Carlo Massullo ITA 5 379 pts
3. Vakhtang Iagorachvili URS 5 367 pts

Team
1. Hungary 15 886 pts
2. Italy 15 571 pts
3. Great Britain 12 276 pts

Tennis

Men:s Singles
1. Miloslav Mecir TCH
2. Tim Mayotte USA
3. Stefan Edberg SWE
Brad Gilbert USA

Men:s Doubles
1. Ken Flach, Robert Seguso USA
2. Emilio Sanchez, Sergio Casal ESP
3. Stefan Edberg, Anders Jarryd SWE
Miloslav Mecir, Milan Srejber TCH

Ben Johnson winning the gold medal he will lose.

Women:s Singles
1. Steffi Graf FRG
2. Gabriela Sabatini ARG
3. Manuela Maleeva BUL
Zina Garrison USA

Women:s Doubles
1. Pam Shriver, Zina Garrison USA
2. Jana Novotna, Helena Sukova TCH
3. Steffi Graf, Claudia Kohde Kilsch FRG
Elizabeth Smylie, Wendy Turnbull USA

Table Tennis

Men:s Singles
1. Yoo Nam-Kyu KOR
2. Kim Ki-Taik KOR
3. Erik Lindh SWE

Men:s Doubles
1. Chen Long Can, Wei Quingguang CHN
2. Ilija Lupulescu, Zoran Primorac YUG
3. Ahn Jae Hyung, Yoo Nam Kyu KOR

Women Singles
1. Chen Jing CHN
2. Li Huifen CHN
3. Jiao Zhimin CHN

Women's Doubles
1. Hyun Jung Hwa, Yang Young-ja KOR
2. Chen Jing, Jiao Zhimin CHN
3. Jazna Fazlic, Gordana Perkucin YUG

Men Shooting

Free Pistol
1. Sorin Babii ROU 660 pts
2. Ragnar Skanaker SWE 657 pts
3. Igor Bassinski URS 657 pts

Rapid-Fire Pistol
1. Afanasi Kouzmine URS 698 pts (world rec.)
2. Ralf Schumann GDR 696 pts
3. Zoltan Kovacs HUN 693 pts

Airgun
1. Taniou Kiriakov BUL 687.9 pts
2. Erich Buljung USA 687.9 pts
3. Xu Maifeng CHN 684.5 pts

Small-Bore Rifle. Prone
1. Miroslav Varga TCH 703.9 pts
2. Cha Young-Chul KOR 703.8 pts
3. Attila Zahonyi HUN 701.9 pts

Airgun, 10 M
1. Goran Maksimovic YUG 695.6 pts
2. Nicolas Berthelot FRA 694.2 pts
3. Johann Riederer FRG 694 pts

Small-Bore Rifle. 3 positions
1. Malcolm Cooper GBR 1279.3 pts
2. Alister Allan GBR 1275.6 pts
3. Kirill Ivanov URS 1275 pts

Moving Target
1. Tor Heiestad NOR 689 pts
2. Huang Shiping CHN 688 pts
3. Guennadi Avramenko URS 686 pts

Trap Shooting
1. Dimitri Monakov URS 222 pts
2. Miroslav Bednarik TCH 222 pts
3. Frans Peeters BEL 219 pts

Skeet
1. Axel Wegner GDR 222 pts
2. Alfonso De Izuarrizaga CHI 221 pts
3. Jorge Guardiola ESP 220 pts

Women Shooting

Airgun, 10 M
1. Jasna Sekaric YUG 489.5 pts
2. Nino Saloukvadze URS 487.9 pts
3. Marina Dobrancheva URS 485.2 pts

Sport Pistol
1. Nino Saloukvadze URS 690 pts
2. Tomoko Hasegawa JPN 686 pts
3. Jasna Sekaric YUG 686 pts

Small-Bore Rifle, 3 positions
1. Silvia Sperber FRG 685.6 pts
2. Vessela Letcheva BUL 683.2 pts
3. Valentina Tcherkassova URS 681.4 pts

Airgun
1. Irina Chilova URS 498.5 pts
2. Silvia Sperber FRG 497.5 pts
3. Anna Maloukhina URS 495.5 pts

Men Archery

Individual
1. Jay Barrs USA 338 pts
2. Park Sung-Soo KOR 336 pts
3. Vladimir Echeev URS 335 pts

Team
1. South Korea 986 pts
2. United States 972 pts
3. Great Britain 968 pts

Women Archery

Individual
1. Kim Soo-Nyung KOR 344 pts
2. Wang Hee-Kyung KOR 332 pts
3. Yun Young-Sook KOR 327 pts

Team
1. South Korea 982 pts
2. Indonesia 952 pts
3. United States 952 pts

Men Yachting

Finn Class
1. Jose Luis Doreste ESP 36.1 pts
2. Peter Holmberg VI 40.4 pts
3. John Cutler NZL 45 pts

470 Class
1. Thierry Peponnet- Luc Pillot FRA 34.7 pts
2. Tynou et Thomas Tyniste URS 46 pts
3. John Shadden-Charlie McKee USA 49 pts

Flying Dutchman Class
1. DEN 31.4 pts (Jorgen Bojsen Moller, Christian Gronborg)
2. NOR 37.4 pts (Olepetter Pollen, Erik Bjorkum)
3. CAN 48.4 pts (Frank McLaughlin, John Willen)

Soling Class
1. GDR 11.7 pts (Jochen Schuemann, Thomas Flach, Bernt Jaekel)
2. USA 11.4 pts (John Kostecki, William Baylis, Robert Billingham)
3. DEN 52.7 pts (Jesper Bank, Jan Mathiasen, Steen Secher)

Tornado Class
1. FRA 16 pts (Jean-Yves Le Deroff, Nicolas Henard)
2. NZL 35.4 pts (Christopher Timms, Rex Sellers)
3. BRA 40.1 pts (Lars Grael, Clinio Freitas)

Windsurfing
1. Bruce Kendall NZL 35.4 pts
2. Jan D. Boersma ANE 42.7 pts
3. Michael Gebhardt USA 48 pts

Star Class
1. GBR 45.4 pts (Michael McIntyre, Philippe Vaile)
2. USA 48 pts (Mark Reynolds, Hal Haenel)
3. BRA 50 pts (Torban Grael, Nelson Falcao)

Women Yachting

470 Class
1. USA 26.7 pts (Allisson Jolly, Lynne Jewell)
2. SWE 40 pts (Marit Soderstrom, Brighitta Bengtsson)
3. URS 45.4 pts (Larissa Moskalenko, Irina Tchounikavskaia)

Volleyball

Men	Women
1. United States	1. Soviet Union
2. Soviet Union	2. Peru
3. Argentina	3. China

FINAL LIST OF MEDALS

Country		Gold	Silver	Bronze	Total
Soviet Union	(URS)	55	31	46	132
German Democratic Republic	(GDR)	37	35	30	102
Unites States	(USA)	36	31	27	94
South Korea	(KOR)	12	10	11	33
Federal Republic of Germany	(FRG)	11	14	15	40
Hungary	(HUN)	11	6	6	23
Bulgaria	(BUL)	10	12	13	35
Rumania	(ROM)	7	11	6	24
France	(FRA)	6	4	6	16
Italy	(ITA)	6	4	4	14
China	(CHN)	5	11	12	28
Great Britain	(GBR)	5	10	9	24
Kenya	(KEN)	5	2	2	9
Japan	(JPN)	5	3	7	14
Australia	(AUS)	3	6	5	14
Yugoslavia	(YUG)	3	4	5	12
Czechoslovakia	(TCH)	3	3	2	8
New Zealand	(NZL)	3	2	8	13
Canada	(CAN)	3	2	5	10
Poland	(POL)	2	5	9	16
Norway	(NOR)	2	3	0	5
Netherlands	(HOL)	2	2	5	9
Denmark	(DEN)	2	1	1	4
Brazil	(BRA)	1	2	3	6
Spain	(ESP)	1	1	2	4
Finland	(FIN)	1	1	2	4
Turkey	(TUR)	1	1	0	2
Morocco	(MOR)	1	0	2	3
Austria	(AUT)	1	0	0	1
Portugal	(POR)	1	0	0	1
Surinam	(SUR)	1	0	0	1
Sweden	(SWE)	0	4	7	11
Switzerland	(SUI)	0	2	2	4
Jamaica	(JAM)	0	2	0	2
Argentina	(ARG)	0	1	1	2
Netherlands Antilles	(ANE)	0	1	0	1
Chile	(CHI)	0	1	0	1
Costa Rica	(CRC)	0	1	0	1
Virgin Islands	(VI)	0	1	0	1
Indonesia	(INS)	0	1	0	1
Iran	(IRN)	0	1	0	1
Peru	(PER)	0	1	0	1
Senegal	(SEN)	0	1	0	1
Belgium	(BEL)	0	0	2	2
Mexico	(MEX)	0	0	2	2
Colombia	(COL)	0	0	1	1
Djibouti	(DJI)	0	0	1	1
Greece	(GRE)	0	0	1	1
Mongolia	(MGL)	0	0	1	1
Pakistan	(PAK)	0	0	1	1
Philippines	(PHI)	0	0	1	1
Thailand	(THA)	0	0	1	1
Total		**241**	**234**	**264**	**739**

OCTOBER

Week 39 1988

Su	Mo	Tu	We	Th	Fr	Sa
						1
2	3	4	5	6	7	8
9	10	11	12	13	14	15
16	17	18	19	20	21	22
23	24	25	26	27	28	29
30	31					

1. Moscow: On retirement of Andrei Gromyko, Mikhail S. Gorbachev becomes new President of Soviet Union (→ 5).

2. Bloomsburg, Pennsylvania: For about an hour, 45 people are trapped hanging upside-down in the middle of a loop on a broken roller coaster.

2. Edwards Air Force Base, California: Space shuttle Discovery returns five astronauts to earth after successful four-day mission (→ 29).

3. Beirut: Kidnappers release Indian Mithileshwar Singh, seized along with three Americans at Beirut University in January 1987 (→ 31).

4. Washington: House falls 11 votes short of overriding President Reagan's veto of textile protection bill.

4. Washington: Saying that they "have no intention of being an accessory to the hoodwinking of the American public," the League of Women Voters withdraws its sponsorship from the presidential debates (→ 5).

4. London: Amnesty International report lists 135 nations guilty of human rights abuses last year.

5. Moscow: New ideology chief urges experiment with market economics, rejects struggle with capitalism (→ 13).

5. Washington: President Reagan unveils cornerstone for new museum dedicated to remembrance of Holocaust.

5. Washington: Reagan administration responds to Soviet proposal to World Court with plan for U.S. and U.S.S.R. to submit a list of disputes for arbitration.

5. Chicago: F.A.A. cuts flights at O'Hare and Midway airports, citing delays and safety problems.

6. New York: Grand jury officially releases report charging Tawana Brawley fabricated rape story.

6. Washington: Pentagon releases $69 billion estimate for S.D.I. deployment, cutting figure in half just in time for election (→ 12).

U.S. rabbi's party is banned in Israel

Oct 5. Israel's Central Election Commission has banned the Kach Party of American emigre Rabbi Meir Kahane from next month's parliamentary elections. Citing his "Nazi-like ideology," the commission used a law banning "racist" or "undemocratic parties" — a measure passed three years ago with the Kahane party specifically in mind. Kahane, who fills the only Kach Party seat in Parliament, has unsuccessfully promoted a variety of bills to legislate the Arabs out of existence in Israel. He would solve the Palestinian problem by ousting all 2.2 million Arabs from Israel, the West Bank and Gaza (→ 23).

Rabbi Meir Kahane, the controversial leader of Israel's Kach Party, which is banned from elections.

Lions win at last

Oct 8. Columbia University, that citadel of learning, has learned that nothing lasts forever — not even a losing streak. After 44 consecutive defeats over a five-year span, Columbia's football team finally won a game, beating Princeton 16 to 13. Swarms of Columbia students ran onto the field and tore down the goalposts as though their team had just won the Rose Bowl (which the Lions did back in 1934). When he was asked at what point he thought his squad would win, the stunned Columbia coach, Larry McElreavy, replied, "About four minutes after the game was over."

Chile cheers as Pinochet yields to plebiscite

A very rare sight: General Pinochet casts his vote at the ballot box.

Oct 6. Thousands of Chileans celebrated in the streets today after General Augusto Pinochet said he would accept his defeat. The announcement came after a count of the votes in a yes-or-no plebiscite in which 43 percent backed an eight-year term for Pinochet and 54.7 percent opposed it. General Pinochet has led Chile during 15 years of often repressive, violent rule in which many dissenters were killed or imprisoned. The opposing factions are now deciding on who their candidates will be in the election which, according to the constitutional provisions, is going to take place late in 1989.

Riot police called as Montenegrins protest

Oct 8. Only days after Serbian nationalists forced the resignation of Vojvodina's government, another of Yugoslavia's eight autonomous provinces and republics was under siege. Thousands of Montenegrins descended on their Parliament building to demand the resignation of government and Communist Party leaders. The rioters were dispersed by policemen using cattle prods and truncheons. The Montenegrins were protesting the sharp deterioration of Yugoslavia's economy, which they say has hit them particularly hard because they are discriminated against by other Yugoslavs (→ 11/21).

Yugoslavia is the latest Communist nation to experience social unrest.

Dozens dead, over 900 hurt in Algeria riots

Oct 7. The Algerian military has declared a state of emergency in Algiers following four days of rioting that killed dozens and wounded 900. The riots, mostly involving youths, were a response to austerity measures that had been imposed by the Algerian government in an attempt to stop rampant inflation and new price increases. More than 4,000 people have been arrested for looting and vandalism. A curfew has been imposed by the military from 10 p.m. until 6 a.m. Even though public demonstrations have been forbidden, a crowd of about 7,000 demonstrators marched in the capital in defiance of the ban. Earlier in the day, Islamic militants clashed with the police at two mosques following the morning prayer. There were fears expressed by public officials that the rioting might spread to other cities. An Air France office was attacked in Oran, the second largest city in Algeria.

Most of the rioters are young people who have been protesting the extremes of wealth and poverty that exist in Algeria. They charge that the weight of the government's new austerity program is falling mostly upon the shoulders of the poor and that the wealthy minority has not been forced to tighten its belts at all. A package of butter that cost the equivalent of 50 cents in January is now selling for $1, and cooking oil that was $2.42 is now priced at more than $4 (→ 11/3).

Protesters in Algeria claim an austerity program hurts the poor most of all.

Debt costs may pass American deficit

Oct 7. Soon, according to government bookkeepers, the interest that the United States Treasury pays on the national debt will exceed the federal budget deficit of $150 billion. The $2 trillion national debt to domestic and foreign investors is now costing interest at the rate of nearly $150 billion per year, an amount that must be paid to the investors before any money can be allocated for other federal projects, such as the space program or welfare. Interest payments have not involved so great a percentage of the United States budget since 1948 (→ 11/11).

Mafia killing again after Sicily trials

Oct 7. Judicial and law enforcement officials in Italy were exultant only 10 months ago when a jury in Palermo convicted 338 people of Mafia crimes in a mass trial. This seeming triumph now appears to have been inconsequential because the resurgent Sicilian Mafia has mounted a terror campaign against the state as well as a series of daylight strikes against underworld rivals. Most disturbing to the Italian government is the recent killing of a senior appellate court judge in Palermo, an apparent violation of the Sicilian taboo against murdering a sitting judge.

Bentsen to Quayle: "You're no Kennedy"

The two rivals for the Vice Presidency battle it out in Omaha, Nebraska.

Oct 5. The angry debate tonight between two senators seeking the Vice Presidency will perhaps be best remembered by remarks about President John F. Kennedy.

It all began when Dan Quayle, the Republican nominee, seeking to discount opposition claims that he is unqualified for top office, argued that he had as much experience as Kennedy did when he became President in 1961.

Lloyd Bentsen, the Democratic nominee, looked askance and, when it came time for rebuttal, turned to his rival and said sternly: "Senator, I served with Jack Kennedy. I knew Jack Kennedy. Jack Kennedy was a friend of mine. Senator, you're no Jack Kennedy." The comment drew both cheers and hoots from the crowd gathered in the Omaha, Nebraska, Civic Auditorium.

Obviously stunned by the Bentsen remark, Quayle replied: "That was really uncalled for, Senator."

"You're the one who was making the comparison, Senator," Bentsen shot back, adding that Kennedy and Quayle were so far apart that the comparison was inappropriate (→ 11).

Koreans filled with pride as Olympics close

Oct 2. South Korea glowed with pride as the Games of the 24th Olympiad closed with traditional pageantry, but there was a bitter aftertaste in some relationships. The Koreans castigated American television coverage of the Games in Seoul and sought to regain face after a near-riot over a Korean defeat in boxing. The host country felt the Americans failed to show proper decorum during the opening parade into the stadium and the Koreans saw the stature of their Games diminished by a furor over the use of steroids. The Soviet team carried off medal honors, even beating the Americans at their own game — basketball. Tight security avoided terrorist attacks of the kind that disrupted the Munich Games in 1972. The runners carrying the Olympic torch to the stadium were threatened by extremists, but riot policemen prevented violence. Said a TV producer, "You say anything wrong about Korean society it's like berating their culture" (→ 18).

Gary Anderson's "Unity" poster symbolizes friendly competition.

Su	Mo	Tu	We	Th	Fr	Sa
						1
2	3	4	5	6	7	8
9	10	11	12	13	14	15
16	17	18	19	20	21	22
23	24	25	26	27	28	29
30	31					

9. New York City: Jay Howell, relief pitcher for L.A. Dodgers, suspended for three days for pine tar in his glove.

10. Jay, Maine: Paper workers decide to end bitter 16-month strike against International Paper.

10. Georgia: Atlanta Falcon defensive back David Croudip dies, apparently a victim of cocaine abuse.

11. Tampa, Florida: International bank holding company is charged with laundering drug money, first such case in which bank itself was indicted (→ 13).

11. Washington: Study finds furloughs were given to 53,000 prisoners all over the country in 1987 and program is considered highly successful.

11. Palo Alto, California: International team of scientists, with computers around the world, succeed in splitting a 100-digit number into two prime factors.

12. San Francisco: Steven Jobs, founder of Apple Computer, unveils Next computer at Davies Symphony Hall.

12. Washington: Sundstrand Corporation fined $115 million for conspiracy to overcharge Pentagon for military supplies; largest fraud settlement by Justice Department (→ 19).

13. London: British high court overturns ban on "Spycatcher," intelligence agent's memoirs that were suppressed as threat to national security.

14. California: Board of Education drops Dick and Jane for novice readers, substituting Aesop, Mark Twain, and modern writers.

14. Washington: Senate finally votes to allow United States to join 97 other nations in treaty outlawing genocide.

14. Raleigh, North Carolina: Two Tuscarora Indians acquitted of seizing newspaper office in February to protest local corruption.

DEATH

9. Felix Wankel, inventor of rotary engine (*1902).

Gorbachev proposes leased private farms

How are you going to keep them down on the farm? Let them lease it.

Oct 13. Faced with chronic and severe food shortages, Soviet leader Mikhail S. Gorbachev has disclosed plans to downgrade state control of collective agriculture. In a meeting with farmers who run experimental private farms, Gorbachev said that "all agriculture, the entire agrarian sector, should follow this path."

The giant collective has been the key to Soviet farming since the 1930's, when Joseph Stalin conducted a decade-long drive to collectivize all agriculture in the Soviet Union. Millions died as a result, victims of Stalin's harsh measures and of starvation. But by 1937, more than 90 percent of Russian peasants were on collectives.

From the start, the collectives have been inefficient and have not produced as much food as required. Small plots, mostly legal and some illegal, have proved to be more productive than the collectives. Under the new system, farmers will be leasing land from the collectives for a period of perhaps 50 years. State-owned and collective farms would remain as regional service centers, providing equipment as well as advice to local private farms.

Not everyone is expected to be happy with the new arrangement. For collective farmers, it will mean an end to their guaranteed incomes. As Gorbachev acknowledged, "No fool is going to work on a lease contract as long as he can have a salary without earning it" (→ 26).

Voters are turned off by presidential race

Oct 11. With the campaign for President now at the halfway point, American voters appear turned off, with many expressing doubts that either man is up to the job and many saying that too much mud is being thrown by both sides.

Those are the findings of a New York Times survey of voters in the pivotal states as the second and last presidential debate nears. Another survey by Time magazine indicates that the gap between the rich and poor has widened during the eight years of the Reagan administration, yet it is uncertain whether this will affect the outcome of the election.

The Times survey shows that many voters feel neither candidate has faced the crucial issues. Typical of the comments were those of Herman Koch, a 69-year-old retired farmer from De Soto, Missouri, whose farm is the site of a marker noting the exact population center of the nation. "They're not coming down and telling us what they're going to do," said Koch, an admirer of President Harry S. Truman.

The Time magazine study found that much of the middle class feels worse off economically than it was eight years ago. Yet, there is no indication that this is doing any harm to the George Bush campaign, despite the efforts by Michael Dukakis to make an issue of the middle-class squeeze (→ 13).

Church finds Shroud of Turin not authenti[c]

Oct 13. New scientific analysi[s] indicates that the Shroud of Turi[n] the cloth Christians believe Jesu[s] was buried in, is not authentic. Th[e] Roman Catholic Church reporte[d] today that this shroud could no[t] have encased Jesus because th[e] linen dated back only as far as th[e] Middle Ages. The new evidence which is based on radiocarbon tests does not explain how an image of [a] face said to resemble that of Jesu[s] appeared on the cloth. The church encouraged Catholics to continue to believe in the "miracles" that the shroud has apparently produced and to honor it as a reminder o[f] Jesus's life on earth.

The holy relic is wholly bogus.

Drug bust nets 120

Oct 13. Police and federal agents took aim at a murderous network of Jamaican drug "posses" last night and today, arresting 120 in a carefully coordinated effort across 20 states. The gangs are believed to control 40 percent of the United States crack market and have been linked to more than 1,400 drug-related murders since 1985, as well as gun trafficking, money laundering and kidnapping. The widespread arrests included the capture of two top-level suspects in New York. But since the heavily armed "posses" are believed to be about 10,000 strong in the United States, this week's counteroffensive may be just one victory in a long war (→ 22).

Peary's notes seem to show he missed Pole

Oct 12. Newly found navigational notes made by Robert E. Peary indicate that he never reached the North Pole during his 1909 expedition and knew it, according to Dennis Rawlins, a Boston astronomer. His conclusion agrees with that of Wally Herbert, a polar explorer, but the two disagree on where and how Peary went wrong.

Writing in the National Geographic magazine, Herbert said Peary's claim to have traveled 296 miles from a base camp to the pole and back in less than eight days was hard to believe. Herbert also noted that Peary's diary contained no information about the 30 hours he and his group spent in the vicinity of the North Pole. Herbert con-

cluded that Peary made a series of navigational errors that left him 30 to 60 miles to the west of the pole.

But Rawlins said his analysis of Peary's handwritten notes, a copy of which he found in the Johns Hopkins University library, show that the explorer stopped 121 miles below the pole and to its east. A key statement in the notes is that Peary saw the sun rising over the horizon in a period of a few minutes. The sun remains at the same altitude all day at the North Pole, so the observation indicates Peary never got there, Rawlins said.

If Peary's claim is disproved, credit for reaching the North Pole first would go to Roald Amundsen, who flew over it in 1926.

Trump the Great Acquisitor buys shuttle

Oct 12. Real estate developer Donald Trump has purchased the shuttle service of Eastern Airlines for a cool $365 million, in cash. Trump said he will rename it after himself. With this acquisition, the developer comes closer to realizing his dream of having a customer take his shuttle to Atlantic City to gamble in his casino, and then fly to New York to stay in his Plaza Hotel and shop in his Trump Tower. Trump said he will work with Continental Airlines, owned by Eastern's parent firm, Texas Air Corporation. Frank Lorenzo, chairman of the Texas airline, wrote provisions into the deal to prevent Trump from ever selling the shuttle to a competitor.

Donald Trump: on top of the heap.

First Arabic writer wins Nobel Prize

Despire his near-blindness, Naguib Mahfouz's literary vision shines.

Oct 13. Citing "works rich in nuance — now clear-sightedly realistic, now evocatively ambiguous," the Swedish Academy of Letters has awarded the Nobel Prize in literature to Naguib Mahfouz of Egypt. The 77-year-old Mahfouz is the first Arabic writer to win this award. He has written 40 novels, several plays, many stories and over 30 screenplays, but his work is largely unknown in Europe and the United States, and his selection came as a surprise. The son of a civil servant, Mahfouz was employed in the Egyptian Civil Service cultural section from 1934 until he retired in 1971. Because he was an ardent supporter of President Anwar Sadat's peace treaty with Israel, his books were banned for a time in many Arab countries (→ 17).

Bush seems cool in second debate

Oct 13. Unlike in his earlier performance, Vice President Bush kept his cool as he exchanged barbs with his Democratic opponent, Governor Michael Dukakis, in their final 90-minute presidential debate in Los Angeles. The candidates quarreled over taxes, crime, defense and which man was responsible for the shrill tone of the campaign. "It's gotten a little ugly out there," said Bush. "It's gotten a little nasty," Dukakis agreed. But he placed the blame on Bush for using labels, especially the word "liberal" (→ 18).

Paisley calls Pope "the Antichrist"

Oct 11. As Pope John Paul II began his speech at the European Parliament in France today, the Northern Ireland Protestant politician the Rev. Ian Paisley stood up and screamed, "I renounce you as the Antichrist!" Quickly, authorities wrestled away Paisley's red sign, which read, "Pope John Paul II — Antichrist" and ejected him. Paisley charged that the Pope was comforting the Irish Republican Army's hunger strikers and that he had given gold crucifixes to "convicted murderers."

Latvians form front to seek autonomy

Oct 9. In an action that would once have been considered criminal, 100,000 Latvians have joined a political front demanding economic autonomy for their republic. Concerned that they are losing their national identity, citizens of the Baltic republic have demanded a restoration of their culture as well as the right to create their own currency and to conduct their own relations with other Soviet republics. This weekend, Moscow allowed Latvian to become the republic's official language (→ 11/16).

Proxmire retiring with a Senate record

Oct 13. The Senate bid farewell this week to William Proxmire of Wisconsin and his Golden Fleece award, a monthly diatribe against federal waste. His all-time favorite: To the National Science Foundation for a $103,000 report on whether gin or tequila makes sunfish more aggressive. The Senate's best-known maverick, Proxmire is calling it quits after 31 years in which he jogged to work, rode herd on the nation's banks, startled colleagues by getting a hair transplant and set a roll-call record by answering 10,500 in a row. Healthy at 72, he plans to stay in Washington.

"Up, up, and away..." Ballooning is becoming popular with Americans as a recreational activity. When the first such flight was made back in 1783, French peasants were so alarmed they set upon the balloon with pitchforks.

OCTOBER
Week 41 1988

Su	Mo	Tu	We	Th	Fr	Sa
						1
2	3	4	5	6	7	8
9	10	11	12	13	14	15
16	17	18	19	20	21	22
23	24	25	26	27	28	29
30	31					

16. United States: Theater community celebrates 100th anniversary of the birth of great American playwright Eugene O'Neill.

17. Stockholm: Americans Gertrude B. Elion and George M. Hitchings and Briton Sir James Black win Nobel Prize in medicine for series of new drugs (→ 18).

18. New York City: South Korean President Roh Tae Woo, addressing United Nations, urges Korean unification and world conference on Korean peninsula (→ 11/23).

18. Los Angeles: Most cigars and some pipe tobacco will get warning label as a result of lawsuit settled today.

18. Fulton, Missouri: At site of Churchill's "Iron Curtain" speech, Vice President Bush says Marxism "is losing its luster" (→ 30).

18. Stockholm: Nobel Prize in economics awarded to Frenchman Maurice Allais for work in market behavior (→ 19).

19. New York City: Grand jury holds Ferdinand and Imelda Marcos in contempt for failing to respond to subpoenas in investigation of charges they embezzled millions before leaving Philippines (→ 31).

19. Johannesburg: Three anti-apartheid leaders, who took refuge in American Consulate after escaping detention 37 days ago, leave with assurances they will be left alone (→ 11/1).

19. Washington: Pentagon halts all Sundstrand contracts after firm's admission of fraud (→ 11/3).

20. Hempstead, Long Island: Mark Gastineau, star defensive lineman for N.Y. Jets, announces he's quitting football.

22. New York City: Two Mexican police officials arrested on charges of conspiring to bring Mexican heroin into the U.S. (→ 11/19).

22. Nicaragua: Hurricane Joan hits Caribbean with great force, leaving 111 dead, thousands homeless, prompting calls for international aid from Nicaragua (→ 24).

Manila gets $962 million in U.S. bases deal

Oct 17. The United States and the Philippines signed an agreement today that allows the United States to operate its military bases in the Philippines in exchange for $962 million in economic and military assistance for 1990-91. The countries had been negotiating for more than 15 months, and the debate about the amount of money has often been heated. The Philippine government had initially asked for $1.2 billion a year.

The United States also agreed to provide $500 million to the Overseas Private Investment Council and the Export-Import Bank for loans and insurance. In addition, the Americans are going to provide $481 million a year to the Filipinos in the form of military and economic aid. This is some two and a half times the amount for the five-year period of 1983-1988.

Signing of the agreement permits the United States to continue to operate its two biggest and most strategically important bases in the Far Pacific, Clark Air Base and the Subic Bay Naval Station. Both bases have been in operation since 1947.

The accord also states that the Philippine government has the authority to prohibit the installation or storage of any nuclear or chemical weapons. An American military spokesman said this would not interfere with the U.S. policy of refusing to confirm or deny the presence of nuclear weapons aboard naval vessels or aircraft. The agreement has not resolved difficulties involving criminal jurisdiction over American military personnel.

Rabbi seeks Christian ministry theme park

Oct 17. Twenty months ago everything at the Christian theme park Heritage USA was business-as-usual. Worshippers were filling the Praise the Lord entertainment facility in Fort Mill, South Carolina, with adulation, and tourists were filling the cash registers.

Then a whirlwind of scandal jolted the community: a sexy Long Island woman, the Rev. Jim Bakker who was caught with her, his teary-eyed wife, Tammy, the minister's remorse, a struggle for power, efforts by the Rev. Jerry Falwell to calm the storm, the Internal Revenue Service, comeback vows, etc.

And now, an Orthodox Jew wants to take charge. Stephen Mernick, who holds rabbinical ordination but does not lead a synagogue, has offered to buy the theme park for $155 million. Mernick, a Canadian businessman, has made several large real estate investments. But without a doubt, this one has received the most attention. There is great speculation about just what a non-practicing rabbi would do with a Christian theme park and an all-Christian cable television network. But as yet, Mernick has not disclosed what he has in mind for the facility (→ 12/13).

A Bible Belt Disneyland now in the midst of a religious identity crisis.

Nancy admits she still borrows dresses

First Lady: caught red-handed.

Oct 17. Despite her promises in 1982 to stop the practice, the First Lady has continued to borrow designer clothes and jewelry in recent years without reporting them. Nancy Reagan's press secretary said that Mrs. Reagan regretted the action, but added that reporting rules had not been violated. However, high government officials are required to disclose gifts of $100 or more per year from any source. Tax experts and designers point out that the practice has given publicity to the chosen designers. Though most of the outfits have been returned, one designer admitted that Nancy still has some of his dresses and that her wearing them "has been a sensation" for his business.

$3.5 billion loan is granted to Mexico

Oct 17. Faced with mounting debts as a result of a plunge in oil prices, Mexico has been granted a short-term loan of up to $3.5 billion from the United States, the largest loan ever made to an indebted nation. Mexico expects to receive longer-term loans from the International Monetary Fund and the World Bank, and the U.S. loan is intended to tide the nation over until negotiations with the multinational agencies are completed. Mexico is the second largest debtor among developing nations.

ellowstone fires w seen as milder

Oct 21. The fires that swept over lowstone Park this summer did less damage than had been ex- ted, park officials said today. rial photos show the fires were tained within 1.4 million of the k's 3.5 million acres, 200,000 er acres than estimated earlier, y said, and less than 1,400 acres re damaged badly enough to de- y all life. Experts who analyzed damage have come to the con- sion that the park will recover hout the need for artificial re- estation or seeding, the officials d. Loss of grass and trees is not at enough to endanger the park's dlife. But the experts said that would take 60 to 100 years to hieve complete recovery.

.S. Congress ends n a note of pride

Oct 22. The 100th Congress end- in the early hours today after ssage of a far-ranging measure to rb the supply of illicit drugs and blic demand for them. With the ection only weeks away, lawmak- s worked nearly around the clock wind up the session, giving final proval to bills to curb lobbying former government officials, ex- nding various tax breaks and in- reasing penalties for insider stock ading. Also passed: a bill naming ay National Asparagus Month.

5 Americans among Nobel Prize winners

Oct 19. Three Americans were awarded the 1988 Nobel Prize in physics today for a 20-year-old ex- periment involving neutrinos, sub- atomic particles with no charge and no mass. The award went to Leon M. Lederman, Melvin Schwartz and Jack Steinberger for using the first laboratory-made beam of neu- trinos to explore the nature of basic forces. The chemistry prize was awarded to Robert Huber, Hart- mut Michel and Johann Deisenhof- er of West Germany for work on photosynthesis. The award in med- icine was shared by Gertrude B. Elion and George M. Hitchings of the United States and Sir James Black of Britain, who were honored for the development of new drugs.

"Happy Birthday to You," for a price

Oct 19. The song "Happy Birth- day to You," one of the most popu- lar in the English language, is up for grabs, along with the publisher, Birchtree, Ltd., which owns the copyright. If you're interested, Birchtree could go for more than $12 million. "Birthday" alone reaps a tidy $1 million a year. As penned by sisters Mildred and Patty Hill in 1892, it was originally called "Good Morning to You" — and went nowhere. The lucrative birth- day lyrics were an afterthought.

Romance is over: Givens divorcing Tyson

Who had the rougher year? Mike Tyson totaled a few cars, fractured several bones and fought three heavyweight bouts. Robin Givens says that her life with the champ "was pure hell." Their marriage seemed to be one long fight.

Oct 19. It seemed like a match made in Celebrity Heaven, a glam- orous beauty-and-the-beast story. She turned men's heads around with her high cheekbones, glitter- ing dark eyes and sleek, sexy body. He turned men's heads around with powerful hooks and jabs. Eight months ago, the world's heavy- weight boxing champion, Michael Tyson, and model-actress Robin Givens were married in a star- spangled wedding.

But soon there was trouble. The couple began bickering. The argu- ments got more violent. She embar- rassed him on television talk shows. He berated her mother and was said to have become suicidal. Now, the romantic saga has come to a close with Givens saying she will grant a divorce and will seek none of the champ's $50-million fortune.

In a prepared statement, she said: "Michael can have his di- vorce. I will not seek nor accept any money for myself." According to Givens's lawyer, Raoul Felder, "The girl didn't want to fight [for money] in the first place."

Howard Weitzman, an attorney for Tyson, said of Givens's deci- sion, "It's a knockout for us." When Tyson was recently asked if he would remarry, he told an inter- viewer, "There are a lot of good woman out there. My mistake was I just didn't find one" (→ 11/16).

$12 million offered and rejected for a gem

Oct 20. It has been an extraor- dinary year for diamonds. Today, at an auction at Christie's in New York, a record price of $12 million was offered, and rejected, for the second largest diamond in the world, a 407.48-carat gem current- ly owned by Marvin Samuels and Louis Glick, New York jewelry dealers, and the Zale Corporation. Yesterday, the record price for a single precious stone was set when an 85.91-carat white diamond sold for $9.3 million. And in March, De Beers announced that it had found in July 1986 the world's biggest uncut diamond, a 599-carat gem dubbed "The Big Rock."

Could be your girl's best friend.

Oct 20. Mickey Hatcher leads the Los Angeles Dodgers to an upset victory over the Oakland A's in five games, to win the 1988 World Series.

OCTOBER

Week 42 1988

Su	Mo	Tu	We	Th	Fr	Sa
						1
2	3	4	5	6	7	8
9	10	11	12	13	14	15
16	17	18	19	20	21	22
23	24	25	26	27	28	29
30	31					

24. Washington: United States bars emergency relief assistance to storm-ravaged Nicaragua.

24. Hackensack, New Jersey: Girl, 18, and cousin, 19, charged with murders of her father and aunt, allegedly with motive of inheriting fortune.

25. Atlanta: Ku Klux Klan and Southern White Knights ordered to pay more than $1 million in damages for disrupting civil rights march in Forsyth County in 1987 (→ 11/3).

26. Moscow: West German Chancellor Helmut Kohl, after three days of talks with top Soviet officials, says they have promised to release all political prisoners before end of year (→ 27).

26. Gila Bend, Arizona: Ten Marines killed as two helicopters crash in training exercise.

30. Sacramento, California: Largest lottery prize, $60.8 million, will be split between three groups of ticket holders.

31. Clackamas County, Oregon: Eldridge J. Broussard's Ecclesia Athletic Association camp revealed to be scene of brutal child abuse.

31. Chicago: Sears reveals major restructuring plan, including sale of Sears Tower, world's tallest building.

31. Warsaw: Government announces it will close financially troubled Lenin Shipyard in Gdansk, birthplace of Solidarity.

31. Beirut: Hostage Terry Anderson appears on videotape, pleading with next President to work for his release.

31. London: Guardian Angels meet with civic groups after founder Curtis Sliwa was slashed while at a London youth center some weeks ago.

DEATHS

24. Henry Armstrong, only boxer ever to hold three world titles at same time (*12/12/1912).

31. John Houseman, actor and producer-director, at 86 (*9/22/1902).

Two whales escape Alaskan ice prison

Oct 26. After more than two weeks in a frigid Arctic enclave, two trapped California gray whales swam to freedom today. A third whale died earlier this week. On October 7, Eskimos came upon the huge whales. They had failed to swim south before a deep freeze isolated them from the ice-free ocean. An expensive, concerted rescue effort ensued. Often receiving as much TV time as the presidential candidates, the whales got help from environmental groups, corporations and both the Soviet and American governments. After futile attempts to smash holes in the ice with helicopter rigs, two Soviet ships tore a path through the frozen sea and the whales swam off.

Save the whales.

Why were nuclear safety gaps unnoticed?

Know your local evacuation signs.

Oct 26. A decades-long policy of neglect and complacency is being blamed for a series of accidents and safety problems that has led to the shutdown of major nuclear-arms facilities across the United States. Reactors at Hanford, Washington, and Savannah River, South Carolina, that produce plutonium and tritium for bombs as well as part of the Rocky Flats, Colorado, weapons plant have been closed in recent months. Formerly secret reports at the Energy Department describe major safety defects in the plants. Energy Secretary John Herrington says an overhaul of policies is needed before they can reopen (→ 11/4).

Over 400 drowned in Philippines typhoon

Oct 25. At least 400 people died in the Philippines when a ferry with 500 aboard sank during a violent ocean storm. The vessel, the Dona Marilyn, was caught in the thick of Typhoon Ruby, which has battered the islands. The boat was a sister ship of the Dona Paz, the ferry that sank last year with a loss of 1,749 passengers. A cargo vessel rescued eight of the Dona Marilyn passengers, and emergency ships are rescuing survivors from many small islands. The overall land toll from fierce winds and flash floods is 70 dead, with some 50,000 homeless. Ruby was the 17th typhoon to hit the Philippines this year.

Storm waters kill many this year.

Soviets abort first space shuttle flight

Oct 29. In an embarrassing moment for the Soviet space program, the first flight of the space shuttle Buran (Snowstorm) was aborted only 51 seconds before it was to be launched, because an emergency evacuation platform did not separate from the rocket. Officials said the mission would be postponed indefinitely while they sought the cause of the failure. The shuttle was to have been put into orbit by the world's most powerful rocket, the 2,000-ton-thrust Energiya. The government greatly publicized the shuttle, showing it nightly on television, but never explaining what its mission would be (→ 11/15).

U.S.S.R. has shuttle troubles too.

Abortion pill furor

Oct 27. A French company that withdrew an abortion pill from the market yesterday reversed its decision today, saying it would obey an order from the French government. The pill, RU 486, has been used in 15 percent of abortions in France since it was marketed last month by Groupe Rousell-Uclaf. Taken under a doctor's supervision, it induces abortion in two weeks. Rousell-Uclaf said it would stop selling the pill because of pressure from abortion foes. But the company, which is owned in part by the French government, resumed sales when the Ministry of Health commanded it to revoke the suspension.

...oviet Union discloses many past deficits

...ct 27. After years of announc-...surpluses at the end of its bud-...report, the Kremlin has admit-...that the Soviet Union has ac-...lly had a long-standing budget ...icit. For 1988, the deficit is ex-...cted to be $58 billion. "This is not ...roblem that has cropped up all ...a sudden," Finance Minister ...ris I. Gostev conceded in his ...dress to the Supreme Soviet, or ...rliament. He said that wasteful ...osidies along with poor manage-...nt were the basic causes of the ...onomic imbalance.

...Although smaller than the Unit-...States deficit of $150 billion, the ...viet deficit makes up a slightly ...ger percentage of the country's ...mestic economic production: 4 ...rcent as compared to the Ameri-...n 3 percent.

...Gostev presented the new $790 ...lion Soviet budget in much more detail than was the case with pre-vious budgets, giving Western ana-lysts a better idea of Soviet leader Mikhail S. Gorbachev's spending priorities. It includes measures that will be popular with Russians, such as spending more money for hous-ing, consumer goods and schools.

To get the budget in balance, the Soviet Union is considering some measures that are radical for a Communist nation. According to Konstantin F. Katushev, Minister of Foreign Economic Relaions, the Soviet Union plans to change its foreign investment laws so that outsiders can own a controlling share of businesses within the Soviet Union. Currently, owner-ship by foreigners is limited to 49 percent. The Russians are also con-sidering introducing a stock market that would be open to workers as well as outsiders (→ 11/6).

...ukakis finally declares that he is a liberal

...Oct 30. Michael Dukakis owned ...o to the "Big L" today, but the ...assachusetts Governor defined it ...his own terms when he said: ..."m a liberal in the tradition of ...ranklin Roosevelt and Harry Tru-...an and John Kennedy."

...For months, Vice President Bush ...ad been trying to pin the liberal ...bel on his Democratic opponent ...r President, but Dukakis, until ...ow, was ducking the issue. Just ...wo weeks ago, he chided Bush dur-...g their final debate for the fre-...uency with which the Vice Pres- ident had used the word "liberal" in describing him. "If I had a dollar, George, for every time you used that label, I'd qualify for one of those tax breaks for the rich that you want to give away."

Dukakis's acknowledgment that he is a liberal came in Fresno, dur-ing a whistle-stop tour of Califor-nia's vote-rich Central Valley. A senior campaign adviser said it was a reminder to Democrats of the rich tradition of their party. Said Kirk O'Donnell: "We think the Demo-crats are coming home" (→ 11/8).

Whistling in the dark, or is the Democratic campaign finally back on track?

Arab talks seek to heal P.L.O.-Jordan rift

Three of the Arab world's most important leaders seeking a unified presence.

Oct 23. Tensions between Jor-dan's King Hussein and the Pales-tine Liberation Organization leader Yasir Arafat reportedly eased dur-ing talks held in the Jordanian port of Aqaba. The meeting was bro-kered by Egyptian President Hosni Mubarak. The negotiations, thus as-sociated with the more moderate Arab nations, sought to paint the P.L.O. in a more reasonable light and in this way to soften the Israeli and U.S. stand against dealing with the group in any Mideast peace con-ference. King Hussein favors a joint Jordanian-P.L.O. delegation for such a parley and Egyptians believe his support is vital to overcoming American and Israeli objections.

The meeting also meant to sway Israel's coming elections by un-dermining Prime Minister Yitzhak Shamir, leader of the Likud Party. Arafat was quoted as being "in fa-vor of a confederation with Jordan" if Israel were prepared to give up the occupied territories, a state-ment clearly tendered to the fol-lowers of Israeli Foreign Minister Shimon Peres, who heads the Labor Party and supports the so-called Jordan option. Peres favors an in-ternational peace conference and territorial concessions by Israel if they bring peace. Shamir, a hard-liner is opposed to both (→ 11/2).

Philip Morris buys Kraft for $13.5 billion

Oct 30. The largest corporate merger to date in American history was announced today as Phillip Morris disclosed its plans to buy Kraft, Inc., for $13.5 billion in cash. The company to be created by the combination will be the largest producer of consumer goods in the world, replacing the current No. 1, the British-Dutch firm of Unilever. Hamish Maxwell, the chief execu-tive officer of Phillip Morris, said that it was purchasing Kraft so that it could compete more effectively in world food markets (→ 11/3).

Not guilty is plea offered by Imelda

Oct 31. In a stunning floor-length turquoise traditional Philip-pine dress and with a strong voice, Imelda Marcos pleaded not guilty in New York City today to charges that include the embezzlement of $108 million from the Philippine treasury to buy Manhattan real es-tate. Former President Ferdinand Marcos remains in Hawaii, citing illnesses. The former first lady of the Philippines, well-known for her extravagances, including a fabulous shoe collection, wore plain black pumps to her arraignment (→ 11/2).

Su	Mo	Tu	We	Th	Fr	Sa
		1	2	3	4	5
6	7	8	9	10	11	12
13	14	15	16	17	18	19
20	21	22	23	24	25	26
27	28	29	30			

1. Tokyo: Japan gives in to international pressure, dropping importation of South African uranium (→ 1).

1. Johannesburg: South Africa bans Weekly Mail, leading opposition newspaper, from publishing for a month (→ 18).

1. Wichita, Kansas: Some 235 people from 12 faiths (mostly Eastern and Native American) meet to establish North American Interfaith Network to work for world peace and the environment; said to be first such gathering since 1983.

2. London: Men's tennis thrown into disarray as top players announce they are forming tour to compete with Grand Prix.

2. New York City: Tobacco heiress Doris Duke says she will post $5 million bail for Imelda Marcos.

3. Brooklyn: Civic groups file lawsuit charging Census Bureau undercounted minorities (→ 7).

3. Washington: Reagan vetoes legislation to protect 1.4 million acres of land in Montana from development.

3. Washington: Norwegian authorities say that some missing heavy water, used to make nuclear weapons, was diverted to India.

3. Hanoi: Vietnamese government turns over to the United States 23 sets of remains purported to be American servicemen.

4. Warsaw: Polish government orders three aircraft from Boeing; first purchase of advanced American planes by Eastern bloc country.

4. New York City: Study finds employers discriminating against legal aliens in effort to stay clear of penalties under new immigration laws.

4. Aiken, South Carolina: Seventeen workers out of 1,400 at Savannah River nuclear arms plant found contaminated by plutonium (→ 18).

4. Washington: Reagan signs legislation enabling United States to ratify the United Nations Genocide Convention.

Thousands of computers infected by virus

Nov 4. A powerful electronic "virus" that sowed chaos throughout a vast network of military, corporate and university computers was eliminated today, according to Defense Department officials.

The virus is the work of Robert T. Morris Jr., a graduate student and the son of a National Security Council expert on computer safety. Intended to be a harmless prank, it was transferred into the Arpanet computer network, an anonymous caller told The New York Times. But a programming error caused it to spiral out of control, reproducing itself so quickly as it spread via datalinks that systems across the nation went down like dominoes.

The virus jammed computers at hundreds of institutions, including Harvard University, the Strategic Air Command, Xerox Corporation and the National Aeronautics and Space Administration. And although it incapacitated systems for hours and caused countless headaches for computer technicians from coast to coast, it is thought that no permanent damage or elimination of files resulted.

Morris: hacked his way to infamy.

Defense officials stressed that no top-security military computers were infiltrated by the virus, but some computer experts questioned assurances that such computers were impervious to sabotage. One said of the Arpanet virus: "I think it's symptomatic of the terrible vulnerability that exists in linked computer systems."

Indian troops put down coup in Maldives

Nov 4. At the crack of dawn yesterday, hundreds of rebels stormed into Male, capital of the Maldives, to overthrow the islands' government. And Indian Prime Minister Rajiv Gandhi responded by sending 1,600 troops to the Indian Ocean republic to defuse the attempted coup. Gandhi's army had little trouble crushing the revolt. News sources estimate that anywhere from 20 to 200 of the rebels were killed; Indian officials say their troops suffered no casualties.

Maldives President Maumoon Abdul Gayoom requested military assistance from Gandhi, who promptly responded. After order was restored, Gandhi told the Indian Parliament, "The attempt to spread terror and undermine peace and stability in our region has been frustrated." It is believed the attackers were expatriate Maldivians trying to oust Gayoom from power. Some of the rebels escaped and are holding hostages aboard a 5,000-ton ship. According to reports, Indian navy boats have encircled the ship and are negotiating for the hostages' release.

The revolt was the second of its kind. In 1983, British mercenaries led by former President Sayed Ibrahim Nasir failed to remove Gayoom. Nasir is believed to be linked to yesterday's attempted coup.

Indian troops in the Maldives.

Expert says buyou may bring on crash

Nov 3. Martin Lipton, a law specializing in corporate takeove has warned that the current fren of mergers and acquisitions v cause another stock market cra "We and our children will pay gigantic price for allowing abus takeover tactics and bootstr junkbond takeovers," Lipton, warned in a recent memorandum his clients. But the Manhatt lawyer's own experiences wi takeovers haven't caused a person crash. He was reported to have ceived more than $20 million cently from Kraft Inc. for tv weeks of takeover discussions wi Philip Morris (→ 12/1).

Algerians vote for political reforms

Nov 3. "It is the beginning change," said one of the millions Algerians who voted today in a re erendum. The vote is expected grant President Chadli Benjedi the power to reform Algeria's pol tical system. Since the Nationa Liberation Front won Algeria's in dependence from France in 1962, has ruled the nation. Planks on th ballot call for a weakening of th front's power. Last month, protest for liberalization turned bloody Dozens of protesters died, prompt ing President Benjedid to fire offi cials who were responsible for po lice violence.

Changing the laws of Algeria.

Close Israeli election calls for coalition

Yitzhak Shamir will need to form a coalition to create his new government.

Nov 2. Voting in Israel's general election ended tonight in a virtual tie. But it appears that Prime Minister Yitzhak Shamir, leader of the right-wing Likud Party, may have enough votes to form a coalition government. Early returns indicate that the Likud Party will hold 39 seats in the Knesset, or Israeli parliament, and the Labor Party, led by Foreign Minister Shimon Peres, will win about 38 seats.

Israel's religious parties, which exist outside the two-party system, will likely throw their support to Likud. Knowing this, Shamir has claimed victory. He told ecstatic supporters, "It seems to us that the situation at the moment allows us to establish this new government at the earliest possible opportunity."

Since a close election in 1984, both Peres and Shamir have run Israel in what has been called a national unity government. Both parties have wanted to end this sharing of power. Analysts who cast doubt on the viability of the two-party system after the 1984 election are now raising similar questions. One political pundit, Daniel Elazar, said, "This is a very strong repudiation of the two major parties" (→ 14).

Recruiting tactics bar Kansas team

Nov 1. The Kansas Jayhawks basked in glory last season as they won the college basketball title. Now, their pride has given way to sorrow as the National Collegiate Athletic Association penalized the team for recruiting violations. The NCAA barred Kansas from postseason play in 1989 and imposed a three-year probation on the champions. Team recruiters offered Memphis State guard Vincent Askew $1,244 in illegal inducements to join the Jayhawks. He was given cash, airline tickets and clothing. Askew reportedly accepted the premiums, but he declined the transfer to Kansas.

Soviets slow move out of Afghanistan

Nov 4. The Soviet Union has announced it is slowing its withdrawal of troops from Afghanistan. According to Deputy Foreign Minister Aleksandr Bessmertnykh, the decision was based on reports that the Afghan guerrillas have violated the terms of disengagement as set in the Geneva accords. The decision ay delay the February 15 deadline for a complete Soviet pullout from the war many refer to as the Soviets' "Vietnam." White House spokesman Marlin Fitzwater expressed the Reagan administration's disappointment, saying the Soviet action "can only increase tension in the region."

Millions paid improperly to consultants

Nov 3. A Defense Department audit has discovered that many of the nation's top defense contractors have been improperly charging the government for millions of dollars in consultant's fees.

The investigation began last August and centered on 60 companies, including such defense giants as General Dynamics, Boeing and the Lockheed Corporation. The auditors discovered that the companies had billed the government for $237 million in consultant's fees over a period of one year. In many cases, however, the companies could not explain what services the consultants had actually provided.

In other instances, the government may have been wrongly charged for consultant's lobbying or publicity fees. The auditors have referred five of the cases they uncovered to criminal investigators, while their report urged an overhaul of Pentagon rules governing the use of contractor consultants.

Talk show creator interviews himself

Nov 4. "I have said more words into a camera and mike than anyone else in the world," says Joe Franklin, the self-proclaimed inventor of the talk show. And he may just be right. Franklin is celebrating his 40th anniversary in broadcasting, after nearly 100,000 interviews that range from such luminaries as Woody Allen and Bing Crosby to the more usual cavalcade of pro wrestlers and lounge singers. A legend among insomniacs, who stare bleary-eyed at his late-night shows, and stand-up comics, who parody his unique delivery, Franklin marked today's milestone by taping his most unusual interview yet, a split-screen tete-a-tete with himself.

Largest chain of theaters expanding

Nov 5. In an age of videotapes and cable TV, what kind of a nut would invest in movie theaters? A very wealthy, successful one. Sane and savvy Canadian entrepreneur Garth Drabinsky owns the rapidly growing Cineplex Odeon theater chain, now the largest in North America. Drabinsky, 39, co-founded Odeon in 1979 with 18 theaters; today there are 1,643. How did he do it? He saw what viewing films at home lacks: class. Who would sit on a frumpy couch and eat cheese puffs when he can be served cups of exotic tea and fresh baked cakes in a luxurious setting? Drabinsky is expanding into movie distribution, anticipating five films to be produced by Robert Redford.

"Dish with Peonies and Butterflies," a piece of ko-kutani ware made in the 17th century by an anonymous artist, is part of the exhibition "Japan: The Shaping of Daimyo Culture 1185-1868," at National Gallery of Art.

Su	Mo	Tu	We	Th	Fr	Sa
		1	2	3	4	5
6	7	8	9	10	11	12
13	14	15	16	17	18	19
20	21	22	23	24	25	26
27	28	29	30			

7. Washington: Supreme Court refuses to challenge lower court ruling that Brooklyn housing project can't limit sale of units to minorities to keep whites from moving out.

7. Las Vegas: Sugar Ray Leonard scores TKO over Donny Lalonde to become second fighter with titles in five weight classes.

8. China: Earthquake two days ago said to kill 600 (→ 9).

9. Peking: Chinese officials ask for international aid, saying 'quake left 100,000 homeless.

9. Washington: Strategic Air Command grounds entire new fleet of B-1 bombers (→ 17).

9. New York City: Matthew Barnwell, arrested for buying crack, is first N.Y. principal held for drug use (→ 14).

10. Washington: Reagan administration publishes new regulations reversing 45-year ban on manufacturing at home.

10. Los Angeles: State Supreme Court delays implementation of insurance rate cuts voted in referendum.

10. Colombo, Sri Lanka: Police fire on demonstrators defying curfew; 15 killed.

10. Washington: Air Force says Stealth bomber's been secretly flown for seven years.

10. United States: Los Angeles Dodgers pitcher Orel Hershiser wins Cy Young award.

11. Baltimore: Scientist Stephen E. Breuning gets 60 days in halfway house for falsifying data on treatment of mentally disabled children.

11. New York City: Sotheby's sells Jasper Johns's "False Start" for $17 million; artist sold it for $1,575 in 1960 (→ 28).

DEATHS

9. John N. Mitchell, convicted for Watergate role while President Nixon's attorney general (*9/15/1913).

12. General Lyman L. Lemnitzer, World War II hero, U.N. commander in Korea and head of Joint Chiefs of Staff, at 89 (*8/29/1899).

Bush elected; Democrats win Congress

George Herbert Walker Bush, to be the 41st President of the United States.

Nov 8. George Herbert Walker Bush was elected President of the United States today, sweeping the South and much of the West to defeat his Democratic challenger, Governor Michael Dukakis. The New England-born patrician, who made his fortune in oil in Texas, is the first sitting Vice President elected to the nation's highest office since Martin Van Buren in 1836.

While retaining control of the White House, Republicans failed to make inroads in the Congress, where Democrats continue to hold substantial margins in both the Senate and the House. Democrats also hold the edge in the nation's governorships.

Shortly after 11 o'clock tonight, Governor Dukakis telephoned the Vice President in Houston to offer congratulations. In his concession speech in Boston, Dukakis told his cheering but saddened supporters: "I know I speak for all of you and the American people. He is our President. We will work with him."

The 64-year-old President-elect, a decorated hero in World War II, will take office next January 20, succeeding Ronald Reagan, the fellow Republican he served as Vice President for eight years. His own running mate, Senator Dan Quayle, will become Vice President.

The campaign just ended was viewed by many voters as one of the most negative in history, with Bush repeatedly rubbing Democratic nerves raw by attacking Dukakis's positions on such issues as the death penalty, prison furloughs, a dirty Boston harbor, the Pledge of Allegiance and liberal leanings. While skirting firm stands of his own on most matters of critical concern to the nation, Bush repeatedly slammed the door on the possibility of any tax increase. By ruling out a tax hike of any kind, even in the face of a huge national deficit, it is likely the Bush Presidency will be marked, at least initially, by intense political struggles (→ 9).

Baker is appointed Secretary of State

Nov 9. President-elect George Bush today chose an old friend, James A. Baker 3rd, to be Secretary of State in his administration. Once a top aide to President Reagan and later the Secretary of the Treasury, Baker had openly sought the job at State, despite his lack of experience in foreign affairs. The 58-year-old former Marine, a smiling Texan noted for his political shrewdness, was tapped for the job at State just a day after the decisive Bush victory. The two men have much in common: Both made fortunes in Texas; both attended Ivy League colleges, Bush at Yale and Baker at Princeton (→ 15).

Worry about Bush depresses market

Nov 11. The stock market took a sharp tumble today and the dollar plummeted overseas in the wake of the election this week of George Bush as President of the United States. Traders explained the twin declines by saying they were more convinced than ever that the Bush administration will favor a weaker dollar. While the financial markets had generally favored the election of Bush, key traders are concerned over whether he will be able to win approval of an economic package that would lower both the nation's budget and trade deficits in view of his persistent opposition to any tax increases (→ 16).

The big winner in the New York City Marathon is Grete Waitz, whose nine victories in the city's race are unequaled in the sport.

akharov visits U.S. ith Soviet consent

Sakharov, physicist and dissident.

Nov 6. Two years ago, Soviet physicist Andrei Sakharov was a virtual prisoner in the city of Gorky. Now he is free not just to leave Gorky, but to venture to the West — with the Kremlin's approval. Sakharov, 67, arrived in the United States today as a Soviet delegate to the Foundation for Survival and Development of Humanity. His outspoken support of human rights and criticism of the invasion of Afghanistan earned him seven years in internal exile, banishment that ended with a friendly phone call from Mikhail Gorbachev in December 1986. During his stay here, the Nobel Prize winner will visit relatives in Boston (→ 30).

Texas chosen for huge atom smasher

Nov 10. The federal government has awarded the project of building the world's largest atom smasher, or superconducting super collider, to the state of Texas. At $4.4 billion, the project would create the largest and most expensive scientific instrument ever, and six other states had lobbied hard for the contract. By accelerating subatomic particles around its 53-mile underground tunnel, and then smashing them together, the scientific device will probe the mysteries of matter and energy.

Cosby grants black college $20 million

Nov 6. Using a sizable part of his earnings as the nation's highest-paid entertainer, Bill Cosby has donated $20 million to Spelman College, a prestigious black women's school in Atlanta. Cosby's grant, the largest ever made to a black college by any individual, was disclosed at a dinner marking the inauguration of Spelman's first woman president, Johnetta B. Cole. According to Ms. Cole, the announcement was greeted by "gasps of wonder, foot-stomping and shouts of jubilation." Cosby, who holds a doctorate in education, termed the gift a challenge to black Americans to support education for blacks. Ms. Cole agreed, noting, "If we can tithe for our churches, we can tithe for our schools."

German quits over speech about Jews

Nov 11. Philipp Jenninger, Speaker of the West German Parliament, has resigned his post after an outcry over a speech he gave last night on anti-Semitism. He claimed his text, delivered on the 50th anniversary of Kristallnacht, the "night of the broken glass" when Jewish shops were destroyed, meant to show how Germans had been "seduced" by Hitler's propaganda. But most Parliament members felt his speech perpetuated interest in Hitler and lacked a tone of contrition.

Fossil 390 million years old is found

Nov 11. Scientists have discovered the oldest known insect in a chunk of fossilized mud excavated in Quebec. The tiny bristletail, a primitive relative of the modern household pest the silverfish, is approximately 390 million years old. Since the creature was by that time well adapted for life on land, the discovery pushes back the date that scientists believe life emerged from the sea by as much as 16 million years, to the late Silurian period, about 421 to 408 million years ago.

Two N.Y. addicts turn up for free needles

Most drug addicts did not get the point of the new anti-AIDS measure.

Nov 8. An experimental program designed to curb the spread of AIDS in New York City by distributing free hypodermic needles has sparked strong reactions from everyone but the addicts it is meant to help. The program has been hailed as a pragmatic solution to the rampant spread of AIDS among the city's 200,000 intravenous drug users, at least half of whom have contracted the disease from contaminated needles. Critics say the program condones drug use, which has especially ravaged minority neighborhoods. As protesters and advocates swamped Health Department offices yesterday, however, only two addicts showed up for the program's opening.

Worst locust plague in 30 years hits Africa

Nov 11. Like a biblical scourge, a massive plague of desert locusts has descended on northern Africa from the Atlantic coast to the Red Sea. It is the worst attack of the insects in 30 years, with individual swarms covering 150 square miles. Such a concentration can ravage crops at a rate of 40,000 tons of food per day. In the west, some croplands were saved when strong winds blew some swarms out to sea; despite a major eradication effort, however, swarms in the east have spread as far away as Iran and Iraq.

The voracious insects threaten to consume everything in sight.

Su	Mo	Tu	We	Th	Fr	Sa
			1	2	3	4	5
6	7	8	9	10	11	12
13	14	15	16	17	18	19
20	21	22	23	24	25	26
27	28	29	30			

14. Jerusalem: After gaining support of Orthodox parties, Yitzhak Shamir is invited to form government (→ 16).

14. Washington: Department of Transportation orders drug tests for four million non-government workers, most extensive such move yet (→ 23).

14. United States: Study shows 55% of newspapers chose not to support presidential candidate, up from 32% in 1984.

14. New York City: Picasso's "Motherhood" sells for $24.8 million, a record for 20th-Century art and third-highest price for a single artwork (→ 28).

15. U.S.S.R.: Soviet space shuttle spends three and a half hours aloft in first flight.

15. Green Bank, West Virginia: Huge, high-tech radio telescope collapses in mysterious accident.

16. Israel: In surprise move, Likud, seeking to avoid becoming beholden to religious right, opens talks with Labor on coalition government (→ 18).

16. New York City: Robin Givens files $125 million libel suit against Mike Tyson.

18. Washington: Reagan issues executive order giving federal government right to draft evacuation plans for nuclear power plants in attempt to circumvent local opposition (→ 22).

18. Pretoria: Four black leaders convicted of treason for inciting opposition to South African apartheid (→ 23).

18. New York City: Mario Biaggi sentenced to eight years in jail and fined $242,000 for role in Wedtech bribery case.

18. Jerusalem: American Jews meet with Shamir to express displeasure over movement to restrict criteria for legitimate conversion to Judaism (→ 30).

19. Philadelphia: Nicodemo Scarfo, reputed mob leader, and 16 associates convicted of murder and extortion.

19. New York City: Pam Shriver beats Steffi Graf 6-3, 7-6, breaking her 46-match winning streak.

Arab state is proclaimed

Chairman Yasir Arafat answers the call of his people for independence.

Nov 14. "In the name of God, in the name of the people, of the Arab Palestinian people, the establishment of the state of Palestine on our Palestinian nation, with its capital in holy Jerusalem." These words, declaring independence, were spoken by Yasir Arafat, chairman of the Palestine Liberation Organization, to the Palestine National Council in Algiers. The state of Palestine is not a concrete reality: Israel occupies the West Bank and the Gaza Strip, as well as the Arab section of Jerusalem. Yet the speech was much more than a gesture; Arafat and the council voted to endorse U.N. resolutions 242 and 338, which implicitly recognize Israel's right to exist. The P.L.O., which endorsed terrorism for decades, now rejects both it and the goal of Israel's destruction. Today's decision could be considered the first giant step in a 40-year stalemate between Israelis and Palestinian Arabs. However, Israel's Prime Minister Yitzhak Shamir is not expected to put any faith in it.

The Palestine National Council, a parliament in exile, voted 253 to 46 last night for U.N. Security Council Resolution 242. The decision fostered a festive mood, and this morning Arafat's speech was greeted by songs and cheers. Palestinians on the West Bank are expected to demonstrate their appreciation when they hear the news later today. In anticipation of trouble, Israel has stepped up security in the region (→ 20).

Palestinians in the occupied territories rejoice around their forbidden flag.

Benazir Bhutto is elected in Pakistan

Nov 17. Educated at Harvard, Oxford and the school of hard knocks (she spent months in government jails), Benazir Bhutto has won a seat in Pakistan's Parliament. And because she heads the Pakistan People's Party, the largest in the country, she will likely be asked soon by President Ghulam Ishaq Khan to form a new government. This would make her at 35 the youngest Prime Minister in the world and the first woman to rule a Moslem nation in centuries. She carries on the legacy of her father, who was elected in 1977, deposed in a military coup and executed. She has assured the army its privileges will be maintained (→ 12/1).

Bhutto will be the first modern woman ruler of an Islamic state.

Third B-1 bomber crashes; crew safe

Nov 17. A B-1 bomber crashed late tonight while attempting a landing in low-visibility weather at Ellsworth Air Force Base in South Dakota. Despite the jet's low altitude, all four crew members were able to parachute to safety. It was the third B-1 lost in 14 months, but as the cause is believed to have been pilot error, the crash will probably not fuel more criticism of the controversial plane, which has been attacked in Congress for design flaws as well as its $283-million-per-plane price tag.

ununu to become Bush's chief of staff

Nov 15. President-elect George Bush has chosen Governor John Sununu of New Hampshire as his White House chief of staff. By reaching outside the Washington establishment, Bush has disappointed some within his inner circle of advisers, who had favored the selection of Craig L. Fuller, a politically savvy Bush aide since 1985. Sununu, a 49-year-old engineer, is credited with helping the Vice President win the crucial New Hampshire primary following a loss in the Iowa caucuses. Meanwhile, the President-elect announced that Nicholas F. Brady would remain as Secretary of the Treasury (→ 12/31).

Million-dollar golf

Nov 14. Golfer Curtis Strange has chipped and putted his way to a million dollars this year. Strange won the Nabisco Championship with a dramatic 4-iron shot and tap-in in sudden death to defeat Tom Kite. Strange, who won the United States Open, collected $360,000 today at the beautiful Pebble Beach, California, course. With the day's take, he became the first golfer ever to earn a million dollars in one year on the PGA Tour. Strange has won four titles this year, three of them in sudden death playoffs.

Estonia declares right to veto Soviet laws

Outside of the Estonian parliament building in the republic's capital of Tallinn, demonstrators gather to voice their support for national autonomy.

Nov 16. The Soviet republic of Estonia acted boldly today, asserting that its legislature has the right to veto Soviet laws. While the declaration of veto power is defiant of Moscow, it seems to fall within the parameters of Soviet tolerance; it was not a call for independence.

The move, adopted unanimously by the Supreme Soviet of Estonia as an amendment to the constitution, was made after weeks of contention with Moscow's plan to diffuse Communist Party power. Soviet leader Mikhail S. Gorbachev's plan to enhance the powers of national legislatures still gives Moscow the right to set national policy and overrule local governments.

Some believe the new Gorbachev program is democratic in nature. But the Estonians see it only as a usurpation of the power of home rule. An estimated 900,000 of Estonia's 1.5 million citizens recently signed petitions opposing the governmental reorganization.

While the other Baltic republics, Latvia and Lithuania, are voicing similar opposition to the plan, Gorbachev has rejected their complaints. He recently denounced regional protest, saying, "We find political extremism of a nationalistic character especially unacceptable." It is expected that Moscow will overturn the action of the Estonians (→ 22).

Fed's chief warns budget cut is vital

Nov 16. In an emphatic warning to President-elect Bush, Federal Reserve Chairman Alan Greenspan said today that an uncurbed budget deficit would mean harsh realities for the economy. Greenspan, who was speaking before the bipartisan National Economic Commission, called "fanciful" those economists advising Bush and President Reagan who maintain that the economy will stay robust with neither spending cuts nor tax hikes. "The deficit has already begun to eat away at the foundations of our economic strength," he said, while stressing that an uncut deficit would lead to either higher interest rates or rising inflation.

Trash TV popular

Nov 16.. TV sleaze reigns supreme. From talk shows, which have featured loudmouth Morton Downey Jr. in a face-to-face screamfest with a stripper, Geraldo Rivera bloodied in a racially inflamed melee and Phil Donahue in drag, to pseudo-news offerings like "A Current Affair," which has re-enacted murders and rapes, anything goes if the ratings soar. Critics have blasted the medium's lurid descent. But as one ex-television executive said, "There would be none of this stuff if it did not have an audience."

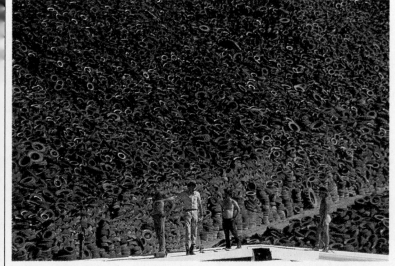

A new problem confronting Americans: What to do with 150 million used tires each year, when the landscape is already littered with two billion.

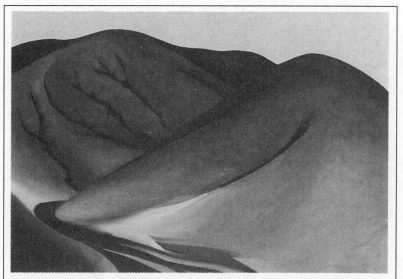

The art of Georgia O'Keeffe is now on display at New York's Metropolitan Museum of Art; above is the artist's work "Red Hills, Grey Sky."

Su	Mo	Tu	We	Th	Fr	Sa
		1	2	3	4	5
6	7	8	9	10	11	12
13	14	15	16	17	18	19
20	21	22	23	24	25	26
27	28	29	30			

20. Cairo: Egypt, after days of deliberation, recognizes Palestinian state (→ 26).

20. Rome: Mother Katherine Drexel, Philadelphia nun who educated blacks and Indians, is beatified by Pope John Paul II.

21. Pristina, Yugoslavia: Ethnic Albanians march for fifth day, protesting proposed changes in constitution.

22. Washington: Federal government, after years of ignoring state regulations, agrees for first time to clean up nuclear weapons facility (in Ohio) to comply with court order.

22. Riga: Latvia votes to reject move to be independent of the Soviet Union (→ 25).

22. Pretoria: South Africa accepts four-nation peace plan for Namibia and Angola, adding there are many details to be worked out (→ 12/13).

23. United States: Biggest air-fare increases in decade go into effect.

23. Johannesburg: Prime Minister Botha commutes death sentences of Sharpeville Six, anti-apartheid activists whose cause has attracted international calls for clemency (→ 24).

23. Washington: Reagan pocket vetoes legislation designed to curb lobbying activities of former government officials, calling the bill excessive.

23. New York City: School board in Bronx suspended, pending inquiry into charges of involvement in drugs, extortion.

24. Vienna: Gaining concessions from Iran, OPEC nations agree to set production quotas; big price rises forecast (→ 28).

25. U.S.S.R.: Military takes control in Armenian capital of Yerevan (→ 26).

26. Washington: Secretary of State Shultz denies P.L.O. chief Yasir Arafat admission to United States to speak at the United Nations (→ 30).

30. Jerusalem: Labor leaves coalition talks with Likud; defection of religious parties from alliance with Likud gives Peres opening to form majority (→ 12/11).

Mulroney wins 2nd term

Nov 22. Prime Minister Brian Mulroney said today he would use the parliamentary majority he won in this week's Canadian election to seek approval of the free-trade pact between his nation and the United States. His election to a second term and pledge to push for the pact most likely will lead to significant changes in world trading in years ahead. The agreement has already been approved by Congress and by Canada's House of Commons but was blocked by Canada's Senate unless Mulroney called a general election. Now that the election is over, key leaders of the opposition Liberal Party said they would allow the trade agreement pact to come to a vote in the Senate.

Mulroney, the voice of free trade.

Kennedy's death is widely commemorated

JFK, the embodiment of charisma.

Nov 22. Everyone over the age of 35 remembers what he or she was doing 25 years ago today. A vibrant young President was visiting Dallas, waving to the crowd, when a sniper's bullet shattered the hopes of a generation. John F. Kennedy was the first President whose career came to life on the television screen; it was strangely fitting that his death be telecast as well. For the past two weeks, in 30 hours of coverage, TV networks have rebroadcast the assassination and reviewed Kennedy's administration, honoring the man for what he did and what he might have done.

Carl Hubbell, great pitcher, is dead at 85

Nov 21. Carl Hubbell, the New York Giants pitcher whose crafty screwball so consistently baffled hitters that he was nicknamed The Meal Ticket, died today of injuries suffered in an auto accident. The Hall of Famer, 85, notched 253 wins for the Giants from 1928 to 1943, including a 1929 no-hitter. He led the team to three pennants and was the National League Most Valuable Player in 1933 and 1936. But Hubbell's most dramatic feat may have been in the 1934 All-Star Game, when he struck out future Hall of Famers Babe Ruth, Lou Gehrig, Jimmie Foxx, Al Simmons and Joe Cronin in succession.

Carl Hubbell baffled batters.

Gas price rise may follow OPEC action

Nov 28. The most influential cartel in the world, the Organization of Petroleum Exporting Countries, completed negotiations today ratifying quota agreements. With the accepted arrangements, quotas were set to limit production, driving the cost of oil up from $12 barrel to $18. The negotiations resolved an impasse with Iran, the second-largest oil producer in OPEC. Iran agreed to allow its former enemy, Iraq, to produce as much oil per day as it does, 2.4 million barrels. The successful accords will likely increase OPEC's international creditability and in the United States raise gas prices, which have not been hiked in years.

Price History

Average annual per barrel price.

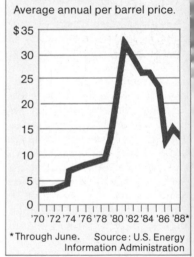

*Through June.   Source: U.S. Energy Information Administration

Mandela will not go back to prison

Nov 24. The South African government has announced that Nelson Mandela, the leader of the African National Congress who has been in prison for 26 years, will not return to jail after he recovers from tuberculosis. But it did not say where he would be sent or if he would remain under guard. Mandela's wife, Winnie, said the announcement was not significant; her husband "still remains a prisoner of the government." The news came on a day when five black South Africans were executed for capital crimes.

Troops detain 1,400 in Armenian capital

Nov 28. Soviet troops moved into Yerevan, capital of Armenia, in an effort to curb ethnic violence in the region. A nighttime curfew has been imposed and army guards and roadblocks are preventing protests in Yerevan. The measures come a day after similar steps were taken by the Russians in Baku, capital of Azerbaijan. Conflict between Moslem Azerbaijan and Christian Armenia has existed for hundreds of years. Recent violence between the two neighboring Soviet republics has killed many. An estimated 20,000 Armenians living in Azerbaijan have fled home and 7,000 Azerbaijanis have become refugees because of the turmoil.

Moscow nullifies Estonian veto plan

Nov 26. The Soviet government has rejected an amendment to the Estonian constitution that gives the Baltic republic veto power over Moscow laws. The recently adopted amendment sent a strong message of Estonian discontent about a plan to restructure the Soviet government. The plan, initiated by Soviet leader Mikhail S. Gorbachev, consolidates power in Moscow. The Soviet rejection of Estonia's action is likely to fuel nationalist movements in Latvia, Lithuania and Estonia (→ 28).

Soviet jamming of U.S. radio is ended

Nov 30. Glasnost, the new Soviet policy of openness, has cleared the air not only for discussion within the Soviet Union, but also for radio broadcasts from outside the country. The Russians began jamming foreign broadcasts in the early 1950's after declaring them tools of subversion. Last year, they took a bold step when they stopped jamming the Voice of America. Today, they opened the airwaves to three more stations, including the American-financed Radio Liberty, which claims to have a Soviet audience of about 16 million (→ 12/1).

Picasso sold for $38 million to Japanese

Nov 28. Pablo Picasso's "Acrobat and Young Harlequin" has been sold for $38 million to a buyer representing a major Japanese department store. The sale, at Christie's of London, set a record for a work created in this century. Despite this staggering fact, the price hardly

Picasso's "Acrobat and Young Harlequin" (1905) sets a 20th-Century record.

partment store is the new owner of "Acrobat," and last year Yasuda Fire and Marine Insurance Company of Tokyo bought van Gogh's "Sunflowers" for $39.9 million.

Impressionist works fetch the highest prices — "Acrobat and Young Harlequin" is from Picas-

surpised the world of auction houses, gallery owners, collectors or artists, who are finding skyrocketing prices almost commonplace in recent years. The Japanese, who are paying essentially 50 cents on the U.S. dollar, are the major buyers, followed closely by the Europeans. Americans with money are far behind. It is often Japanese companies rather than individuals making purchases — the Mitsukoshi de-

so's Rose period — although works by contemporary artists like Jasper Johns are also popular. Why the heavy investments in art? The works appreciate rapidly and confer status on the owner. But some point to another factor: their value transcends cultural and national borders. And that is why museums, increasingly priced out of the market, regret that these universal pleasures are enjoyed by just a few.

Arafat denied visa to address the U.N.

Nov 30. The United States found itself in almost total isolation today as 151 United Nations members protested America's decision to prevent Yasir Arafat from addressing the General Assembly. The Reagan administration informed the assembly on the 26th that "to protect our national security" the United States would not grant Arafat a visa. The United Nations has given the U.S. government 24 hours to reconsider its decision. No Reagan official has given any indication that it will be reversed; therefore, the United Nations will likely meet outside the United States to debate the Palestinian question this year.

Several U.N. representatives expressed deep disappointment over the U.S. decision, in light of recent diplomatic overtures by Arafat, chairman of the Palestine Liberation Organization. Two weeks ago in Algiers, Arafat proclaimed Palestine an independent state in a declaration worded to recognize implicitly the right of Israel to exist. For this reason, traditional supporters of U.S. policy such as Australia and Canada voted for the U.N. resolution, although they did object to its harsh wording. Britain abstained, leaving only the U.S. and Israel to vote against the Arab-backed resolution. Before the week is out, Arab representaives are expected to propose the assembly meet in Geneva. Little opposition is expected (→ 12/14).

Korean apologizes, goes to monastery

Nov 23. Former South Korean President Chun Doo Hwan was driven by limousine to a mountain monastery outside Seoul today, where he will presumably seek forgiveness from Buddha for his political abuses. Chun apologized to the public on television this morning, admitting to misuse of funds during his eight-year rule. He said he would return $23 million to the public; however, opposition leader Kim Dae Jung has stated that his savings are in "billions of dollars." He warns President Roh Tae Woo against granting Chun clemency.

97

DECEMBER
Week 48 1988

Su	Mo	Tu	We	Th	Fr	Sa
				1	2	3
4	5	6	7	8	9	10
11	12	13	14	15	16	17
18	19	20	21	22	23	24
25	26	27	28	29	30	31

1. Washington: Department of Health and Human Services reports that over 4,000 of nation's 15,000 nursing homes hand out drugs to patients without prescriptions.

1. United States: Federal officials announce arrest of 52 people in major crackdown on suspected Sicilian Mafia members dealing drugs in U.S.

1. Moscow: Kremlin says it has opened way to emigration of some 50 dissidents by classifying them as no longer in possession of state secrets.

1. Washington: President Reagan rules out pardon for Oliver North, but insists government has a duty to withhold classified documents that might harm state security (→ 6).

1. Pakistan: Benazir Bhutto becomes first woman Prime Minister of modern Moslem nation.

2. Moscow: Chinese Foreign Minister Qian Qichen and Gorbachev announce plans for Chinese-Soviet summit early next year that would end three decades of mutual alienation.

5. Fort Mill, Sorth Carolina: Jim Bakker and former aide charged with defrauding some 150,000 contributors to PTL club of more than $4 million for personal use.

5. Los Angeles: Geologists have found two major faults under most densely populated areas of city, including Beverly Hills and Santa Monica.

5. London: Lorin Maazel, director of Pittsburgh Symphony, is first to conduct all nine Beethoven symphonies in one day, leading three orchestras at Royal Festival Hall.

5. New York City: Boris Becker beats Ivan Lendl 5-7, 7-6, 3-6, 6-2, 7-6 in four-hour, 42-minute Masters final.

6. Washington: Prosecutors in Oliver North case restrict charges to Iran-contra affair, dropping allegations North used money for personal use.

8. Mauritania: United States government plane on African relief mission is shot down by unidentified missile.

Gorbachev pledges major troop cuts

Dec 7. With his usual flair for the dramatic, Soviet leader Mikhail S. Gorbachev may have reversed the course of East-West relations in one bold stroke today, by pledging a substantial unilateral cut in conventional arms in Eastern Europe.

Speaking before the United Nations General Assembly, Gorbachev said that within two years the Red Army would be cut by 500,000 men and 10,000 tanks, representing about 10 percent of total military manpower and over one-fourth of Soviet tanks in Eastern Europe. In an ideological turnaround perhaps equally as startling, Gorbachev also rejected 70 years of Marxist dogma on the class struggle with capitalism. "The world economy is becoming a single organism," said Gorbachev, who, as he tries to restructure the Soviet economy, can only benefit from lessening the drain of military spending.

While many Western leaders were quick to point out that the reductions will still leave the Soviet Union with a marked advantage in Europe, President Reagan, at a New York lunch with the Soviet leader, said, "Naturally, I heartily approve." President-elect Bush, upstaged by Gorbachev's diplomatic coup, simply said, "I support what the President says."

But New Yorkers didn't lack enthusiasm. When the leader of the Soviet Union stepped from his limousine tonight, Times Square crowds erupted in cheers (→ 10).

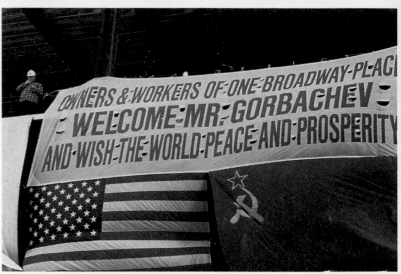

The Big Apple bids Mikhail Gorbachev a warm welcome to Broadway.

Three of the world's most important men confer on Governors Island.

Soviet skyjackers give up in Israel

Dec 3. Five Soviet skyjackers, whom Israeli Defense Minister Yitzhak Rabin called "simple criminals," surrendered today in Tel Aviv. Armed with small weapons, they had seized a school bus in the Caucasus yesterday and were granted a cargo plane and $3 million in exchange for the lives of 31 hostages. According to a crew member on the plane, the hijackers were not Jews, "just people who wanted to fly out of the Soviet Union." Rabin said they would be sent home "if there is a proper request to extradite them."

Soviets switch some party power to voters

Dec 1. Mikhail S. Gorbachev's efforts to move his nation past the entrenchments of Stalinism received a boost today when the Supreme Soviet legislature approved a limited transfer of power from the Communist Party to a new, popularly elected legislative body.

Under the plan, a 2,500-member Congress of People's Deputies would be formed by elections on March 26, with officials limited to 10-year terms. It would be the highest state body, wielding broad power over economic and social policies. Gorbachev also fortified his own position through the creation of the powerful new post of President, which he is likely to fill while retaining his job as General Secretary of the party. By taking absolute power away from the party, which has resisted many of Gorbachev's socioeconomic reforms, the Soviet leader could establish a more secure base of support.

The changes will "open a new chapter in the development of Soviet statehood and democratization," Gorbachev said today. Despite the plan's overwhelming passage, some intellectuals and leaders of minority national groups feared that the plan's populist overtones masked a dangerous monopoly on power for Gorbachev.

Quake devastates Soviet Armenia; death toll huge

Dec 10. A powerful earthquake that rumbled through Soviet Armenia Wednesday morning has devastated the region, leaving in its wake a landscape of ruin and despair, with a death toll officials feared could well exceed 40,000.

The first of two major, closely spaced shocks struck at 11:41, centered in the northwest portion of the region. Within moments, the temblor — at 6.9 on the Richter scale, the worst to strike the area in over 80 years — reduced entire towns and cities to heaps of rubble. Flimsily constructed schools, factories, homes and hospitals were toppled instantly with deadly effect, as thousands were crushed or entombed. Leninaken, Armenia's second largest city at 290,000 people, was 80 percent destroyed, with Kirkovan, a city of 150,000, suffering comparable levels of destruction. Spitak, a town of 30,000 located directly adjacent to the earthquake's epicenter, was completely leveled. The town just "doesn't exist anymore," remarked one stunned observer.

Mikhail S. Gorbachev, just 24 hours after his historic U.N. address, abruptly cut short his New York visit and flew to Moscow, then Leninaken, to direct relief efforts in the stricken region, which has been convulsed in recent months by ethnic strife and nationalist rebellions. But Soviet authorities were reeling from the vast scope of the new Armenian trage-

Poor building practices are to blame for the total ruin of some areas.

Christmas joy will be in short supply this year in Christian Armenia.

dy. An estimated 500,000 numbed survivors wandered the streets and countryside of the region, their homes ravaged, while tens of thousands of injured severely strained scarce medical resources. Though the faint cries of victims trapped within collapsed buildings echoed hauntingly for hours, cranes and other rescue equipment were in such short supply that very few lives could be saved.

Unlike disasters that have befallen the Soviet Union in previous years, the Armenian calamity was reported in all of its shocking reality on Soviet television, and the images of desolation wrought by the earthquake sparked an unprecedented outpouring of assistance from Western nations. Underscoring the superpower thaw so carefully coaxed by Gorbachev earlier in the week, the Soviet government accepted American aid for the first time since World War II. And last night, the first cargo plane, carrying rescue teams and equipment, left New York for Armenia.

But long after the victims are buried and the rebuilding process begun, the effects of the earthquake may linger, not only among the grieving, traumatized survivors, but for Gorbachev's ambitious economic restructuring. At a cost expected to be in the tens of billions of rubles, the disaster, like the Chernobyl nuclear accident before it, will undermine an already shaky Soviet economy (→ 12).

Nabisco bought out for record $25 billion

Dec 1. Wall Street's most bitter and costly takeover battle ended late last night when the leveraged buyout firm of Kohlberg, Kravis, Roberts and Company won its bid for RJR Nabisco Inc. with an audacious $24.88 billion offer.

It was the largest sum ever paid in a buyout, nearly double the previous record $13.4 billion paid for the Gulf Oil Corporation by Chevron Corporation in 1984. But in an angered response typical of the six-week bidding war, Kohlberg, Kravis's closest rival, an investment group teaming RJR Nabisco executives with the Wall Street firm of Shearson Lehman Hutton,

claimed that its own offer had topped the winner's. The $25.42 billion bid lost out, the group said, due to unfair bidding practices.

The food division of RJR Nabisco, the nation's 19th-largest company, owns such brand-name products as Ritz crackers, Oreo cookies and Planters nuts. But since the leveraged buyout will leave the company with a staggering $22.8 billion debt, Kohlberg, Kravis may be forced to sell off some of these food businesses. The debt burden has raised some eyebrows in Congress, where hearings into Wall Street's leveraged buyout mania are expected next year.

Rock and roller Roy Orbison is dead at 52

Dec 6. "Roy's ballads were always best when you were alone and in the dark," Bruce Springsteen said of his idol Roy Orbison in 1987. Elvis Presley simply called him "the greatest singer in the world." Orbison, whose haunting tenor and introspective lyrics brought a new emotional depth to rock and roll in the late 50's and early 60's, died today at 52 of a massive heart attack. With his trademark black suits and dark glasses, Orbison cut a solitary contrast to rock's early innocence; he graced the airwaves with gems like "Only the Lonely," "Oh, Pretty Women" and "In Dreams."

Orbison, one of the greats, is gone.

DECEMBER
Week 50 1988

Su	Mo	Tu	We	Th	Fr	Sa
				1	2	3
4	5	6	7	8	9	10
11	12	13	14	15	16	17
18	19	20	21	22	23	24
25	26	27	28	29	30	31

11. Jerusalem: Labor and Likud parties resume talks to forge coalition government (→ 19).

11. Morocco: Polisario Front, leftist guerrilla rebel group, apologizes for attack on American relief planes that killed five, saying the planes were mistaken for Moroccan military C-130's.

12. Lompoc, California: Anthony Provenzano, ex-chief of Teamsters union in New Jersey, dies at 71 while serving prison sentence for racketeering.

12. Washington: Congressman Dan Coats appointed by governor to fill Dan Quayle's Indiana Senate seat.

12. Washington: Immigration officials announce plan to root out aliens arriving from Nicaragua and send them back if they cannot prove "well-founded fear of persecution."

13. Florennes, Belgium: United States removes last cruise missiles from Belgium, making it first country cleared of intermediate-range missiles under INF Treaty.

13. Columbia, South Carolina: Federal bankruptcy judge orders PTL assets sold to Stephen J. Mernick, Toronto real estate developer and Orthodox Jew, for $65 million.

14. Stockholm: Swedish police arrest suspect in 1986 slaying of Prime Minister Olof Palme.

15. Bronx, New York: Larry Davis, acquitted in 1986 shootout with police, gets five to 15 years on weapons charges.

15. Hanoi: Vietnam gives United States 38 sets of remains, believed to be American servicemen, largest group yet.

15. United States: Study indicates that one in 15 high school senior boys use anabolic steroids.

16. Dallas: Federal Judge Jack Hampton is quoted in the Dallas Times Herald as saying that he gave the killer of two homosexuals light sentences because "I put prostitutes and gays at about the same level."

U.S.-P.L.O. talks begin

Dec 16. Robert Pelletreau, the American Ambassador to Tunis, met in Carthage for one hour and 40 minutes with Yasir Abed Rabbo of the Palestine Liberation Organization today, just two days after the United States dropped its 13-year ban on contact with the P.L.O.

"It is our hope that this dialogue, as it develops, will lead to peace," the American envoy said, adding that the discussions were "practical and characterized by seriousness of purpose." Abed, the head of the P.L.O. delegation, called the session "constructive and fair."

After the meetings, details of which were not made available, Abed also issued a strong attack on Israel and a defense of the year-long Palestinian uprising. "We're here to achieve the goals of the uprising," he said. "It will end with the establishment of a Palestinian state with Jerusalem as its capital."

In the Mideast, reaction to the U.S.-P.L.O. meeting was favorable. Syria and Iran, however, rejected the talks, saying peace should be achieved by force.

The meeting would not have taken place if not for the secret intermediary role of Sweden. On the 14th, Ulf Hjertonsson, deputy chief of mission at the Swedish Embassy in Washington, helped to smooth out problems in wording unacceptable to the U.S. that were included in a statement to be read by Yasir Arafat at a news conference in Geneva. Arafat read the statement and President Reagan accepted it.

Arafat calls for peace parley with Israel

Dec 14. In a speech yesterday to the United Nations General Assembly in Geneva, Yasir Arafat urged Israel to negotiate with the Palestine Liberation Organization.

In the speech, delivered in Geneva because the P.L.O chairman had been denied an American visa, Arafat called for "a serious effort" to convene an international peace conference on the Middle East under U.N. auspices. He said the "occupied Palestinian lands" under Israeli control should be placed under U.N. supervision, with a U.N. peacekeeping force sent in to "protect the people" and oversee "Israeli withdrawal." In return, the P.L.O would strive for a "comprehensive settlement among the parties in the Arab-Israeli dispute, including the state of Palestine, Israel and other neighbors." The settlement, Arafat said, would be based on U.N. Security Council Resolutions 242 and 338 and should guarantee "the right to exist in peace and security for all."

"The Palestine National Council," Arafat proclaimed in the address, "has also reaffirmed its rejection of terrorism in all its forms, including state terrorism ..."

Reaction to the speech was swift. In Israel, Prime Minister Yitzhak Shamir called Arafat's peace offer nothing more than deceptive "double talk" intended to "create an

Yasir Arafat: wants to talk peace.

impression of moderation."

The United States said the speech failed to meet American conditions for engaging in talks with the P.L.O. But after Arafat held a news conference in Geneva today and said he accepted "the right of all parties concerned in the Middle East conflict to exist in peace and security" and renounced "all forms of terrorism, including individual, group and state terrorism," the U.S. changed its position. President Reagan has authorized the start of a "diplomatic dialogue" with the P.L.O., which he said had met U.S. conditions for direct talks (→ 16).

Relief plane bound for Armenia crashes

Dec 12. A Soviet military transport plane on a rescue mission ha crashed approaching Leninaken one of the cities in Armenia dev astated by last week's earthquake The death of nine crew members and 69 military personnel adds more grief to the already known loss o 45,000 lives from the earthquake Even before the crash, the Soviet press had shown a new toughness in criticizing rescue efforts, which it asserts are hampered by disorganization. Meanwhile, the earthquake exacerbated ethnic grievances as Armenian protesters clashed with army troops. "To behave like this at such a time," said Soviet leader Mikhail Gorbachev, "what sort of morals do these people have?"

3 commuter trains collide in London

Dec 12. At least 36 persons died in south London this morning when a packed commuter train plowed into the rear of a train stopped ahead of it. An empty train coming the other way then struck the wreckage. "There were pieces of bodies lying all over the place in the wreckage," said an ambulance worker. The cause of the accident was a "technical fault following preparatory work in connection with re-signaling."

$1.1 billion paid for baseball on TV

Dec 14. CBS, seeking to improve its poor ratings performance, has won exclusive rights for four years to televise 12 major league baseball games during each regular season, plus the All-Star Game, the league playoffs and the World Series. The award, which will pay 26 teams $1.1 billion, was announced by Peter Ueberroth, the baseball commissioner, who said that "it may be the largest network sports transaction in the history of the medium." Laurence Tisch, CBS president, said he was "thrilled" with the deal, and Neil Pilson, president of CBS Sports, called it "a lifelong dream."

Socialist Spain is paralyzed by strike

Dec 14. Nearly eight million out of a total workforce of 10 million stayed off their jobs in Spain today, halting commerce, industry and transportation throughout the nation. The one-day strike indicates that there is widespread dissatisfaction with the economic policies of the Socialist government of Prime Minister Felipe Gonzales.

"This is a historic work stoppage, never before seen in our country," said one union official, pointing to the probability that Gonzales will have to alter his policies or call elections earlier than those scheduled for 1990. For two years, union leaders have complained that the government's anti-inflation campaign and a prolonged economic boom have benefited business rather than labor. In fact, relations between the Socialist Party and its union allies have eroded to the point that the unions for the first time joined Communist-led organizations in sponsoring the strike.

Agreement reached on Namibia's freedom

The latest adherent to this year's pullout trend are Cubans, leaving Angola.

Dec 13. In a negotiating process overseen by the United States and begun nearly eight years ago, South Africa, Angola and Cuba have reached an agreement providing for independence for Namibia (formerly South-West Africa) and the pullout of all Cuban troops from Angola, beginning next April 1.

The accord, signed in Brazzaville, capital of the Congo, envisions a key role for United Nations peacekeeping forces, both in securing Namibian independence and verifying Cuban troop withdrawals from Angola. It also represents a major foreign policy success for the Reagan administration in its final days.

Fiber-optic cable spans the Atlantic

Dec 14. A new era of faster, clearer global communications dawned today when the first fiber-optic telephone cable across the Atlantic Ocean went into service, vastly increasing the number of calls that can be handled simultaneously. Using pulses of laser light to send voice and computer information, the new cable can carry 40,000 calls at one time, double the number carried before by three copper cables.

Installed at a cost of $362 million over a period of six months, the new cable is a joint venture of 29 telephone firms in North America and Europe. The American Telephone and Telegraph Company will operate it. An AT&T spokesman said that the cable was not expected to reduce prices, but that a variety of new services as well as transmissions free of distortions and delays would result. People in the United States made 4.7 billion minutes of overseas calls last year.

Van Gogh paintings stolen from museum

Dec 12. Three paintings by Vincent van Gogh, "Dried Sunflowers," "Weaver's Interior" and a version of his renowned "Potato Eaters," have been stolen from the Kroller-Muller National Museum, which houses one of the world's largest collections of the Dutch artist's work, in Otterlo, The Netherlands. This version of "Potato Eaters," which depicts peasants eating a frugal meal, was a painted sketch, preliminary to the completion of the work in 1885. No estimated value of the stolen paintings was available.

Illnesses can be diagnosed by satellite

Dec 17. A visit to the doctor may be changing. In an experiment in South America and Miami, Florida, such medical images as X-rays and cat scans are captured in a computer system, identified, catalogued and filed in a database and then transmitted by phone lines and a satellite. A South American patient, whose local medical services are inadequate, is thus diagnosed by doctors in Miami, who can then determine whether to fly him to the United States for treatment. Previously, patients made expensive trips to Miami for diagnosis alone.

A painted sketch of "Potato Eaters" is the most notable of the stolen works.

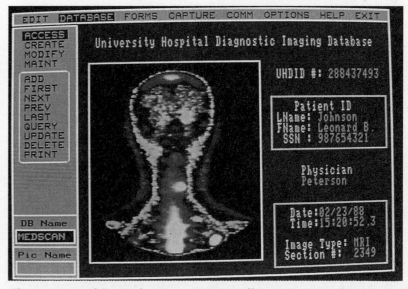

The money saved by not having to transport all patients to the diagnosis site can help free more financial resources to provide better care to more people.

Su	Mo	Tu	We	Th	Fr	Sa
				1	2	3
4	5	6	7	8	9	10
11	12	13	14	15	16	17
18	19	20	21	22	23	24
25	26	27	28	29	30	31

18. Washington: World Bank report says that Third World nations have given record amount of money in loan repayments to wealthy countries this year.

19. Washington: A federal official reports that the No. 9 killer of children between 1 and 4 years old is AIDS.

19. Richmond, Virginia: Electoral College officially makes George Bush and Dan Quayle the next President and Vice President, with 426 votes to Dukakis and Bentsen's 111.

20. Chicago: Jesse Jackson says that term 'black' is outdated, and should be replaced with the ethnic description 'African American.'

20. UNICEF annual report says that 500,000 children died in 1988 in developing nations as a result of reversals in 40 years of progress.

21. Washington: Federal judge sets date for the conspiracy trial of Oliver North as January 31, 1989 (→ 31).

21. U.S.S.R.: Two Soviet cosmonauts set a human endurance record by completing a 366-day stay in space.

22. Washington: Scientists report they have succeeded in implanting AIDS virus in genetically altered mice.

23. Cairo: A book, possibly world's oldest, is discovered in child's grave; most complete book of psalms ever unearthed.

23. Beirut: Palestinian guerrillas and Shiite militiamen agree to end their feud.

23. Rome: Pope meets with Yasir Arafat and takes noncommittal stance in Israeli-Palestinian conflict, saying the two sides both have "an identical, fundamental right to their own homelands."

23. Washington: Budget officials say hidden losses in U.S. loan portfolios are huge, and will be a large financial burden on taxpayers for years.

DEATH

20. Max Robinson, first black to anchor network news, at 49 of AIDS.

Pan Am 747 crashes in Scottish town

Speculation abounds that a terrorist bomb caused the airplane to crash.

The citizens of Lockerbie had no warning of the terror falling from the skies.

Dec 21. A Pan Am Boeing 747 has crashed in the village of Lockerbie, Scotland, with 258 people aboard. The airline reported that it knew of no survivors. There was no immediate indication of the cause of the crash, although it appears to have been an on-board explosion or a structural failure.

The plane was flying at 31,000 feet, from London to New York, when it disappeared from radar and fell onto two rows of houses, setting them on fire. Pan Am officials said it was the worst single-plane disaster in the airline's history, and Britain's Prime Minister Margaret Thatcher said it was the worst air disaster in British history.

Among those on board Pan Am World Airways Flight 103 was the chief administrative officer of the U.N. Council for Namibia, Bernt Carlsson of Sweden, as well as 38 people from Syracuse University.

According to Pan Am, there were 243 passengers on board and 15 crew members. A Pan Am spokesman said there was "no sign at all" of adverse weather that might have been a factor in the crash. A British military spokesman said there had been no midair collision with another plane.

Witnesses said the huge aircraft left a deep crater where it came down, near a gas station. "I was driving past the filling station when the aircraft crashed," said one. "The whole sky lit up and the sky was actually raining fire" (→ 28).

"Happy Birthday" is bought by Warner

Dec 20. The largest music publisher in the world, Warner Chappell, a division of Warner Communications, has agreed to pay $25 million to buy Birchtree Ltd., owner of the song "Happy Birthday to You." The old favorite, an essential part of every birthday party, generates about $1 million a year in royalty fees, a relatively modest amount because it is virtually impossible to enforce the copyright on the song. Warner will no longer be entitled to royalties after the year 2010, when, under federal law, the copyright will expire.

Baron moves his art collection to Spain

Dec 20. Baron Hans Heinrich Thyssen-Bornemisza has reached an agreement with the Spanish government that will allow more than 800 artworks in his extensive collection to be moved to Spain for 10 years. The Thyssen collection, which includes 1,400 paintings, is considered the second largest, most valuable private collection in the world, after that of England's Queen Elizabeth II. Under the agreement, the Baron will head a foundation to oversee the collection, most of which will be housed at Madrid's Prado Museum, and he will receive $5 million annually as compensation.

Valuable art bound for Spain.

Canada okays trade pact

Dec 24. A new relationship of historic importance between the United States and Canada will go into effect on January 1, 1989, as a result of action taken today in Canada's House of Commons. It voted 141 to 111 to give approval to the Canada-United States free-trade accord, which will create a free market of 270 million people over a 10-year period. The current $130 billion in annual trade between the U.S. and Canada is the world's largest between two nations.

The agreement will abolish all remaining tariffs, and eliminate or lower a variety of restraints on trade in energy and agriculture, investments and other service industries. Experts foresee an increase of 1 percent in the U.S. gross national product and a 4 or 5 percent rise in Canada. Supporters of the pact also hope to match the new competitiveness in Western Europe, where 12 nations with a combined population of 320 million are preparing to eliminate trade barriers.

Prime Minister Mulroney, who was re-elected on a platform supporting the free-trade pact, said in his closing speech to the Commons, "Canadians have decided. They chose the broad avenue of confidence over the blind alley of fear. They chose an instrument that promises more jobs and more wealth for future generations of Canadians over the poverty of protectionism."

Bess Myerson acquitted of all charges

Dec 22. Bess Myerson, former Miss America and Cultural Affairs Commissioner of New York City, and two other defendants have been found not guilty of all charges in a conspiracy, fraud and bribery case in New York. The central issue in the trial, which captured media attention for two months, was whether a city job that Ms. Myerson gave to a judge's daughter was a bribe to induce the judge to cut temporary alimony payments in the divorce case of Ms. Myerson's lover.

Elizabeth Dole will be Secretary of Labor

Dec 24. Elizabeth Hanford Dole, a Washington insider who was Secretary of Transportation in the Reagan administration, has been selected by President-elect Bush as Secretary of Labor. The choice was welcomed by union officials as well as liberals in Congress, who feel it may portend better relations with organized labor in coming years.

With the exception of the posts of Energy Secretary and drug czar, Bush has completed his choices to fill the Cabinet and to serve as his top aides. They include: James Baker, Secretary of State; Nicholas Brady, Secretary of the Treasury; John Sununu, chief of staff; Richard Thornburgh, Attorney General; Lauro Cavazos, Education Secretary; Richard Darman, head of the Office of Management and Budget; Clayton Yeutter, Secretary of Agriculture; Jack Kemp, Secretary of Housing and Urban Development; Louis Sullivan, Secretary of Health and Human Services; William Reilly, administrator of the Environmental Protection Agency, and Samuel Skinner, Secretary of Transportation. Edwin Derwinski will be the first Secretary of the Department of Veterans Affairs.

Dole is the only female Secretary.

Israeli parties form coalition government

After weeks of often difficult negotiations, Peres and Shamir agree to cooperate — at a time when Israel will perhaps be put to its severest test.

Dec 19. Leaders of Israel's Labor and Likud parties have agreed to form a new coalition government to be headed by Prime Minister Yitzhak Shamir. The agreement comes after seven weeks of discussions.

By agreeing to form a coalition, the two largest Israeli parties seemed to rule out negotiating with the Palestine Liberation Organization, even though the United States has chosen to do so. This suggests that new strains might develop between Israel and its main supporter, the United States. By excluding Israel's small religious parties, the new coalition also prevented changes in laws dealing with the Sabbath and with the controversial question of who is regarded as Jewish.

Stock firm to pay $650 million fine

Dec 21. Drexel Burnham Lambert, the Wall Street investment firm, has agreed to plead guilty to six felony counts and pay a $650 million penalty. It was the largest settlement in history of federal securities law violations.

If approved by the Justice Department, the settlement will include admissions of mail fraud, wire fraud and securities fraud, and confirm government charges that Drexel Burnham Lambert, with Ivan F. Boesky, the Wall Street speculator who pleaded guilty in 1986, broke the law by illegally trading on inside information and improperly concealing the ownership of stock in more than a dozen deals between 1984 and 1986.

The proposed settlement was reportedly accepted by Drexel executives in large part because they feared that a criminal charge of racketeering could cripple the firm by freezing its assets (→ 29).

Pollsters ask: Are Americans happy?

Dec 24. Most Americans are happy with the state of the nation as well as with their own lives, according to the results of one recent poll. But another index says that perhaps they shouldn't be.

According to a Gallup Poll, 56 percent of the public this year is satisfied "with the way things are going in the U.S.," up from 45 percent last year. And even most of the 40 percent who are not satisfied with the nation's course indicated that they are satisifed with their personal lives.

At the same time, an index of social health developed by the Fordham Institute for Innovation in Social Policy shows that social problems in America have worsened in 13 areas, from teen-age suicide to the widening income gap, while only three areas — infant mortality, the high-school dropout rate and poverty among the elderly — have shown improvement this year.

Su	Mo	Tu	We	Th	Fr	Sa
				1	2	3
4	5	6	7	8	9	10
11	12	13	14	15	16	17
18	19	20	21	22	23	24
25	26	27	28	29	30	31

26. Washington: Energy Department report expresses pessimism over nuclear industry's ability to fulfill the nation's need for tritium, primarily used for military purposes.

26. China: Nanking is site of large demonstration against African students.

27 Cairo: Egyptian government says President Mubarak's willingness to visit Israel depends on Israeli willingness to meet with the P.L.O.

27. Beeville, Texas: Bush aides say that the President-elect bagged some birds while on his annual quail hunt here.

29. United States: Joint Council on Economic Education says that more than half of American high school students are lacking in basic economic knowledge.

29. United States: Traveler's newsletter International Living rates the United States as the best place in the world to live, fourth year in a row.

29. Tripoli: Marie-Laure and Virginie Betille, 7 and 6 years old, are free after being held hostage by Palestinians for more than a year and being released several days ago.

29. Washington: Justice Department will investigate Washington, D.C., Mayor Marion S. Barry Jr. for possible complicity in city's drug trade.

29. Boston: Federal judge delays a hostile takeover attempt because of concern over ability of Drexel Burnham Lambert to finance deal following its declaration that it will pay insider-trading fine.

29. Washington: Government announces it will bail out five savings institutions in Texas and California at cost to taxpayers of $7 billion.

30. Moscow: Yuri M. Churbanov, son-in-law of former Soviet leader Leonid Brezhnev, sentenced to 12 years in labor camp for accepting bribes.

31. Washington: U.S. government accuses West German firm, Imhausen-Chemie, of helping Libya build chemical weapons plant.

Bomb downed Pan Am jet

Searching for clues amid the debris.

Dec 28. The Pan Am jumbo jet that crashed in Scotland last week was blown apart by a powerful plastic explosive device, British investigators said today. Two parts of the framework of a luggage pallet, the metal rack in which luggage is stored, showed "conclusive evidence of a detonating high explosive," the investigators said.

The bomb was most probably planted in the forward hold of the aircraft, blowing the nose section from the fuselage, according to a researcher on terrorism at Aberdeen University who has been quoted by the Associated Press.

Scotland Yard's anti-terrorist squad and the United States Federal Bureau of Investigation are leading a criminal investigation into the crash, which killed all 259 people aboard and 11 more on the ground in Lockerbie, Scotland.

Authorities in the United States, meanwhile, said they are planning tougher security measures, including the searching of luggage of more passengers at 103 airports in the Middle East and Europe.

Speculation about who would want to plant a bomb on the aircraft has included Palestinian terrorists loyal to Abu Nidal, who oppose the Palestine Liberation Organization's opening of a dialogue with the United States, as well as pro-Iranian groups seeking revenge for the accidental American downing of an Iranian airliner over the Persian Gulf last July.

Michael Yardley, a British expert on terrorism, has speculated that the bomb contained Semtex, a high-performance explosive that British authorities say has come into Libyan hands recently.

"Much investigative work remains to be done to establish the nature of the explosive device," the investigators said in a statement, "what it was contained in, its location in the aircraft and the sequence of events immediately following its detonation."

"Year of the Dragon," commemorating the year 1988, by artist Qin DaHu, is part of an ongoing exhibit of contemporary realist art from the People's Republic of China at GWS Galleries in Southport, Connecticut.

Plan to close army bases is proposed

Dec. 29. In order to save $5.6 billion over 20 years, a federal commission has proposed a comprehensive plan to close 86 U.S. military bases and partly shut five more. About 21,000 jobs would be eliminated in the process. In January, Defense Secretary Frank Carlucci is expected to approve the plan. Congress then has 45 days after March 1 to block it; otherwise, it will automatically take effect, and base closings will commence in 1990. The plan has raised some opposition in Congress, particularly among members whose areas will be hit by the base closings, but most lawmakers agree that it will probably go into effect.

Billiard parlors are on the rebound

From Houston to Minneapolis and Boston to Miami, pool halls are back, with yuppies leading the way. While there was a time when expertise at a billiard table was a sign of a misspent youth, now it is a status symbol. Recently, Manhattan has seen the opening of four plush pool parlors, and equipment manufacturers are trying to meet demand. Playing pool is relatively cheap and an easy way to meet people.

Social Security leads in relieving poverty

Dec 27. A Census Bureau study indicates that Social Security is the federal government's most effective weapon in the war on poverty and reduces inequality in America more than the tax system. According to the report, the most comprehensive effort ever made to measure the role of government in redistributing income, Social Security benefits lifted 15.1 million out of poverty in 1986, reducing the number of poor from 50.6 million to 35.5 million. They also were responsible for cutting the poverty rate among the elderly, to 14 percent from 47.5 percent. Meanwhile, the study said, "taxes had a relatively minor effect on the redistribution of income."

Lawyers call Reagan and Bush to testify

Dec 31. Vice President Bush and President Reagan were subpoenaed yesterday to testify as defense witnesses for Oliver L. North at his trial on conspiracy charges stemming from the Iran-contra affair. The trial is set to begin on January 31, 1989, 11 days after President-elect Bush will take office as President. The White House has begun drafting documents seeking to overturn the subpoenas. One expert on constitutional law has said that President-elect Bush would have a strong claim to immunity from testifying, based on legal precedents. Reagan's position, he added, would be weaker once he leaves the Presidency.

Boom in Japanese electronics business

Despite increasing competition from such other Asian nations as South Korea, Taiwan and Singapore, Japan's electronics industry grew at its fastest pace in four years in 1988. Factory revenues from all types of electronics products, from videocassette recorders to radios, soared 12.9 percent, to 21.2 trillion yen, or about $170 billion at current exchange rates. With the exception of computers, the United States is no longer considered a factor in the electronics industry.

Noguchi, legendary sculptor, dies at 84

Dec 30. Isamu Noguchi, one of the greatest sculptors of the 20th Century, died of heart failure today in New York at the age of 84. Born in Los Angeles of a Japanese father and American mother, and raised in Japan, Noguchi sought in his work to synthesize contemporary Japanese sensibilities and those of the past. For him, clay, wood and stone remained elemental, even sacred, as he believed they contained the energies of nature. His sculpture gardens, commissioned for parks from Houston to Jerusalem, were total artistic environments, filled with large abstract pieces. Among his great works are "White Sun" and "Slide Mantra."

Homelessness spills into many suburbs

Suburban areas surrounding the nation's major cities are struggling to cope with an increase in homelessness. In these areas, where the price of housing far outstrips people's ability to pay, most of the homeless are families, usually single mothers and their children. But, living in wooded areas and abandoned cars, they are often less visible than the urban homeless. "Homelessness is growing," said one suburban official. "It is not a problem that is going to go away."

Rain and gloom were in keeping with this year's Christmas observations in Bethlehem. Jesus's birthplace is in the Israeli-occupied West Bank, and the continuing Palestinian revolt canceled most celebrations in the town.

Filmmakers made funny flicks this year

It was a fine year for comedy, as movie directors rediscovered the fact that most people want to have a good laugh when they see a film.

"Bull Durham" was an offbeat look, with some very funny moments, at the shabby world of minor league baseball. Susan Sarandon and Kevin Costner starred. The star of "Who Framed Roger Rabbit," meanwhile, was the special-effects wizard who integrated cartoon characters and live action. "Beetlejuice" featured comic-book ingenuity and a fine performance by Michael Keaton as a punk demon. Michael Caine and Steve Martin were hilarious as "Dirty Rotten Scoundrels," as were Arnold Schwarzenegger and Danny DeVito as "Twins." And "The Naked Gun" was in a category of its own: nonsense.

Perhaps the brightest spot on the comic horizon was "Working Girl," an old-fashioned story directed by Mike Nichols, starring Melanie Griffith and Harrison Ford. And then, of course, there was the popular Tom Hanks as an adult-sized child in "Big."

There was plenty of fare for the serious-minded. "Mississippi Burning," with Gene Hackman, is about the murder of three civil rights workers in 1964. And "Wings of Desire," from German director Wim Wenders, is an eerie, romantic fairy tale about an angel who falls to earth and falls in love. It's funny too.

Sarandon hit a box-office home run.

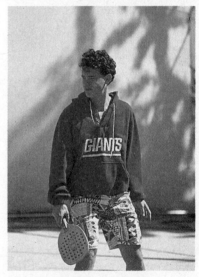

Tom Hanks was also big this year.

Popular music is back on a social track

The musical sensation of the year is Tracy Chapman, whose songs on such social problems as poverty and racism lit up the charts. "Fast Car" and "Talkin' Bout a Revolution," from her first album, reveal a depth of feeling reminiscent of the protest songs of the 1960's. Ms. Chapman was discovered as a student at Tufts University, when a classmate's father, a music publisher, helped her sign up with Elektra/Asylum records. "Her songs were wonderful melodies with important lyrics," he remembered. "That was enough. But when I saw her in front of an audience! When she smiled, everyone smiled. When she was serious, you could hear a pin drop."

"Fast Car" drove Tracy onto charts. ▷

The World's Nations

This section gives brief updated facts on each nation's geographical location, population, area, language, religion, political status, and membership in international organizations. The head of state and head of government are also named. Figures provided for Gross National Product (GNP) and population are the latest available. Currency values are based on May 30, 1988, indicative rates. The texts provide a short summary of the main events of 1988. A list of abbreviations used is provided on page 123.

Afghanistan

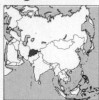

Central Asia
251,773 sq. mi
Pop: 8-10m.
UN

Capital: Kabul (Pop: 2m.)
Official languages: Pushtu, Dari (Persian)
Religion: Moslem (Shiah, Sunni)
Political status: People's republic
Head of state: Najibullah (since 1987)
Head of government: Sultan Ali Kishtmand (since 1981)
GNP per capita: $250 (1985)
Currency: afghani ($1 = 50.60)

The signing in Geneva on April 14 of a U.S. and Soviet-guaranteed peace agreement did not lead to an end of the bloodshed in war-torn Afghanistan. The historic peace accord marked the start of the process of withdrawal of the 115,000 Soviet troops which had rolled into Afghanistan in December 1979. Under the terms of the accord, all Soviet forces must be out by February 15, 1989. Soviet losses during the war against the Western-backed Afghan rebels, or mujahedeen, are estimated at more than 20,000 men. Well over a million Afghans died in a war that spilled over into Pakistan, soured superpower relations and blocked significant improvement of links between Moscow and Beijing. The Soviet pullout was marked by an upsurge in rebel attacks on Soviet and Afghan army positions, particularly Kabul. Bomb and rocket attacks increased during the summer. The Soviet Union, citing repeated mujahedeen violations of the U.N.-sponsored Geneva accord, "temporarily halted" its troop pullout in November. This prompted the United States to call on Afghan rebels to refrain from attacks on Soviet troops.

Albania

Southeastern Europe
11,101 sq. mi
Pop: 3.08m.
UN, WP

Capital: Tirana (Pop: 206,000)
Official language: Albanian
Religion: officially atheist
Political status: Socialist people's republic
Head of state: Ramiz Alia (since 1982)
Head of government: Adil Çarçani (since 1982)
GNP per capita: $930 (1986)
Currency: lek ($1 = 5.51)

Albania, isolated from the outside world for decades, in 1988 further opened up. In June, a party of 100 students was allowed to visit Yugoslavia, while in October Hungary said it was ready to start talks on an exchange of ambassadors with Albania.

Algeria

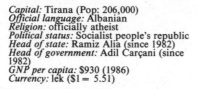

North Africa
919,595 sq. mi
Pop: 22.6m.
UN, AL, OAU, OPEC

Capital: Algiers (Pop: 1,721,607)
Official language: Arabic
Religion: Sunni Moslem
Political status: Socialist republic
Head of state: Chadli Bendjedid (since 1979)
Head of government: Kasdi Merbah (since 1988)
GNP per capita: $2,430 (1984)
Currency: Algerian dinar ($1 = 5.21)

President Chadli Benjedid in November appointed Health Minister Kasdi Merbah, 50, as premier, a month after violent rioting led to a referendum in which voters approved broad reforms. According to official figures, 176 people died in the riots.

Andorra

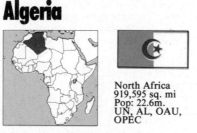

Southern Europe
180 sq. mi
Pop: 42,712

Capital: Andorre la Vieille
Official language: Catalan
Religion: Roman Catholic
Political status: Principality
Heads of state: The Spanish Bishop of Urgel, Mgr. Joan Marti y Alanis, and

French President François Mitterrand
Head of government: Josef Pintat Solans (since 1986)
GNP per capita: $9,000
Currencies: French franc and Spanish peseta

A medieval necropolis containing about 100 skeletons of people who died between the 12th. and 15th. centuries was discovered in August near the Sant Joan de Casselles chapel.

Angola

Southwestern Africa
481,351 sq. mi
Pop: 8.96m.
UN, OAU

Capital: Luanda (Pop: 960,000)
Official language: Portuguese
Religions: Roman Catholic 55%, Protestant 9%, animist 34%
Political status: Socialist people's republic
Head of state: José Eduardo dos Santos (since 1979)
GNP per capita: $500 (1985)
Currency: kwanza ($1 = 29.92)

Following lengthy talks with the United States, South Africa and Cuba, Angola agreed in November to a plan calling for the phased withdrawal of some 55,000 Cuban troops sent to help Angola fight South African-backed rebels.

Antigua and Barbuda

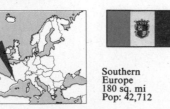

Caribbean
171 sq. mi
Pop: 81,500
UN, OAS, Caricom, CW

Capital: St John's (Pop: 30,000)
Official language: English
Religion: Christian (mostly Anglican)
Political status: Constitutional monarchy
Head of state: Queen Elizabeth II
Head of government: Vere C. Bird (since 1981)
GNP per capita: $1,990 (1984)
Currency: Eastern Caribbean dollar ($1 = 2.70)

The 13 leaders of the English-speaking Caribbean Community in October agreed to abolish nearly all trade barriers between their nations, thus establishing a free-trade zone in the economically-buffeted region.

Argentina

South America
1,073,358 sq. mi
Pop: 31.06m.
UN, LAIA, OAS

Capital: Buenos Aires (Pop: 9,927,404)
Official language: Spanish
Religion: Roman Catholic 92%
Political status: Federal republic
Head of state: Raul Alfonsin (since 1983)
GNP per capita: $2,470 (1984)
Currency: austral ($1 = 4.60)

In October, the government set elections for May 1989. The poll will mark the first time a presidential term has been completed in the last 36 years. Earlier, a court sentenced three former members of the military junta to 12 years in jail for their role in the 1982 war with Britain over the Falklands. In April, a U.S. court ordered a former Argentine general to pay damages of $21 million to a man he allegedly tortured. Rebel army troops in December seized the country's largest military base.

Australia

South Pacific
2,966,200 sq. mi
Pop: 15.97m.
UN, ANZUS, CW, OECD

Capital: Canberra (Pop: 286,000)
Official language: English
Religions: Anglican 36%, other Protestant 25%, Roman Catholic 33%
Political status: Federal constitutional monarchy
Head of state: Queen Elizabeth II
Head of government: Robert Hawke (since 1983)
GNP per capita: $11,172 (1984)
Currency: Australian dollar ($1 = 1.39)

Britain's Queen Elizabeth II in April attended ceremonies marking the 200th. anniversary of British settlement in the former convict colony. It was the Queen's 12th. official visit to Australia and was followed by several other British royal visits. In September, a Darwin court quashed the convictions of an Australian couple for the 1980 death of their baby daughter, closing the book on the celebrated "dingo murder" case as a miscarriage of justice. In November, it was announced that AIDS has killed 525 Australians, 24 of them women. In the same month, Australia and China signed a major five-year agreement to cooperate in space technology. This was seen by Canberra as a big boost for Australia's fledgling space industry.

Austria

Western Europe
32,376 sq. mi
Pop: 7.57m.
UN, EFTA, OECD

Capital: Vienna (Pop: 1,481,399)
Official language: German
Religions: Roman Catholic 84.3%, Protestant 5.6%
Political status: Federal parliamentary republic
Head of state: Kurt Waldheim (since 1986)
Head of government: Franz Vranitsky (since 1986)
GNP per capita: $12,297 (1986)
Currency: schilling ($1 = 11.85)

Chancellor Franz Vranitsky firmly condemned in November the "fanatics of Vienna" who took part in the 1938 "Crystal Night" Nazi wave of pogroms during which 30 Austrian Jews were massacred.

Bahamas

Caribbean
5,353 sq. mi
Pop: 235,000
UN, OAS, CW, Caricom

Capital: Nassau (Pop: 135,437)
Official language: English
Religions: Baptist 29%, Anglican 23%, Roman Catholic 22%
Political status: Constitutional monarchy
Head of state: Queen Elizabeth II
Head of government: Sir Lynden O. Pindling (since 1967)
GNP per capita: $7,950 (1984)
Currency: Bahamian dollar ($1 = 1)

The long-running investigation of premier Lynden Pindling for alleged drug trafficking dragged on. The Bahamian attorney general said a drug runner's claim that Mr. Pindling had accepted bribes was "incredible".

Bahrain

Middle East
265.5 sq. mi
Pop: 416,275
UN, AL, GCC

Capital: Manama (Pop: 121,986)
Official language: Arabic
Religion: Moslem 85%, Christian 7.3%
Political status: Emirate
Head of state: Isa bin Sulman Al-Khalifa (since 1961)
Head of government: Khalifa bin Sulman Al-Khalifa (since 1973)
GNP per capita: $11,708 (1985)
Currency: Bahrain dinar ($1 = 0.377)

Bahrain in November became the 138th. signatory to the international nuclear non-proliferation treaty. In October, Bahrain and Qatar agreed to end a border dispute over the tiny Gulf island of Fasht al-Dibel.

Bangladesh

Southern Asia
55,598 sq. mi
Pop: 104.1m.
UN, CW

Capital: Dhaka (Pop: 3,440,147)
Official language: Bangla
Religions: Moslem 80%, Hindu, Buddhist, Christian
Political status: Presidential republic
Head of state: Hossain Mohammad Ershad (since 1983)
Head of government: Moumoud Ahmed (since 1988)
GNP per capita: $140 (1986)
Currency: Taka ($1 = 31.43)

The ruling Jatiya Party won a huge majority in a March 3 parliamentary vote. In September, Bangladesh's worst floods in living memory killed some 2,000 people, with 29 million people being made homeless. A December cyclone left at least 1,500 dead and 16,000 people missing.

Barbados

Caribbean
166 sq. mi
Pop: 253,055
UN, CW, OAS, Caricom

Capital: Bridgetown (Pop: 7,466)
Official language: English
Religions: Anglican 70%, Methodist, Moravian, Roman Catholic
Political status: Constitutional monarchy
Head of state: Queen Elizabeth II
Head of government: Erskine Sandiford (since 1987)
GNP per capita: $4,560 (1984)
Currency: Barbados dollar ($1 = 2.11)

An alert was issued in October following the arrival in Barbados of grass-hoppers which posed a threat to crops. The insects had migrated across the Altantic after causing devastation in many parts of Africa.

Belgium

Western Europe
11,778 sq. mi
Pop: 9.86m.
UN, EEC, NATO, OECD

Capital: Brussels (Pop: 973,499)
Official languages: French, Dutch, German
Religion: mostly Roman Catholic
Political status: Constitutional monarchy
Head of state: King Baudouin I (since 1951)
Head of government: Wilfried Martens (since 1981)
GNP per capita: $7,870 (1984)
Currency: Belgian franc ($1 = 35.28)

In May, Belgian premier Wilfried Martens named a center-left cabinet, ending more than six months of life without a government. A major row erupted with Britain in December over Belgium's refusal to extradite an Irish priest sought by London for suspected terrorist links.

Belize

Central America
8,866 sq. mi
Pop: 171,000
UN, Caricom, CW

Capital: Belmopan (Pop: 3,500)
Official language: English
Religions: Roman Catholic 62%, Protestant 28%
Political status: Constitutional monarchy
Head of state: Queen Elizabeth II
Head of government: Manuel Amadeo Esquivel (since 1985)
GNP per capita: $1,200 (1985)
Currency: Belize dollar ($1 = 2)

Belize and Guatemala agreed in May to set up a permanent commission with British participation to work out a treaty ending a long-time territorial dispute between the two Central America nations.

Benin

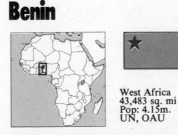

West Africa
43,483 sq. mi
Pop: 4.15m.
UN, OAU

Capital: Porto Novo (Pop: 208,258)
Official language: French
Religions: Mainly animist, Christian, Moslem
Political status: Socialist people's republic
Head of state: Ahmed Kerekou (since 1972)
GNP per capita: $250 (1983)
Currency: franc CFA ($1 = 286)

Benin celebrated in October the 16th. anniversary of the 1972 revolution, amid a continuing economic crisis. In May, the United States expressed concern about an increasing Libyan presence in the country.

Bhutan

South Asia
18,000 sq. mi
Pop: 1.3m.
UN

Capital: Thimphu (Pop: 15,000)
Official languages: Dzongkha, Lhotsam (Nepali), English
Religions: Buddhist 75%, Hindu 25%
Political status: Monarchy
Head of state: Jigme Singye Wangchuk (since 1972)
Head of government: Council of ministers
GNP per capita: $140 (1984)
Currency: Ngultrum ($1 = 13.05)

The young ruler of the tiny Himalayan kingdom, King Jigme Singye Wangchuck, in October formally wed four sisters whom he had privately married nine years ago and with whom he has had eight children.

Bolivia

South America
424,165 sq. mi
Pop: 6.25m.
UN, LAIA, OAS

Capital: Sucre (legal), La Paz (de facto; pop: 881,404)
Official languages: Spanish, Quechua, Aymara
Religion: Roman Catholic 95%
Political status: Presidential republic
Head of state: Victor Paz Estensoro (since 1985)
GNP per capita: $400 (1985)
Currency: boliviano ($1 = 2.21)

In August, U.S. Secretary of State George Shultz escaped an assassination attempt in La Paz. A self-styled "nationalist commando" later claimed responsibility for placing a powerful bomb close to Mr. Shultz's motorcade. He had earlier strongly condemned the effects of the international traffic in Bolivian cocaine. The U.S. in October sent military helicopters to help Bolivia stamp out the drug trade. The extreme-left "Shining Path" terrorist group in 1988 continued its attacks on government and civilian targets.

Botswana

Southern Africa
220,000 sq. mi
Pop: 1.13m.
UN, CW, OAU

Capital: Gaborone (Pop: 96,000)
Official languages: English, Setswana
Religions: Bahai, Moslem, Hindu, Christian
Political status: Presidential republic
Head of state: Quett Ketumile Joni Masire (since 1980)
GNP per capita: $920 (1983)
Currency: pula ($1 = 1.68)

During a September visit, Pope John Paul II said Botswana was "an island of peace in a troubled sea". Tensions with South Africa remained very high in 1988, as Botswana denounced apartheid policies.

Brazil

South America
3,286,487 sq. mi
Pop: 141.3m.
UN, LAIA, OAS

Capital: Brasilia (Pop: 411,305)
Official language: Portuguese
Religion: Roman Catholic 89%, Protestant 6.6%, Spiritualist
Political status: Federal republic
Head of state: José Sarney (since 1985)
GNP per capita: $1,740 (1986)
Currency: cruzado ($1 = 99.20)

President Sarney in March scored a political victory when the National Assembly approved a U.S.-style presidential system. After some 20 months of bargaining, the National Congress in October put a new constitution into effect, a step hailed as crucial in the country's transition to democracy. But the economic crisis raged on, with 1988 inflation approaching 800 per cent. An October wave of strikes halted work in 17 of the government's 26 departments. In November municipal elections, Mr. Sarney's Brazilian Democratic Movement Party suffered a major set-back when leftist parties won control of a number of Brazil's most important cities, including Sao Paulo, the country's largest and wealthiest.

Brunei

Southeast Asia
2,226 sq. mi
Pop: 221,900
UN, CW, ASEAN

Capital: Bandar Seri Begawan (Pop: 63,868)
Official languages: Malay, Chinese
Religions: Moslem 63%, Buddhist 14%, Christian 10%
Political status: Sultanate
Head of state: Sultan Muda Hassanal Bolkiah Mu'izzadin Waddaulah (since 1967)
GNP per capita: $15,989 (1985)
Currency: Brunei dollar ($1 = 2.01)

In July, thirty-four political prisoners, mostly foreign students, were freed after swearing allegiance to Sultan Hassanal Bolkiah. In August, oil-rich Brunei offered billions of dollars in aid to the Philippines.

Bulgaria

Southeastern Europe
42,823 sq. mi
Pop: 8.95m.
UN, CMEA, Warsaw Pact

Capital: Sofia (Pop: 1,114,962)
Official language: Bulgarian
Religions: mostly Orthodox, Moslem 7%
Political status: Socialist people's republic
Head of state: Todor Zhivkov (since 1971)
Head of government: Georgi Atanasov (since 1986)
GNP per capita: $6,460
Currency: lev ($1 = 0.82)

Bulgarians elected 25.87 per cent of non-party candidates in March local elections, while the Communist Party had a 60.78 share of the poll. A multiple choice of candidates was being offered to voters for the first time since the communists came to power at the end of World War II. Bulgaria, previously regarded as one of the most conservative communist bloc countries, in 1988 was in the forefront of socialist states adopting policies linked to Soviet leader Mikhail Gorbachev's economic and social reforms, or "perestroika".

Burkina Faso

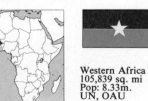

Western Africa
105,839 sq. mi
Pop: 8.33m.
UN, OAU

Capital: Ouagadougou (Pop: 442,223)
Official language: French
Religions: animist 45%, Moslem 43%, Christian 12%
Political status: Presidential republic
Head of state: Blaise Compaoré (since 1987)
GNP per capita: $160 (1984)
Currency: franc CFA ($1 = 285.66)

Burkina Faso's President, Captain Blaise Compaoré, in October lashed out at the "anarchy" among the ranks of the country's armed forces, vowing to reform the army set up by his predecessor Thomas Sankara.

Burma

Southeast Asia
261,228 sq. mi
Pop: 37.85m.
UN

Capital: Rangoon (Pop: 2,458,712)
Official language: Burmese
Religion: Buddhist
Political status: Socialist people's republic
Head of state: U San Yu (since 1981)
Head of government: Saw Maung
GNP per capita: $180 (1983)
Currency: kyat ($1 = 6.25)

General Ne Win, who had seized power in a military coup in 1962, stepped down on July 23 amid rising discontent with his rule. On September 18, the military seized power after two months of often violent mass demonstrations and strikes against 26 years of authoritarian one-party rule by the Burma Socialist Program Party. Western experts set the death toll at around 400. Before being ousted, the government of President Maung Maung ordered all members of the military and state employees to quit the BSPP. A military government led by General Saw Maung said in late September that it would hold multi-party elections, but only after law and order had been restored.

Burundi

Central Africa
10,759 sq. mi
Pop: 4.92m.
UN, OAU

Capital: Bujumbura (Pop: 272,000)
Official languages: Kirundi, French
Religions: Roman Catholic 60%, traditional tribal beliefs 32%
Political status: Presidential republic
Head of state: Pierre Buyoya (since 1987)
Head of government: Adrien Sibomana (since 1988)
GNP per capita: $250 (1984)
Currency: Burundi franc ($1 = 118.28)

Massacres between Hutu and Tutsi tribesmen in August left 5,000 dead, according to government figures. Diplomats said up to 50,000 may have died. On October 19, Adrien Sibomana became premier.

Cambodia

Southeast Asia
69,898 sq. mi
Pop: 6.23m.
UN

Capital: Phnom Penh (Pop: 500,000)
Official language: Khmer
Religions: Theravada Buddhism, Roman Catholic and Moslem minorities
Political status: People's republic
Head of state: Heng Samrin (since 1979)
Head of government: Hun Sen (since 1985)
GNP per capita: no accurate estimate available
Currency: riel ($1 = 100)

The year saw considerable progress in diplomatic efforts to settle the Cambodian conflict, with Vietnam promising to withdraw 50,000 of its estimated 120,000 troops by the end of the year. Hanoi also announced in May that all the Vietnamese troops which invaded Cambodia in 1978 would be repatriated by the end of 1990 at the latest. Foreign observers were to be allowed to witness the pullout in December. This was conducted by land, sea and river routes. Vietnam said in June its intervention in Cambodia had cost the lives of some 25,000 Vietnamese troops. In October, President Reagan met with Cambodia's resistance leader Prince Norodom Sihanouk, who was ousted in a 1970 U.S.-backed coup. Mr. Reagan echoed Prince Sihanouk's call for an international peace conference on the Cambodian issue.

Cameroon

Western Central Africa
179,558 sq. mi
Pop: 9.88m.
UN, OAU

Capital: Yaoundé (Pop: 435,892)
Official languages: French, English
Religions: animist 39%, Roman Catholic 21%, Moslem 22%, Protestant 18%
Political status: Presidential republic
Head of state: Paul Biya (since 1982)
GNP per capita: $800 (1983)
Currency: franc CFA ($1 = 285.66)

President Paul Biya celebrated the sixth anniversary of his November 6, 1982 rise to power, calling on the population to continue its efforts aimed at overcoming the country's severe economic crisis.

Canada

North America
3,553,357 sq. mi
Pop: 25.4m.
UN, NATO, OECD, CW

Capital: Ottawa (Pop: 819,263)
Official languages: English, French
Religions: Roman Catholic, Protestant
Political status: Parliamentary monarchy
Head of state: Queen Elizabeth II
Head of government: Martin Brian Mulroney (since 1984)
GNP per capita: $12,940 (1984)
Currency: Canadian dollar ($1 = 1.26)

Canada's conservative Prime Minister Brian Mulroney won a clear-cut parliamentary majority in hotly-contested November 21 elections. The election was essentially fought on the issue of a free trade agreement with the United States. After his victory, Mr. Mulroney said he would call parliament back in December to enact the pact. He vowed to implement the trade accord on schedule on January 1, 1989. Opponents of the accord said it would reduce Canada to being an "economic colony" of the United States. Canada's business community strongly supported the pact, which will, over the next decade, eliminate almost all hindrances to the flow of trade between Canada and the U.S. In September, the U.S. Senate approved the free trade accord in an 83 to 9 vote. Following the success of the 1988 Winter Olympics in Calgary, Victoria was awarded in September the 1994 Commonwealth Games. In June, relations with Moscow took a turn for the worse, when a wave of tit-for-tat expulsions of diplomats broke out. In September, Mr. Mulroney signed an agreement making the Indian Dene tribe the biggest private landowners in North America. It was to recover rights lost in 1899. In October, Canada authorized a U.S. ship to navigate the contested Northwest Passage.

Cape Verde

Atlantic
1,557 sq. mi
Pop: 350,000
UN, OAU

Capital: Praia (Pop: 37,676)
Official language: Portuguese
Religion: Roman Catholic 98%
Political status: Republic
Head of state: Aristides Maria Pereira (since 1975)
Head of government: Pedro Verona Rodrigues Pires (since 1975)
GNP per capita: $320 (1983)
Currency: escudo Caboverdiano ($1 = 73.42)

In September, Justice Minister Jose Araujo stepped down, citing bad health. In October, the government began a wide-ranging review of the trouble-plagued and increasingly criticized state-run health service.

Central African Republic

Central Africa
240,324 sq. mi
Pop: 2.78m.
UN, OAU

Capital: Bangui (Pop: 473,817)
Official language: French
Religions: animist beliefs 57%, Roman Catholic 20%, Protestant 15%, Moslem 8%
Political status: Presidential republic
Head of state: André Kolingba (since 1981)
GNP per capita: $280 (1984)
Currency: franc CFA ($1 = 285.66)

The government in November categorically denied reports that it had allowed several thousand tons toxic waste from Western Europe to be dumped in the country in exchange for pay-offs to senior officials.

Chad

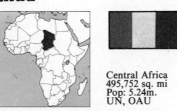

Central Africa
495,752 sq. mi
Pop: 5.24m.
UN, OAU

Capital: N'Djaména (Pop: 511,700)
Official languages: French, Arabic
Religions: Moslem 44%, animist 38%, Christian 17%
Political status: Presidential republic
Head of state: Hissène Habré (since 1982)
GNP per capita: $88 (1984)
Currency: franc CFA ($1 = 285.66)

Chad and its northern neighbor Libya in October restored full diplomatic ties after a six-year break. Both sides pledged to respect a late 1987 cease-fire which ended a drawn out and violent border dispute.

Chile

South America
284,520 sq. mi
Pop: 12.07m.
UN, LAIA, OAS

Capital: Santiago (Pop: 4,318,305)
Official language: Spanish
Religions: Roman Catholic, Protestant, Jewish
Political status: Presidential republic under a military regime
Head of state: Augusto Pinochet Ugarte (since 1974)
GNP per capita: $1,590 (1984)
Currency: Chilean peso ($1 = 244.51)

General Augusto Pinochet lost an October bid to remain in power until 1997 after 54.68 per cent of voters said "no" to eight more years of power for the President. However, General Pinochet refused to step down right away, although the Chilean leader is constitutionally bound to hold open presidential elections by December 1989 at the latest. The plebiscite was marred by arrests and violent police reprisals against Chileans opposed to Gen. Pinochet's continued rule. The election results led to widespread celebration after 15 years of military rule. In mid-October, Chile rejected a U.S.

request for $12 million in compensation for the killing of Orlando Letelier, a Chilean exile leader assassinated in Washington in 1976.

China

East Asia
3,682,131 sq. mi
Pop: 1,072.2m.
UN

Capital: Beijing (Peking; pop: 5.86m.)
Official language: Chinese
Religions: officially atheist; Confucianism, Buddhism, Taoism
Political status: People's republic
Head of state: Li Xiannian (since 1983)
Head of government: Li Peng (since 1987)
GNP per capita: $250 (1986)
Currency: Renminbi yuan ($1 = 3.72)

A new and younger government, featuring reformists close to senior leader Deng Xiaoping, took the reins of power in China in April. There were growing calls for the retirement of Mr. Deng, who despite his 84 years and pledges to step down continued to run the country. Faced with record inflation and potential social unrest, Chinese leaders found themselves divided over what road to take, with the most cautious demanding that political stability be put ahead of reforms. In March, the United States said it would resume sales of high technology to China, thus ending a five-month embargo, because Washington was satisfied that Beijing was not selling Silkworm anti-ship missiles to Iran. In November, the government said there will be as many as 1.27 billion Chinese in the year 2000, some 70 million more than officially predicted in 1980. China's first-ever sex-education exhibition was held in Shanghai in October. A devastating November earthquake in southwestern China killed about 750 people and seriously injured 3,400 others. More than 700,000 houses were destroyed and damage was estimated at over $110 million.

Colombia

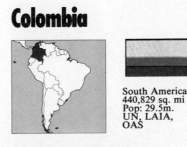

South America
440,829 sq. mi
Pop: 29.5m.
UN, LAIA, OAS

Capital: Bogota (Pop: 4,185,174)
Official language: Spanish
Religion: Roman Catholic
Political status: Democratic presidential republic
Head of state: Virgilio Barco Vargas (since 1986)
Head of government: Cesar Gaviria Trujillo
GNP per capita: $1,129 (1986)
Currency: peso ($1 = 273.60)

Police in May raided what was probably the biggest cocaine processing plant in the country, seizing 6,000 pounds of the drug. In October, government and opposition leaders agreed on constitutional reforms.

Comoros

Indian Ocean
719 sq. mi
Pop: 422,500
UN

Capital: Moroni (Pop: 20,112)
Official languages: French, Arabic
Religions: Moslem (Sunni) 99%, Christian
Political status: Federal Islamic republic
Head of state: Ahmed Abdallah Abderemane (since 1978)
GNP per capita: $290 (1985)
Currency: Comorian franc ($1 = 285.66)

The Islamic republic celebrated the 13th. anniversary of its independence in July amid a deep economic crisis. The World Bank in October said it would increase its credits to the impoverished island nation.

Congo

Central Africa
132,046 sq. mi
Pop: 2.18m.
UN, OAU

Capital: Brazzaville (Pop: 595,102)
Official language: French
Religions: Roman Catholic 54%, Protestant 24%, animist 19%, Moslem 3%
Political status: People's republic
Head of state: Denis Sassou-Nguesso (since 1979)
Head of government: Ange-Edouard Poungui (since 1984)
GNP per capita: $1,140 (1984)
Currency: franc CFA ($1 = 285.66)

A delegation of U.S. businessmen and congressional leaders visited Brazzaville in November to discuss U.S. investment possibilities. The government meanwhile pressed ahead with its austerity measures. In October, the wages of 15,000 ruling party officials were cut by ten per cent as part of the regime's austerity drive.

Costa Rica

Central America
19,730 sq. mi
Pop: 2.66m.
UN, OAS

Capital: San José (Pop: 241,464)
Official language: Spanish
Religion: Roman Catholic
Political status: Democratic republic
Head of state: Oscar Arias Sanchez (since 1986)
Head of government: Rodrigo Arias Sanchez
GNP per capita: $1.280 (1984)
Currency: colone ($1 = 73.45)

The hurricane Joan hit Costa Rica in October, killing at least 25 people and leaving a trail of devastation behind. Earlier, Costa Rica accused a group of Panamanian soldiers of having illegally crossed the border.

Cuba

Caribbean
44,206 sq. mi
Pop: 10.19m.
UN, CMEA, OAS

Capital: Havana (Pop: 2,014,800)
Official language: Spanish
Religions: Roman Catholic, Methodist, Baptist
Political status: Socialist republic
Head of state: Fidel Castro Ruz
GNP per capita: $2,696 (1981)
Currency: peso ($1 = 0.79)

The Pentagon in March acknowledged that Cuban forces possessed some Frog-7 nuclear-capable missiles, but stressed none had been equipped with nuclear warheads. In June, the worst flooding in 25 years killed over 20 people and ended 10 years of drought. A Cuban gunboat in October seized the ship carrying New Zealand's America's Cup entry. In September, relations with Britain soured after a Cuban diplomat was expelled from London in a bizarre incident in which he shot an alleged deserter from Cuba's secret service. Calling it an act of U.S. provocation, Mr. Castro decorated the diplomat.

Cyprus

Southern Europe
3,572 sq. mi
Pop: 673,100
UN, CW

Capital: Nicosia (Pop: 163,700)
Official languages: Greek, Turkish
Religions: Greek Orthodox 80%, Moslem 19%
Political status: Republic
Head of state: George Vassiliou (since 1988)
GNP per capita: $5.703 (1986)
Currency: Cyprus pound ($1 = 2.19)

Independent candidate George Vassiliou won February presidential elections. Despite some progress, hopes for an early reunification of Cyprus faded in November.

Czechoslovakia

Central Europe
49,383 sq. mi
Pop: 15.5m.
UN, CMEA, Warsaw Pact

Capital: Prague (Pop: 1,194,000)
Official languages: Czech, Slovak
Religion: Roman Catholic 24%
Political status: Federal socialist republic
Head of state: Gustav Husak (since 1975)
Head of government: Ladislav Adamec (since 1988)
GNP per capita: $8.700 (1985)
Currency: Czech koruna ($1 = 5.15)

In a major October government reshuffle, Ladislav Adamec replaced Lubomir Strougal as premier. The 70th anniversary of Czechoslovakia's founding was celebrated for the first time in decades in late October.

Denmark

Northern Europe
16,631 sq. mi
Pop: 5.12m.
UN, EEC, NATO, OECD

Capital: Copenhagen (Pop: 622,275)
Official language: Danish
Religion: Lutheran 90%
Political status: Constitutional monarchy
Head of state: Queen Margrethe II (since 1972)
Head of government: Poul Schlueter (since 1982)
GNP per capita: $7,533 (1985)
Currency: krone ($1 = 6.45)

Conservative Prime Minister Poul Schlueter formed a new coalition government in June following inconclusive elections focusing on Denmark's role in NATO and its decision to ban nuclear ships from Danish ports.

Djibouti

Northeastern Africa
8,960 sq. mi
Pop: 470,000
UN, AL, OAU

Capital: Djibouti (Pop: 250,000)
Official languages: French, Arabic
Religion: mostly Moslem
Political status: Presidential republic
Head of state: Hassan Gouled Aptidon (since 1977)
Head of government: Barkat Gourad Hamadou (since 1978)
GNP per capita: $760 (1984)
Currency: Djibouti franc ($1 = 177)

Western aid was rushed to Djibouti in October to help it fight the spread of crop-ravaging locusts. In November, a man was arrested for a two-month-long wave of bomb attacks on power stations and government offices. His motives were not clear.

Dominica

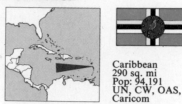

Caribbean
290 sq. mi
Pop: 94,191
UN, CW, OAS, Caricom

Capital: Roseau (Pop: 20,000)
Official language: English
Religion: Roman Catholic 80%
Political status: Republic
Head of state: C.A. Seignoret (since 1983)
Head of government: Mary Eugenia Charles (since 1980)
GNP per capita: $970 (1983)
Currencies: French franc, £ sterling and East Caribbean $ ($1 = EC$2.70)

Dominica's leaders in July objected to U.S. government attempts to indict Panamanian strongman General Manuel Antonio Noriega on charges of drug trafficking.

Dominican Republic

Caribbean
18,700 sq. mi
Pop: 6.6m.
UN, OAS

Capital: Santo Domingo (Pop: 1,313,172)
Official language: Spanish
Religion: Roman Catholic
Political status: Presidential republic
Head of state: Joaquin Balaguer (since 1986)
GNP per capita: $1,090 (1984)
Currency: peso oro ($1 = 4.97)

President Joaquin Balaguer, blind and aged 80, seeemed set to seek a sixth term in office in the 1990 elections. In September, Hurricane Gilbert left five dead in its wake.

Ecuador

South America
104,505 sq. mi
Pop: 9.64m.
UN, LAIA, OAS, OPEC

Capital: Quito (Pop: 1,110,248)
Official languages: Spanish, Quechua
Religion: Roman Catholic
Political status: Presidential republic
Head of state: Leon Febres Cordero (since 1984)
GNP per capita: $1,160 (1985)
Currency: sucre ($1 = 386)

Ecuador's annual inflation rate h a record of 77.4 percent in 1988, whi the foreign debt stood at over $1 billion. In October, the president o the High Court was assassinated b an unknown assailant.

Egypt

North Africa
386,900 sq. mi
Pop: 49.28m.
UN, AL, OAU

Capital: Cairo (Pop: 6,205,000)
Official language: Arabic
Religions: Sunni Moslem 90%, Coptic Christian 7%
Political status: Presidential republic
Head of state: Hosni Mubarak (since 1981)
Head of government: Atef Mohamed Naguib Sidki (since 1986)
GNP per capita: $466 (1984)
Currency: Egyptian pound ($1 = 0.70)

Egyptian novelist and short story writer Naguib Mahfouz was awarded the 1988 Nobel Prize for Literature in October. In November, the U.S. and Egypt agreed to co-produce the M-1 tank in a further tightening of U.S.-Egyptian military ties.

El Salvador

Central America
8,236 sq. mi
Pop: 5.48m.
UN, OAS

Capital: San Salvador
Official language: Spanish
Religion: Roman Catholic
Political status: Presidential republic
Head of state: José Napoléon Duarte (since 1984)
GNP per capita: $880 (1985)
Currency: colon ($1 = 5)

President José Napoléon Duarte fought a losing battle with terminal cancer. Presidential elections were set for March 19, 1989, as the war with leftist rebels, which has already claimed 65,000 lives, dragged on. The leftist alliance named former exile Guillermo Ungo as its candidate.

Equatorial Guinea

West Africa
10,831 sq. mi
Pop: 384,000
UN, OAU

Capital: Malabo (Pop: 10,000)
Official language: Spanish
Religions: mostly Roman Catholic, Protestant
Political status: Presidential republic
Head of state: Teodoro Obiang Nguema Mbasogo (since 1979)
GNP per capita: $420 (1983)
Currency: franc CFA ($1 = 286)

This former Spanish colony celebrated the 20th. anniversary of its independence in October. A worldwide drop in cocoa prices had a severe effect on the hard-hit economy, forcing the country to look for aid.

Ethiopia

Northeastern Africa
471,800 sq. mi
Pop: 46m.
UN, OAU

Capital: Addis Abada (Pop: 1,412,575)
Official languages: Amharic, Galla
Religions: Moslem 45%, Ethiopian Orthodox 40%
Political status: People's democratic republic
Head of state: Mengistu Haile Mariam (since 1977)
Head of government: Fikre-Selassie Wogderess (since 1987)
GNP per capita: $110 (1984)
Currency: birr ($1 = 2.07)

Already facing a violent, 27-year-old rebellion in the province of Eritrea, continued nationwide famine and a devastating plague of locusts, Ethiopia in 1988 was hit by its worst epidemic of malaria in 25 years. In November, the government launched a major economic and agricultural reform program aimed at the country's ailing economy.

Fiji

South Pacific
7,076 sq. mi
Pop: 714,000
UN

Capital: Suva (Pop: 71,255)
Official language: English
Religions: Christian 42%, Hindu 33%, Moslem 6%
Political status: Republic
Head of state: Ratu Sir Penaia Ganilau (since 1987)
Head of government: Ratu Sir Kamisese Mara (since 1987)
GNP per capita: $1,700 (1985)
Currency: Fiji dollar ($1 = 1.46)

The discovery in June of a cache of Soviet arms led the government to step up security measures. Fijian leader Sitiveni Rabuka and premier Ratu Sir Kamisese Mara vowed to fight subversion. In September, Australia threatened to cut aid after tension rose between Canberra and Suva.

Finland

Northern Europe
117,615 sq. mi
Pop: 4.93m.
UN, NC, OECD, EFTA

Capital: Helsinki (Pop: 487,581)
Official languages: Finnish, Swedish, Lappish
Religion: Lutheran 89.2%, Greek Orthodox 1.1%
Political status: Democratic parliamentary republic
Head of state: Mauno Koivisto (since 1982)
Head of government: Harri Holkeri (since 1987)
GNP per capita: $14,302 (1986)
Currency: Finnmark ($1 = 4.08)

President Mauno Koivisto, a Social Democrat, on March 1 began his second six-year term. He had failed to win an absolute majority in the elections held the previous month.

France

Western Europe
211,968 sq. mi
Pop: 55.62m.
UN, EEC, OECD

Capital: Paris (Pop: 2,188,918)
Official language: French
Religion: Roman Catholic 76%, Moslem 4.5%, Protestant 1.4%
Political status: Parliamentary republic
Head of state: François Mitterrand (since 1981)
Head of government: Michel Rocard (since 1988)
GNP per capita: $9,280 (1985)
Currency: French franc ($1 = 5.71)

France's voters had a particularly busy year: they were called to the polls a total of seven times. In May, Socialist candidate François Mitterrand defeated conservative presidential hopeful Jacques Chirac. The extreme-right National Front led by Jean Marie Le Pen was the chief victim of June legislative elections. It secured just one seat of the 32 it had held in the previous National Assembly. In May, three French hostages in Beirut returned to an emotional welcome in Paris. The three, a journalist and two diplomats, had been held hostage for three years. Also in May, 19 Melanesian separatist militants died on the French South Pacific territory of New Caledonia when French troops attacked to free hostages they had been holding in a cave. In June, pro-independence and loyalist leaders on New Caledonia signed accords designed to restore peace to the archipelago. The pact was approved by a majority of voters in a referendum held in France in November. Prince Charles and Princess Diana of Britain made a highly successful November visit to Paris.

Gabon

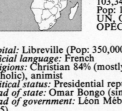

Central Africa
103,346 sq. mi
Pop: 1.22m.
UN, OAU, OPEC

Capital: Libreville (Pop: 350,000)
Official language: French
Religions: Christian 84% (mostly Roman Catholic), animist
Political status: Presidential republic
Head of state: Omar Bongo (since 1967)
Head of government: Léon Mébiame (since 1975)
GNP per capita: $4,250 (1983)
Currency: franc CFA ($1 = 285.66)

By late 1988, Gabon was set to export its own manganese for the first time. Previously, this resource was exported via the Congo. The ore was to be shipped from a new port.

Gambia

West Africa
4,127 sq. mi
Pop: 698,817
UN, OAU, CW

Capital: Banjul (Pop: 44,188)
Official language: English
Religions: Moslem 70%, Christian, animist
Political status: Republic
Head of state: Dawda Kairaba Jawara (since 1970)
GNP per capita: $170 (1984)
Currency: dalasi ($1 = 7.27)

Gambia and Senegal in October agreed to set up a free-trade zone. By late 1988, Gambia had recorded a total of 52 cases of AIDS, half of which had resulted in death.

Germany (East)

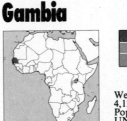

Central Europe
41,827 sq. mi
Pop: 16.6m.
UN, CMEA, Warsaw Pact

Capital: East Berlin (Pop: 1,223,309)
Official language: German
Religions: Protestant 80.5%, Roman Catholic 11%
Political status: Socialist republic
Head of state: Erich Honecker (since 1976)
Head of government: Willi Stoph (since 1976)
GNP per capita: $10,400 (1985)
Currency: GDR mark ($1 = 1.69)

East Germany's government acted quickly to stamp out all attempts at Soviet-style reforms and openness, known as "perestroika" and "glasnost". In November, Berlin banned a Soviet magazine and several Soviet films. These were deemed "too daring" by East Germany. The number of East Germans fleeing to the West rose sharply in 1988.

Germany (West)

Central Europe
96,025 sq. mi
Pop: 61m.
UN, EEC, NATO, OECD

Capital: Bonn (Pop: 290,800)
Official language: German
Religions: Protestant 49%, Roman Catholic 44.6%
Political status: Federal republic
Head of state: Richard von Weizsäcker (since 1984)
Head of government: Helmut Kohl (since 1982)
GNP per capita: $10,300 (1985)
Currency: deutsche Mark ($1 = 1.69)

A mine disaster, West Germany's worst in 26 years, claimed 51 lives in June. In August, young West German dare-devil Matthias Rust came home after spending 14 months in a Soviet prison for landing his light aircraft in Red Square. On his return, he was stripped of his pilot's licence. Also in August, a mid-air catastrophe at the U.S. base of Ramstein killed 70 people, most of them spectators attending an air show. The accident occurred when Italian Air Force jets collided during a stunt-flying display. This prompted West Germany to impose a permanent ban on all military air shows. In October, West Germany's right-wing heavyweight politician Franz Joseph Strauss died, leaving a power vacuum on the right. The political scene was rocked by a major row in November when parliamentary speaker Philip Jenninger praised Adolf Hitler and appeared to partly justify the Nazi's treatment of Jews, in a speech to commemorate the 50th. anniversary of the 1938 "Crystal Night" pogroms against the Jews. The speech caused a walkout by dozens of parliamentarians of all political persuasions. The incident came at an embarrassing moment for Chancellor Helmut Kohl.

In January, West Germany and its World War II foe, France, decided to create a joint army brigade. The force will have a total of 4,200 men based in West Germany.

Ghana

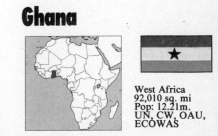

West Africa
92,010 sq. mi
Pop: 12.21m.
UN, CW, OAU, ECOWAS

111

Capital: Accra (Pop: 964,879)
Official language: English
Religions: Christian 52%, Moslem 13%, traditional beliefs
Political status: Republic
Head of state: Jerry John Rawlings (since 1981)
GNP per capita: $390 (1986)
Currency: cedi ($1 = 183)

Ten people, including a woman, were sentenced to death in October for the witchcraft murder and decapitation of three villagers. Campus unrest led to the three-month shut-down of two large universities.

Greece

Southeastern Europe
50,949 sq. mi
Pop: 9.97m.
UN, EEC, NATO, OECD

Capital: Athens (Pop: 1,082,126)
Official language: Greek
Religion: Greek Orthodox 98%
Political status: Democratic parliamentary republic
Head of state: Christos Sartzetakis (since 1985)
Head of government: Andreas Papandreou (since 1981)
GNP per capita: $3,300 (1985)
Currency: drachma ($1 = 135.30)

The year ended on a sour note for premier Andreas Papandreou. After undergoing heart surgery in London, he announced he was divorcing his U.S.-born wife of 37 years to marry a 34-year-old former stewardess. His socialist government also found itself embroiled in a major multi-million-dollar financial scandal.

Grenada

Caribbean
120 sq. mi
Pop: 88,000
UN, CW, OAS, Caricom

Capital: St George's (Pop: 4,788)
Official language: English
Religions: Roman Catholic, Anglican, Methodist
Political status: Constitutional monarchy
Head of state: Queen Elizabeth II
Head of government: Herbert Blaize (since 1985)
GNP per capita: $940 (1984)
Currency: Eastern Caribbean dollar ($1 = 2.70)

A U.S. presidential delegation led by Secretary of the Navy William Ball in October attended ceremonies held at Saint George's to mark the fifth anniversary of the U.S. military intervention in Granada. In a message, President Ronald Reagan paid homage to the 19 U.S. servicemen who died on the island in 1983, and to Grenada's economic progress.

Guatemala

Central America
42,042 sq. mi
Pop: 8.99m.
UN, OAS, Caricom

Capital: Guatemala City (Pop: 1.3m.)
Official language: Spanish
Religion: Roman Catholic
Political status: Presidential republic
Head of state: Vinicio Cerezo Arevalo (since 1986)
GNP per capita: $1,150 (1985)
Currency: quetzal ($1 = 1)

At least nine people died in a failed coup attempt in June at a military base, barely a month after a similar bid was put down peacefully. Continued human rights violations were reported by the Catholic Church.

Guinea

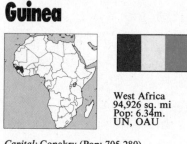

West Africa
94,926 sq. mi
Pop: 6.34m.
UN, OAU

Capital: Conakry (Pop: 705,280)
Official language: French
Religions: Moslem 69%, tribal beliefs 30%, Christian 1%
Political status: Presidential republic
Head of state: Lansana Conté (since 1984)
GNP per capita: $300 (1984)
Currency: Guinea franc ($1 = 440)

President Lansana Conté in November denied reports he had been the target of an October assassination attempt. General Conté also called for a "Basic Law" to be drafted to replace the existing constitution.

Guinea-Bissau

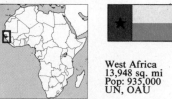

West Africa
13,948 sq. mi
Pop: 935,000
UN, OAU

Capital: Bissau (Pop: 109,214)
Official language: Portuguese, Crioulo
Religions: Moslem 30%, Christian 5%
Political status: Republic
Head of state: Joao Bernardo Vieira (since 1980)
GNP per capita: $180 (1983)
Currency: peso ($1 = 650)

Guinea-Bissau's most senior citizen, and one of the oldest men in the world, died in October at the ripe old age of 139. Born in 1849, he left seven widows and 14 children.

Guyana

South America
83,000 sq. mi
Pop: 812,000
UN, Caricom, CW

Capital: Georgetown (Pop: 188,000)
Official language: English
Religions: Christian 52%, Hindu 34%, Moslem 9%
Political status: Presidential republic
Head of state: Hugh Desmond Hoyte (since 1985)
Head of government: Hamilton Green (since 1985)
GNP per capita: $510 (1984)
Currency: Guyana dollar ($1 = 10)

The presence of at least 10,000 refugees from neighboring Suriname continued to be a heavy strain on Guyana's economy. The refugees had fled a 1986 outbreak of fighting in the former Dutch colony.

Haiti

Caribbean
10,700 sq. mi
Pop: 5.3m.
UN, OAS

Capital: Port-au-Prince (Pop: 449,831)
Official language: French
Religions: Roman Catholic, Voodoo
Political status: Presidential republic
Head of state: Prosper Avril (since 1988)
GNP per capita: $320 (1983)
Currency: gourde ($1 = 5)

It was a tumultuous year for Haiti, starting with the election in January of Leslie Manigat as President. By May, violent anti-government protests spread. In June, General Henri Namphy took power. He was ousted in September by Lt. Gen. Prosper Avril. In November, the commander of one of Haiti's most feared battalions was allegedly poisoned.

Honduras

Central America
43,277 sq. mi
Pop: 4.3m.
UN, OAS

Capital: Tegucigalpa (Pop: 571,400)
Official language: Spanish
Religions: Roman Catholic
Political status: Presidential republic
Head of state: José Azcona Hoyo (since 1986)
GNP per capita: $750 (1984)
Currency: lempira ($1 = 2)

Honduras accused Nicaraguan forces of invading its territory in March, prompting a build-up of U.S. forces. In October, Hurricane Joan ripped through Hunduras, leaving devastation and some 15 dead.

Hungary

Central Europe
35,911 sq. mi
Pop: 10.62m.
UN, CMEA, Warsaw Pact

Capital: Budapest (Pop: 2.08m.)
Official language: Hungarian
Religions: Roman Catholic 49%, Protestant 23.5%
Political status: Socialist people's republic
Head of state: Karoly Grosz (since 1987)
Head of government: Miklos Nemeth (since 1988)
GNP per capita: $2,150 (1983)
Currency: forint ($1 = 47.05)

In May, the Communist Party's General Secretary Karoly Grosz succeeded Janos Kadar as top leader. In late November, Miklos Nemeth, a progressive young economist, was appointed Prime Minister, as the nation moved towards a more open political and economic system.

Iceland

North Atlantic
39,758 sq. mi
Pop: 244,009
UN, OECD, NATO, EFTA, NC

Capital: Reykjavik (Pop: 91,394)
Official language: Icelandic
Religion: Evangelical Lutheran
Political status: Parliamentary republic
Head of state: Vigdis Finnbogadottir (since 1980)
Head of government: Thorsteinn Palsson (since 1987)
GNP per capita: $11,410 (1985)
Currency: krona ($1 = 39.46)

A sharp downturn in the economy, partly due to falling world fish prices, led in September to calls for a freeze in wages and prices and a devaluation. In London, Miss Iceland was crowned Miss World in November.

India

Southern Asia
1,222,713 sq. mi
Pop: 748m.
UN, CW

Capital: New Delhi (Pop: 5,714,000)
Official languages: Hindi, English
Religions: Hindu 82.7%, Moslem 11.2%, Christian 2.6%, Sikh 1.9%, Buddhist, Jain
Political status: Federal parliamentary republic
Head of state: R. Venkataraman (since 1987)
Head of government: Rajiv Gandhi (since 1984)
GNP per capita: $2260 (1983)
Currency: rupee ($1 = 13.05)

Sikh separatist killings continued in Punjab, while India's year-old peace efforts in Sri Lanka were hampered by well-armed Tamil guerrillas. The July 1987 Indo-Sri Lanka peace accord remained bogged down. In November, premier Rajiv Gandhi kicked off a year of celebrations to mark the birth centenary of Jawaharlal Nehru, his grandfather. Two October airline disasters left some 170 dead. India's shortest man in October claimed that no one in the world could undercut his stature of just 63 centimeters (25.2 inches).

Indonesia

Southeast Asia
741,098 sq. mi
Pop: 172m.
UN, ASEAN, OPEC

Capital: Jakarta (Pop: 6,503,449)
Official language: Bahasa Indonesian
Religion: Moslem 78%, Christian 11%, Buddhist, Hinduist
Political status: Presidential republic
Head of state: Gen. Raden Suharto (since 1968)
GNP per capita: $510 (1986)
Currency: rupiah ($1 = 1660)

General Suharto was re-elected for a fifth term as President, Prime Minister and Defense Minister. Two village women, attacked and buried by robbers in September, crawled out of their graves to report the crime.

Iran

Middle East
634,724 sq. mi
Pop: 49.86m.
UN, OPEC

Capital: Tehran (Pop: 6,022,078)
Official language: Farsi (Persian)
Religion: Moslem (Shi'a 96%, Sunni 3%)
Political status: Islamic republic
Head of state: Sayed Ali Khamenei (since 1981)
Head of government: Hosein Musavi-Khamenei (since 1981)
GNP per capita: $1,690 (1986)
Currency: rial ($1 = 67.81)

In April, U.S. warships demolished two Iranian oil rigs in the Gulf in retaliation for an Iranian attack on a U.S. frigate. On July 3, a U.S. Navy cruiser shot down an Iranian jetliner in the Gulf, killing all 290 people on board, in what the White House called a "terrible tragedy". Iranian gunboats continued to attack Gulf shipping. In October, prospects for the release of three British hostages in Lebanon and two Britons held in Iran brightened following the restoration of full diplomatic ties between London and Tehran. Iran and Iraq in August implemented a cease-fire and began United Nations-sponsored talks aimed at settling their eight-year conflict. Despite this, the two sides remained far apart on a troop withdrawal to international boundaries, demarcation of the frontier and navigation rights in the Shatt al-Arab, Iraq's only outlet to the sea. The exchange of prisoners of war got under way in late November, but soon hit snags. Iran and Iraq held an estimated 100,000 POWs. In October, Britain called off its Gulf naval escort patrol which had ensured the safety of vessels flying the Union Jack in the Gulf. The United States said in November it was maintaining the state of emergency declared in 1979 in its relations with Iran.

Iraq

Middle East
167,925 sq. mi
Pop: 17.09m.
UN, AL, OPEC

Capital: Baghdad (Pop: 2,183,760)
Official language: Arabic
Religions: Moslem 64%, Christian 2%
Political status: Socialist presidential republic
Head of state: Saddam Hussein at-Takriti (since 1979)
GNP per capita: $2,140 (1984)
Currency: Iraqi dinar ($1 = 0.311)

Some 5,000 civilians were killed by Iraqi forces in a March attack on a Kurdish village north of Baghdad. Iraq was widely accused of having used chemical weapons. In August, an estimated 130,000 Kurds fled Iraq into Turkey. In October, the U.S. Senate voted to impose sanctions on Iraq. Britain expelled two Iraqi diplomats for spying in October. Despite this, London said it would almost double its credits to Baghdad in 1989. President Saddam Hussein in November ordered his eldest son tried for the murder of a presidential guard.

Ireland

Western Europe
26,600 sq. mi
Pop: 3.54m.
UN, EEC, OECD

Capital: Dublin (Pop: 915,115)
Official languages: Irish (Gaelic), English
Religions: mostly Roman Catholic, Church of Ireland, Presbyterian, Methodist
Political status: Parliamentary republic
Head of state: Patrick Hillery (since 1976)
Head of government: Charles Haughey (since 1987)
GNP per capita: $4,040 (1985)
Currency: Irish pound ($1 = 1.58)

James Joyce's "dear dirty Dublin" celebrated its 1,000th. anniversary in style this year. In the first ever speech to the Irish Parliament by a French head of state, President François Mitterrand in February stressed France and Ireland's commitment to a unified Europe. In April, U.S. Representative Joe Kennedy met Irish premier Charles Haughey and lambasted Britain's position on Northern Ireland. Also in April, a Dublin court jailed a man for 40 years for the kidnapping of a wealthy dentist. In July, an Irish prisoner serving a life term for the murder of Britain's Lord Mountbatten in 1979 staged an unsuccessful jailbreak attempt. A major Anglo-Irish dispute erupted in November over a former Irish priest wanted by Britain for suspected terrorist links; Patrick Ryan sought refuge in Ireland after being allowed to travel from Belgium. The emigration of young people seeking work abroad resulted in Ireland's first population drop since 1961. In October, the European Court of Human Rights ruled that Irish law on homosexuality violated the right to privacy.

Israel

Near East
8,017 sq. mi
Pop: 4.33m.
UN

Capital: Jerusalem (Pop: 468,900)
Official languages: Hebrew, Arabic
Religions: Jewish 82%, Moslem 13%
Political status: Parliamentary republic
Head of state: Chaim Herzog (since 1983)
Head of government: Yitzhak Shamir (since 1986)
GNP per capita: $6,350 (1986)
Currency: new shekel ($1 = 1.58)

Violent Palestinian protests on the Israeli-occupied territories of the West Bank and Gaza Strip continued all year, leaving more than 330 people dead and hundreds injured. Israel came under increased criticism for its handling of the uprising. The situation in the occupied territories weighed heavily on November elections in which voters refused to give an overall mandate to either of the two main parties: Premier Yitzhak Shamir's conservative Likud bloc and the Labor Party headed by the Foreign Minister Shimon Peres. The inconclusive result gave right-wing religious parties a major say in politics. In March, former Israeli nuclear expert Mordechai Vanunu was sentenced to 18 years in prison for divulging nuclear secrets to a British newspaper. In November, Israel dismissed P.L.O. chief Yasir Arafat's declaration of an independent Palestinian state on the West Bank and Gaza as propaganda. In December, five Soviets, who had hijacked a busload of children and traded them for $2 million and an aircraft, surrendered after flying to Israel.

Italy

Southern Europe
116,319 sq. mi
Pop: 57.3m.
UN, EEC, NATO, OECD

Capital: Rome (Pop: 2,815,457)
Official language: Italian
Religion: Roman Catholic
Political status: Parliamentary republic
Head of state: Francesco Cossiga (since 1985)
Head of government: Ciriaco De Mita (since 1988)
GNP per capita: $6,096 (1984)
Currency: lira ($1 = 1,244)

Ciriaco De Mita in April formed Italy's 48th. post-war government. In Sicily, an October wave of Mafia murders left some 20 dead. In November, an inquiry into a mysterious 1980 airline disaster was opened.

Ivory Coast

West Africa
124,503 sq. mi
Pop: 10.60m.
UN, OAU

Capital: Abidjan (Pop: 1.85m.)
Official language: French
Religions: Moslem 24%, Christian 32%, animist 44%
Political status: Presidential republic
Head of state: Félix Houphouët-Boigny (since 1960)
GNP per capita: $720 (1983)
Currency: franc CFA ($1 = 285.66)

The economic crisis in Ivory Coast deepened markedly in 1988 due to a drop in world cocoa prices. The World Bank in November threatened to cut off its aid to the impoverished West Africa nation.

Jamaica

Caribbean
4,411 sq. mi
Pop: 2.3m.
UN, OAS, CW, Caricom

Capital: Kingston (Pop: 524,638)
Official language: English
Religion: mostly Protestant
Political status: Constitutional monarchy
Head of state: Queen Elizabeth II
Head of government: Edward Seaga (since 1980)
GNP per capita: $909 (1986)
Currency: Jamaican dollar ($1 = 5.50)

Hurricane Gilbert cut a huge swath of devastation through Jamaica in September, killing over 30 people and leaving 500,000 homeless. Damage stood at $8 billion. The U.S. and Western Europe sent disaster aid.

Japan

Northwestern Pacific Ocean
145,874 sq. mi
Pop: 121.67m.
UN, OECD

Capital: Tokyo (Pop: 8,354,000)
Official language: Japanese
Religions: Buddhist, Shintoist
Political status: Parliamentary monarchy
Head of state: Emperor Hirohito (since 1926)
Head of government: Noboru Takeshita (since 1987)
GNP per capita: $13,447 (1985)
Currency: yen ($1 = 128.5)

As the year drew to a close, all Japan's eyes were turned to the Imperial Palace, where aging Emperor Hirohito was fighting for his life. The prospect of his death sent shock waves through the country and millions of people followed the daily health bulletins. Crown Prince Akihito was to succeed the emperor. Prime Minister Noboru Takeshita in November celebrated the start of his second year in office. Even his critics acknowledged that he had made a good job of running the country and standing up to domestic protectionist pressures. He defused trade conflicts with the U.S. and Western Europe. Many also said he successfully tackled his responsibilities as the leader of the West's second biggest economy. In November, Mr. Takeshita pushed through the lower house of the Diet a package aimed at reforming Japan's tax system. The victory was seen as a boost to his chances for another two-year term once his first expires in October 1989. On December 7, the Nikkei stock index hit 3,009 points, the first time ever it had gone over 3,000 points. By late 1988, Japan's trade surplus stood at $95.6 billion.

Jordan

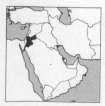

Middle East
34,443 sq. mi
Pop: 3,500,000
UN, AL

Capital: Amman (Pop: 777,500)
Official language: Arabic
Religion: Sunni Moslem 80%
Political status: Constitutional monarchy
Head of state: King Hussein II (since 1952)
Head of government: Zaid Rifai (since 1985)
GNP per capita: $1,900 (1984)
Currency: dinar ($1 = 0.344)

Jordan continued to be an active participant in the often-fragile Middle East peace process in 1988. In July, King Hussein announced that he was cutting administrative and legal links with the Israeli-occupied West Bank. The monarch met with Palestine Liberation Organization leader Yasir Arafat and Egyptian President Hosni Mubarak in October for talks focusing on future P.L.O.-Jordanian relations. Jordan was among the first nations to recognize the Palestinian state proclaimed by Mr. Arafat in mid-November.

Kenya

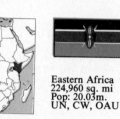

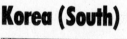

Eastern Africa
224,960 sq. mi
Pop: 20.03m.
UN, CW, OAU

Capital: Nairobi (Pop: 827,800)
Official language: Kiswahili
Religions: Protestant 19%, Roman Catholic 27%, other Christian 27%, Moslem 6%, tribal beliefs 19%
Political status: Presidential republic
Head of state: Daniel arap Moi (since 1978)
GNP per capita: $280 (1985)
Currency: Kenya shilling ($1 = 15.87)

President Moi was sworn in for a third five-year term in March. In April, cattle rustlers killed 191 villagers. The government said that wildlife poachers would be shot on sight. In September, British Foreign Secretary Sir Geoffrey Howe praised Kenya's human rights record.

Kiribati

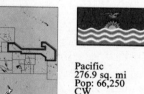

Pacific
276.9 sq. mi
Pop: 66,250
CW

Capital: Tarawa (Pop: 24,598)
Official language: English
Religions: Protestant, Roman Catholic
Political status: Presidential republic
Head of state: Ieremia Tabai (since 1979)
GNP per capita: $390 (1985)
Currency: Australian dollar ($1 = 1.39)

On July 12, the central Pacific islands of Kiribati, formerly known as the Gilbert and Ellice Islands, celebrated the ninth anniversary of their independence as a republic.

Korea (North)

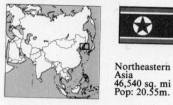

Northeastern Asia
46,540 sq. mi
Pop: 20.55m.

Capital: Pyongyang (Pop: 1.28m.)
Official language: Korean
Religions: Buddhist, Chondoist, Christian
Political status: Democratic people's republic
Head of state: Kim Il Sung (since 1972)
Head of government: Li Gun Mo (since 1986)
GNP per capita: $1,180 (1985)
Currency: won ($1 = 0.94)

A well-rehearsed outpouring of revolutionary fervor swept North Korea in September as it celebrated the 40th anniversary of its founding. In April, the country cut back its military spending to spur the economy.

Korea (South)

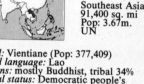

Northeastern Asia
38,232 sq. mi
Pop: 41.8m.

Capital: Seoul (Pop: 9,645,824)
Official language: Korean
Religions: animist, Buddhist, Confucianist, Christian
Political status: Presidential republic
Head of state: Roh Tae-Woo (since 1988)
Head of government: Lee Hyun-jae (since 1988)
GNP per capita: $2,850 (1987)
Currency: won ($1 = 761)

Chun Doo-Hwan was succeeded as President by Roh Tae-Woo in February. He was the first leader to relinquish power democratically in the history of South Korea. Mr. Chun had to apologize for abuse of power in November, saying he was ready to face punishment. The opposition captured an unprecedented combined majority of seats in April National Assembly elections. In August, Seoul successfully hosted the 1988 Olympics, which were snubbed by North Korea. In October, a woman who makes tear gas, used by police to break up anti-regime riots, became South Korea's top 1987 taxpayer.

Kuwait

Middle East
6,880 sq. mi
Pop: 1.77m.
UN, AL, OPEC, GCC

Capital: Kuwait (Pop: 60,525)
Official language: Arabic
Religion: Sunni Moslem 78%, Shia Moslem 14%, Christian 6%
Political status: Emirate
Head of state: Shaikh Jabir al-Ahmad al-Jabir al-Sabah (since 1977)
Head of government: Shaikh Saad al-Abdullah as Salim as Sabah (since 1978)
GNP per capita: $11,510 (1985)
Currency: dinar ($1 = 0.278)

Kuwait and other members of the six-nation Gulf Cooperation Council in mid-June signed a major economic cooperation pact with the EEC.

Laos

Southeast Asia
91,400 sq. mi
Pop: 3.67m.
UN

Capital: Vientiane (Pop: 377,409)
Official language: Lao
Religions: mostly Buddhist, tribal 34%
Political status: Democratic people's republic
Head of state: Phoumi Vongvichit
Head of government: Kaysone Phomvihane (since 1975)
GNP per capita: $220 (1984)
Currency: new kip ($1 = 350)

Soviet-backed Laos and U.S. ally Thailand signed a cease-fire in February, ending two months of fighting over a border dispute. Hundreds of Thai and Laotian soldiers died.

Lebanon

Near East
4,036 sq. mi
Pop: 3.5m.
UN, AL

Capital: Beirut (Pop: 702,000)
Official language: Arabic
Religions: Moslem (Sunni, Shiite, Druze), Christian (mostly Maronite and Greek Orthodox)
Political status: Parliamentary republic
Head of state: vacant
Head of government: vacant
GNP per capita: no reliable figures available
Currency: Lebanese pound ($1 = 370)

1988 was another difficult year for Lebanon, with continued hostage-taking, car-bombings, political paralysis and a spiraling economic crisis. In April, 66 people were killed in Tripoli by a massive bomb attack. Palestinian attacks into northern Israel brought repeated reprisal air raids on Palestinian camps. By year's end, more than 20 foreigners were being held hostage. Lebanon failed to elect a president to replace Amin Gemayel in September. This led to the formation of rival Christian and Moslem dominated governments.

Lesotho

Southern Africa
11,720 sq. mi
Pop: 1.63m.
UN, CW, OAU

Capital: Maseru (Pop: 109,382)
Official languages: Sesotho, English
Religions: Roman Catholic 44%, Protestant 49%
Political status: Constitutional monarchy
Head of state: King Moshoeshoe II (since 1966)
Head of government: Gen. Justin Lekhanya (since 1986)
GNP per capita: $470 (1984)
Currency: loti ($1 = 2.11)

Pope John Paul II's visit in September was marred by a hostage drama, when a group of unidentified armed men seized a bus containing pilgrims, two of whom died in a police rescue operation.

Liberia

West Africa
42,989 sq. mi
Pop: 2.5m.
UN, ECOWAS, OAU

Capital: Monrovia (Pop: 425,000)
Official language: English
Religions: Moslem 26%, Christian, traditional beliefs
Political status: Presidential republic
Head of state: Samuel Kanyon Doe (since 1980)
GNP per capita: $490 (1984)
Currency: Liberian dollar ($1 = 1)

President Samuel K. Doe called in November for greater international pressure against South Africa's apartheid policies. Liberia in November freed two Americans accused of plotting to overthrow Mr. Doe, who said the release was a sign of his goodwill towards U.S. President-elect George Bush. The two Americans were to have been tried for treason.

Libya

North Africa
679,358 sq. mi
Pop: 3.96m.
UN, AL, OAU, OPEC

Capital: Tripoli (Pop: 858,000)
Official language: Arabic
Religion: Sunni Moslem 97%
Political status: Socialist people's state
Head of state: Muammar Qadhafi (since 1969)
GNP per capita: $7,180 (1985)
Currency: dinar ($1 = 0.28)

In October, the U.S. accused Libya of building a chemical weapons factory. Tripoli denied the charge, saying it was willing to attend a 1989 international conference on banning chemical arms. Also in October, Libya formally ended its six-year border conflict with neighboring Chad.

Liechtenstein

Western Europe
61.8 sq. mi
Pop: 27,400
EFTA

Capital: Vaduz (Pop: 4,606)
Official language: German
Religions: Roman Catholic 87%, Protestant 8.6%
Political status: Constitutional monarchy
Head of state: Prince Francis Joseph II (since 1938)
Head of government: Hans Brunhart (since 1978)
GNP per capita: $15,000 (1984)
Currency: Swiss franc ($1 = 1.39)

In January, free public transport was introduced throughout Lichtenstein for a twelve-month trial period. The move was aimed at reducing the level of atmospheric pollution.

Luxembourg

Western Europe
998 sq. mi
Pop: 369,500
UN, EEC, NATO, OECD

Capital: Luxembourg (Pop: 76,640)
Official languages: Luxemburgish, French, German
Religion: Roman Catholic 95%
Political status: Constitutional monarchy
Head of state: Grand Duke Jean (since 1964)
Head of government: Jacques Santer (since 1984)
GNP per capita: $12,990 (1985)
Currency: Luxembourg franc ($1 = 35.28)

A big financial scandal which was sparked off by the bankruptcy of a building firm led to a member of the Luxembourg Parliament being given a five-month suspended prison sentence in mid-October.

Madagascar

Indian Ocean
226,658 sq. mi
Pop: 10.57m.
UN, OAU

Capital: Antananarivo (Pop: 662,585)
Official languages: Malagasy, French
Religions: Christian 50%, Moslem 3%, animist 47%
Political status: Republic
Head of state: Didier Ratsiraka (since 1975)
Head of government: Victor Ramahatra
GNP per capita: $250 (1984)
Currency: Malagasy franc ($1 = 1,277.6)

Madagascar's President vowed in November that elections would be held in 1989, adding he would seek a third mandate. In September, the International Olympic Committee said Madagascar would be sanctioned for boycotting the 1988 Games.

Malawi

Southern Africa
36,325 sq. mi
Pop: 7.1m.
UN, CW, OAU

Capital: Lilongwe (Pop: 186,800)
Official languages: Chichewa, English
Religions: mostly Christian, Moslem 7%
Political status: Presidential republic
Head of state: H. Kamuzu Banda (since 1966)
GNP per capita: $210 (1983)
Currency: kwacha ($1 = 2.53)

Close relations with South Africa were further strengthened in 1988, with leaders of both nations saying they intended to increase cooperation. Malawi is the only African state to have diplomatic ties with Pretoria.

Malaysia

Southeast Asia
127,317 sq. mi
Pop: 16.5m.
UN, ASEAN, CW

Capital: Kuala Lumpur (Pop: 937,875)
Official language: Malay
Religions: mostly Moslem, Buddhist, Hindu, Christian
Political status: Federal constitutional monarchy
Head of state: Sultan Mahmood Iskandar (since 1984)
Head of government: Mahathir Mohamad (since 1981)
GNP per capita: $1,870 (1985)
Currency: ringgit ($1 = 2.58)

A brand-new coral island about the size of four tennis courts rose up from the sea off the Malaysian coast in May. The newcomer was called Pulau Batu Hairan, or Surprise Rock Island. In November, premier Mahathir Mohamad defused a potentially serious political crisis by offering cabinet posts to two figures who had played key roles in an April 1987 leadership struggle.

Maldives

Indian Ocean
115 sq. mi
Pop: 189,000
UN, CW

Capital: Malé (Pop: 46,334)
Official language: Divehi
Religion: Moslem
Political status: Presidential republic
Head of state: Maumoon Abdul Gayoom (since 1978)
GNP per capita: $470 (1985)
Currency: rufiyaa ($1 = 10.10)

President Maumoon Abdul Gayoom began a third five-year term in November after surviving a bloody attempt to overthrow his government. Mr. Gayoom blamed "foreign terrorists" and "invading mercenaries".

Mali

West Africa
478,832 sq. mi
Pop: 8.73m.
UN, OAU

Capital: Bamako (Pop: 404,022)
Official language: French
Religions: Sunni Moslem 90%, animist 9%, Christian 1%
Political status: Presidential republic
Head of state: Moussa Traoré (since 1969)
GNP per capita: $150 (1983)
Currency: franc CFA ($1 = 285.66)

Mali's President, General Moussa Traoré, said at a November ceremony marking the 20th. anniversary of his rise to power that the army had seized power in 1968 to stave off political, economic and social chaos. He stressed that the main challenge for Mali now was economic rather than political problems. Also in November, a presidential decree ordered the release of some 240 prisoners.

Malta

Southern Europe
121.9 sq. mi
Pop: 343,334
UN, CW

Capital: Valletta (Pop: 9,263)
Official languages: Maltese, English
Religion: Roman Catholic
Political status: Democratic parliamentary republic
Head of state: Paul Xuereb (since 1987)
Head of government: Eddie Fenech Adami (since 1987)
GNP per capita: $3,103 (1984)
Currency: Lira Maltija ($1 = 3.05)

A Palestinian was sentenced to a 25-year jail term in November for his role in a 1985 hijack drama in which a total of 61 people were killed.

Mauritania

West Africa
398,000 sq. mi
Pop: 2.01m.
UN, AL, OAU

Capital: Nouakchott (Pop: 500,000)
Official languages: Arabic, French
Religion: Sunni Moslem 99%
Political status: Republic
Head of state: Maaouia Ould Sidi Mohamed Taya (since 1984)
GNP per capita: $450 (1985)
Currency: ouguiya ($1 = 72.41)

President Maaouia Ould Sidi Mohamed Taya said in November that his West African nation would support the struggle for the independence of Namibia. A jailed former health minister died in a Nouakchott prison in November.

Mauritius

Indian Ocean
787 sq. mi
Pop: 1.041m.
UN, CW, OAU

Capital: Port Louis (Pop: 138,482)
Official language: English
Religions: Hindu 53%, Christian 30%, Moslem 13%
Political status: Constitutional monarchy
Head of state: Queen Elizabeth II
Head of government: Aneerood Jugnauth (since 1982)
GNP per capita: $1,150 (1983)
Currency: rupee ($1 = 12.85)

The former British Indian Ocean colony in March celebrated the 20th. anniversary of its independence. Several African nations criticized continued trading links between Mauritius and South Africa.

Mexico

North America
756,198 sq. mi
Pop: 76m.
UN, OAS, LAIA

Capital: Mexico City (Pop: 12,932,116)
Official language: Spanish
Religion: Roman Catholic 92.6%
Political status: Federal republic

Head of state: Carlos Salinas de Gortari (since 1988)
GNP per capita: $2,200 (1984)
Currency: peso ($1 = 2,300)

President Reagan and Mexico's outgoing President Miguel de la Madrid in February held their sixth and final summit meeting. In June, the U.S. recalled its ambassador to Mexico and expressed its anger over the freeing of a Puerto Rican nationalist wanted in the U.S. for terrorism. July presidential elections were won by Carlos Salinas de Gortari with 50.7 per cent of the vote, amid charges of fraud. President-elect George Bush met Mr. Salinas in November in a bid to smooth the troubled U.S.-Mexican relationship. In October, the U.S. said it would grant Mexico $3.5 billion to help it cope with reduced oil revenues. Mexico's massive foreign debt stood at $104 billion.

Monaco

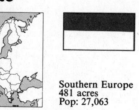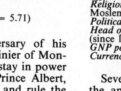

Southern Europe
481 acres
Pop: 27,063

Capital: Monaco
Official language: French
Religion: Roman Catholic
Political status: Constitutional principality
Head of state: Prince Rainier III (since 1949)
Head of government: Jean Ausseil (since 1985)
GNP per capita: $10,000
Currency: French franc ($1 = 5.71)

As the 40th. anniversary of his reign neared, Prince Rainier of Monaco said he planned to stay in power until his son, Crown Prince Albert, was ready to take over and rule the tiny but wealthy principality.

Mongolia

Eastern Asia
605,022 sq. mi
Pop: 1.97m.
UN, CMEA

Capital: Ulan Bator (Pop: 479,500)
Official language: Mongolian
Religion: Tibetan Buddhist Lamaism
Political status: People's republic
Head of state: Jambyn Batmunkh (since 1984)
Head of government: Dumaagiyn Sodnom (since 1984)
GNP per capita: $940 (1978)
Currency: tugrik ($1 = 3.36)

Despite the late 1987 withdrawal of one division of about 10,000 Soviet troops from Mongolia, an estimated 65,000 Soviet military personnel remained stationed there in 1988. Relations with China improved in 1988.

Morocco

North Africa
177,116 sq. mi
Pop: 23m.
UN, AL

Capital: Rabat (Pop: 841,800)
Official language: Arabic
Religions: Sunni Moslem 98%, Christian 2%
Political status: Constitutional monarchy
Head of state: Hassan II (since 1961)
Head of government: Azzeddine Laraki (since 1986)
GNP per capita: $500 (1984)
Currency: dirham ($1 = 8.06)

After a 12-year rift over the disputed Western Sahara, Morocco and Algeria resumed their diplomatic ties in May. The following month, the border between the two North African nations was reopened.

Mozambique

Southern Africa
308,642 sq. mi
Pop: 14.54m.
UN, OAU

Capital: Maputo (Pop: 882,800)
Official language: Portuguese
Religions: animist 60%, Christian 18%, Moslem 16%
Political status: People's republic
Head of state: Joaquim Alberto Chissano (since 1986)
GNP per capita: $90 (1986)
Currency: metical ($1 = 454)

Several Western nations accused the anti-government Renamo rebels of massacring hundreds of thousands of civilians. In a June move to normalize church-state relations, the government said it would return all church property nationalized after the country's independence in 1975. During a September visit, Pope John Paul II called for an end to the bloody conflict in Mozambique.

Namibia

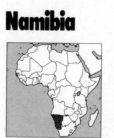

Southern Africa
318,261 sq. mi
Pop: 1,184,000

Capital: Windhoek (Pop: 110,644)
Official languages: Afrikaans, English
Religions: Protestant, traditional beliefs
Political status: South African-controlled territory
Head of state: Louis Pienaar (since 1985)
GNP: $1.2 bil. (1985)
Currency: South African rand ($1 = 2.86)

Some 10 years after the U.N. ruled that South Africa's occupation of Namibia was illegal, independence for the mineral-rich territory at last seemed a possibility. Pretoria in November approved a regional peace plan for Namibia's independence. January 1, 1989 was set as the target date for implementing the plan.

Nauru

Pacific
8,108 sq. mi
Pop: 8,042
CW

Capital: Yaren (Pop: 4,000)
Official languages: Nauruan, English
Religions: Roman Catholic, Protestant
Political status: Republic
Head of state: Hammer DeRoburt (since 1978)
GNP per capita: $0,091 (1985)
Currency: Australian dollar ($1 = 1.39)

The tiny South Pacific island territory of Nauru, which became independent in January 1968, developed its close trade links with Australia and New Zealand in 1988.

Nepal

South Asia
56,827 sq. mi
Pop: 16.63m.
UN

Capital: Kathmandu (Pop: 235,160)
Official language: Nepali
Religions: Hindu 90%, Buddhist 5%, Moslem 3%
Political status: Constitutional monarchy
Head of state: Birendra Bir Bikram Shah Dev (since 1972)
Head of government: Marich Man Singh Shrestha (since 1986)
GNP per capita: $170 (1983)
Currency: Nepalese rupee ($1 = 21)

A March soccer-stadium stampede left some 75 people dead. An August earthquake killed more than 700 people. British parliamentarians in November held talks with Nepalese leaders over the future of the elite Gurkha troops in the British army.

Netherlands

Northwestern Europe
16,163 sq. mi
Pop: 14.62m.
UN, EEC, NATO, OECD

Capital: Amsterdam (Pop: 682,702)
Official language: Dutch
Religions: Roman Catholic 36%, Dutch Reformed 19%
Political status: Constitutional monarchy
Head of state: Queen Beatrix (since 1980)
Head of government: Ruud Lubbers (since 1982)
GNP per capita: $8,500 (1984)
Currency: guilder ($1 = 1.89)

Three British soldiers were killed in two May 1 attacks claimed by the Irish Republican Army. The I.R.A. said the killings were revenge for the earlier slaying of three I.R.A. members by British forces in Gibraltar.

New Zealand

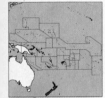

South Pacific
103,736 sq. mi
Pop: 3.3m.
UN, CW, OECD

Capital: Wellington (Pop: 351,400)
Official language: English
Religions: Anglican, Presbyterian, Roman Catholic, Methodist
Political status: Constitutional monarchy
Head of state: Queen Elizabeth II
Head of government: David R. Lange
GNP per capita: $5,276 (1985)
Currency: New Zealand dollar ($1 = 1.51)

New Zealand in 1988 protested repeatedly and strongly against the continued French nuclear testing on the South Pacific atoll of Mururoa. Relations with the United States also remained clouded by New Zealand's firm anti-nuclear stance.

Nicaragua

Central America
49,363 sq. mi
Pop: 3.5m.
UN, OAS

Capital: Managua (Pop: 903,998)
Official language: Spanish
Religion: Roman Catholic 91%
Political status: Republic
Head of state: Daniel Ortega Saavedra (since 1984)
GNP per capita: $960 (1985)
Currency: new cordoba ($1 = 10)

In late March, Nicaragua released political prisoners as the first step of a cease-fire accord reached with the U.S.-backed contra rebels. President Reagan said in October he was giving up his efforts to obtain additional military aid for the contras before his term expires. In November, Managua postponed until 1990 municipal elections due in 1989. The government said it could not afford to hold the poll. Hurricane Joan hit Nicaragua in October, caused 250 deaths and disappearances and damages estimated at more than $900 million.

Niger

West Africa
458,075 sq. mi
Pop: 6.6m.
UN, OAU

Capital: Niamey (Pop: 399,100)
Official language: French
Religions: Moslem 97%, animist
Political status: Republic
Head of state: Ali Seybou (since 1987)
Head of government: Hamid Algabid (since 1983)
GNP per capita: $240 (1985)
Currency: franc CFA ($1 = 285.66)

President Ali Seybou stated in November that general elections would be held in late 1989, when he ends his first term in office. He did not rule out staying on for a second term, if the voters asked him to do so.

Nigeria

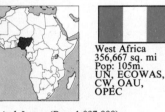

West Africa
356,667 sq. mi
Pop: 105m.
UN, ECOWAS, CW, OAU, OPEC

Capital: Lagos (Pop: 1,097,000)
Official language: English
Religions: Moslem 48%, Christian 34%
Political status: Federal republic
Head of state: Ibrahim Babangida (since 1985)
GNP per capita: $730 (1986)
Currency: Naira ($1 = 4.23)

Nigerian leader General Ibrahim Babangida said in October he was committed to reducing military involvement in politics as the nation moves gradually towards a return to civilian rule in 1992.

Norway

North. Europe
125,049 sq. mi
Pop: 4.2m.
UN, EFTA, NATO, NC, OECD

Capital: Oslo (Pop: 451,099)
Official language: Norwegian
Religions: mostly Evangelical Lutheran, Roman Catholic
Political status: Constitutional monarchy
Head of state: King Olav V
Head of government: Gro Harlem Brundtland (since 1986)
GNP per capita: $16,400 (1986)
Currency: krone ($1 = 6.38)

Norwegian premier Gro Harlem Brundtland reshuffled her minority Labor government in June after it was defeated in a parliament vote. In September, the resort of Lillehammer, north of Oslo, was chosen for the 1994 Winter Olympic Games.

Oman

Middle East
105,000 sq. mi
Pop: 1.2m.
UN, AL, GCC

Capital: Muscat (Pop: 250,000)
Official language: Arabic
Religions: Ibadhi Moslem 75%, Sunni Moslem
Political status: Sultanate
Head of state: Qaboos bin Said (since 1970)
GNP per capita: $7,080 (1985)
Currency: Rial Omani ($1 = 0.385)

Further progress was made in 1988 toward settling a long-running border dispute with Marxist South Yemen. In mid-November, nearly 100 cases of polio were reported in Oman.

Pakistan

South Asia
307,293 sq. mi
Pop: 102.2m.
UN

Capital: Islamabad (Pop: 201,000)
Official languages: Urdu, English
Religions: Moslem 97%, Christian, Hindu
Political status: Federal Islamic republic
Head of state: Ghulam Ishaq Khan (since 1988)
Head of government: Benazir Bhutto (since 1988)
GNP per capita: $390 (1983)
Currency: rupee ($1 = 17.59)

An early April blast at a munitions depot in Islamabad killed 100 people and destroyed hundreds of tons of U.S. arms. The arms were reportedly destined for anti-Soviet Afghan rebels. In mid-April, Pakistan signed an Afghan peace accord which is to lead to the total pullout of Soviet forces from Afghanistan by February 1989. General Zia ul-Haq, Pakistan's longest-serving leader, was killed in an August plane-crash allegedly caused by sabotage. An October outburst of ethnic violence in Karachi left more than 300 dead. On December 2, Benazir Bhutto, who gave up a jet-setting life to avenge her father, overthrown in a coup by Gen. Zia in 1977 and executed in 1979, was sworn in as Prime Minister. She thus became the first woman to govern a Moslem country. Ms. Bhutto, 35, headed the first democratically-elected government since her father's ouster. She immediately announced the restoration of fundamental rights and lifted the state of emergency in force since President Zia's death.

Panama

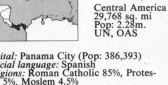

Central America
29,768 sq. mi
Pop: 2.28m.
UN, OAS

Capital: Panama City (Pop: 386,393)
Official language: Spanish
Religions: Roman Catholic 85%, Protestant 5%, Moslem 4.5%
Political status: Presidential republic
Head of state: Manuel Solis Palma (since 1988)
GNP per capita: $2,060 (1985)
Currency: balboa ($1 = 1)

Relations between Panama and the United States hit rock bottom in early 1988, after the Reagan administration tried unsuccessfully in February to force out Panamanian Defense Forces chief Manuel Antonio Noriega, indicted on U.S. drug conspiracy charges in Miami. In March, Washington sent 2,000 more troops to Panama and a coup bid against General Noriega failed. Despite the crippling effects of a clampdown on Panamanian assets in the U.S. and trade with that country, General Noriega clung tenaciously to power. Alleged links between General Noriega and the U.S. intelligence services loomed large in the 1988 U.S. presidential elections.

Papua New Guinea

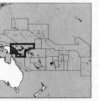

Pacific
170,702 sq. mi
Pop: 3.48m.
UN, CW

Capital: Port Moresby (Pop: 123,624)
Official language: English
Religions: Protestant 63%, Roman Catholic 31%, local religions
Political status: Constitutional monarchy
Head of state: Queen Elizabeth II
Head of government: Rabbie Namaliu (since 1988)
GNP per capita: $751 (1986)
Currency: kina ($1 = 0.90)

Premier Paias Wingti was ousted by opposition leader Rabbie Namaliu in July. Mr. Wingti said he would cooperate with the new government. A major September mud-slide killed 75 villagers in Morobe province.

Paraguay

South America
157,042 sq. mi
Pop: 3.79m.
UN, LAIA, OAS, LAES

Capital: Asuncion (Pop: 729,307)
Official languages: Spanish, Guarani
Religion: Roman Catholic 97%
Political status: Presidential republic
Head of state: Alfredo Stroessner (since 1954)
GNP per capita: $1,175 (1984)
Currency: guarani ($1 = 320)

President Alfredo Stroessner won his eighth five-year term in February elections marred by reports of fraud. In October, the government denied persistent rumors that President Stroessner, 75, was gravely ill.

Peru

South America
496,222 sq. mi
Pop: 20.2m.
UN, LAIA,
OAS

Capital: Lima (Pop: 5,258,600)
Official languages: Spanish, Quechua
Religion: Roman Catholic over 90%
Political status: Republic
Head of state: Alan Garcia Perez (since 1985)
Head of government: Guillermo Larco Cox (since 1987)
GNP per capita: $970 (1985)
Currency: inti ($1 = 33.00)

President Alan Garcia in March unveiled a new economic policy, saying it was based on a "war footing" economy. All non-essential government spending programs were cut back in a bid to stem runaway inflation. A nationwide wave of strikes in November forced the government to lift a controversial decree limiting salaries. Security forces continued to battle Shining Path extreme-left guerrillas. In September, archeologists discovered a major cache of 1,500-year-old artifacts at a burial site northwest of Lima.

Philippines

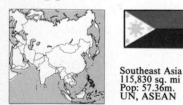

Southeast Asia
115,830 sq. mi
Pop: 57.36m.
UN, ASEAN

Capital: Manila (Pop: 1,630,485)
Official languages: Pilipino
Religions: Roman Catholic 83%, Protestant 9%, Moslem 5%
Political status: Republic
Head of state: Corazon C. Aquino (since 1986)
GNP per capita: $614 (1986)
Currency: peso ($1 = 21.10)

President Corazon Aquino marked the 1,000th. day of her presidency on November 21, as the Philippines faced persistent economic woes, a communist insurgency, high level corruption and threats from rightist extremists in the military. Relations

with the U.S. improved after the October signing of a pact allowing U.S. forces to continue using two huge bases in exchange for increased aid. President Reagan said he would urge his successor to launch an ambitious international plan to rehabilitate the Philippine economy from 1989. Two late 1988 typhoons killed some 700 people and caused damage estimated at over $250 million.

Poland

Eastern Europe
120,628 sq. mi
Pop: 37.6m.
UN, CMEA,
Warsaw Pact

Capital: Warsaw (Pop: 1,649,000)
Official language: Polish
Religion: Roman Catholic 93%
Political status: Socialist republic
Head of state: Wojciech Jaruzelski (since 1985)
Head of government: Mieczyslaw Rakowski (since 1988)
GNP per capita: $56,420 (1985)
Currency: zloty ($1 = 675.93)

Several thousand Poles marched through the streets of Warsaw in April to commemorate the 45th. anniversary of the city's Jewish ghetto uprising. In October, Poland's new Prime Minister, 61-year-old Mieczyslaw Rakowski, who is a long-time foe of the banned Solidarity trade union, issued a stern warning that he was prepared to call in the army to prevent "social anarchy". A government decision to shut down the historic Gdansk shipyards sparked off a wave of nationwide labor unrest. Prime Minister Margaret Thatcher in November became the first British premier to visit Poland and the first Western leader to meet Solidarity chief Lech Walesa in Gdansk.

Portugal

Southwestern
Europe
35,516 sq. mi
Pop: 10.29m.
UN, NATO,
OECD, EEC

Capital: Lisbon (Pop: 807,937)
Official language: Portuguese
Religion: Roman Catholic 94.5%
Political status: Parliamentary republic
Head of state: Mario Soares (since 1986)
Head of government: Anibal Cavaco Silva (since 1985)
GNP per capita: $2,190 (1983)
Currency: escudo ($1 = 138.33)

A huge blaze in August burned down much of Lisbon's historic district of Baixa, which was rebuilt after a 1755 earthquake. Portugal's roads remained the most deadly in Europe, with more than 2,500 deaths in 1988.

Qatar

Middle East
4,415 sq. mi
Pop: 371,863
UN, AL, OPEC,
GCC

Capital: Doha (Pop: 190,000)
Official language: Arabic
Religion: Moslem 95%
Political status: Emirate ·
Head of state: Khalifa bin Hamad Al-Thani (since 1972)
GNP per capita: $22,940 (1984)
Currency: riyal ($1 = 3.64)

Drilling began off Qatar's coast in August at a well which was reported to contain the world's largest reserves of natural gas. Drilling operations were being carried out by a large Franco-American consortium.

Romania

Southeastern
Europe
91,699 sq. mi
Pop: 22.7m.
UN, CMEA,
Warsaw Pact

Capital: Bucharest (Pop: 1,975,808)
Official language: Romanian
Religions: Orthodox 80%, Roman Catholic 6%
Political status: Socialist republic
Head of state: Nicolae Ceausescu (since 1967)
Head of government: Constantin Dascalescu (since 1982)
GNP per capita: $2,540 (1981)
Currency: leu ($1 = 4.25)

Apparently irked by U.S. calls for improvement in human rights policies, Romania in February said it no longer wanted preferential trading links with Washington. In September, the government watered down a controversial resettlement plan that was to have involved the levelling of thousands of small villages.

Rwanda

Central Africa
10,169 sq. mi
Pop: 6.32m.
UN, OAU

Capital: Kigali (Pop: 156,650)
Official languages: French, Kinyarwanda, Kiswhahili
Religions: Christian 68%, traditional 23%, Moslem 9%
Political status: Republic
Head of state: Juvenal Habyarimana (since 1975)
GNP per capita: $257 (1984)
Currency: Rwanda franc ($1 = 75.46)

President Juvenal Habyarimana, became in October the sole candidate for late December presidential elections. Rwanda's meagre resources were hit by the arrival of 40,000 refugees from massacres in Burundi.

St Christopher and Nevis

Caribbean
103 sq. mi
Pop: 47,000
UN, CW, OAS,
Caricom

Capital: Basseterre (Pop: 14,283)
Official language: English
Religion: Protestant 76.4%, Roman Catholic 10.7%
Political status: Constitutional monarchy
Head of state: Queen Elizabeth II
Head of government: Kennedy A. Simmonds (since 1983)
GNP per capita: $820 (1983)
Currency: East Caribbean dollar ($1 = 2.70)

Saint Christopher and Nevis was spared major damage to housing and agriculture in September when Hurricane Gilbert went on a rampage through the Caribbean.

St Lucia

Caribbean
238 sq. mi
Pop: 143,600
UN, CW, OAS,
Caricom

Capital: Castries (Pop: 45,763)
Official language: English
Religion: Roman Catholic 86%
Political status: Constitutional monarchy
Head of state: Queen Elizabeth II
Head of government: John Compton (since 1982)
GNP per capita: $1,105 (1985)
Currency: East Caribbean dollar ($1 = 2.70)

There was disagreement in July when Caribbean Community members, including St. Lucia, did not agree on whether to suspend Haiti's observer status with the group.

St Vincent and the Grenadines

Caribbean
150 sq. mi
Pop: 138,000
UN, CW, OAS,
Caricom

Capital: Kingstown (Pop: 33,694)
Official language: English
Religions: Anglican 47%, Methodist 28%, Roman Catholic 13%
Political status: Constitutional monarchy
Head of state: Queen Elizabeth II
Head of government: James Mitchell (since 1984)
GNP per capita: $860 (1983)
Currency: East Caribbean dollar ($1 = 2.70)

St. Vincent in January broke its diplomatic ties with North Korea. In June, Canada granted aid to safeguard St. Vincent's forests.

San Marino

Southern Europe
24.1 sq. mi
Pop: 22,638

Capital: San Marino (Pop: 4,363)
Official language: Italian
Religion: Roman Catholic 95%
Political status: Republic
Heads of state: Two co-regents appointed every 6 months
Currency: Italian lira

The mountainous city-state of San Marino, the world's smallest republic, became the 22nd. member of the Council of Europe in late 1988.

Sao Tome and Principe

Atlantic Ocean
387 sq. mi
Pop: 113,000
UN, OAU

Capital: Sao Tome (Pop: 34,997)
Official language: Portuguese
Religion: Roman Catholic 80%
Political status: Republic
Head of state: Manuel Pinto da Costa (since 1975)
GNP: $31 mil. (1983)
Currency: dobra ($1 = 73.47)

The army crushed a coup attempt against President Manuel Pinto da Costa in March, killing two opponents of the government.

Saudi Arabia

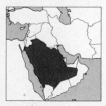

Middle East
849,400 sq. mi
Pop: 11.52m.
UN, AL, GCC, OPEC

Capital: Riyadh (Pop: 666,840)
Official language: Arabic
Religion: Sunni Moslem 85%, Shiite 15%
Political status: Kingdom
Head of state: King Fahd ibn Abdul Aziz (since 1982)
GNP per capita: $8,000 (1985)
Currency: rial ($1 = 3.75)

Saudi Arabia cut its diplomatic ties with Iran in April. In July, Riyadh concluded a huge arms deal with Britain including warplanes and navy vessels following U.S. refusals to supply certain weapons.

Senegal

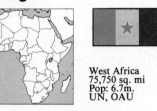

West Africa
75,750 sq. mi
Pop: 6.7m.
UN, OAU

Capital: Dakar (Pop: 978,553)
Official language: French
Religions: Moslem 91%, Christian 6%, animist 3%
Political status: Republic
Head of state: Abdou Diouf (since 1981)
GNP per capita: $360 (1984)
Currency: franc CFA ($1 = 285.66)

Following his overwhelming election victory in February, President Abdou Diouf invoked emergency powers when reports of large scale vote fraud led to widespread rioting.

Seychelles

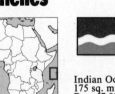

Indian Ocean
175 sq. mi
Pop: 67,000
UN, CW, OAU

Capital: Victoria (Pop: 23,000)
Official languages: Creole, English, French
Religion: Roman Catholic 96%
Political status: Republic
Head of state: France Albert René (since 1977)
GNP per capita: $2,320 (1984)
Currency: Seychelles rupee ($1 = 5.31)

A treasure hunt began in July to find gold and silver worth $200 million allegedly buried by 18th. century French pirate Olivier Le Vasseur.

Sierra Leone

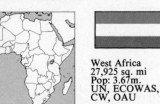

West Africa
27,925 sq. mi
Pop: 3.67m.
UN, ECOWAS, CW, OAU

Capital: Freetown (Pop: 554,243)
Official language: English
Religions: tribal 52%, Moslem 39%, Christian 8%
Political status: Republic
Head of state: Joseph Saidu Momoh (since 1988)
GNP per capita: $380 (1983)
Currency: leone ($1 = 30.65)

Siaka Probyn Stevens, who ruled Sierra Leone for 17 years, died in May. His hand-picked successor, Major General Joseph Momoh, in October said that he would not tolerate anti-government "subversion".

Singapore

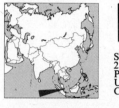

Southeast Asia
238.7 sq. mi
Pop: 2.59m.
UN, ASEAN, CW

Capital: Singapore (Pop: 2,500,000)
Official languages: Chinese, Malay, Tamil, English
Religions: Buddhist, Taoist, Moslem, Hinduist, Christian
Political status: Parliamentary republic
Head of state: Wee Kim Wee (since 1985)
Head of government: Lee Kuan Yew (since 1959)
GNP per capita: $6,630 (1986)
Currency: Singapore dollar ($1 = 2.01)

Relations with Washington soured in May after Singapore accused a U.S. diplomat of "gross interference" in its domestic affairs. In July, premier Lee Kuan Yew proposed that an international panel resolve the row. British Prime Minister Margaret Thatcher held talks with Mr. Lee in July. Singapore's leader was re-elected for an eighth term in September with 61.8 percent of the vote. He promised to resign sometime after turning 65 in late September.

Solomon Islands

Pacific
10,640 sq. mi
Pop: 270,000
UN, CW

Capital: Honiara (Pop: 26,000)
Official language: English
Religions: Protestant 76%, Roman Catholic 19%
Political status: Constitutional monarchy
Head of state: Queen Elizabeth II
Head of government: Ezekiel Alebua (since 1988)
GNP per capita: $640 (1983)
Currency: Solomon Island dollar ($1 = 2.03)

Ezekiel Alebua became the new Prime Minister following the resignation in late 1987 of Sir Peter Kenilorea, who was accused of accepting French aid to rebuild his own village, which had been hit by a cyclone.

Somalia

Northeastern Africa
246,201 sq. mi
Pop: 6.11m.
UN, AL, OAU

Capital: Mogadishu (Pop: 250,000)
Official languages: Somali, Arabic
Religion: Sunni Moslem 99%
Political status: Republic
Head of state: Mohammed Siyad Barre (since 1969)
Head of government: Mohammed Ali Samater
GNP per capita: $250 (1983)
Currency: Somali shilling ($1 = 100.00)

Drought affected many regions of Somalia in 1988. The country also had to cope with the devastation caused to agriculture by hordes of locusts. Refugees from neighboring Ethiopia continued to flood in.

South Africa

Southern Africa
433,678 sq. mi
Pop: 23.39m.
UN

Capital: Pretoria (Pop: 528,407)
Official languages: Afrikaans, English
Religion: Mainly Christian
Political status: Republic
Head of state: Pieter Botha (since 1978)
GNP per capita: $2,500 (1984)
Currency: rand ($1 = 2.86)

Although it ended on a positive note, 1988 was another difficult year for South Africa, which began its third year of emergency in June. The far-right Conservative Party won two by-elections in March. This was a setback for President Pieter Botha's limited race reforms. Pretoria defiantly told U.N. members to "do your damnedest" to try to force change in South Africa. Three anti-apartheid leaders in October left the U.S. Consulate in Johannesburg after holing up there for over a month. A controversial labor law banning "politically motivated" strikes was implemented in September. Segregated local elections held in October were marred by a low black turnout and a far-right challenge to the government. Year-long feuding between black factions in Natal left some 600 people dead. The November killing of six blacks by a white neo-Nazi led to South Africa's first ever banning of a white supremacist group. On November 22, Pretoria approved an historic plan to bring independence to Namibia and a Cuban troop pullout from Angola. In November, South Africa moved toward the freeing of veteran anti-apartheid leader Nelson Mandela, who has served 26 years of a life sentence for sabotage.

Spain

Southwestern
Europe
194,884 sq. mi
Pop: 38.9m.
UN, NATO,
EEC, OECD

Capital: Madrid (Pop: 3,188,297)
Official language: Spanish
Religion: Roman Catholic
Political status: Constitutional monarchy
Head of state: King Juan Carlos I
Head of government: Felipe Gonzalez
Marquez (since 1982)
GNP per capita: $5,198 (1986)
Currency: peseta ($1 = 113.49)

. Anglo-Spanish ties, often troubled by a dispute over Gibraltar, took a big step forward in September when Margaret Thatcher became the first British premier to visit Spain. In December, the U.S. and Spain signed an eight-year military accord.

Sri Lanka

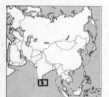

South Asia
25,332 sq. mi
Pop: 15.8m.
UN, CW

Capital: Colombo (Pop: 587,647)
Official language: Sinhala
Religions: Buddhist 69%, Hindu 15%, Christian 7%, Moslem 7%
Political status: Republic
Head of state: Junius R. Jayawardene (since 1978)
Head of government: Ranasinghe Premadasa (since 1978)
GNP per capita: $361 (1984)
Currency: Sri Lankan rupee ($1 = 30.85)

A 1987 peace accord with India failed to end the bloodshed in Sri Lanka, which continued to be paralyzed by the vicious conflict between separatist Tamil guerrillas and the Sinhalese-dominated government. More than 700 Indian troops were reported killed since the July 1987 peace pact. In September, Tamil gunmen killed a cabinet minister. Armed men belonging to a secretive Marxist group, the JVP, resurfaced in October, butchering 45 Sinhalese, mostly government employees who had defied a JVP order to stay away from work. It was the worst attack against civilians in 18 months.

Sudan

North Africa
967,500 sq. mi
Pop: 25.55m.
UN, AL, OAU

Capital: Khartoum (Pop: 476,218)
Official language: Arabic
Religions: Moslem 73%, animist 18%, Christian 9%
Political status: Republic
Head of state: Ahmad Ali al-Mirghani (since 1986)
Head of government: Sadiq al-Mahdi (since 1986)
GNP per capita: $400 (1983)
Currency: Sudanese pound ($1 = 4.50)

A terrible famine continued to stalk Sudan, where more than four million people were reported to be starving. International efforts to rush relief supplies to the affected zones were hampered by the 24-year-old conflict between the predominantly Moslem north and the Christian and animist south. More than a million people have already died in the war between government forces and rebels of the Sudanese People's Liberation Army led by Col. John Garang.

Suriname

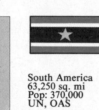

South America
63,250 sq. mi
Pop: 370,000
UN, OAS

Capital: Paramaribo (Pop: 67,905)
Official languages: Dutch, English
Religions: Moslem, Hindu, Christian
Political status: Republic
Head of state: Ramsewak Shankar (since 1988)
GNP per capita: $2,980 (1984)
Currency: Suriname guilders ($1 = 1.79)

Fighting broke out between rebels led by Ronnie Brunswijk and government troops in June, ending a truce struck in late 1987 following Suriname's first free elections after seven years of military rule.

Swaziland

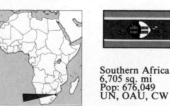

Southern Africa
6,705 sq. mi
Pop: 676,049
UN, OAU, CW

Capital: Mbabane (Pop: 23,109)
Official languages: Swazi, English
Religions: Christian 77%, traditional 23%
Political status: Monarchy
Head of state: King Mswati III
Head of government: Sotja E. Dlamini (since 1986)
GNP per capita: $730 (1984)
Currency: emalangeni ($1 = 2.11)

King Mswati III, aged 20, married the 19-year-old daughter of an Anglican priest in October. She became his fifth wife. A witch-doctor was sentenced to death in November for the ritual killing of a young boy. In October, Swaziland denounced border incursions by South African forces.

Sweden

Northern
Europe
173,731 sq. mi
Pop: 8.4m.
UN, EFTA,
OECD

Capital: Stockholm (Pop: 663,217)
Official language: Swedish
Religion: Lutheran 95%
Political status: Constitutional monarchy
Head of state: King Carl XVI Gustaf
Head of government: Ingvar Carlsson (since 1986)
GNP per capita: $11,977 (1985)
Currency: Swedish krona ($1 = 5.99)

The fate of farm animals became a hot issue as the government approved a "bill of rights" for barnyard beasts. In April, the U.S. and Sweden marked the 350th. anniversary of the arrival of Swedes in America.

Switzerland

Western Europe
15,943 sq. mi
Pop: 6.5m.
EFTA, OECD

Capital: Bern (Pop: 301,100)
Official languages: German, French, Italian, Romansh
Religions: Roman Catholic 47.6%, Protestant 44.3%
Political status: Federal state
Head of state: Otto Stich (since 1988)
GNP per capita: $14,030 (1985)
Currency: franc ($1 = 1.39)

Britain's Prince Charles escaped badly shaken but unhurt in March when an Alpine avalanche buried one of his closest friends. In mid-November, a Swiss national was taken hostage in Lebanon.

Syria

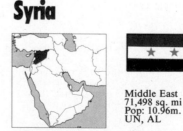

Middle East
71,498 sq. mi
Pop: 10.96m.
UN, AL

Capital: Damascus (Pop: 1,251,028)
Official language: Arabic
Religions: Sunni Moslem 90%
Political status: Republic
Head of state: Hafez al-Assad (since 1971)
Head of government: Mahmoud Zubi (1987)
GNP per capita: $2,000 (1984)
Currency: Syrian pound ($1 = 30.00)

Syria continued to play a major military and political role in strife-torn Lebanon, as pro-and anti-Syrians clashed in Beirut. Syria's influ-ence over events in Lebanon contributed to a political stalemate there following Lebanon's failure to elect a president in September.

Taiwan

East Asia
13,969 sq. mi
Pop: 19.5m.

Capital: Taipei (Pop: 2.56m.)
Official language: Chinese
Religions: Buddhist, Taoist, Christian
Political status: Republic
Head of state: Lee Teng-hui (since 1988)
Head of government: Yu Kuo-hwa (since 1984)
GNP per capita: $3,748 (1986)
Currency: New Taiwan dollar ($1 = 28.63)

A wind of change swept through the ruling Kuomintang leadership in July, reflecting an urge for reform and greater democratization. Relations with mainland China continued to improve. In September, Taipei authorized direct trade with China. For the first time since 1949, a Taiwan trade delegation visited Moscow in October. U.S.-Taiwan trade tensions heightened after Washington enacted trade restrictions in August.

Tanzania

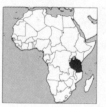

Eastern Africa
364,886 sq. mi
Pop: 23.2m.
UN, CW, OAU

Capital: Dodoma (Pop: 47,703)
Official languages: Kiswahili, English
Religions: Moslem 33%, Christian 40%
Political status: Republic
Head of state: Ndugu Ali Hassan Mwinyi (since 1985)
Head of government: Joseph S. Warioba (since 1985)
GNP per capita: 210 (1984)
Currency: Tanzanian shilling ($1 = 92.82)

Tanzania finally reached agreement with the International Monetary Fund in November after months of hard bargaining. This meant that the IMF would back the Tanzanian government's austerity measures.

Thailand

Southeast Asia
198,456 sq. mi
Pop: 52.5m.
UN, ASEAN

Capital: Bangkok (Pop: 5,446,708)
Official language: Thai
Religions: Buddhist 95%, Moslem 4%
Political status: Constitutional monarchy
Head of state: King Bhumibol Adulyadej (since 1946)
Head of government: Prem Tinasulanonda (since 1980)
GNP per capita: $720 (1985)
Currency: baht ($1 = 25.26)

A Chicago, Illinois, museum in November returned a 1,000-year-old sandstone temple carving to Thailand, thus ending a lengthy dispute between Bangkok and Washington. Thai officials said the artifact was stolen by U.S. soldiers during the Indochina War in the 1960s. Late November flooding and mudslides left an estimated 1,000 dead, mainly in a province south of Bangkok. The government appealed for international assistance, saying the disaster was among the worst natural calamities Thailand had ever endured.

Togo

West Africa
21,925 sq. mi
Pop: 3.16m.
UN, ECOWAS, OAU

Capital: Lome (Pop: 366,476)
Official language: French
Religions: animist 46%, Christian 37%, Moslem 17%
Political status: Republic
Head of state: Gnassingbe Eyadema (since 1967)
GNP per capita: $280 (1983)
Currency: franc CFA ($1 = 285.66)

The West African nation on September 23 marked the second anniversary of the attempted overthrow of Gen. Gnassingbe Eyadema's regime, allegedly carried out by commandos from nearby Ghana.

Tonga

South Pacific
289 sq. mi
Pop: 94,535
CW

Capital: Nuku'alofa (Pop: 28,899)
Official languages: Tongan, English
Religions: Christian 90%
Political status: Constitutional monarchy
Head of state: King Taufa'ahau Tupou IV (since 1965)
Head of government: Prince Fatafehi Tu'pelehake (since 1965)
GNP per capita: $580 (1986)
Currency: pa'anga ($1 = 1.39)

The tiny South Pacific Kingdom of Tonga was granted a low-interest loan of $2.3 million by the United Nations International Agricultural Development Fund in July. The aid was for Tonga's fishing industry.

Trinidad and Tobago

Caribbean
1,978 sq. mi
Pop: 1.22m.
UN, Caricom, CW, OAS

Capital: Port-of-Spain (Pop: 58,400)
Official language: English
Religions: Christian 48.6%, Hindu 25%, Moslem 5.9%
Political status: Republic
Head of state: Noor Hassanali (since 1986)
Head of government: Arthur Robinson (since 1986)
GNP per capita: $6,360 (1985)
Currency: Trinidad and Tobago dollar ($1 = 3.60)

Faced with a worsening economic situation, the government in November dismissed 25,000 of the 60,000 government employees. This move came after an August devaluation of the currency by 15 percent.

Tunisia

North Africa
59,664 sq. mi
Pop: 7.32m.
UN, AL, OAU

Capital: Tunis (Pop: 596,654)
Official language: Arabic
Religion: mainly Moslem
Political status: Republic
Head of state: Zine el Abidine Ben Ali (since 1987)
Head of government: Hedi Baccouche (since 1987)
GNP per capita: 1,250 (1985)
Currency: dinar ($1 = 0.82)

Abu Jihad, the Palestine Liberation Organization's second in command, was assassinated in Tunis in April. The killing was allegedly carried out by Israeli commandos. In November, President Zine el Abidine Ben Ali said general elections would be held in 1989 rather than in 1991.

Turkey

Southeastern Europe
300,947 sq. mi
Pop: 50.67m.
UN, NATO, OECD

Capital: Ankara (Pop: 2,251,533)
Official language: Turkish
Religion: Moslem 98.2%
Political status: Republic
Head of state: Kenan Evren (since 1980)
Head of government: Turgut Ozal (since 1983)
GNP per capita: $1,020 (1986)
Currency: Turkish lira ($1 = 1,183)

In February, Turkey became the first nation to ratify the European Convention on torture. This came a month after a U.N. body put Turkey on a blacklist of countries practising torture. Prime Minister Turgut Ozal escaped virtually unharmed from a spectacular June assassination bid in which 13 people were injured. Mr. Ozal vowed to stay on as premier in September despite nearly 65 percent of voters rejecting constitutional reforms proposed by his government. He had earlier promised to resign if the vote went against him. A June landslide killed 63 people. In August, an estimated 130,000 Kurds fleeing from Iraqi air strikes on their camps streamed across the border into Turkey. Sheltering and feeding the refugees posed a major problem.

Tuvalu

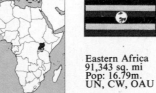

South Pacific
9.5 sq. mi
Pop: 8,229
CW

Capital: Funafuti (Pop: 2,620)
Official languages: Tuvaluan, English
Religion: Protestant
Political status: Constitutional monarchy
Head of state: Queen Elizabeth II
Head of government: Tomasi Puapua (since 1981)
GNP per capita: $500 (1984)
Currency: Australian dollar

The former British Protectorate of Tuvalu celebrated the 10th. anniversary of its independence on October 1. Money sent home by Tuvaluans working abroad remained among the islands' chief sources of income.

Uganda

Eastern Africa
91,343 sq. mi
Pop: 16.79m.
UN, CW, OAU

Capital: Kampala (Pop: 458,423)
Official languages: English, Kiswahili
Religions: Christian 62%, Moslem 6%
Political status: Republic
Head of state: Yoweri Museveni (since 1986)
Head of government: Samson Kisekka (since 1986)
GNP per capita: $230 (1984)
Currency: Uganda shilling ($1 = 60.10)

Ugandans celebrated the 26th. anniversary of independence from Britain in October amid political uncertainty and a continued rebel insurgency in the north. The government sought to rebuild the country's wrecked infrastructure. British, Italian and Chinese firms did brisk business rebuilding roads.

Union of Soviet Socialist Republics

Eurasia
8,649,496 sq. mi
Pop: 284.5m.
UN, CMEA, Warsaw Pact

Capital: Moscow (Pop: 8,715,000)
Official language: Russian
Religions: Christian, Moslem, Jewish, Buddhist
Political status: Federal union
Head of state: Mikhail Gorbachev (since 1988)
Head of government: Nicolai Ryzhkov (since 1985)
Head of Communist Party: Mikhail Gorbachev (since 1985)
GNP per capita: $6,000 (1985)
Currency: ruble ($1 = 0.60)

The year ended in tragedy, when a devastating December earthquake hit Armenia, killing tens of thousands of people. The extent of the disaster was such that President Mikhail Gorbachev had to cut short a visit to New York and cancel trips to Britain and Cuba. It was not all smooth sailing for Mr. Gorbachev, despite a string of successes at home and abroad. On the political front, he consolidated his hold on the reins of power, pushing his main critics and rivals to the sidelines and adding the title of President to his powerful post as General Secretary of the Communist Party in October. Hard-line opponents of Mr. Gorbachev's reform policies of "perestroika" and "glasnost" were replaced by reform-minded officials. The wind of change also blew through the economy: waste, a top-heavy bureaucracy, fraud and chronic inefficiency were targeted by the authorities. There was progress on the human rights front with the freeing of a number of political prisoners. Soviet space technology took a big step forward with the November maiden flight of the shuttle Buran (Snowstorm).

On the international front, the Soviet Union won acclaim for the April signing of a peace accord in Afghanistan. Moscow agreed to withdraw all its troops from that country by February 1989. Mr. Gorbachev travelled widely to the West and the Third World. In December, he held his final meeting with outgoing President Ronald Reagan. The improvement of relations with Washington was marred by a dispute over alleged Soviet bugging of the U.S. Embassy in Moscow.

However, regional nationalism and ethnic strife, which spread from the Baltic to the Caucasus, became a major problem. Year-long tension and clashes between Armenians and Azerbaijanis left dozens dead and forced Mr. Gorbachev to send in the army to try to restore calm in the disputed Nagorny Karabakh region. The Kremlin's authority was defied in the Baltic republics of Latvia, Estonia and Lithuania, where demands for greater autonomy reached a crescendo in November.

United Arab Emirates

Middle East
32,300 sq. mi
Pop: 1.77m.
UN, AL, GCC, OPEC

Capital: Abu Dhabi (Pop: 670,125)
Official language: Arabic
Religion: Moslem 90%
Political status: Federation of emirates
Head of state: Sheikh Zayed bin Sultan Al Nahyan (since 1971)
Head of government: Sheikh Rashid bin Said al-Maktoum (since 1979)
GNP per capita: $19,270 (1985)
Currency: dirham ($1 = 3.67)

The world-wide drop in oil prices seriously affected the United Arab Emirates in 1988, leading the Gulf state to impose budgetary restrictions in a bid to cut down the growing $3 billion dollar deficit.

United Kingdom

Northwestern Europe
94,226 sq. mi
Pop: 55,78m.
UN, CW, EEC, NATO, OECD

Capital: London (Pop: 6,800,000)
Official language: English
Religions: Church of England, Roman Catholic
Political status: Constitutional monarchy
Head of state: Queen Elizabeth II
Head of government: Margaret Thatcher (since 1979)
GNP per capita: $7,860 (1985)
Currency: pound sterling ($1 = 1.77)

Former British spy Kim Philby, who passed secrets to the Kremlin while ostensibly working for British intelligence, died in Moscow in May. A terrible North Sea oil rig disaster killed 167 people in July, when the Piper Alpha platform, owned by the U.S. firm Occidental Petroleum, exploded. One man was killed when a fire swept through another North Sea drilling rig in September, bringing calls for tighter safety measures.

Conservative Prime Minister Margaret Thatcher's government in October lost a drawn out fight to stop the publication of "Spycatcher", the memoirs of a former British intelligence agent. In November, the government introduced legislation to make unauthorized disclosure of information by a member of the intelligence service a criminal offense.

Controversy erupted following the shooting of three members of the Irish Republican Army by British soldiers in Gibraltar. In September, a jury in the British colony returned a verdict of "lawful killing" at an inquest into the March shootout. In November, two top managers of London's Un-

derground system resigned prior to the publication of a damning report on a 1987 fire at Kings Cross station which left 31 people dead.

Mrs. Thatcher, likening herself to Genghis Khan, in October strongly denounced moves by Brussels for a more centralized European Economic Community, stressing that she intended to remain a staunch ally of the United States. In November, the "Iron Lady" visited Washington, where she bade an emotional farewell to outgoing President Reagan. Also in November, Britain and Iran ended a 17-month freeze in their ties by agreeing to resume full relations. Despite this, three British hostages, including Anglican Church envoy Terry Waite, were still being held by pro-Iranian groups in Lebanon. In October, Neil Kinnock was re-elected leader of Britain's opposition Labour Party, despite dissent over the party's nuclear disarmament policy. The Scottish National Party won a stunning upset victory in a November by-election in Glasgow.

United States

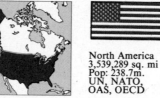

North America
3,539,289 sq. mi
Pop: 238.7m.
UN, NATO, OAS, OECD

Capital: Washington D.C. (Pop: 638,333)
Official language: English
Religions: Protestant 56%, Catholic 36.7%, Jewish
Political status: Federal republic
Head of state: Ronald Reagan (since 1981)
GNP per capita: $16,710 (1986)
Currency: dollar

The race to succeed Ronald Reagan dominated the political year with George Bush defeating the Republican challenge of Robert Dole and Michael Dukakis emerging from the Democratic pack to defeat the spirited campaign of Jesse Jackson. As Mr. Reagan entered the final stretch of his eight years in office, he won Senate approval in May for the historic December 1987 U.S.-Soviet treaty on the scrapping of all medium-range nuclear missiles. It was the first major superpower arms treaty to win Senate approval since 1972 and contributed to the success of Mr. Reagan's visit to Moscow in early June. However, continued work on the futuristic and costly "Star Wars" project caused new tension with the Kremlin. In November, the Pentagon unveiled its B-2 "Stealth" bomber designed to streak unnoticed past enemy radar. A major bribes and fraud scandal rocked the Defense Department in July, leading to suspension of payments on a billion dollars worth of defense contracts.

Relations between the Reagan administration and the U.N. had their ups and downs in 1988. In September, Mr. Reagan ordered the payment

of nearly $520 million in current and past dues to the cash-strapped U.N. But in November, a U.S. decision to bar P.L.O. chief Yasir Arafat from entering New York to adress the U.N. brought international condemnation.

October marked the first anniversary of Wall Street's cataclysmic "Black Monday". Although the situation that prompted the record 508-point drop in the Dow Jones index receded in 1988, financial markets were still awaiting the return of the small investor.

The U.S. roared back into space in September as the shuttle Discovery completed the first U.S. manned space mission since the Challenger disaster 32 months earlier.

President-elect George Bush, who was to take office on January 20, 1989, faced tough challenges. Among the major hurdles confronting him are the gargantuan national debt, a stubborn budget deficit, continued strife in Central America, trade tensions with Asia, a deadlocked Middle East peace process and rapidly changing relations with Soviet leader Mikhail Gorbachev.

Uruguay

South America
72,172 sq. mi
Pop: 2.95m.
UN, LAIA, OAS

Capital: Montevideo (Pop: 1,237,227)
Official language: Spanish
Religion: Roman Catholic 66%
Political status: Republic
Head of state: Julio Maria Sanguinetti (since 1985)
GNP per capita: $1,800 (1984)
Currency: Nuevo Peso ($1 = 304)

A Montevideo cinema showing the controversial film "The Last Temptation of Christ" was hit by a November arson attack. President Sanguinetti in November approved an anti-inflation plan. Police nabbed eight people for a baby-selling racket.

Vanuatu

South Pacific
5,700 sq. mi
Pop: 141,000
UN, CW

Capital: Vila (Pop: 15,000)
Official languages: Bislama, English, French
Religion: Christian 80%
Political status: Republic
Head of state: Ati Sokomanu (since 1980)
Head of government: Walter Lini (since 1980)
GNP per capita: $350 (1981)
Currency: Vatu ($1 = 103)

Vanuatu in 1988 headed toward a reconciliation with its former colonial power, France, after years of discord over the issue of independence for the neighboring French South Pacific territory of New Caledonia.

Vatican City

Southern Europe
108.7 acres
Pop: 1,000

Capital: Vatican City
Official languages: Italian, Latin
Religion: Catholic
Head of Roman Catholic Church: Pope John Paul II (since 1978)
Secretary of State: Cardinal Agostino Casaroli (since 1979)
Currency: lira ($1 = 1,244)

The Vatican in June excommunicated renegade French Archbishop Marcel Lefebvre for violating church rites. This marked the first schism in the Roman Catholic Church in more than a century.

Venezuela

South America
352,143 sq. mi
Pop: 17.32m.
UN, LAIA, OAS, OPEC

Capital: Caracas (Pop: 1,816,901)
Official language: Spanish
Religion: Roman Catholic
Political status: Republic
Head of state: Jaime Lusinchi (since 1984)
GNP per capita: $2,680 (1985)
Currency: bolivar ($1 = 29.40)

Ruling party candidate Carlos Andres Perez, who was Venezuela's president from 1974 to 1979, won an easy victory in December 4 elections, defeating his rival Eduardo Fernandez. Mr. Perez will succeed President Lusinchi on February 2, 1989.

Vietnam

Southeast Asia
127,245 sq. mi
Pop: 61.95m.
UN, CMEA

Capital: Hanoi (Pop: 2,600,000)
Official language: Vietnamese
Religions: Buddhist, Taoist
Political status: Socialist republic
Head of state: Vo Chi Cong (since 1987)

Head of government: Du Muoi (since 1988)
GNP per capita: $300 (1984)
Currency: dong ($1 = 368)

Vietnam in May pledged to withdraw 50,000 of its estimated 120,000 troops from Cambodia by the end of 1988. Relations with the U.S. improved following a July accord for former Vietnamese prisoners to emigrate to the United States. Great progress was made this year on the issue of U.S. servicemen still believed missing in Vietnam. Fierce November typhoons caused major damage.

Western Samoa

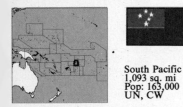

South Pacific
1,093 sq. mi
Pop: 163,000
UN, CW

Capital: Apia (Pop: 33,170)
Official languages: Samoan, English
Religions: Congregationalist 47%, Roman Catholic 22%, Methodist 16%
Political status: Constitutional monarchy
Head of state: King Malietoa Tanumafili II
Head of government: Tofilau Eti Alesana (since 1988)
GNP per capita: $770 (1985)
Currency: tala ($1 = 1.00)

February general elections resulted in the defeat of Va'ai Kolone. The new premier, Tofilau Eti Alesana, head of the Human Rights Protection Party which has been ousted in December 1985, took office in April.

Yemen (North)

Middle East
73,300 sq. mi
Pop: 6.53m.
UN, AL

Capital: San'a (Pop: 277,817)
Official language: Arabic
Religion: Moslem (Sunni 39%, Shi'a 59%)
Political status: Republic
Head of state: Ali Abdallah Saleh (since 1978)
Head of government: Abdel Aziz Abdel Ghani (since 1983)
GNP per capita: $510 (1983)
Currency: riyal ($1 = 9.88)

North Yemen's leader, Colonel Ali Abdallah Saleh, accepted a third term as head of state on July 17, soon after submitting his resignation and asking the Consultative Assembly to choose a new president.

Yemen (South)

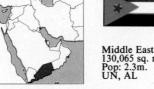

Middle East
130,065 sq. mi
Pop: 2.3m.
UN, AL

Capital: Aden (Pop: 318,000)
Official language: Arabic
Religions: mostly Moslem, Christian, Hindu
Political status: People's democratic republic
Head of state: Haidar al-Attas (since 1986)
Head of government: Yasin Sa'id Nu'man (since 1986)
GNP per capita: $500 (1985)
Currency: dinar ($1 = 0.343)

In May, South Yemen's government marked the 25th. anniversary of its revolution, as it sought to solidify its legitimacy by improving ties with its Horn of Africa neighbors.

Yugoslavia

Southern Europe
96,835 sq. mi
Pop: 23.27m.
UN

Capital: Belgrade (Pop: 1,470,073)
Official languages: Serbo-Croat, Macedonian, Slovene
Religions: Orthodox 41%, Roman Catholic 32%, Moslem 12%
Political status: Federal socialist republic
Head of state: Lazar Mojsov (since May 1987)
Head of government: Branko Mikulic (since 1986)
GNP per capita: $5,600 (1985)
Currency: dinar ($1 = 1,353)

Nearly 40 years after Yugoslavia was kicked out of the Socialist bloc by Moscow, Soviet leader Mikhail Gorbachev in March visited Belgrade, ending the ideological rift. A wave of often-violent Serbian nationalism left the country facing its worst crisis since Marshal Josip Broz Tito's death in 1980. Yugoslavia's eight million Serbs, led by Serbian Communist Party chief Slobodan Milosevic, demonstrated repeatedly to back their demands for greater control over the autonomous provinces of Kosovo and Vojvodina. The ethnic unrest came on top of a disastrous economic situation, with inflation reaching 250 percent and high unemployment.

Zaire

Central Africa
905,365 sq. mi
Pop: 31.78m.
UN, OAU

Capital: Kinshasa (Pop: 2,653,558)
Official language: French
Religions: mostly Roman Catholic, Protestant, Moslem
Political status: Presidential republic
Head of state: Marshal Mobutu Sésé Séko (since 1965)
Head of government: Mabi Mulumba (since 1987)
GNP per capita: $160 (1983)
Currency: zaïre ($1 = 143.55)

Pope John Paul II in April warned the bishops of Zaire against what he said was a rising trend to polygamy in their country. He urged Zairians to reject polygamy, adding this was harmful to Christian marriages.

Zambia

Southern Africa
290,586 sq. mi
Pop: 7.12m.
UN, CW, OAU

Capital : Lusaka (Pop: 538,469)
Official language: English
Religions: Christian 66%, Moslem
Political status: Republic
Head of state: Kenneth David Kaunda (since 1964)
Head of government: K.S.K. Musokotwane (since 1985)
GNP per capita: $410 (1984)
Currency: Kwacha ($1 = 8.05)

Zambians faced five more years of stiff belt-tightening after President Kenneth Kaunda was sworn in for his sixth term of office in October. Mr. Kaunda has led Zambia since its 1964 independence from Britain.

Zimbabwe

Southern Africa
150,699 sq. mi
Pop: 8.64m.
UN, CW, OAU

Capital: Harare (Pop: 656,100)
Official language: English
Religions: mostly Anglican and Roman Catholic
Political status: Republic
Head of state: Robert G. Mugabe (since 1987)
GNP per capita: $780 (1984)
Currency: Zimbabwe dollar ($1 = 1.74)

Zimbabwe President Robert Mugabe in April declared an amnesty for all the country's dissident rebels in a bid to further strengthen the merger of the opposition Zimbabwe African Peoples Union, led by rival politician Joshua Nkomo, into his ruling Zimbabwe African National Union. This brought new hope for an end to years of anti-government violence.

Abbreviations					
	AL	Arab League		LAES	Latin American Economic System
	ANZUS	Australia, New-Zealand, U.S.		LAIA	Latin American Integration Association
	ASEAN	Association of South East Asian Nations		NATO	North Atlantic Treaty Organization
	Caricom	Caribbean Community and Common Market		NC	Nordic Council
	CFA	African Financial Community currency		OAS	Organization of American States
	CMEA	(or Comecon) Council for Mutual Economic Assistance		OAU	Organization of African Unity
	CW	The Commonwealth		OECD	Organization for Economic Cooperation and Development
	ECOWAS	Economic Community of West African States		OPEC	Organization of Petroleum Exporting Countries
	EEC	European Economic Community		UN	United Nations
	EFTA	European Free Trade Association		WP	Warsaw Pact
	GCC	Gulf Cooperation Council			

General Index

125

Photo Credit Index